ISLAMIC DIVORCE IN NORTH AMERICA

ISLAMIC DIVORCE IN NORTH AMERICA

A *Shari'a* Path in a Secular Society

Julie Macfarlane

OXFORD
UNIVERSITY PRESS

OXFORD

UNIVERSITY PRESS

Oxford University Press, Inc., publishes works that further
Oxford University's objective of excellence
in research, scholarship, and education.

Oxford   New York
Auckland   Cape Town   Dar es Salaam   Hong Kong   Karachi
Kuala Lumpur   Madrid   Melbourne   Mexico City   Nairobi
New Delhi   Shanghai   Taipei   Toronto

With offices in
Argentina   Austria   Brazil   Chile   Czech Republic   France   Greece
Guatemala   Hungary   Italy   Japan   Poland   Portugal   Singapore
South Korea   Switzerland   Thailand   Turkey   Ukraine   Vietnam

Copyright © 2012 by Oxford University Press, Inc.

Published by Oxford University Press, Inc.
198 Madison Avenue, New York, New York 10016

www.oup.com

Oxford is a registered trademark of Oxford University Press

Library of Congress Cataloging-in-Publication Data
Macfarlane, Julie.
Islamic divorce in North America : a *Shari'a* path in a secular society / Julie Macfarlane.
   p.   cm.
Includes bibliographical references and index.
ISBN 978-0-19-975391-8 (hardcover : alk. paper)
1. Divorce (Islamic law)—North America. I. Title.
KBP558.32.M33A34   2012
340.5'9097—dc23   2011031281

9 8 7 6 5 4 3 2 1
Printed in the United States of America
on acid-free paper

To Sibyl

You are my sunshine.

And the rest you know.

CONTENTS

Acknowledgments   ix

Introduction   xiii

1. Muslim Identity in the West   3

2. A Primer on Islamic Family Law   19

3. Getting Married   40

4. Staying Married   70

5. Marital Conflicts and Abuse   102

6. Getting Divorced   141

7. The Consequences of Divorce   177

8. Legal Issues for Islamic Marriage and Divorce   210

9. Looking Forward   240

Appendix A: Marriage Contracts   263

Appendix B: Divorce Ruling on Verbal Delegated Talaq   267

Appendix C: Faskh *Ruling*   269

Notes   271

Glossary   301

Index   303

ACKNOWLEDGMENTS

A book of this kind—taking the subject of Muslim marriage and divorce in North America and turning it inside out, looking under the surface themes carried by the press and the assumptions of a largely uninformed public discourse—is only possible with the input and support of many people.

My first and primary acknowledgements are to my research subjects. I am so grateful for their trust in me, and their willingness to share both personal stories and contentious professional perspectives. Whether an imam, a community worker, a marriage therapist, or a divorced person, each one of the 212 people interviewed for this book took a courageous step in talking to me frankly and honestly about the taboo of divorce in the Muslim community. They told me over and over again that they spoke out despite the risk of potential disapproval and judgment by others because they believed it was important for their community to begin to talk openly about marital conflict and divorce, and especially about the impact on women. Many community leaders, including imams, demonstrated their commitment to the well-being of their communities by supporting my work and promoting my contact with their members. I sincerely hope that these individuals will find in this book the beginnings of the honest and open debate that they crave, and that they can now take forward in their own families, mosques, and communities.

I was fortunate to be assisted throughout the five years of this project by three extraordinarily able research assistants. Aisha Amjad deserves special acknowledgement. Aisha's energy and commitment to what sometimes felt like an impossible project in the early stages was inspirational. Aisha has a genius for conveying her passion on this (or any!) subject and for persuading even the most recalcitrant and skeptical individual that they will enjoy talking to her. Her intimate understanding of the Muslim community, and her deft touch in the most sensitive situations, was invaluable in helping me to steer a course through many shoals of controversy. Aisha and I know how hard we had to work for participation at the beginning of this project—we drove and flew hundreds of miles together and had many adventures—and we share the satisfaction of what we ultimately achieved. Sibyl Macfarlane, my eldest daughter, completed the coding of the interviews and assisted me with editing and footnoting as the manuscript emerged (at the same time that she completed her graduate work in religious studies). To be able to work with your own child and realize how much you can learn from their adult intellect is a real gift. In the final stretch, Lindsay Trevelyan was patient, painstaking, and everlastingly resourceful in completing the footnotes and finalizing the manuscript. I am so appreciative of her continuing commitment to finishing this project long after she ended her time at the law school. I had many insightful conversations with all three of these fabulous young women throughout the project—about the interpretation of data, about the research methodology, and above all about what we were discovering meant to them, as young women, Muslim and non-Muslim. These conversations challenged me, made me think and rethink again and again, and deepened my own analysis.

Many people who were not direct participants in the study provided the community and institutional support that enabled the research to take shape. On numerous occasions we visited a region or a mosque in order to speak about the research and solicit participation and were generously hosted by wonderfully kind people. Critical introductions were facilitated for me many times by influential individuals who encouraged others to participate in the research. While I cannot mention everyone here, I want to say a special thanks for believing in this project to Saleema Abdul-Ghafu, Salma Abugideiri, Abdullah An-Naim, Ben Davis, Anver Emon, Bruce Elman, Alia Hogben, Faisal Kutty, Elena Meloni, Asifa Quraishi, Farid Senzai, and Sadia Shakir. I am especially grateful to Katherine Bullock, who believed in this project right from the very beginning, allowed me to ask her any question, no matter how dumb, and always helped me to reach a better understanding. Thanks also to my brilliant team of readers—Aisha, Sibyl and Lindsay but also Katherine Bullock, Suzanne Ghais, Beth Johnstone, Alfred Mamo, Bernie Mayer, Andy Schephard, Damhnait Rumney and Debbie Donovan.

I thank the Social Science and Humanities Research Council of Canada (SSHRC) for its generous financial support of this project, and in particular for providing the teaching relief (sadly, no longer part of their program) without which I would still be out in the field trying to fit data collection around my teaching responsibilities. I hope that SSHRC will continue to try to develop a funding model that will enable empirical researchers to complete complex projects of this kind; many questions go unanswered without this type of research. I also appreciate the financial and moral support of the Institute for Social and Policy Understanding, as well as the guidance of Farid Senzai, ISPU's research director, and the work of its staff who set up numerous meetings and introductions for me. I am proud of my association with this terrific organization. Thanks also to Oxford University Press, in particular Cynthia Read for her support of this project, Lisbeth Refield, and my copy editor, Stacey Hamilton.

My ability to work and produce research is made possible by the support and love of my family and close friends. As if I needed reminding, my diagnosis with breast cancer in June 2010 underscored this. My stepson Mark was with us when we received the diagnosis, and I am grateful for his quiet compassion and support. My three daughters, Hopey, Ellie, and Sibyl, stood by my side with fortitude and an apparently bottomless belief in my ability to get through my treatments and finish my book (and they were right!). My friends (human, canine and equine) at the barn, in my wonderful community of Kingsville, and scattered around the globe—you know who you are—showed me that the love of others is the greatest gift of all. It is what has made completing this project, only slightly delayed, possible.

Ironically, having spent so much time trying to find the right words to write this book, I do not have the right words to tell my husband, Bernie Mayer, how lucky I am to have him in my life. Everyone who knows me knows this. Bernie allowed many people and in particular my beloved daughters to feel that I was always in safe, secure hands throughout some frightening months. He was willing to humor me when I insisting on typing during my chemotherapy treatments— one hand on the keyboard, the other attached to an IV—and on every other interminable visit to the hospital, doctor, and emergency room because he knew that working on this book was part of what would keep me going. Just as important, he developed some excellent grooming skills to enable me to go on riding when I was too weak to take care of these tasks myself. For these and a million other acts of kindness and love—thank you.

I hope that the work of all these people and many others will be rewarded by a more informed and open conversation about marital conflict and divorce in Muslim families. This book is forthright about the challenges they face, but with a vibrant dialogue and strong leadership, anything is possible. Contemporary, progressive models of Islamic family life are already emerging from the experiences of young Muslim men and women growing up in North America. Many of these individuals stepped out of their "comfort zone" in order to make this book possible. It is my passionate hope that when they read this book their non-Muslim friends and neighbors will be prepared to reciprocate, enabling us to better understand both our differences and our many similarities.

Julie Macfarlane
Kingsville, May 2011

INTRODUCTION

For many people, the image of Islamic law is laden with fear. Over the past five years, each time I told a non-Muslim that I was conducting an empirical study of Islamic marriage and divorce, their reaction was surprise, alarm, and in some cases horror. Many expressed dismay, revulsion even, that I ("I thought you were a feminist!") would devote myself to this area of study. When I tried to explain the research I was doing I was asked over and over, "You mean, they *have* divorce?" and often (accompanied now by laughter) "Don't they just stone the women?" These reactions to my study and to me reflect pervasive public stereotyping of Muslims and largely uninformed public–policy making about the use of Islamic legal processes.

Issues that implicate Islamic values, culture, traditions and law are increasingly prominent in the public discourse of non-Muslim countries, including Canada and the United States. This debate follows the migration of Muslim communities to North America and Europe, beginning after the colonization of their countries of origin in the nineteenth century and continuing today. These new, displaced communities are as diverse as the Muslim world. Living in non-Muslim societies where Muslims are members of a fragmented and still relatively "new" community, they face complex and sometimes painful questions of identity. How do Muslims retain their Islamic identity in a non-Muslim state? How do they meet both their Islamic responsibilities and the obligations of citizenship in their new states? How does a secular state accommodate Muslim religious and cultural beliefs and values? These are dense and complicated questions, and their discussion is often controversial inside Muslim communities. They have been further reframed—divisively, unhelpfully—by rising public fears about Islam since the events of 9/11.

This book is concerned with a hitherto unexamined question about the religious, cultural and social identity of North American Muslims:

their recourse to Islamic marriage and divorce. In the United States and Canada these operate as private ordering processes outside the formal legal system. Nonetheless, they are widespread and used by many North American Muslims. Religious divorce in particular is the subject of a mostly "stealth" debate inside the Muslim community, especially among women. Between 2006 and 2010 I interviewed 212 Muslim men and women ("Muslim" as it is used throughout this book refers to any individual who identifies as a Muslim, whatever their level of personal observance) living in the United States and Canada in which they described their perspectives on Islamic marriage and divorce. Just over 100 of these interviews were with divorced men and women who described their personal experiences with disarming openness and in considerable depth. These interviews show that despite their lack of legal efficacy, Islamic marriage and divorce processes are very important for Muslims across a range of cultural, class and educational backgrounds. Islamic marriage is easily secured by signing a *nikah*, or Muslim marriage contract. Obtaining an Islamic divorce is much more difficult, but for some Muslims it is a vital symbol of legitimacy and closure. This group is not simply delineated as the religiously observant—many of those who described the importance of Muslim marriage and divorce did not attend mosque regularly, nor did they consider themselves to be especially "religious."[1] Their attachment to these processes is explained by a complex—and often idiosyncratic—blend of identity, culture and family values as well as religious traditions.

The personal stories told by divorced men and women—which are presented here with changed names in order to protect individual identities but in all other details remain faithful to the story I was told—offer a window into the motivations and experiences of those seeking religious approval for their decision to end their marriage. Some live in communities where divorce still carries a profound social stigma, especially for women. Imams, scholars, social workers and therapists working with Muslim families provide further perspectives—about the use of Islamic family law principles, as well as attitudes towards family issues ranging from gender roles to spousal incompatibility to domestic violence and abandonment. Each quotation and every story in this book comes directly from one of the 212 respondents, although direct attribution is omitted from this text. Together their experiences and insights provide a detailed, textured and diverse picture of Muslim family life in North America.

Islamic Marriage and Divorce and *Shari'a*

Immigrant communities frequently experience discrimination and alienation, and their relative powerlessness may mean exclusion from life in the economic and social "mainstream." For Muslims in North America, a sense of exclusion and difference has deepened since the events of 9/11, reinforcing their common experience and stimulating a mentality of "closing ranks." Historically, many immigrants maintain both their common connection and their connection to their country of origin by continuing to practice their religious and cultural traditions; many established communities continue to take pride in maintaining traditional processes. The most important passages of life—birth, marriage, divorce, death—are the repositories of this continuing connection. Moments of crisis and transition often lead to reaffirmation of emotional and behavioral touchstones. When it comes to dealing with life's crises, it is commonplace for individuals to feel that they must "get it right" by resorting to traditional practices that they and their families believe will ensure that they have met their religious and moral obligations, both outwardly and inwardly.

The meaning and rituals associated with these events represent the traditions and roots of family life for many Muslims living in non-Muslim countries. Most Muslims understand the inspiration for the principles and processes they adopt as *shari'a*, or "The Way" (meaning the principles that govern a Muslim way of life). *Shari'a* takes many different forms of observance among Muslims, but all Muslims understand *shari'a* to describe their personal responsibilities as a Muslim, whether or not they live in a Muslim state. The idea of *shari'a* is meaningful to Muslims of all levels of observance. Interpretations of what is expected and efforts to satisfy these expectations operate at a very personal, often private level among individuals who are not traditionally observant, as well as among those who are more publicly committed to their faith (for example, they attend prayers regularly at the mosque). Some North American Muslims have previously lived under repressive regimes which assert that they govern using "*shari'a*" law, and in which brutal punishments are imposed by law enforcement or the army, and this is sometimes reflected in their fears about the emergence of a similar self-styled *shari'a* in North America. Outside these experiences, the majority of Muslims have a positive understanding of *shari'a* as a framework for Islamic values and providing guidelines for living as a "good" Muslim—including their personal rights, responsibilities towards others and towards God, and faith obligations.

In contrast, the word *shari'a* is associated in Western public discourse almost exclusively with the violent and frequently misogynist jihadist movement that has "stolen" the public understanding of Islam.[2] Media reports of "Islamic *shari'a*" focus on accounts of cruel criminal punishments and anti-women laws in Saudi Arabia and Iran, extremist theocracies which are presented as representative of mainstream Islam; or extra-governmental regimes in regions of Pakistan, Afghanistan, Somalia and Nigeria. There are numerous examples of respected media sources describing *shari'a* as "flogging criminal[s] in public, forcing women to cover themselves with burkahs" and flogging and stoning as a "strict interpretation" of Islam.[3] The very mention of *shari'a* raises deep fears among non-Muslims in the West. Each time I have stood up to speak about this research at an academic conference in the last five years I registered the immediate alarm on the faces of my audience when I mentioned *shari'a*. When I asked my (largely non-Muslim) audiences what they understand by *shari'a* their responses were consistent: cruel penal punishments, the oppression of women, a general tone of rigidity and authoritarianism. When I shared these experiences with a sympathetic colleague, also a university professor, she told me the story of a student who came to her proposing that he write a paper on the *shari'a* law debate then taking place in Ontario. When the professor asked the student what he knew about *shari'a* law, he replied, "Well, nothing, but I know that it's a really bad thing."

Understanding what *shari'a* really means to Muslims in North America in contrast to its representation in the public discourse was central to this research. I wanted to explore how Islamic marriage and divorce is practiced in North America and how it enables individual men and women to feel that they have behaved "Islamically" and appropriately. My goal was to get behind media portrayals of Muslims and *shari'a* and examine the lived experiences of Muslims in North America, in order to replace fear and speculation with some hard data.

How This Study Was Conducted

This study was conceived following the 2003–2005 "*shari'a* debate" in Ontario, when public alarm at the disclosure that mosques were conducting Muslim marriages and divorces eventually led the government to announce that they were "banning" recourse to Islamic law. Frustrated by the absence of information about the format and outcomes of these processes and the experiences of those using them, I began to contact imams and leaders in the Muslim community to explore their willingness to facilitate some data collection. They were immediately on-board. The study would proceed to conduct in-depth interviews with imams, religious scholars, community leaders, social workers and divorced men and women. Face-to-face data was gathered principally in Detroit/Dearborn; Los Angeles; Toronto; Windsor/London; Ottawa; and London, England. In addition, many telephone interviews were conducted with individuals in cities all over the United States and Canada. Approximately 75 percent of the data was collected from respondents in the United States, and 25 percent from Canada. No pervasive differences in respondents' experiences were noted between the two jurisdictions, and data presented here does not distinguish between these two countries.

The primary objective of the study was to document, using a qualitative approach, how North American Muslim communities manage divorce by exploring private family and third party processes—including reconciliation efforts, family conferences, the intervention of the imams and the eventual pronouncement of divorce—and their relationship to legal divorce. I wanted to better understand the various motivations of both the users and the facilitators of processes for marital counseling and divorce. To this point, there had been almost no data collection or formal monitoring of the practice of Islamic divorce in Muslim communities in North America. I quickly learned that I would need to understand the meaning of the related system of Islamic marriage (*nikah*) in order to properly understand the role and meaning of Islamic divorce. Numerous respondents reminded me of this point: "The *nikah* was based on *shari'a*—so when we end it naturally we should use *shari'a*. Otherwise why have a *nikah*; why not just have a legal marriage?"

The phenomenon of Islamic marriage and divorce is located within a plethora of wider social, legal and religious issues that arise for relocated Muslim communities. I had not anticipated the extent to which gathering such a large amount of data on divorce would expose many of the systemic causes of marital conflict within marriage and the wider social and cultural forces at play in these communities. In the course of the study I stumbled across many embedded issues, including the common causes of marital conflict, the social role of the imams and other religious leaders, attitudes towards other interventions in family life (by police, social workers, counselors), and the relationship between Islamic law and the formal legal system. Each represents a potential site of conflict and tension for Muslims who hold at least two overlapping identities—as citizens of the United States or Canada and as Muslims. Interviews illuminated the broader changes taking place within diverse Muslim communities as they adjust not only to life in the West, but also to more systemic changes in societal norms. This helped me to understand that North American Islamic identity is being shaped not only by religious but also by cultural and societal factors—for example, attitudes towards the equal participation of women in work and education, gender roles and expectations within marriage (for example, how to structure a contemporary marriage partnership where both spouses work outside the home), the role of the extended family in choosing a marriage partner, and attitudes towards divorce itself.

Different interview formats were used for the three major respondent subgroups (imams and other facilitators of divorce processes; divorced men and women; and community specialists [social and community workers, therapists and mental health professionals, lawyers]). Semi-structured interviews lasted between 30 and 120 minutes. All interviews were noted contemporaneously, including transcribing many direct quotations. Audio recording was avoided because it seemed to alienate some early respondents and generally reduced respondent comfort with sharing sensitive personal data. When quotations are presented from interviews all references to a particular respondent have been removed, although the context makes the position of the individual (an imam, a divorced person, a social worker, and so on) and often their gender clear.

Every quotation in the book which is not referenced to a scholarly source comes from a study respondent. The data was analyzed using the NVivo 7 software[4] and a variety of other manual coding and analysis processes, including the development of individual story synopses for the 101 divorced men and women, a model for distinguishing different process narratives, financial and legal outcomes distinguishing between shorter and longer marriages, participant motivations and a typology based on a number of variables the different roles played by the imams.

Getting Started

After a four-month immersion course in Islamic family law, I began by interviewing the imams, widely regarded as the "gatekeepers" of religious divorce by their community. I eventually interviewed forty-one imams or religious leaders, representing both Sunni and Shia communities, and all five schools of Islamic jurisprudence.[5] They described to me the process they adopted for counseling warring couples and how they responded to requests for divorce (almost always from women). There was no correlation between the overall approach adopted and whether the imam was Sunni or Shia, or had been educated in a particular school of jurisprudence (despite the certainty with which many respondents assured me that I would find clear differences in approach). Far more significant than school or sect were the imams' values regarding family life, a woman's role in the family and sometimes the degree of conservatism of his community (which may lead him to refuse divorce when the law would technically allow it).

I also conducted interviews with seventy Muslim social workers and community workers, marriage counselors, therapists and other mental health professionals, religious scholars and academics and Muslim family lawyers (the "community specialists"). These professionals described the practices they saw among their own clients, and the continuing desire for Islamic processes. They provided me with valuable insights into the ways in which their communities were evolving and how some traditional views—for example, the role of the extended family in marriage choices and lifestyle choices and the exceptionalism of divorce—were changing. They described the connection between their own work with Muslim families and that of the imams (of whom they were often critical). A few social work and mental health professionals worked closely with an imam, either by screening cases or taking referrals. In other cases there was no coordination at all between, for example, the work of a Muslim family lawyer or a Muslim social services agency, and the local mosque.

Personal Stories

After the first eighteen months, having laid a foundation of knowledge from my interviews with imams and community specialists, I began to focus on gathering the personal stories of men and women who had experienced divorce. This proved to be a difficult group to access, and I explored many different avenues to reach divorcées and divorcés. Interviewees were solicited via imams and other professionals, presentations in mosques and community centres, the project website (www.islamicdivorce.org) and a Facebook page ("Islam and Divorce: What Do You Think?"). The website was very successful in bringing in study participants, the Facebook page (reflecting a widespread tentativeness about speaking publicly about divorce) less so. I also used a snowballing approach, especially effective among divorced women who always knew at least one other divorcée to whom they referred me.

The study eventually collected detailed personal accounts of marital conflict, efforts at reconciliation, and steps to obtain both religious and civil divorce from 101 individuals (describing a total of 104 marriages). The majority (80 percent) of personal stories came from women, probably because they are required to be more proactive than men in obtaining permission for divorce. Of the 101 respondents who spoke about their marriage(s), approximately half came to North America as an adult (often to study), one quarter as a young child, while the other 25 percent were born in the United States or Canada. This was a highly educated group, with approximately half identifying themselves as professionals (lawyers, doctors, dentists, financial specialists, research scientists, academics and others) holding professional and/or graduate qualifications, and almost all the remainder holding college or university degrees.

Divorced men and women also came from all ethnic groups. Almost 20 percent of the marriages were cross-cultural. Half the sample identified as South Asian (predominantly Indo-Pakistani), nearly 30 percent said that their families came originally from the Middle East and just under 10 percent identified as African (primarily from North Africa and the Horn of Africa). Just 6 percent were African-American. This breakdown is close to the estimated ethnic breakdown in the North American Muslim population; the one group that may be underrepresented is African-American and African-Canadian Muslims.[6] There may also be an underrepresentation of Caucasian converts to Islam (just 3 percent of this sample), with one recent U.K. study finding that this group is growing rapidly there.[7] Both personal experiences and process characteristics of marriage and divorce are sometimes related to particular ethnic groups, and I have noted where this was pervasive. For the most part, there was a great deal of similarity among the experiences of all 101 divorced men and women, regardless of their ethnic origins.

How This Book Is Organized

Organizing the study data in this book has been challenging, since I wanted to set the context in which Islamic marriage and divorce takes place in North America, as well as provide "dense description" of the processes themselves. The book begins with a review of some of the most important challenges facing the Muslim community in North America—their status as "newcomers," preserving their religious and cultural identity and the impact of public fear of Islam. Chapter two introduces the reader to Islamic law as a system and describes the most important legal principles that govern marriage and divorce. It describes the relationship between *shari'a*—general guidelines for behavior—and Islamic law, which concerns rights and obligations to family and others. Offering a primer on Islamic law makes me vulnerable to the criticism that I am oversimplifying a complex system, while to others this material may seem very theoretical. However I believe that a basic knowledge of the design and structure of Islamic law, its roots in *shari'a* (often conflated with law) and the evolution of Islamic laws over centuries of migration is important to understanding its meaning and importance to modern-day Muslims. I have tried to make this section of the book highly accessible to those without prior knowledge of Islamic law.

Chapters three through seven present what respondents told me about getting married, staying married, marital conflict, getting divorced and the consequences of divorce. These chapters explore each of these life-changing events through personal accounts of love, marriage, conflict, despair, divorce and hope. Chapter eight reviews the present state of the law in the United States and Canada in relation to Islamic marriage and divorce and includes the experiences of respondents who found themselves as litigants. Chapter nine offers recommendations directed at policy makers who must confront the relationship between private Islamic processes and the law of the state, as well as other recommendations to enhance the fairness, consistency and modernity of Islamic marriage and divorce, addressed primarily to Muslim communities.

While a qualitative study cannot offer scientific generalizations, many strong and consistent themes emerge from the data. There is evidence of widespread use of Islamic marriage and divorce processes in North America, on a similar scale to studies conducted in the United Kingdom[8] and western Australia.[9] It is clear that commitment to using Islamic marriage and divorce processes is not explained simply by religious observance but that these processes reflect the contemporary blending of religious practice into cultural identity and subjective life. North American Muslims want to be able to use both informal Islamic processes as well as formal legal procedures, and the vast majority see no incompatibility between these and no reason to choose between them (almost all the respondents were married legally as well as in an Islamic ceremony, and sought both a legal and a religious divorce). Almost none of the total of 212 respondents (including imams, community leaders, divorced men and women and other professionals) advocated a formal legal status for Islamic family law, preferring to maintain two systems which together meet their needs as both Muslims and Americans or Canadians. The respondents help us to understand the relationship among religious, family, cultural and ideological values in their lives, and encourage us to reflect on our own. It is my hope that these realities—and not our fears or assumptions—will shape social and legal policy in the future.

The Research Journey

When I began this research, I had virtually no knowledge at all of Islam and only a few close friends who were Muslim, none of whom were strictly observant. Educated in the United Kingdom in the 1970s, I learned only about the tenets of Christianity, although my family members are not practicing Christians. Upon being funded to undertake this study, I began reading widely about Islam, Islamic law and Islamic family law, but I was woefully ill prepared for my first forays into the world I hoped to explore. A Muslim woman who has been a great supporter throughout this project met me for the first time shortly after my third interview with an imam. As I grasped her hand enthusiastically in greeting in the parking lot where we met, she looked at me directly and enquired, "Have you been shaking the hands of the imams too?" My affirmative confirmed what we both suspected—that I was almost completely unschooled in the etiquette required to build trust with my research subjects.

Gradually I learned what to expect and how to behave. I stopped assuming that I should shake hands, instead pressing my open palm against my chest in greeting and waiting until a hand was offered to me. Some of the imams I interviewed left the door of their office open or sat what seemed like very far away from me, in order to feel comfortable meeting with a woman alone. If I interviewed an imam in my office I offered tea first and coffee second. Occasionally when I conducted an interview in a mosque I was asked to cover my head. After several disastrous episodes in which helpful ladies at the mosque lent me a scarf which I endeavored to "fit" in the bathroom (I was completely incompetent, and the *hijab* always slid off my head partway through the interview), my research assistant (the dedicated and endlessly innovative Aisha Amjad) bought me a "ready-made" *hijab* which I simply had to slip on. These simple adjustments in my own expectations and behavior in order to respect rudimentary customary norms seemed the least I could do when venturing into a world that was not mine and asking probing questions about its values, beliefs and conventions. More often than not, the imams assured me that there was no need for me to wear *hijab* as a nonbeliever, but if they felt more comfortable talking to a woman who was covered, I had no difficulty meeting this need.

If the imams and scholars and social workers and divorced men and women I interviewed over the four years of the fieldwork were baffled by my interest in Islamic marriage and divorce, they were too polite to say so. Divorce was a difficult subject for all respondents to talk about, either because of a personal experience of a broken marriage or because of their concerns about rising levels of divorce within a community that prizes family stability. At a family fair during the first year of the study I set up a stall with information about the research in the hope of drawing in participants to talk about their experiences of divorce. Three hours later it felt as if I was surrounded by a force field—no one had ventured up to the stall. I tried walking around the fair and offering leaflets (which included words such as "divorce," "marital conflict," and "dissolving your marriage") directly to people, but they reacted as if they were being handed a burning coal. Finally, one woman approached the stall and began talking (loudly and looking around as she spoke) about her marriage and divorce—she was followed by a number of increasingly emboldened others. This pattern of women coming forward slowly to begin with, but then with increasing confidence, was repeated over and over. When I spoke at mosques, the women would rush forward to ask questions and talk about their experiences when the men departed for the prayer hall or became otherwise engaged. At one mosque I asked to be introduced to the "sisters group" to solicit their perspectives on divorce. The imam assured me that they would be much too shy to talk about the subject to a non-Muslim, but I asked if I might at least try. After the imam had introduced me to the group, and before he had reached the door to leave, all the women began talking at once, raising their hands and calling out their opinions about marriage and divorce. The imam lowered himself slowly into a chair at the back of the room where he remained for the next hour, listening with a dazed expression and ignored by the women, who didn't stop talking for an instant.

Constraints on talking about sensitive issues to a non-Muslim affected all my introductory conversations with potential respondents, men and women alike. Concerns about sharing personal information with an unknown outsider often surfaced in last-minute cancellations, difficulty reaching people by telephone and dozens of unanswered e-mails. One of the first imams I interviewed in the United States told me that most people in his community would assume I was either "from the immigration department, from the FBI, or a journalist," none of whom were people that Muslims were likely to be eager to talk to. One mosque almost 1,000 kilometres from my home base suggested that I first fly out for a visit in order to see if they were comfortable talking with me, and then they would decide if I could come back on a different occasion and ask them questions. When I explained that I did not have enough funding for two separate trips, they relented, and I conducted a number of valuable interviews on my one and only trip there. Another mosque that initially expressed interest in participating in the research later wrote—following a period of intensely Islamophobic news coverage in that region—that it "no longer seeks to cooperate in 'studies.' Even though I know you have the best of intentions, the willing ignorance that society likes to live in would make involvement a waste of time." This was a commonly expressed sentiment—that no matter how much information was brought to light in the course of research to "normalize" Islamic practices, they would always be demonized by the public culture and especially by a hostile media. After some follow-up and further dialogue, this mosque did in fact agree to talk to me, and the individuals I met there were extremely helpful and cooperative. I fully understood their hesitancy and that of others who were concerned about my "agenda." My only recourse throughout was to be fully transparent. I explained many times that my goal was not to somehow "evaluate" Islamic marriage and divorce but to understand it better through the stories of those who chose to go through these processes (and sometimes those who objected to the use of Islamic divorce). If asked, I acknowledged my own feminist values. But I would stress that as a researcher it was not my responsibility to judge—and certainly not to pre-judge—but to fairly and authentically present what I had learned.

My experiences impressed upon me over and over the "outsider" character of life as a Muslim in North America, no matter how long one's family has been established here. While I visited some beautiful mosques in affluent neighborhoods, the location and style of some of the facilities at which I conducted interviews and discussions—community centres, mosques, and other meeting places—were far more humble. I frequently found myself driving around and around—an industrial estate, or a rural area with farm-only buildings—looking for a venue and questioning myself, "Surely it can't be here?" A resourceful community takes any opportunity to establish space, but its settings are often less than glamorous. Some premises are dilapidated. A degree of anonymity is often preferred—security is a big concern in some locations. One inner-city Muslim community centre operating on a minimal budget uses cheap sound monitors normally affixed to babies' cots as security; I conducted a number of interviews there with these buzzing away in the background. Another day a terrific crash turned out to be the floor collapsing in an upstairs room used by the centre's social workers.

I crossed the U.S.–Canada border innumerable times in the course of the study—often by car, from Windsor to Detroit—and each time faced the question of whether disclosing my purpose in entering the United States would result in suspicion and delays. Hearing the stories of the difficulties faced by many of my subjects in crossing the same border I resolved that I would not use my privilege to avow a more innocuous purpose ("I'm going shopping") but that I would be open about where I was going (usually to a mosque or Islamic centre) and why. In this small way I took on a little outsider status myself, vicariously. Ironically, my privilege still protected me—with puzzled expressions ("you're studying *what*?"); the border officials waved me through. My own experience of outsider status was significantly increased by the reaction of some of my friends and colleagues to my new research project. Their certainty that Islamic marriage and divorce "must be bad" was based on little or no actual knowledge. I had expected this attitude to prevail in the public discourse but was shocked at its prevalence among educated elites. When I described many of the women I interviewed as highly educated professionals I was frequently asked, "So women are allowed to go to work?" The extent of this ignorance and prejudice reveals the deep roots and tolerance of Islamophobia in our present culture, including academia.

A number of the divorced men and women I interviewed had never told their full story before—not even to family members—and many found the experience liberating and therapeutic: "It means a lot to me that the experiences I had will matter somewhere. I have never shared my life's story with anyone the way I did with you. [S]ince speaking with you . . . it is as if a healing occurred in being able to tell you my story." Some interviews lasted for hours, and many women and men stayed in touch with me as they resolved various aspects of their lives post-divorce. It was a privilege to be able to provide a sympathetic ear to these individuals. Their response to telling their stories—captured by the woman quoted above—also points to a significant unmet need. The study website (www.islamicdivorce.org) continues to receive a steady flow of enquiries about Islamic divorce—what the "rules" are, where to obtain a religious divorce—and highlights the need for a service for men and women which can provide not only technical information (several sites already provide legal advice,[10] and I was careful not to do so) but also empathy and practical information (for example, where to go to talk to a sympathetic imam).

This book is about what Islam means to Muslims of all levels of observance— what it means to have a strong value system or belief in our lives. My goal was to provide information drawing on real-life experiences rather than assumptions or stereotypes for both Muslims and non-Muslims, before they rush to judgment about the place of Islamic family law in a non-Muslim state. The stories of those who have sought divorce and navigated its personal, religious and community shoals illuminate the disparate goals, motivations and of Muslims for whom Islamic marriage and divorce are meaningful. Research is about uncovering and understanding things that we do not know and cannot, therefore, understand. This was an incredible journey of discovery for me. I hope that this book will bring those insights to life.

ISLAMIC DIVORCE IN NORTH AMERICA

1 MUSLIM IDENTITY IN THE WEST

"Muslim communities in the West have a captive mentality—they are still captive to the traditions back home. They have one foot in North America and one foot in the air."

The identity of Muslims in the West must be understood in the context of the immigrant experience. The Muslim diaspora began with the journey from Medina to Mecca in 628, and continues into the twenty-first century. Following colonization in the nineteenth century, poverty and conflict led to waves of migration from Muslim countries to the West. Immigrants come from dozens of countries and from multiple cultural and ethnic groups. Among the first generation, past experiences of life in a Muslim country are similarly diverse—growing up in Kabul, Afghanistan, or in Amman, Jordan, or in Riyadh, Saudi Arabia, or on the West Bank, are very different experiences. At the same time many Muslims who have migrated to the West share some similar values and experiences, for example conservative norms about gender roles, limited experience with political democracy, and a strong identification with an extended family system. Once they arrive in the West, they find themselves both newcomers and outsiders.

The Newcomer

The establishment of Muslim communities in the West is a relatively recent development. The number of Muslims living in the European Union has doubled in ten years and is now 4 percent of the total population (10 percent in France, 5.4 percent in The Netherlands). It is estimated that by 2050 Muslims will constitute 20 percent of those living in the European Union.[1] Muslim communities are smaller but growing in North America. The U.S. Census does not collect data on religious identification, but estimates of the Muslim American population range between 1 and 3 million (the latter would be 1 percent of the U.S. population). The 2001 Canadian Census showed that 1.8 percent of Canadians was Muslim.[2] The number of converts is also growing significantly. One U.K. study estimates that the number of converts has doubled over the last ten years.[3] Studies suggest that as many as 30 percent of those who regularly attend mosque in the United States are converts, the majority African Americans.[4] Muslim communities in North America are extremely diverse and include South Asians, Arabs, Africans, East Europeans, and African Americans.

The bottom line is that "Islam is the fastest growing religion in America and Europe."[5] This brings challenges for both Muslims and their new countries of residence. The "newness" of Muslim communities in the West means that institutions, including government, courts and public services, are frequently unfamiliar with Islam and vulnerable to stereotypes, especially negative and prevalent since 9/11. At the same time, Muslim communities are struggling with their place—economic, social and political—within their new states. One Muslim scholar suggests that the emphasis on collectivism in Muslim cultures adds "a stronger need for group acceptance from the host society."[6] Muslims must balance a desire to maintain close ties with their country of origin and a strong cultural identity with the need to adapt to the conventions and expectations of life in the West. For immigrants there are reminders everywhere of the difference between their life in their country of origin and the surrounding North American culture. Should they embrace the difference or stand apart from it? Some advocate integration and the abandonment of "folkloric village customs" by "dinosaur village communities." Others respond by retreating into familiar beliefs and customs.

"[Muslim] families that come to the United States face huge adjustments. For example, they see their neighbor washing their car in the driveway wearing a bikini. Some families respond by marrying their daughters very young, wearing *hijab* and generally becoming more conservative."

It makes intuitive sense that a feeling of belonging to an ethnic or cultural group other than one's state of residence is strongest among first-generation immigrants.[7] Historically theories of ethnicity have assumed that long exposure to a majority culture will result in assimilation and loss of a distinctive ethnic identity.[8] There is growing evidence of the continuing vibrancy and distinctiveness of cultural religious and ethnic identity, in particular under certain conditions.[9] A 2002 Statistics Canada study found that a continuing commitment to cultural traditions and customs was significantly higher among first-generation South Asians (of whom one-third are Muslim) compared with Chinese Canadians and

African Canadians.[10] The data in this book demonstrates the tenacity of Muslim identity over several generations of assimilation—via education and socialization—in North America. Currently, the majority of the Muslim population in North America is born overseas. A 2007 Pew survey reported that approximately two-thirds of adult Muslims living in the United States were born elsewhere, and 39 percent have come to the United States since 1990.[11] A persistent question is what does this mean for the citizen loyalty of the newcomers? A 2006 Pew Survey found that 81 percent of British Muslims think of themselves as Muslims first rather than as British,[12] raising predictable concerns over their citizenship commitment; in the 2007 study a lower but still significant percentage of American Muslims (47 percent) considered themselves "Muslim first."[13] Similar studies among Christian Americans who consider themselves "Christians first"[14] suggest that this identification correlates with levels of religiosity or religious observance rather than lack of patriotism. This interpretation is reinforced by a 2009 Coexist/Pew study which found that British Muslims are highly patriotic in the sense that they strongly support British institutions.[15] This study supports this picture of dual but compatible loyalties. Few Muslims in this study appear to experience any tension between their commitment to Canadian or American citizenship and their Muslim identity. Many respondents assert strong loyalty to their faith, their culture and their citizenship. Few see themselves as having to choose between being Muslim and being American. "I love America . . . but I love to see always to see the right way in Islam. It is possible to hold loyalty to both."

Muslim communities in non-Muslim states are not only growing in numbers, they are developing particular cultural identities and roles within their new states. The assertion of religious and cultural identity for newcomers inevitably requires the drawing of boundaries and the creation of "insider" spaces.[16] For Muslims in North America these boundaries are typically defined in terms of Muslim family life, including, for example, a preference for finding a marriage partner within the community (Statistics Canada reports that marriage outside the community runs at only 13 percent in South Asian communities compared with 43 percent among African Canadians),[17] as well as continuing recourse to traditional rituals of Islamic marriage and divorce. The creation of an Islamic "space" for marriage and divorce rituals is an important assertion of identity even for more secular Muslims, essential to a feeling of well-being and belonging. For more conservative Muslims, their response to the perceived moral permissiveness of Western culture takes the form of a sustained effort "to assert Muslim culture aggressively and maintain the boundaries around Islam."[18] Both these groups are reflected in the study data.

The Outsider

As cultural communities develop identity by establishing space for private religious practices, the mainstream community designates them as "The Other." Yvonne Haddad notes that "America, although a nation of immigrants, is nonetheless not particularly fond of them, no matter where they come from or what they believe in."[19] This problem is worse for those who look different to the majority and are subject to what Sherene Razack calls "race thinking"[20]—the construction of social hierarchies based on race and group membership. Muslims become "outsiders" in North America almost unconsciously as social norms expect and permit categorization on the basis of race. Frequently, the response to Islam and Muslims "is underpinned by the idea that modern, enlightened, secular peoples must protect themselves from pre-modern, religious peoples whose loyalty to tribe and community reigns over their commitment to the rule of law."[21] Consciousness of "outsider" status among North American Muslims has been heightened since 9/11 by the increased hostility and fear of non-Muslims, who associate them with the threat of violence.

Many of the 212 people interviewed for this study volunteered that their lives had changed, usually for the worse, since 9/11, and this reality colored almost every conversation.[22] Women who were accustomed to wearing *hijab* without attracting attention now found themselves the subject of intense scrutiny and sometimes hostility; imams spoke of the need for increased security at the mosque and concern about strangers; and many others described the experience of fielding questions from friends, neighbors and media which sometimes feel less than open-minded and sometimes intrusive and hostile. Concerns about the consequences of growing Islamophobia are most acute among parents of young children. "We are, in fact, far more scared and disgusted about what happened (on 9/11) than non-Muslims, because it affects our children."

Signs of preoccupation with the "threat of Islam" are all around us, so continuous that we barely register them. It was, perhaps, inevitable that the terror of 9/11 would excite fear of an unknown "Other," but this fear is continuously reinforce by public figures and popular culture. In the United Kingdom, the fiction writer Martin Amis has conducted a long public campaign against Islam, describing Muslims as "less civilized" and non-Muslims as "morally superior."[23] In Canada, journalist Mark Steyn wrote in *Maclean's Magazine* in 2006 that the population growth among Muslims threatened a "take-over" that would lead to apocalyptic violence and terror worldwide.[24] Several of the Republican candidates for the presidential nomination in 2011 publicly declared that they would not include Muslims in their cabinet.[25] From the perspective of those most fearful of Islam and hostile towards Muslims, the battle is now engaged. New sites for conflict emerge on an almost weekly basis—the row over the construction of a Muslim community centre some blocks away from "Ground Zero" in New York City (described by popular radio host Rush Limbaugh as "a victory monument");[26] Qur'an burning stunts orchestrated by a Florida pastor;[27] and efforts to force the Detroit suburban bus network to carry billboards asking, "Leaving Islam? Fatwa on your head? Is your family or community threatening you?"[28] Invoking the principle of invidious comparison, one scholar has suggested that the constant attacks on Islam meet an important need for Westerners: ". . . they act as a foil to make us look good."[29]

One strategy a minority group can adopt in the face of such hostility is withdrawal, further entrenching outsider status.[30] This may take many forms, including a falling back on familiar norms and customs and a reassertion of identity. An alternate strategy is to increase efforts at mutual understanding and integration. Many of the Muslim leaders interviewed for this study believed a commitment to greater openness and communication with non-Muslims to be critical. "Muslim communities since 9/11 are much more willing to speak up and open doors to outsiders. This is essential."

Shari'a for Muslims in the West

One of the most intense sites of fear and suspicion of Muslims by the West is Islamic *shari'a*. The media's portrayal of *shari'a* as a brutal penal regime or a misogynist legal system is very different to the understanding that the vast majority of Muslims have of *shari'a*. For them, following *shari'a*—the normative principles governing the Muslim way of life, from prayer to fasting to family law—is an expression of Muslim identity. The literal meaning of the Arabic word *shari'a* is "The Way" (the names given to the Jewish Talmud and the Tao carry a very similar meaning). *Shari'a* encompasses all aspects of an individual's personal life and life choices. It represents the complete body of principles for daily living and includes rules for personal observance as well as personal conduct in every aspect of life.

Shari'a principles derive from an interpretation of the Qur'an and the Sunna (reports of the behaviors, habits and practices of the Prophet Mohammed as recorded by his Companions) by jurists living in the seventh and eighth centuries. The substance of *shari'a* is controversial among Muslims because of concerns over the validity of these interpretations and because of the particular historical contexts in which *shari'a* emerged (for example, women in seventh-century Arabia had few rights). There has never been uniformity regarding what constitutes *shari'a*; Abdullahi An-Na'im argues that what is accepted as *shari'a* has always been—and will always be—negotiable.[31] The scope of personal discretion within *shari'a* is a source of controversy. Some Muslims argue for a homogeneous and singular "right" approach to *shari'a*, insisting that certain behaviors are non-negotiable and are required to be a "good Muslim." Others adopt a more private approach to adherence and understand compliance as a matter of personal conscience. The majority accept that there may be differences in approach among Muslims but assume a body of core principles such as treating others with respect, dealing fairly and staying close to God.

Shari'a represents the unity of Islam; as one imam expressed this to me, "Without *shari'a*, Muslims would not be Muslims." It also reflects its extraordinary diversity. Another scholar told me, "There is a *shari'a* for every . . . Muslim." Despite differences in approach and observance, there is a persistent consciousness of *shari'a* among Muslims. Muslim scholars are paying increasing attention to the idea of a progressive twenty-first-century *shari'a* that reflects the ideals of Islam in a contemporary context. Asserting that equality and social justice are core principles of *shari'a*, many leading Muslim scholars argue that *shari'a* can and should continue to evolve in a way that meets contemporary needs and norms.[32] Many of the imams and scholars interviewed for this study share this conviction: "*Shari'a* is . . . not fixed in seventh-century Medina. . . . [I]t is a growing tree."

Strictly speaking, *shari'a* is not law (whatever its source) but a code of personal behavior. *Shari'a* refers to a Muslim way of life and beliefs, whereas *fiqh* refers to Islamic laws.[33] I shall describe the rules that govern family law as Islamic family law, rather than the more generic *shari'a*. There may be some overlap; for example, some parts of *shari'a* that are concerned with family relationships have found their way into law—but these are separate concepts. Western media, many non-Muslims and even some Muslims constantly conflate *shari'a* and Islamic law. This may reflect the fact that Islam does not distinguish between laws and ethics or between religion and morality.[34] All rules for personal conduct are understood to come from and relate to God. Violation of a formal law is an offence against society and also against God. Whether or not an individual is actually caught breaking a law, he is still accountable to God for his behavior. This means that for practical purposes, whether a particular principle is contained in law or derives from *shari'a* may not be important for Muslims. While recognizing that some respondents drew no such distinction either in theory or in practice, I shall try to distinguish between *shari'a* and Islamic law. Aside from trying to use both expressions accurately, the distinction is important to the debate over which rules are divinely ordained, and which can change and evolve.

Another often-repeated assumption of the public debate is that Muslims desire the imposition and enforcement of so-called *shari'a* law in North America. A further implication is that eventually *shari'a* will come to be applied to non-Muslims also— one highway billboard displayed prominently along U.S. highways in 2009 ominously predicted "*Shari'a* Is Coming." There is an assumption that support among Muslims for *shari'a*—compliant behaviors (for example, Islamic marriage and divorce)—represents an aggressive antagonism towards local laws and norms. The only study that gives credence to the claim that Muslims want Islamic law to govern in their adopted countr ies was conducted in the United Kingdom in 2007 by the Policy Exchange think tank.[35] Policy Exchange claimed that 37 percent of 16–24 year-olds questioned in a telephone survey said that they would prefer to be governed by *shari'a* law. This claim attracted considerable controversy when subsequent reporting exposed that much of the study data was fraudulent.[36]

Interviews conducted for this study found a very different—and more complex—attitude towards the application of Islamic law in North America. First, the only area in which respondents were concerned with applying Islamic law to their own lives was in relation to family matters (marriage and divorce) and, occasionally, financial decision making.[37] No one interviewed for this study ever suggested that they wanted the extension of the most notorious penal regimes described as "*shari'a*" to North America. This is hardly surprising since the majority of respondents regarded these regimes as aberrant and lacking in Qur'anic authority. Consistent with these findings are repeated public comments by many Muslim leaders, including the then-director of CAIR (Council on American-Islamic Relations) Oklahoma who commented during the 2010 campaign for the Oklahoma amendment on *shari'a* law that "I know no American Muslims who would like to see *shari'a* law implemented in the U.S."[38]

All the respondents in this study understand their private choices of Islamic marriage and divorce as separate from the formal legal system. They consistently draw a distinction between God's law—which they regard as a matter for their personal conscience rather than public adjudication—and the law of the state or "human law." The overwhelming majority of respondents expressed a desire to be able to continue to access their Islamic traditions in a private, informal system, and also to be able to use the legal process.

Islamic Marriage and Divorce

"In the absence of physical institutions of Islam and paradigms of *shari'a*, Muslims create their own 'Islamic imagination' as a substitute for those institutional elements."

In common with other immigrant groups that share their sense of "newcomer" and "outsider' status, many North American Muslims exercise an "Islamic imagination"—encompassing religious principles, cultural norms and personal values—in approaching life's critical transitions, such as birth, marriage, divorce and death. The specifics of the processes themselves, especially divorce, vary widely. The *nikah*, or Muslim marriage contract, is widely used, and many couples resort to a simple boilerplate. The contract describes the commitment that the spouses are making to one another and to God in their union. It also includes a description of the *mahr*—the traditional wedding gift that passes from husband to wife—and implicitly embeds Islamic family law principles in relation to property (usually kept separate in a Muslim marriage) and support. There is a widespread presumption that a Muslim couple will marry using a *nikah*. For some the *nikah* represents a deep religious commitment, while others sign the marriage contract mostly to satisfy their parents, or to give a nod to tradition. Many barely read the terms before signing, or discuss whether they and their spouses share the same understanding of Islamic family law, which may lead to future disappointments and conflicts.

Islamic divorce is more complex and much more diverse. There is no single process. Some Muslims go to their imam, who may take one of many different approaches. Others go to a trusted family member for advice or convene a discussion between the two families, and yet others practice self-help by informing themselves about their rights and responsibilities in Islamic law. Yet others choose to go to a lawyer and ask for Islamic elements to be included in their separation agreement. There is no single or uniform set of governing principles applied to the dissolution of marriage; there are minor differences between different schools of law but much larger differences in the way in which the law is applied, for example, the grounds on which women may obtain divorce.

The phenomenon of Islamic divorce is supported by the belief of the individual that he or she is now divorced in God's eyes. There is no "certified" documentation, formal proceeding or third-party qualification. If an individual believes that she or he is Islamically divorced—following a discussion with an imam, an agreement with their spouse or family or simply by default after certain conditions have been met—then essentially she or he is. Despite the psychological rather than the formal legal nature of the phenomenon, the need to secure religious approval for the ending of a marriage is critical to closure and moving forward after divorce for many Muslims, especially (although not only) for women. In the absence of a quantitative study it is difficult to assess the extent of recourse to religious divorce, but it is clearly both vibrant and commonplace among North American Muslims.

Religion, Religious Practice, Culture and Identity

"The religion gives the women the rights—but the culture will abuse them."

As Muslims in the West struggle to define their identity, both inward and outward, they constantly confront choices about the organization and values of their family life—how to get married, how to structure their family life and roles within their family, whether to stay married and how to get divorced. In the process, they juggle multiple obligations—religious, cultural and familial—as well as their personal aspirations and goals for life in North America. The relationship between these obligations is often complex.

Some respondents describe their choice of an Islamic process and principles as motivated by their religious beliefs.

> "This is my life. Everything I do is according to what God tells us to do in the Qur'an. . . . I could not imagine any other way."
> "I refer everything to what pleases Allah."

In other cases, the expectations of community and family—to stay in a marriage, to try again, to keep the family together—give rise to an equally strong sense of obligation, especially for women. Sometimes these types of family and cultural obligations are difficult to distinguish from religious beliefs. In others, respondents clearly distinguish cultural and religious beliefs.

> "There is an unconscious burden on women. This is not Islam, this is the culture."

Many community leaders acknowledge that their influence is dependent in part on their cultural authority and knowledge, and some go so far as to suggest that Muslims are more attached to their culture than to their religion. Religious dogma is sometimes used to explain behavior that seems to have little to do with Islamic principles but is culturally justified and accepted. The most frequent example of this is male assertion of power and control over women, often their wives, but also their sisters, mothers and others. Some men taunt their wives with what they assert is their failure to behave as a "good Muslim woman," knowing this to be a powerful psychological tool. The use of claimed religious proscriptions—described by one researcher as "spiritual abuse"[39]—to control a partner and justify violence is often prevalent in communities that privilege male power and authority.[40] Lack of education on Islamic rights and responsibilities worsens the problem. "Women are given a lot of rights in Islam, but people are not educated on them and get influenced by culture."

In the midst of marital conflict, individuals must balance their desire to escape an unhappy relationship with their need to feel that they have acted appropriately in their own eyes and in the eyes of their family. In the process, they will construct what their religion means for them individually and socially. Appeal to religious principles—however these are constructed—offers an attractive external rationalization. Religious rationalization must also be compatible with cultural norms and assumptions (for example, tolerance for divorce) and personal aspirations (for example, the ending of an unhappy marriage). What respondents understand as religious principle reflects their formal knowledge but is also integrated with their cultural consciousness, including traditions from their countries of origin and customs within their own family systems. The lines between what they understand to be religiously proscribed and their embedded cultural beliefs are continually blurred. The significance of cultural beliefs and tolerances is clear in the range of attitudes towards divorce that emerge from the interviews. While Islam has permitted divorce for a variety of reasons since the seventh century, respondents constantly refer to cultural barriers that sometimes prevent even consideration of such a step. "It's not acceptable in our culture—period." Many respondents struggle—both practically and emotionally—with the tensions and even overt contradictions between religion and culture as sources of authority and significance in their lives.

This struggle is related to another theme of this book, which is the changing nature of what we think of as "religious practice." Historically, religion has been associated with external observances. Researchers have noted a shift from a "life-as" model that is motivated by obedience to external authority to a "subjective-life" model where the primary source of personal satisfaction is psychological well-being, rather than the fulfillment of duties owed to religious authorities.[41] Many of those who turn to religious authorities for divorce are not conventionally observant and would not describe themselves as "religious" but regard religious approval as important for their own sense of conscience, their Muslim identity and in order to meet the expectations of their communities. Rather than expressed publicly in observance rituals, this identity is expressed as a private consciousness that connects personal spirituality to a sense of personal well-being—for example, "I was not strictly observant but I turned to Allah and found strength as I remembered him more." It is also articulated as an obligation to the community, which requires them to meet cultural expectations and respect cultural traditions.[42]

If our understanding of religious practice is expanded to include a subjective, private consciousness, our understanding of how personal obligations are formed changes also. Religion becomes only one marker among many others, including culture, gender and race, instead of the sole criterion. Whereas religious norms are given and imposed by external authorities, cultural norms are generated and sustained—and modified—within families and communities. An almost limitless diversity is possible. The private nature of some religious practice may provide psychological protection for individuals whose behavior defies community norms—for example, going through with divorce when there are strong taboos against this. For these respondents, the most important standard for personal behavior is a "recognition of self"[43]—meeting their own needs as a Western Muslim, male or female, however they understand these —rather than conformity with either religious proscription or cultural expectations.

Watershed Debates

The question of the place and status of "*shari'a* law" has ignited contentious debate in many Western countries. The focus of these debates has varied—from the wearing of the *hijab*, to the building of mosques, to the recognition of Islamic tribunals—but the essential question is the same. Do Muslims in the West accept "Western" values and processes or do they prefer *shari'a*? The assumption is that this is a forced choice—either/or—and that parallel loyalties are impossible. These controversies reflect a high level of public alarm about Islam and have cast Muslims in the West as a threat to public safety and stability. They have alienated many Muslims who feel unfairly scrutinized, and caused divisions within the Muslim community. Muslims who do not regard themselves as especially religious or observant have become drawn into these debates because the attacks on expression—wearing *hijab,* establishing new mosques, using an Islamic arbitrator—appear to them as attacks on symbols of their Muslim identity as much as on their religion. Because Muslims do not distinguish between personal morality and law and understand *shari'a* to govern all aspects of their lifestyle and choices, "attacks on Shariah can often be misconstrued by Muslims as an attack upon their core values."[44] Interviews in this study constantly reinforce this sense of unfair scrutiny and differential treatment. "Why should I not be able to follow my process which fits with my values when others can follow theirs?"

Each controversy that arises has been constructed in the public discourse as a collision between religious beliefs (entrenched in *shari'a*) and citizenship loyalties, often framed by the media as a struggle between religious fundamentalists and progressive Muslims, and between Islam and Christianity (synonymous herewith a Western value system). Watershed debates over Islam and *shari'a* took place in Ontario in 2003–2005 and in the United Kingdom in 2008. These controversies are more accurately framed as debates over identity, and specifically the process of identity construction for Muslims in the West and their differences as "the Other."[45]

Ontario (2003–2005)

The existence of informal dispute resolution processes—described as "Islamic courts" or "Muslim tribunals"—reported to be relying on *shari'a* law sparked widespread public alarm in Ontario, Canada, in September 2003. The catalyst was an announcement by a small Ontario-based group called Darul-Qada, led by Syed Mumtaz Ali, a lawyer and arbitrator, calling for the legal recognition of Islamic tribunals offering arbitrations applying Islamic family law. After the story first appeared in the *Canadian Law Times*,[46] sensationalist media coverage ensued. As Catherine Morris described it, "Three days later, the first line of an American news story proclaimed that 'Canadian judges soon will be enforcing Islamic law, or *Shari'a*, in disputes between Muslims, possibly paving the way to one day administering criminal sentences, such as stoning women caught in adultery.'"[47] The story was picked up by news media around the world from the United States to Turkey.

In fact, similar demands had been made for more than a decade, first by the Canadian Society of Muslims (of which Mumtaz Ali was president) and then by the Islamic Institute of Civil Justice or *Darul-Qada* (also headed by Mumtaz Ali). There had been some limited earlier press coverage[48] and an effort to lobby the 1994 Ontario Civil Justice Review, but the issue attracted little interest until 2003.[49] A poorly understood reality—the Ontario Arbitration Act of 1991 already recognized decisions of faith-based arbitrators including Jewish and Ismaili tribunals—obscured the debate from the outset.[50] The Act allowed for the recognition of decisions of a religious tribunal, which meant that an award by an arbitrator based on faith principles was recognized as having the same status as any other arbitral award under the act. An award by a religious arbitrator was subject to the same (limited) grounds of appeal (that the applicant was treated fairly, that proper process was followed), although the parties to arbitration may waive their rights to any appeal. Significantly, there is no record of any arbitral award from a Muslim arbitrator ever being appealed using the Act.[51]

Nonetheless, the Ontario and wider Canadian news media presented the *Darul-Qada* proposal as something new and different than the status quo. Newspaper articles constantly referred to the Ontario government considering "the introduction of *shari'a* law into family law disputes" and "the enforcement of *shari'a* law." Religious divorce that referred to the principles of Islamic family law was already taking place in private processes conducted by imams and a few self-described arbitrators. Recourse to Islamic marriage and divorce was regarded as opting out of the legal system—those who used such processes were labeled "un-Canadian" by some media.[52] Islamic divorce processes were inaccurately described (first by Ali and then by the press) as "arbitration tribunals," but they bear little or no resemblance to a formal arbitration. There is no formal hearing or evidence presented, no legal representation of the parties, only rarely a written agreement to arbitrate, and no record of the proceedings (aside from the outcome, in some cases). Instead, an informal meeting takes place in either the imam's office or the family home, where the imam talks with one or sometimes both spouses, and sometimes their family members. The misnomers "arbitration" and "tribunal" imbued these informal private processes with an aura of authority and structure which further elevated public alarm.

The advance sought by the *Darul-Qada* may have been political and symbolic rather than legal. If this was the objective, it backfired badly, instead creating a climate of public fear and moral panic and dividing the Muslim community in Ontario. Opposition to the proposal, especially from the Canadian Council of Muslim Women (CCMW), became more organized and more vocal.[53] The CCMW lobby attracted widespread support from feminist organizations and women's groups, reflecting the conviction that faith-based divorce mediation or arbitration would be inherently damaging to women. One columnist in a national newspaper described the use of Islamic law to determine divorces as "about the best idea since female foot-binding."[54] In June 2004 the Ontario government announced it would establish a public enquiry to examine the proposals made by *Darul-Qada* and to solicit the input of all interested parties, including other communities operating religious tribunals. The report which followed[55] recommended continuing recognition of religious tribunals by the Arbitration Act but adding regulations under the act to allow for greater monitoring of family arbitrators at-large. The recommendations were widely praised by Muslim groups including the Canadian Islamic Congress and CAIR-CAN (Canadian Council on American-Islamic Relations), although the CCMW was "disappointed," arguing that family matters should be removed from the purview of arbitration altogether. The debate was not informed by any empirical data on how divorce processes were being conducted, what "arbitration" and "mediation" meant in this context, or how the outcomes of Islamic divorce compared with those ordered by the courts. This did not prevent some journalists and scholars from making definitive pronouncements on whether or not the outcomes of such processes (for example) infringed human rights, ran contrary to principles of freedom and democracy or infringed the Canadian Charter of Rights and Freedoms.[56]

Intense media coverage continued into 2005, and the debate became increasingly divisive both inside and outside the Muslim community. Protests and counter - protests began outside the Ontario Parliament buildings in Queen's Park. In September 2005 the Ontario premier, Dalton McGuinty, announced that he would amend the Arbitration Act to remove the recognition of religious arbitration.[57] The McGuinty statement was widely reported as a "ban" on "*shari'a* law." What McGuinty actually said in his statement was, "I've come to the conclusion that the debate has gone on long enough. There will be no *shari'a* law in Ontario, there will be no religious arbitration in Ontario, there will be one law for all Ontarians." He went on to say that he would never deny Ontarians "the right to seek advice from anyone in matters of family law, including religious advice." However the widespread reporting of his statement as a "ban" was never corrected by the government and conveyed the widespread impression (appealing to popular opinion which was registering 63 percent opposed to religious arbitration[58]) that recourse to Islamic divorce was now illegal in Ontario.

Sources close to the premier say that his announcement—made on a Sunday—took them completely by surprise. An adviser to the premier told me that "the loudest voices carried the day." These were a "strange alliance" between an anti-immigration, anti-Muslim lobby and Muslim anti-*shari'a* activists. The amendments to the Arbitration Act passed in 2006 removed any access to the civil courts to either appeal or enforce a decision of a religious arbitrator, including divorces arbitrated or mediated by imams in mosques.[59] The same amendments removed access to the courts for family arbitrations conducted by the Jewish Bet Din, leading to a storm of protest from the Jewish community. One rabbi commented, "Because *shari'a* was at odds with modern values, they took it out on the Jews."[60] At the same time the government established regulations which incorporated many of the Boyd recommendations by placing new requirements on *any* family arbitrator who wished to bring his or her awards within the purview of the act (for example, access to independent legal advice and screening for domestic violence). If the imams wished to bring themselves within the purview of the act, they would have to comply with these regulations. Presumably the hope was that this would act as an incentive to provide such safeguards. None of the imams or other respondents I interviewed for this study gave this serious consideration. I quickly discovered Muslim men and women had little interest in their religious outcomes being recognized by Ontario law. The point of their seeking a religious divorce was in almost all cases a matter of spiritual beliefs, values, culture and identity. For a legal divorce, they went to the courts.

Media coverage, and in particular the widely reported "ban" on *shari'a* law in Ontario, convinced some Muslims that they could no longer go to their imams for divorce, although the practice resurged within a year. This debacle added to the sense of mistrust between the Muslim and non-Muslim communities in Ontario, an unease that continues today.

The United Kingdom (2008)

In February 2008 the archbishop of Canterbury, Rowan Williams, delivered a speech on the place of Islam in contemporary British political and legal culture. In his speech, Williams referred to the work of the U.K. Shari'a Councils (as well as Jewish tribunals) and reflected on the possible extension of legal recognition to such bodies to enable them to function as a parallel legal system. Williams argued that Muslims in a non-Muslim state have multiple affiliations and identities. They should not have to choose between cultural identity and citizenship. British Muslims, Williams argued, are told by their own communities that choosing outside their cultural identity is a betrayal and by non-Muslims that choosing outside their citizenship identity is a betrayal. He warned that this presentation as a stark choice—"your culture or your rights"—threatened to alienate and ghettoize these communities.[61]

The speech provoked a media storm. There were widespread calls for the archbishop's resignation.[62] Members of Parliament described Williams as "totally unfit for the role he undertakes" and his comments as "unhelpful" and fermenting "social chaos."[63] Newspaper articles referred to the "un-British" character of those Muslim men and women who sought Islamic divorce.[64] The interpretation—repeated over and over in the press—was that the archbishop was advocating brutal penal punishments such as those applied by Taliban authorities in the most unstable parts of the Muslim world.

The substance of the speech—which went on to discuss in a detailed and scholarly manner the various arguments for and against recognizing a parallel Islamic jurisdiction—was important, but the reaction to it was perhaps even more revealing. Despite the care that Williams took to limit the discussion to the resolution of family matters and to explain the dynamic and evolving character of *shari'a* and its adaptability to a contemporary context, the response to the speech demonstrated that "you can barely use the word Shariah because of what people associate with it, which for a practicing Muslim is quite difficult because they don't see it in that light."[65] This fear and bias leaked into the reporting of the speech; the archbishop was widely described as "calling for Islamic law" (he was proposing reframing a debate over private customary systems) and the "imposition" of *shari'a* (he was exploring the possibility of choice by Muslims).

The day after the speech, Williams was described as "shocked" by the extent of the hostility expressed against him by members of the Church and the British government.[66] A spokesperson for the Muslim Public Affairs Committee UK described the climate as "hysteria" (while trying to draw attention to the lack of interest among most British Muslims for a separate Islamic legal system).[67] In remarks made a few days later, Williams warned against a "stand-off" between Muslims and non-Muslims based on conscience, setting up a clash of values that appears non-negotiable. This was precisely the framing that the speech argued against by suggesting that multiple loyalties and affiliations in a multicultural society do not have to cancel one another out. Ironically, in calling for more understanding of shared citizenship values and efforts to promote interfaith and community cooperation, the archbishop's comments vividly illuminated the fault lines.

The reframing of the real message of Williams's speech led some Muslims to wonder if an open-minded debate is even possible at this time. Is it possible, as Williams suggested, "to look at this with a clearer eye and not imagine . . . that we know exactly what we mean by *Shari'a*?"[68] Despite negativism and a parlous lack of information, significant public interest exists in engaging in the discussion over relations between Muslims and non-Muslims in the West. A first step must be to better understand the underlying principles of a Muslim identity, expressed in *shari'a* and Islamic law, and its continuous expression and development via the Muslim diaspora. Recourse to Islamic marriage and divorce in the West represents one site for the evolution of this identity, and a closer look at the meaning and practice of these processes offers many important insights into the formation and substance of Muslim identity in the West. First, the development of Islamic law, and its principles on marriage and divorce, provides a historical and ideological context for these practices.

2 A PRIMER ON ISLAMIC FAMILY LAW

This is not a book about Islamic law, but the practice of Muslim marriage and divorce in North America. Nonetheless, understanding the relationship between theory—here Islamic family law—and practice is a critical part of making sense of how Muslims exercise their "Islamic imagination." This chapter offers a basic framework for understanding the systems characteristics of Islamic law and the fundamental principles of Islamic marriage and divorce. These principles are refracted through the practice of the imams who in practice substitute for Islamic judges in North America. As the following chapters reveal, the imams are highly pragmatic in the application of Islamic law principles, adapting them to many different circumstances. In their continuing recourse to Islamic marriage and divorce, North American Muslims are creating their own, contemporary, versions of Islamic family law. In the process, a modern Western Muslim identity is emerging.

How Islamic Law Has Developed
A Personal Moral Code

In Islam, all rules for conduct are understood to come from and relate to God, whether framed as a legal or a personal moral obligation. Islam does not distinguish between laws and ethics, or between religion and morality.[1] *Shari'a* is a matter for the personal conscience of every Muslim, "a matter between the individual and God, to be settled on the Day of Judgment."[2] The spirit in which one conducts oneself is as important as what one actually does, and the "intention" of the actor is more important than whether or not they have broken or complied with a law. "God knows and sees actual intention."[3] Many respondents spoke about their need to have a clear conscience about the spirit in which they handled marital conflict and its consequences (for example, working as hard as possible at reconciliation, being kind and just in settling financial affairs), as well as following what they understood Islamic law required of them. In the face of an outcome that feels unfair, this brings some consolation: "I know that if I am right, I will be rewarded one day. . . . This is the right way to behave as a Muslim. . . . Allah is there and Allah sees."

Primary Sources

The Qur'an, the Sunna and *hadith* represent the three primary sources for the development of Islamic law or *fiqh*. The Qur'an contains between 80 and 600 verses (estimates vary) that suggest legal principles or rules.[4] Since Mohammed was illiterate, the Qur'an was written down by the Companions of the Prophet, who also created other textual sources for Islam. Principal among these are the Sayings of the Prophet or *hadith*, which are understood as narratives of "what the Prophet had said, done or tacitly approved,"[5] and the Sunna of the Companions of the Prophet, which are examples of exemplary conduct—"established conduct, rooted in past practice"[6]—taken from the Prophet's own life. In the first century after the death of the Prophet, a largely oral tradition was gradually translated into *hadith* and Sunna and also integrated the adjudications of the first *caliphs* (rulers) and *qadis* (judges). Debates over the authenticity of *hadith* continue to be a source of contention among scholars. Shia Muslims do not rely on the same *hadith* and Sunna as Sunni Muslims because they have a different belief about the appropriate succession of leaders from the Prophet and hence a different position on which Companions and Successors are credible and authoritative. This leads to some differences between Sunni and Shia jurisprudence.

How Law Developed Out of Shari'a

In the decades and then the centuries after the death of the Prophet, *shari'a* was developed with reference to the Qur'an and the Sunna. Some rules based on these textual sources emerged as *fiqh*, or laws, in an effort to practicalise in daily life the principles of the Qur'an. These scholars (historically known as the *ulama*) wielded significant power in the Muslim world during the centuries following the life of the Prophet. Muslim jurists—the *ulama* or community of scholars— determined which *shari'a* principles should be formalized as law, as well as their substance. One commentator describes the development of Islamic jurisprudence as "the science of interpretation of both Qur'an and Sunna."[7] Where the Qur'an was silent on a particular point, *fiqh* would be developed where necessary from caliphal law or the rulings of the *ulama*. The ruler or *caliph* relied upon the edicts of the *ulama* to give legitimacy to his claim to rule according to the will of God.[8] The jurists authored the legal treatises and *fatwa* (rulings on particular questions) that formed the substance of early *fiqh*. Although the *ulama* were never a formal part of government, they became a potent political force in the Islamic state because they exercised control over the development of *fiqh* and, by extension, *shari'a*.

In developing *fiqh*, the *ulama* focused on social and family obligations within *shari'a*. Not all *shari'a* is suitable for translation into law—with its attendant enforcement mechanisms—because so much of it relates to a personal relationship with God. Where the duty is owed to God—for example, the obligation to fast—atonement of any breach takes place between the individual and God. Where *shari'a* creates a social obligation to others—for example, a father's obligation to financially support his children—it may be enforced by law. Thus *fiqh* is a subset of *shari'a*. Within *shari'a*, there is a distinction between "the rule which is enforced by the law as applied by the courts, and the rule which finds its sanction only at the Bar of eternity."[9]

An Islamic Legal Method

To ensure that *fiqh* is faithful to the core principles of *shari'a*, a number of doctrinal principles and tools have emerged over the centuries to guide the development of Islamic law.[10] These constitute an Islamic jurisprudence, or legal method. When they authored legal treatises, or adjudicated conflicts using *fatwa* or authoritative opinions, the first jurists built on original legal principles to further develop the law. They did so by constructing and applying a methodology of interpretation that was increasingly formalized as a legal method and used to explain interpreting and perhaps extending the law. Jurists argued that by following an established jurisprudential method to address ambiguities and resolve conflicts they could ensure that *fiqh* remained faithful to the core principles of *shari'a*.[11] In this way, Islamic law has been able to grow and to adapt to changing and unanticipated situations via the authoritative opinions of jurists. Contemporary *fatwa* are the continuation of this tradition, but their status and authority are unclear—and certainly diminished—in a modern Western state.

Contemporary Muslim scholars continue to debate these interpretive tools. The guiding principles of interpretation of Islamic law are described collectively as *ijtihad* (effort), acknowledging the role of human reasoning in trying to interpret and apply the law. One of the most important is *ijma*, or consensus, which roughly translates that the law should reflect the shared opinion of the community. Some Islamic jurisprudence limits the notion of consensus to the established scholarly community, or *ulama*, although Imam ash-Shafi'i and Malik ibn Anas, both of whom founded schools of law, also looked at the practice of the wider community in reaching an opinion.[12] How far this included the views of women is not clear, but when the search for consensus is limited to the *ulama*, the rules developed inevitably reflect its men-only membership.

Another important tool to emerge during the first 100 years of Islamic jurisprudence was *qiyas*, or reasoning by analogy. *Qiyas* constrains judicial speculation by developing a system of precedent in which new cases are bound by the reasoning of previous cases. At the same time it permits the extension of the law by analogy when a new circumstance can be brought within the scope of the original reasoning and reflect the purpose of the law. For example, "Wine drinking . . . is prohibited by explicit text. The cause for the prohibition is the intoxicating effect, hence in whatever this cause is found prohibition will become applicable."[13]

A system of precedent may be justified by the need to constrain judicial activism—it may also be used to control the status quo. In the eyes of some, *qiyas* is an effort to enable an unbroken line between principles derived from an historical *shari'a* and the application of the same principles to contemporary cases; in this way human reasoning can always be traced back to a divine source.[14] A further safeguard is that jurists must consider the consensus among them over the particular principle. In all these ways, *qiyas* is similar in process and purpose to *stare decisis*, or "let the decision stand," in the common law system, where judges apply the same reasoning and subsequent principle (the *ratio decidendi*) to similar fact cases—it also shares the same mixed motivation. It can be used either conservatively to limit the development of the law, or to justify extending it.

Jurisprudence and Decision Making

The four major Sunni schools of law are Hanbali, Hanifi, Maliki and Shafi'i. The major Shia school is Jafiri. The schools adopt somewhat different approaches to the interpretation of the sources and therefore have some slight variation in laws. Each school recognizes the Qur'an as the primary source of law, but Sunni jurists also look to the *hadith* and the Sunna (differences exists between Sunni and Shia theologians over which *hadith* authors are credible). Historically, different schools of jurisprudence have held sway in different parts of the modern Muslim world. For example, the Hanbali school is dominant in Saudi Arabia, the Maliki school in North Africa, the Hanifi school in India and Pakistan and the Shafi'i school in Indonesia and Southeast Asia. The Hanifi and Maliki schools are geographically the most widespread. Although all Muslims formally recognize all five schools of law, anyone who has lived in a Muslim country is likely to assume a preference for the particular school that dominated that legal culture.

The substance of *fiqh* is often controversial among Muslims, and Islamic family law continues to develop in Muslim countries via judicial decision making, pressure for law reform and discourse among jurists. There is a long tradition of contextualization which is rarely constrained by school-based orthodoxies. An-Na'im suggests that in practice, "judges and legislators first decide what the rule should be, and then go into an arbitrary 'fishing' expedition for nominal support among any of the schools or scholars . . . that they can find."[15] While some jurists might take issue with the description of "arbitrary," An-Na'im's assertion fits with observations that have long been made by scholars studying the practice of Islamic law in Muslim countries. Laurence Rosen in his classic study of Moroccan *sharia* courts concludes that these courts give wide discretion to the judges, or *qadis*. He suggests that this exemplifies the central role of negotiation as a cultural norm—especially in the construction and constant renegotiation of social relationships of all kinds—and the importance of context in judgment and decision making, especially in family matters.[16]

In North America, in the absence of universally accepted Islamic legal institutions that can authoritatively interpret the law or develop precedent, discussions often centre on relatively minor differences among the five schools. I was frequently asked whether the practice of Islamic divorce I was documenting was affected by the different juristic allegiances of the scholars and imams, with the assumption that the answer to this question would be yes. This was clearly not the case. The interpretation and application of Islamic law by North American imams appears to adopt the same tradition of contextualization described by Rosen and others. While individuals and communities occasionally express their preference for a particular school of law, and may seek out imams who are conversant (perhaps as a result of their own religious education) with this school, these preferences appear to be cultural and related to personal comfort rather than tied to any particular expectations of substantive differences in outcome.

I found very little evidence of any school-based differences in decision making among the imams. Instead, I came across numerous examples of pragmatic choices that matched the desired outcome in any one case with whatever legal theory could provide a rationale. As a group, imams are extremely pragmatic about their application of Islamic law. Almost all emphasize the need to make the solution fit the problem. As one imam told me, "We are not here to be Hanifi, Maliki et cetera—but to be human beings." Another imam commented, "As a Muslim living in the West I cannot afford to follow just one school. I must construct a modern approach that responds to the reality of the contemporary West and in particular the difference between the reality of the seventh and the twenty-first century—and the diversity of [Muslim] communities." A strong theme of pragmatism underlies the decisions made as well as an effort to fit the desired solution to the rules, rather than the other way around ("we make it fit"). Most of the imams see Islamic law as a guide—"Islamic legal texts do not tell you what you should be doing, but delineating [*sic*] the absolute minimum"—and do not regard it as a constraint to sensible, just and practical outcomes. "Ninety percent of decisions in *shari'a* are discretionary because they are based on personal circumstances."

Any jurisprudential differences are less significant in decision making than personal and cultural orientations towards issues of family structure and gender roles which are "part of a wider network of legal and social relations as perceived by jurists."[17] The approach of the imams to substantive questions about marital relations and especially women's rights reflects their attitude towards these issues as a social rather than a legal matter and influences how far they are prepared to go in problem-solving in any one case. Those determined to find a way to address a marital problem—for example, abandonment by a husband who has remarried, or a *talaq* (divorce) uttered in haste and now regretted—do so regardless of the laws that might have been interpreted as a constraint upon them.

> One imam described the story of a couple divorced using an irrevocable *talaq*, who now wished to be together again as a married couple. The Islamic law generally requires that where a couple have been divorced using *talaq*, they cannot remarry until the wife has married another man, and then is divorced from him (the intention is to discourage the hasty use of *talaq*).
>
> In this case, the imam reasoned, it would be unkind to force the wife to marry another man simply in order to enable her remarriage to her first husband. It would be unfair to the man she married instrumentally—and it would be hard on both the wife and her first husband who simply wished to be together again. To achieve this result, the imam found a technical defect (as he described it) with the way in which *talaq* had been pronounced. This allowed him to declare that the couple had never been divorced and could continue to live together, happily married.

God's Word or Man's Law?

Individual problem solving aside, the potential for innovation and development is critical to the future of Islamic law. This raises the question of the nature of *fiqh*, and whether it is understood as the immutable word of God—or a man-made system derived from Quranic sources inherently adaptable to modern conditions and context. What support is there in Islamic jurisprudence for either view?

Historically, the *ulama's* exercise of discretionary judgment in developing the law was understood as more than merely the expression of their scholarly authority, but as a process whereby the scholars revealed the word of God to ordinary

Muslims. By assessing the appropriate outcome in the case of a conflict, or elaborating the scope and substance of an existing law, the jurists claimed to be articulating divinely ordained rights and obligations that could be traced back to the original texts. This assertion of "natural law"—the idea that certain Islamic rights and obligations are determined by God and revealed through jurisprudence—shores up the authority of the *ulama* and stifles both challenge and change. A natural law tradition in Islamic jurisprudence stands in contrast to the positivist tradition that dominates most Western legal systems which argues that man-made reasoning, however sophisticated or enlightened, "cannot arrive independently at the law of God."[18]

Some contemporary Muslim scholars still claim that *fiqh* is "God-given."[19] Their normative authority is explained by their use of an accepted procedure or methodology, described above, for determining the "correct" outcome. In this way juristic discretion is cloaked in the justification that they speak "in God's name." There were echoes of this when I asked imams about the source of their authority to provide rulings on divorce. A typical comment from one imam was that he gave his "best reading of God's advice," trying to reflect the spirit of *shari'a* and using appropriate tools for interpretation. In common with many others, he differentiated this "reading" from what he called his "personal advice" to the spouses, based on their particular situation, which he might also offer. Whether the imams really intend to assert that their interpretation is the "word of God" is unclear, but certainly this is how some Muslims regard the nature of the advice they receive. Others challenge such claims to speak "in God's voice" by the imams, often referring to their variable qualifications and education in Islamic law.

The *ulama's* claim to be the mouthpiece of God enabled them to innovate and develop the law while maintaining their authority and legitimacy. As one writer points out, "In legal cultures, opinions that assert a continuity of doctrine have a greater claim to legitimacy and authoritativeness than novel doctrines that represent a clear and sharp break with the established doctrines."[20] Similar concerns lie behind the rationale provided by contemporary imams. Most contemporary scholars describe Islamic law as a man-made creation derived from divine sources.[21] While most Muslims believe the core principles of *shari'a* to be divine and immutable, *fiqh* is derivative, man-made, and can change according to time and place. Tariq Ramadan describes the development of practical principles from the corpus of *shari'a* as "the work of human intellect."[22] The goal is to develop laws which respond to contemporary conditions yet are faithful to the essence of *shari'a*, characterized by the pursuit of justice, equality, and respect for other human beings.[23] Ramadan offers a distinction between "the universal principles to which the Muslim consciousness must seek to be faithful through the ages and the practice of those principles, which is necessarily relative, at any given moment in history."[24] The articulation of these "universal principles" is elusive, but the imam quoted in the following passage makes an eloquent effort:

> "*Sharia* is basically two principles—justice and fairness leading to rights—and compassion and mercy leading to negotiation. Whatever laws there are must be true to this framework—to restore justice and create harmony and peace."

If no distinction is drawn between *shari'a* and *fiqh*, change in the law becomes both impermissible and unthinkable. "The resistance to accept[ing] modern day Islam is because some people think that would be like changing God's word." Many Muslims—including many of the respondents—made no distinction between *shari'a* and Islamic law. Since most Muslims regard *shari'a* as divine revelation the immutable law of God (a more controversial perspective is that *shari'a* itself is malleable and subject to changing conditions), the failure to distinguish *shari'a* from fiqh constrains meaningful law reform. Ziba Mir-Hosseni, an empirical researcher, notes this problem: "In Muslim consciousness these two are so much intertwined that to make any meaningful distinction entails the risk of questioning the very notion of a divinely ordained law."[25]

Alternately, if *fiqh* is understood as a human intellectual endeavour, guided by divine sources, there is plenty of potential for development and change. Islamic law can evolve from historical models into a form that reflects the particular conditions of life in North America for Muslim men and women. A code developed by male scholars in the seventh and eighth centuries embeds many assumptions—most obviously the appropriate role of women in the family system and wider society—that are out of place today. *Fiqh* as it operates in Muslim countries with Islamic courts draws on a variety of interpretive tools to develop organically in order to meet new social conditions. Modernists argue that the origins of Islamic jurisprudence make it clear that the intention was that the legal system should be constantly adaptable, serving as a guiding moral order for Muslims. Many scholars argue that Islamic jurisprudence is explicitly designed to allow for constant adaptation as the consequence of diaspora.

> "Islam is an intellectual tradition that allows people to find themselves in a new social space."

Ongoing law reform is necessary to ensure that Islam stays relevant to the lives of Muslims, whenever and wherever they might live. To argue that Islamic law is unchangeable "in effect is saying that Allah did not foresee this. It is up to us to understand how these laws apply to contemporary circumstances." This means that the development of *fiqh* is the responsibility of Muslims who must "make a best effort to reach for and understand the eternal law." As Islamic scholars have described this, "Islamic law is a human product subject to error, alteration, development and nullification"[26] and "a work of human intellect."[27]

This understanding of the structure and nature of Islamic law is in stark contrast to the Western media perception of *shari'a* as an archaic, strict and inflexible system. Reportage is dominated by a focus on Islamic traditionalists, whose ideas appear the most extreme and bizarre to Western audiences. These ideas are epitomized, among others, by the Wahhabist sect in Saudi Arabia[28] and Taliban regimes in Afghanistan and parts of Pakistan, Nigeria and Somalia. These groups are highly resistant to what they see as the dilution of classical Islamic law by "Western" (equated with modernist) ideas and norms. Their calls for a "return to *shari'a*" usually suggest a return to a more traditional version of *fiqh* that predates colonization and focuses on controlling behaviors that were unknown in the time of the Prophet—for example, smoking, driving (at least by women) and listening to modern music. Traditionalists and reformers have debated the potential of Islamic law to evolve and change over many centuries. In the tenth century, some jurists argued for "closing the doors" (*ijtihad*) on any further interpretation of Islamic law, asserting that it had reached a "perfect" form. In practice, the doors did not close, and legal reform and innovation continues up to the present day. Traditionalists continue to argue that juristic innovation is only possible on questions that have not been decisively resolved, which for some jurists is as small as 10 percent of the law. Much contemporary Islamic scholarship is highly critical of this perspective, emphasizing instead the capacity—and the necessity—for *fiqh* to evolve and adjust to modern conditions.[29] Unfortunately the attention given to a small number of traditionalist groups by the Western media ensures their continuing influence on Muslims and reinforces the impression that *"shari'a"* is inflexible and antimodern.

To explore the extent to which they understand Islamic law as capable of modernization, I asked the imams how they dealt with cases in which the wife was the primary breadwinner, something unanticipated in seventh-century Arabia. The classical law assumes that all financial responsibility lies with the husband. How might an Islamic divorce settlement be negotiated under these modern-day circumstances? None of the imams referred to any specific doctrinal tool or new principles, but instead described a case-by-case approach. Most maintained that classical principles, such as the default primary financial responsibility of the husband, could not be altered. They also clearly wished to minimize any conflict between contemporary and traditional expectations of family structure. These twin concerns were easily accommodated by inviting the wife to volunteer financial support to her husband where this was appropriate, and/or voluntarily waiving her own rights to support (like the common law system, Islamic law allows for any right to be voluntarily waived or renegotiated). Each of the imams I questioned offered a pragmatic solution along these lines. The main difference lay in the degree to which some saw it as their responsibility to modernize the law, while others were much more cautious and less comfortable about discussing change.

Islamic Family Law

Much of *fiqh* focuses on family, property and inheritance matters, and this body of laws is known as Islamic family law. Islamic family law is what remains of a more comprehensive legal system including commercial and land laws that existed in Muslim countries prior to nineteenth-century colonization. Before colonization, the scholarly treatises and *fatwas* of the *ulama* were determined by the content of Islamic law throughout the Ottoman Empire, which included much of today's Middle East, Eastern Europe, Russia and North Africa. After colonization, the legal systems in many Muslim countries were codified (formalized in written codes) and either adopted, or integrated with, the commercial and property laws of the colonizing power. This left the family law system—the laws relating to marriage, divorce and inheritance—relatively untouched. These areas comprise the bulk of contemporary Islamic law. "Private" law—family law—was regarded as relatively politically unimportant,[30] and maintaining Islamic family law avoided possible confrontation between modern Islamic governments and their respective *ulama*.[31]

As a result, marriage and divorce in Muslim countries continue to be regulated according to modified versions of classical Islamic law, with some late twentieth- and twenty-first-century reforms designed to enhance the rights of women (for example, the expansion of grounds for judicial release from marriage for women, protection against unreasonable divorce by their husbands, and restrictions on polygamous marriages).[32] The last thirty years have seen important reforms in countries such as Morocco, Turkey, Tunisia and Egypt. Even more conservative jurisdictions such as Pakistan and Iran have introduced reforms to protect women from some of the harshest aspects of the classical law (such as unilateral *talaq* and limited post-divorce spousal support).[33] In North America, Islamic family law cannot develop systematically in the absence of courts or other legal institutions, which means that the type of advice given by imams is often limited to a classical or traditional understanding of family rights and obligations and does not benefit from the modernization taking place in some Muslim countries. Nonetheless, some creativity and modernization is taking place in an ad hoc fashion. In any case, even the most radical contemporary reforms have not altered the essential elements of Islamic family law that are familiar to many North American Muslims. The two most important pillars of the family law system are the rules that concern marriage and divorce.

The Marriage Contract, or *Nikah*

Many North American Muslims marry using a Muslim marriage contract, or *nikah*, as well as completing the formal legal registration of their union. The meaning of the *nikah* to those who use it is described in detail in chapter three. The basic legal principles governing the contract, including its essential elements, are set out here.

Marriage Procedure

Islamic law stipulates that a marriage contract can be made only with the consent of both parties.[34] Even in seventh-century Arabia, adult women were required to consent to marriage—in some circumstances a *wali*, or guardian, could consent to marriage for a child bride. Classical Islamic law allowed for marriage at the time of puberty or the onset of menses;[35] such marriages would be unlawful in North America. I did not come across any examples of marriage under the age of majority (although a few respondents had been married overseas at a younger age in a marriage subsequently recognized by a North American court). Islam prohibits forced marriage but distinguishes between it and arranged marriage. In the latter case the parents and the young person confer on an appropriate partner, and the parents help their son or daughter to make this decision—not insist upon it. There should still be a real choice exercised by the young person. The ideal is a dialogue process between the two families. "There needs to be a synergy between two families, they will be intertwined—this is part of the process." Respondents' comments show that some cultural norms elevate family loyalty over personal autonomy and blur the distinction between forced and arranged marriage. Some of these experiences are described in chapter three.

Most schools of Islamic law require a woman to obtain consent to her marriage from her *wali*, who may be her father or another appointed person.[36] It is the responsibility of the *wali* to ensure that the woman is married with adequate protections and to look out for her interests—for example, ensuring she has a sufficient *mahr*. Some cultural practices place the *wali* in a position of authority where he may effectively veto the marriage. Marriage requires the presence of two witnesses. At least one of the witnesses must be a man.[37]

The Contract and Its Terms

Islamic law allows Muslim men and women to freely contract in any way that varies their traditional rights and responsibilities, and the marriage contract is no exception. The opportunities presented by the device of the *nikah*, therefore, are almost limitless. The marriage contract can cover both rights and reasonable expectations during the marriage, and responsibilities should the marriage end. In practice, couples may be reluctant to discuss potential sources of future conflict and their advisers—their families and the imams—often share that reluctance. In some cultures, it is assumed that the terms of the *nikah* will be taken care of by the bride's family—most likely her father—and that the couple will not even see the contract until they are asked to sign it.[38]

The standard *nikah* used by many couples defaults to the classical Islamic law. Its preamble typically refers to the fact that husband and wife will govern their relationship by *shari'a*. For example:

"All the rights and obligations expressed or implied hereunder are according to the *Shari'ah* derived from the Qur'an, Sunnah, Qiyas and Ijma' as codified by prominent Muslim Jurists."[39]

"Our marriage shall be in accordance to *Sharia'h* (Islamic Law)" and "Our living habits (inside and outside the home) shall be in accordance with Islam."[40]

Because the substance of *shari'a* is a subject of contention, statements such as these have a variety of interpretations and possible meanings. It is generally assumed that a marriage contract adopts the classical position of Islamic family law in relation to marital property, spousal and child support on divorce, custody and perhaps polygamy. Less clear is how *shari'a* relates to expectations regarding work and education for women, and other aspects of modern family life.

There is no concept of common or shared matrimonial property in Islam. Classical Islamic law dictates that the property and assets of each partner remain his or her own.[41] A standard form *nikah* entrenches this principle unless it is expressly altered by agreement. Custody of children under the age of puberty generally remains with the mother; over the age of puberty the default is that formal legal custody reverts to the father. As the classical position, this might be read into the *nikah* absent a provision to the contrary. Another potential implied term is the right of a Muslim man to take up to four wives, despite the fact that many modern scholars and some imams argue that this is inappropriate in contemporary North America.[42] To avoid this assumption, the *nikah* can provide for what will happen if there is marital infidelity, which can be defined however the couple wishes. For example, if the *nikah* defines fidelity as commitment to a single wife, polygamy would be a clear breach of the marriage vows. The *nikah* can also be drafted to trigger a renegotiation of conventional custody arrangements, or the classical approach to spousal support upon divorce (which is not provided beyond the period of the *iddat*, or waiting period, usually three months).

Important issues for modern couples arise in relation to expectations and norms about the role of the woman, including her access to education and work outside the home. What does signing a boilerplate *nikah* mean for these questions? The most frequently cited Quranic verse regarding a husband's authority (in Arabic, *qiwama*) over his wife is translated in various ways, but the two consistent concepts are male superiority (described as "in charge"[43]) and the role of men as providers for women. For example:

"Men are the protectors and maintainers of women because God has given the one [more strength] than the other, and because men can support them from their means."[44]

The parallel concept of wifely obedience derives from the same verse. The implicit bargain is that the wife accepts her husband's authority in return for his responsibility to take care of her practical needs. This verse reflected the reality of gender roles in marriage in seventh-century Arabia. Ideas about the demonstration of both authority and obedience have subsequently developed through Islamic jurisprudence—not coincidentally, the work of male jurists. The result was far-reaching limits on women's choices and behavior, sometimes extending beyond the family system to justify male authority in social and political spheres.[45] Esposito states the classical legal position as follows: "[The husband] is entitled to exercise his marital authority by restraining his wife's movements and preventing her from showing herself in public. This restriction of the wife mirrors the prevailing medieval social customs of veiling and seclusion of women, practiced in order to protect their honour."[46] These ideas linger in a few contemporary Islamic legal systems. In Saudi Arabia, married women can only travel outside the country with the permission of their husbands (they share their travel documentation). Another disturbing example are the "houses of obedience" which have existed at various times in Egypt, Lebanon and Iran, which allow husbands to force their "disobedient" wives to cohabit with them.[47] One female respondent[48] was terrified of returning to her native Lebanon without the divorce she asked four different imams to grant her from her abusive husband because she believed she might be incarcerated in such a "house."

Without explicit clauses to the contrary, and isolated from reformist jurisprudence in Muslim countries, the *nikah* in North America may be understood as entrenching classical expectations of wifely "obedience," as well as limiting women's expectations of work and education. A small group of women told me that they had assumed that their husbands would not interpret their *nikah* in this way—but they were wrong. Other women wished that they had used the opportunity of the *nikah* to clarify these expectations and actually negotiate the "terms" of the marriage. By far the most common regret over the substance of the *nikah* was in relation to divorce rights. A boilerplate *nikah* entrenches the gendered inequality of the classical Islamic law which gives the husband a unilateral right to divorce his wife but places limits on such a right for the wife. In order to displace this assumption, some *nikah* include a clause in which the husband delegates the right of divorce to his wife (*talaq al-tafwid*). A small number of female respondents described adding such a clause, some only following a struggle; many more wished in hindsight that they had done so. Such a delegation can also be agreed verbally at the time of the *nikah*. See appendix A for an example of a divorce based on a verbal agreement to a delegated *talaq*.

The *Mahr*

The *mahr*, or wedding gift, is a required element of the marriage contract; without it the contract is not valid in Islamic law.[49] The *mahr* is understood in Islamic jurisprudence as a form of contractual consideration, payable by the husband to the wife. The *mahr* may be immediate (given at the time of the marriage) or deferred and payable at the time of the husband's death or if the couple divorce. A deferred *mahr* is in effect monetary insurance for the wife, giving her the right to payment if her husband dies or if the marriage ends. In these cases payment of the *mahr* may look similar to a lump-sum payment either agreed or ordered by a court in the civil system. One important difference is that in Islamic law the amount of the *mahr* is predetermined and set out in the *nikah*, so that it is not related to assets accumulated throughout the marriage (which remain the legal property of each spouse). If the marriage was contracted a long time before, it may not represent a reasonable settlement by the time of the divorce. The range of customary practices means that the *mahr* may be much more, or far less, than the amount a court would award as a lump-sum payment upon divorce. A significant *mahr* may offset many of the other financial disadvantages a woman may suffer on divorce, but the amount of the *mahr* is entirely at the discretion of the parties to the *nikah* (or their families). To qualify as "consideration" for the contract, the *mahr* does not have to have a monetary value, only a value to the parties. I have come across cases where the *mahr* was substantial—up to $100,000—and others in which it had no monetary value at all (for example, a love poem). The *mahr*—along with all other types of financial support after marriage in the classical Islamic law—is payable only from the husband to the wife. This may cause practical problems in families where the wife is the principal or sole bread-winner.

There are many different cultural traditions surrounding the promise to pay a *mahr*. Some communities favor the practice of deferred *mahr* and others prefer to have the *mahr* payable at the time of the marriage to give the woman some immediate financial independence from her husband. In some communities the *mahr* is customarily small, while others make more extravagant promises, seen as evidence of the family's social status and the husband's commitment to his bride. A woman may also agree to waive her right to a *mahr* altogether. This is most common in second marriages, or where there is an agreement to substitute certain other rights. One female respondent agreed to forgo a *mahr* in exchange for a clause that stipulated that if her husband remarried it must be to a widow or a person in need, not a virgin.

If the marriage ends at the initiative of the wife but with her husband's agreement (*khula*), the wife must usually provide something of value—described as consideration—in exchange for her release from the marriage. This is typically the forfeiture of the *mahr*, although some scholars and imams point to a Quranic verse which anticipates the potential for husbands to use *khula* as a means of divorcing their wives without paying the *mahr*.[50] Some suggest that a deferred *mahr* must still be paid—or a paid-up *mahr* retained—where the divorce is the result of ill treatment by the husband.[51] These cases are often contentious, and the practice of the imams varies considerably.

Social workers and others working with Muslim families and communities frequently expressed concerns to me about the *mahr*. The undertaking may look good on paper, but in practice it is often difficult to persuade a man that he must pay. Some men appear to believe that the undertaking is symbolic only, despite the fact that the promise they make is memorialized in a contract and often witnessed by hundreds of wedding guests. In one case, the lawyer for a husband who was resisting payment of the *mahr* argued that when his client made his promise to pay a deferred *mahr*—in front of hundreds of witnesses at his wedding celebration—he did not regard it as a "real" promise, but a part of a ritual without moral or legal meaning. Another woman told me that her husband refused to pay the *mahr* until his Muslim lawyer took him to the side and reminded him that it was his Islamic obligation. This reluctance to keep the promise made is exacerbated by the approach of the courts in the United States and Canada, which have historically been reluctant to enforce the *mahr*, deeming the *nikah* a contract for a religious purpose and therefore—unlike a prenuptial agreement—unenforceable. This has led some imams to develop *nikah* that use wording that minimizes the religious aspects of the ceremony and emphasizes the contractual nature of the

undertakings being made. These drafting approaches to avoid enforceability problems have yet to be tested at higher court levels, and uncertainty continues over whether an application based on contract for a recalcitrant husband to pay the *mahr* will succeed (see the discussion in chapter eight). If the court cannot be relied upon as an enforcement mechanism, the moral suasion of the imam may be the most significant factor in securing payment.

Islamic Divorce

In Islamic law, the binding contract that is made when the spouses sign the *nikah* can only be undone by divorce. In Muslim countries, most forms of divorce must be processed by a court. In the absence of Islamic courts, many North American Muslims seek the approval of a religious leader, usually an imam, to break their *nikah* vows. Others follow a private ritual, based on their personal knowledge of Islamic law, that allows them to feel satisfied that they are "really" divorced in the eyes of God. Approval for divorce is especially important for women, who unlike their husbands (who are permitted more than one wife[52]) cannot remarry unless they are Islamically divorced. Also unlike their husbands, they cannot divorce without "permission," either from their husband or a third party. Where a husband will not give permission, Muslim courts have developed judicial annulment procedures to dispense with his consent and award a divorce. In North America, the imam substitutes for the *qadi* or Muslim judge.

Despite the importance placed upon marriage and family life, divorce has been permitted in Islam since the seventh century. Divorce is described in a well-known *hadith* as the "most hated permitted thing."[53] Acknowledging that some marriages fail, the Qur'an sets out the basis for ending a union. These verses are mostly concerned with the procedures for divorce, the right of men to divorce their wives, the right of women to divorce with the permission of their husbands, and the requirement that divorced women be treated fairly.[54] A number of additional stories in *hadith* describe the Prophet permitting both men and women to divorce, even in apparently "trivial" circumstances, where continuing in the marriage would cause one or the other great unhappiness. The most widely cited of these is the story of Jamilah. Jamilah, the wife of Thabit, told the Prophet, "I cannot find fault with [my husband] regarding his morals or faith, but I cannot bear him."[55] The Prophet told her to return to Thabit what he had given her upon marriage (an orchard) and granted her a divorce. The implication seems to be that if couples cannot be happy together, even if there is no objective reason such as ill treatment or infidelity, they should be allowed to separate.

Talaq: Divorce by the Husband

While both men and women can request divorce, there are significant differences between their procedural rights. The right to determine a divorce unilaterally is afforded only to the husband, described in Arabic as *talaq*. This rule means that in practice, a husband may reject his wife without any effort at reconciliation or dialogue and end the marriage by the simple recitation of the required words. For most Muslims, this does not even require the presence of witnesses.[56] A number of verses in the Qur'an make clear that any marital conflict should be discussed and negotiated, with the assistance of family arbiters or others if necessary, and reconciliation sought wherever possible. However, the unilateral structure of *talaq* allows such a dialogue to be sidestepped if there is no will to pursue it. In North America—unlike many Muslim countries where a *talaq* must be registered with the court and notice given formally to the wife—a husband who wishes to divorce his wife does not need the help of any third party, as long as he is sufficiently knowledgeable to be able to utter the required words in the appropriate form. If he chooses to proceed without any third-party consultation he may also avoid any pressure to consider reconciliation or negotiation, pressure that is almost always placed on his wife, who must seek permission for divorce.

The pronouncement "I divorce you" signals the beginning of a temporary state of separation, during which the husband and wife are required to live apart in the same house for the period of *iddat* (for a menstruating woman this is three menstrual cycles or around three months). The purpose of the *iddat*, or "waiting period," is to ensure that the wife is not pregnant by her husband[57] and to give the couple the opportunity to reconsider and possibly reconcile. The husband continues to have the responsibility of taking care of his wife during this period.[58] All schools agree that divorce does not become irrevocable until the husband has pronounced *talaq* three times. This means that even after the end of the *iddat*, if only one or two *talaqs* have been given, the divorce is still revocable—that is, the couple may reconcile and live together again as man and wife without the need for a new *nikah*. The divorce only becomes irrevocable once *talaq* has been pronounced a total of three times; and effective once the couple has not been sexually intimate for a total of three months, with this time running from the first pronouncement of *talaq*. After a third and irrevocable *talaq*, the husband cannot change his mind and remarry his former wife unless she marries another man,[59] and then gets divorced or becomes widowed. The device of the *iddat*, and the requirement for three pronouncements of *talaq*, are intended to ensure that decisions are not made hastily and that *talaq* is not pronounced simply as a bluff, or to punish or traumatize the wife.

Considerable controversy exists among jurists over whether or not the pro-nouncement of *talaq* can be repeated three times on the same occasion and still be valid.[60] This would mean that the subsequent period of *iddat* does not offer a gen-uine opportunity to reconcile, because the third *talaq* is irrevocable. This frus-trates the intention of the three stages of *talaq*, which are intended to allow some time for "cooling off" and change of heart. Some imams explicitly advise men that a same-time triple *talaq* is not valid in Islamic law, in order to slow the process down and ensure there is some space for reflection and discussion. A small number of female respondents report being given *talaq* three times in one pronounce-ment, including a woman who was left a triple *talaq* on her telephone answering machine. Having collected a range of scholarly opinions, this woman was eventu-ally satisfied that this was a valid divorce. There is further jurisprudence regarding what form of words needs to be used in order for the uttering of divorce to be "valid," including both the words used and the intention behind them;[61] for ex-ample, some schools are clear that a *talaq* pronounced in anger, or in a state of in-toxication, is not valid, whereas others regard any such pronouncements as valid.[62]

If divorce is effected by *talaq,* the wife generally keeps any marriage gifts and remains entitled to her *mahr*, if it was deferred.[63] A number of Quranic verses exhort husbands who divorce their wives to treat them "equitably" and "with kindness."[64] However, most jurists agree that the provision of spousal support is limited to the duration of the *iddat*. Some imams encourage the negotiation of a longer period of support, applying civil law principles and citing the Quranic exhortation to "kindness," but there is no direct support in classical Islamic law for this. The classical legal position was developed at a time when divorced women would have expected to return to their families upon divorce and their male relatives would have been expected to take financial responsibility for them. It represents one of the clearest examples of divergence between Islamic law and civil law.

Unlike his ex-wife, minor children remain the financial responsibility of the husband after divorce. The amount payable varies widely. Some imams refer to the child support guidelines in their jurisdiction when setting a monthly or weekly amount. Others simply pull a number out of the air or adopt a proposal from either party. Yet others do not discuss the financial consequences of divorce at all. This subject is discussed in detail in chapter seven.

Khula: Divorce Requested by the Wife

The wife's right to initiate divorce is known as *khula*, and its form and limits are described by all the schools of law. Like the concept of *talaq*, the concept of *khula* is drawn from the primary sources of Islamic law, including at least one Quranic verse[65] and *hadith* such as the story of Jamilah. The principle of *khula* requires the wife to "buy" her freedom from the marriage, usually by returning the *mahr*, although there are arguable exceptions to this also, for example when the husband ill treats the wife and effectively forces her to seek divorce.[66] The "price" of buying one's freedom from the *nikah* may vary; anything considered sufficient consideration to be a *mahr* would also qualify as consideration for *khula*.

Khula is often described as "divorce by mutual consent" since it assumes the agreement of the husband to the request for divorce made by his wife. In other words, there is no absolute right to *khula*, only the right to seek permission. The request must be based on a reason, and there is inevitable controversy over what is a "good" reason. Some imams appear to suspect the motivation of almost any request for divorce coming from the wife, assuming it to be based on some trivial or flimsy rationale, and prefer to urge "patience" or "prayer." Others consider that the jurisprudence is sufficiently flexible to enable them to seek permission from the husband on almost any grounds when the wife believes that she cannot continue in the marriage. This view is supported by scholars who argue that stories such as that of Jamilah make it clear that spouses should not have to remain married when they are unhappy, that a husband is not entitled to unreasonably refuse a request for divorce from his wife, and that she cannot be forced to remain as his wife against her will. Another well-known *hadith* describes Barira's husband—a slave named Mughith—following after his wife and weeping, because she no longer wanted to be married to him. The Prophet said to Barira, "Why don't you return to him?" When Barira asked the Prophet, "Do you order me to do so?" he said, "No, I only intercede for him." Barira said, "I am not in need of him."[67] We are told that while the Prophet grieved for the broken heart of Barira's husband, Mughith, "he did not contradict her" and gave Barira her freedom. This story implies that there is some potential for pressure to be placed on the husband—usually by an imam or by a family member—to grant permission for divorce when conditions appear appropriate. Unless the husband is agreeable to divorce, it is common for a third party, usually an imam, to become involved in decisions about *khula*. The wife may go to him for advice, and he may act as a go-between in initiating dialogue between husband and wife.

Faskh: Annulment of Marriage

If a husband will not agree to release his wife from her vows, a judge may substitute his own permission for that of her husband. Confusingly, some jurists still refer to this imposed decision as *khula*,[68] whereas others more accurately describe it as judicial annulment of marriage, or *faskh*. Divorce via annulment is widely offered by Islamic courts in Muslim countries. The grounds for such an application vary among the schools of law and between modern family law jurisdictions. Typically they include ill treatment of the wife and/or harm caused by the husband (this would include any domestic violence), failure to financially maintain the family (another form of "harm") or abandonment (caused, for example, by imprisonment or desertion).[69] Some jurisdictions are now adopting broader criteria for judicial annulment—for example, simple incompatibility—reflecting the Quranic principle that women should not be forced to remain unhappily married.

In North America, sympathetic imams will as a practical matter offer to approve divorce for women in situations where they cannot secure the permission of their husband, often describing this as *khula*. Strictly speaking, where a third party substitutes their approval for the permission of a husband they are offering *faskh*. Of course, imams are not judges, but they are trying to help women left in "limping marriages" whose husbands refuse to participate in any discussion of divorce. Whereas Muslim men can move on and remarry, women remain trapped within a nonexistent marriage. As one imam expressed it, "*Shari'a* would not allow this type of suffering." Without *faskh*, the only advice that North American imams could give to these women would be to travel to a Muslim country in order to obtain a divorce from the courts there. The emergence of regional panels of imams who will consider and award annulments is a sign of movement away from ad hoc decision making by individual imams and towards a more structured form of extrajudicial annulment in North America.

Islamic Law in Twenty-First-Century North America

The tradition of the Islamic law system is that it can establish "the grounds upon which negotiation can proceed,"[70] rather than a closed system of reasoning. The law is often used to rationalize a common-sense solution, rather than to point to a precise outcome. In this way, Islamic law reflects the culture and context of the setting in which it is applied, as well as the particular problems of the individual parties.

In the absence of Muslim courts and institutions that might contribute innovations and modernizations, the way in which Islamic family law is used in North America to conduct marriage and divorce processes follows the same tradition. For example, the practice of annulments is currently largely idiosyncratic to individual imams who assume a quasi-judicial authority in order to assist women in limping marriages—their motivation is to "make it fit" rather than strictly apply the letter of the law. Community cultural traditions have a significant influence on both the ritual of marriage and divorce and the particular application of the Islamic law. This distinction between what Tariq Ramadan calls "religious judgment and its cultural garb"[71] is often difficult to make. Many of the stories in this book reflect the relationship between religious and cultural beliefs. In these accounts we recognize what another researcher describes as "confrontations between the spheres of the sacred and the mundane."[72] When Muslims in North America seek legal advice on marriage and divorce, they are expressing not only religious values but also a multilayered cultural identity that reflects the relationship among their faith, their personal values and the secular society in which they live as Muslims. The remainder of this book explores these experiences and examines what they tell us about the evolving identity of Islam in North America.

3 GETTING MARRIED

"It doesn't matter how North American you are, it still matters so much to us that we do Islamic marriage and divorce. Even second and third generation immigrants, you always have your foot in your parents' hang ups, however Westernised you are."

Celebrating Muslim Marriage

Islam offers an understanding of love, marriage and family, embraced and adapted by Muslim men and women across the world. Despite significant diversity of practice, there are important unifying principles. There is a widespread desire for an Islamic identity among Muslims living in North America, however observant or secular they might be. In the absence of formal Islamic institutions and legal structures, the celebration of marriage offers an opportunity to remember and recommit to both traditions and beliefs.

"I don't know anyone who wouldn't get a nikah"

The single thread that runs throughout any discussion of Islamic marriage and family life is the marriage contract, or *nikah*. The *nikah* is a written contract signed by the parties in the presence of two witnesses. Only 2 of the 104 marriages in this study did not have a *nikah*.[1] Signing a marriage contract as a part of a wedding (or engagement) ceremony is a relatively simple procedure. This is usually a simple template, provided by the mosque or widely available on the Web.[2] One young imam who as a university student worked with other young Muslims on his campus told me, "I don't know anyone who wouldn't get a *nikah*."

It is easy to understand why more traditionally "religious" Muslim families—those who attend mosque on a regular basis, observe feasts and fasts, make *zagat* (charity contributions) and perhaps go on *haj* (pilgrimage to Mecca)—would be committed to using the *nikah* as an expression of their faith. "This is a system of belief—it is more than culture which you can walk away from—it is belief, which you cannot be without. So if you want to be married you have to use the *nikah.*" Marriage in Islam is not a religious sacrament; in contrast to Christianity and common law, marriage is understood as a contractual commitment.[3] However, Islam also teaches that marriage is a means of drawing closer to God. This means that many Muslims talk about the commitment they make in the *nikah* as a promise made not only to one another (as they sign the contract) but also to God. The preamble to the *nikah* always includes a call to God: "In the name of Almighty Allah." In this way, the *nikah* contract "realizes the essence of Islam."[4]

> "The *nikah* binds people together in the eyes of God. It is not only a legal document. It is binding also in a different way, a sacred covenant."

As one woman described it to me: "We are in this to become better Muslims and to further our faith. We move forward towards God, not away from God." For such couples, signing the *nikah* is an expression of faith and a statement of their commitment to Islam as well as to their spouse. To ensure that they both understood and accepted this commitment, she and her husband-to-be spent their first time alone together immediately before they signed their *nikah* in a private moment of reflection.

> Tarik and Shireene took a brief private moment away from the bustle of the engagement party where they were to sign their *nikah*, in order to be sure that they were truly able to make this commitment to one another and to God. Their families had arranged their marriage, and the young couple had spent relatively little time together until this point. They did not know each other very well at all. What they were seeking in that moment of solitude was not more knowledge of one another—but the certainty that this was a shared commitment that they could make both to one another and to God. This was based not on knowledge of one another, but on what they knew about each other's faith and values. Tarik told me, "We sat in silence with no one else present amid all the chaos. We found that commitment."

Not all North American Muslim couples understand their marriage as a religious commitment, yet many still use the *nikah*. Many young Muslims who understand their lifestyle to be relatively secular acknowledge the structures and rituals of their faith at important moments of transition. Which may inspire reaffirmation of emotional and behavioral touchstones, even for those whose faith commitment usually lies dormant. "The average Muslim person knows this [having a *nikah*] naturally, it is just part of how life is, even when they are not 'good' Muslims, they take these rules very seriously." Some of the imams with whom I spoke grumbled that many of the people they see for a *nikah* ceremony they never see at prayers, but as one acknowledged, "Even if they are secular [Muslims], they don't want to mess with sensitive family issues. . . . They want to do it right." The desire for an Islamic identity is often disassociated from religious adherence. This is well understood among religious leaders; "*Shari'a* has a role to play even in secular households for this reason." This means that sons and daughters who consider themselves less devout than their parents commonly make a *nikah* when they marry. While this is ostensibly to please their parents, they often acknowledge that an Islamic marriage ceremony meets their own needs for an affirmation of Islamic identity and values.

> Fashia and Qasif were clear that they couldn't contemplate getting married without a *nikah*. Born and raised in Canada, both are young professionals with a very different lifestyle from their parents—both are working professionals—but they were committed to having a traditional Muslim marriage ceremony and signing a *nikah*.
>
> Neither Fashia nor Qasif are traditionally observant, but the principles of their faith are very important to them. They feel that without a *nikah*, it would simply not be permissible, in the eyes of God or their community, for them to be together. The *nikah* is "the only way for us to be married and recognized in the eyes of God, our family." In making this commitment Fashia understood herself and Qasif to be making a promise to one other—rather than a contract with God, as some understand the marriage promise. But God—represented by norms and principles—is still a presence. "It is a contract with each other, but guided by our shared values and beliefs." She added: "The substantive content of the *nikah*—what it says—is far less important to me than its symbolic value—that is, what it represents." For Fashia and Qasif having a *nikah* makes their relationship "real," that is, recognized as appropriate and welcomed both by family and, more abstractly, by God.

The *Nikah* Is the "Real" Marriage

The *nikah* is rarely used as a substitute for a civil marriage license; instead most couples both sign a *nikah* and get a license. The *nikah* is not a legal marriage in North America (although in some jurisdictions the officiator has the authority to oversee both the religious commitment and the legal registration in a single ceremony).[5] In 95 percent of the cases in this study, both a *nikah* and a civil license were included in the marriage formalities (not necessarily at the same time). Most individuals considered legal registration to be an obvious step, so that the legal system in their place of residence would regard them as husband and wife. The imams are generally proactive in ensuring that Muslim couples understand that they must also get a civil marriage license, and in fact many will not officiate at a *nikah* until the couple obtains a civil marriage license.

Despite this, most respondents understood the signing of the *nikah* rather than the legal registration of their marriage to be their meaningful commitment to one another. They saw this part of the process as their "real" marriage, and the civil license simply a formality that had to be completed. This became even clearer when the question of divorce arose; "The *nikah* was the true marriage and this was the fire that kept going, and the civil divorce did not end this because it was only paperwork." In a few cases where the marriage was not legally registered, one spouse later denied the marriage in order to gain a legal advantage. For Bita, whose story follows, this was traumatic and disorienting.

> When Bita was still a high school student, she married her high school sweetheart—like her, a Muslim—with a *nikah*. The couple did not obtain a civil marriage license, although Bita imagined that they would eventually register the marriage.
>
> Bita almost immediately became pregnant with their child. At the same time the marriage very quickly began to go wrong. Her husband was very controlling and emotionally abusive. His family, as her parents had feared, held much more traditional views on marriage and women's education than they did. Her husbands' parents did not want Bita to continue with her education, but she was determined to do so.
>
> After the baby was born, her husband told Bita that he wanted to divorce her and applied for custody of the child. Bita's own parents persuaded her to agree to give up custody of her baby to her husband and his family. They thought that this would give Bita a better chance at further education.
>
> In court, Bita's husband denied that they had ever been married. There was of course no legal record of their marriage. Bita however understood them to be married, and fully committed to one another, in Islam. The court accepted the fact that they were not legally married and quickly made the order for custody. Bita told me that she was on the stand for "one minute," and she was not represented by counsel. Ten years later, Bita still vividly recalled the shock of the denial of her marriage and her feeling of

complete powerlessness when she heard her husband tell the court this. "I said nothing. I was traumatized. For me the real marriage was the *nikah*, but he could deny this in court with impunity."

"All you need is a nikah"

Reliance on a *nikah* alone appears to be mostly limited to particular communities where it has become the usual practice. I came across two such communities that offer an interesting contrast. In Highland Park, Michigan, it is common to find African-American Muslims who have been married using a *nikah* but did not legally register their marriage. In Toronto and Ottawa, the Somalian Canadian community that has migrated to Ontario during the last fifteen years rarely uses a civil license and relies instead on the *nikah*. One imam in this community estimates that up to 85 percent of his members married using a *nikah* have no civil marriage license.

Interestingly, the reasons for this practice appear to be quite different in each case. Highland Park is home to an African-American Muslim community suffering high levels of poverty and unemployment. The community has a historical and contemporary unease with state institutions in general and the legal system in particular. As one local community worker put it, "Our relationship with the law and the courts as African-Americans? Not good." Residents face numerous disincentives to legal registration, and many prefer to remain "beneath the radar" to avoid bringing themselves to the attention of the state (for example, to avoid debt, criminal charges or identification of illegal status). As another respondent put it,

> "The real question that Muslims here ask themselves is 'what are the advantages to me of going on the record?' On the other hand, there are many dangers for example, scrutiny of immigration status, restrictions on polygamy and other intrusions."

This may be the same question that African-American Christians and members of other religious and ethnic groups ask themselves in the alienated climate of Highland Park, and it is not exclusive to Muslim Americans; it is a symptom of poverty and alienation, rather than religious orientation. One social worker in this community told me that a civil ceremony is an option mostly taken up by those who are concerned about providing any children of the marriage with legal status and protection. In fact, the state of Michigan, in common with other states, allows for child support (and other legal rights including inheritance) to be ordered when the parents of the child are not legally married, but requires proof of paternity in the absence of a voluntary admission by the father.[6] The social worker's comment indicates that while it is possible within the law to take the necessary steps to obtain a court order in the absence of an admission of paternity, it is unlikely that such action would be taken because of the general disinclination among this community to participate in legal processes. In order to protect children and secure their legal relationship to each parent, a legal registration of marriage is the easier and least onerous option. It is also clear that when legal registration of a marriage does take place, it does not change the perspective of this group that God (and not the state) represents "the highest court of law."

Among Canadian-Somalis in Toronto and Ottawa, the reluctance to obtain a civil license for marriage appears largely based on their sense that the legal procedure is irrelevant, adding nothing to the signing of a *nikah*. Several respondents told me they could see "no point" in registering their marriage. It would not mean that they felt "married," which they appeared to associate exclusively with signing the *nikah* and not at all with a state procedure such as registration. Several divorced women and men in this community told me that they could see no reason to change their practice in the future. For childless couples living in jurisdictions (like Ontario) that recognize common law status for the purposes of financial settlement, there may be no real advantage to registration.[7] Myine, a resident of Ontario, told me, "As a common law partner, I am still entitled to rights [she obtained both child and spousal support via the courts even though she was not legally married to her partner]—so why bother?" Myine's approach assumes a comfort with presenting oneself to the court as a "common law" partner, but it is unclear how many Muslims would be comfortable with this characterization (partnership without a formal commitment would be regarded as *haram*, or prohibited, in Islamic law). Myine's attitude may be explained by the widespread use of *nikah*-only marriages in her community, as well as a greater tolerance for divorce in North African Muslim communities. In contrast Amira, a South Asian Muslim living in the same jurisdiction as Myine who was left in dire financial straits by her husband of ten years, chose not to take this step.

> Amira was married with a *nikah* only. It was a second marriage, and she had no *mahr*. Amira had twin daughters from an earlier marriage who had lived with her and her husband. When I asked why she had not registered their marriage, she told me, "[My husband] kept saying that we would get a civil license after our *nikah*, but he didn't follow through and I didn't want to insist."

Amira told me that her husband was abusive and controlling. He bor-rowed money from her in order to purchase a matrimonial home, but later sold the house and they moved into a rental property. After ten years, he left her.

Amira contacted me when she received a letter from a law firm repre-senting her husband. In that letter, her husband's lawyer ordered her to vacate their shared home in three months' time (the rent had been paid for this period, representing the *iddat*). The letter further stated that her hus-band would not be responsible for paying utilities and other bills from the date of the letter, and went on to inform her that there would be no sup-port payable, property division or claim on her husband's pension. Amira was upset and frightened at this sudden turn of events. She had a little money to pay the rent for "a few months" but was without any other source of support. Her husband did not offer any support for the children, now aged twelve.

Amira's friends and family urged her to go to Legal Aid to try to "get him back financially." She could have presented their relationship as common law and sought support. However, Amira was clear that she did not want to do this. She saw making a claim this way as prolonging the conflict with her husband—"we haven't discussed this"—rather than asserting her rights, and she just wanted out of the marriage. When I con-tacted her again nine months later, Amira had moved out of her home with her daughters and had moved into a small apartment in a poor area. She was hoping to move to live with her extended family. She and her ex-husband seemed to be coming to an informal understanding: "He is trying to make it up to me, buying me groceries, paying the rent."

She was just scraping by.

An individual married by *nikah* only who lives in a jurisdiction that does not recognize common law marriage for the purposes of financial settlement faces some serious practical consequences.[8] For example, for those married using a *nikah* only in Highland Park, the state of Michigan will not recognize their mar-riage, nor will the state enforce a claim for financial relief from anyone not legally married.[9] Most (although not all) respondents appeared to be aware that without registration the local legal system would not recognize their marriage, although they may not fully understand all the subsequent implications. Where they would not consider recourse to the legal system to resolve problems in any case (like Amira above), many felt it was unimportant to have this option. Of course, the absence of a legal marriage need not mean there is no negotiation regarding a fair outcome in the ending of the relationship, in the spirit of the Quranic exhortation to "release them in a just manner."[10] However, as in Amira's case, the fact that Islamic marriage is not recognized as a legal union may lead some men and their legal advisers to assume they can dispense with such responsibility.

Other Ways to Use the *Nikah*: Trial Marriage and Multiple Marriages

Reliance on a *nikah* alone arises in two other contexts. The first is to legitimize sexual relationships in a "trial marriage" before a final formal commitment is made.[11] One-on-one dating is avoided among all but the most secular Muslims, although courtship in larger social groups if often permitted. A few communities approve the use of a *nikah* to enable a young couple to begin a sexual relationship which may not end in marriage; this is a form of "legalized dating," or "trial marriage."

> "It's like [some] Western parents' attitudes towards their children using marijuana. They should be able to experiment in their bedroom—as long as . . . it is only a *nikah*; Islamically they can be together now—why not let them be together and experiment? Islam believes that it is natural to have physical expression of love, and the *nikah* enables them to do this."

This convention is limited to particular communities, and some imams told me that they would not officiate under these circumstances. Those who do facilitate "trial marriages" see them as socially beneficial devices to allow young people to "try out" marriage, and to avoid the pressure and recriminations of a broken marriage in the event that the partners are not yet ready for a final commitment. In some communities, the trial may facilitate courtship but not sexual relations.

> "In my community many couples have a legal marriage proceeding and then begin to court or date. If the relationship ends at this stage—before consummation—there is no shame. I encourage relationships that are not working to end peacefully at this stage. If the relationship continues, it is formalized in a marriage ceremony."

The practice of trial marriage is controversial in the Muslim community. An even more contentious area is the facilitation (by an imam or other celebrant) of a *nikah* for a couple when the man is already married to another woman. To avoid a charge of bigamy, men who are already legally married may use a *nikah* alone when they contract for a further marriage. Polygamy is still practiced among some North American Muslims. While it is rarely discussed openly, in some communities it appears to be broadly accepted and formal legal constraints regarded as socially unimportant. A daughter of a polygamous marriage told me that for her father, "The idea that this was bigamy would not have been at all important to him. This was common [practice] in his circle." Few of the imams I interviewed wanted to say much on this topic, and since this was not an explicit part of my research agenda, I trod carefully. Most acknowledged, some readily, that they were aware that polygamous marriages continued to be contracted, but none was prepared to say that they played any role in them—as one would expect, given the legal implications of such an admission. A few imams spoke in very critical tones of others whom they named as sanctioning polygamous marriages. Overall, however, the attitude among the imams appears to be that many turn a blind eye to this practice, and only a few are prepared to speak out against it. Both reactions suggest significant social pressure to allow multiple marriages.

A small number of imams went on the record to speak in defense of polygamy. In each case, the same rationale was offered: multiple marriage is a "better" alternative than having secret mistresses, and an approach that ensures acknowledged paternity for any children of the relationship. Some imams suggested that polygamy is simply a cultural reality for Muslim communities and should not be understood as an issue of morality. One imam cited to me the example of a famous and beautiful Lebanese pop singer who agreed to become a man's second wife "just because she loved him." He explained that it is culturally accepted for a woman to choose (as in this case) to "share" her husband with another woman and still have a fulfilling and satisfying relationship.

Among religious scholars I found a greater willingness to be explicit about discomfort with polygamy. Several scholars made the point that while the Qur'an permits polygamy—it was an established part of social customs in seventh-century Arabia before the revelations of the Prophet—it certainly does not require it. Multiple marriage at the time of the Prophet appears to have been a response to historical conditions (the number of women who were left widowed by war). Many of these same scholars made the further observation that the Quranic stipulation that all wives must be treated equally[12] probably renders the practice impossible in twenty-first-century North America, at least where polygamous families wish to integrate into a wider social community, which would be difficult if they established a visible residence for multiple wives and children. Several also made the point that since Muslims are obligated to live by the laws of their host country or residence,[13] and since it is unlawful to make more than one legal marriage at one time in either the United States or Canada, formally avoiding bigamy by using only a *nikah* breaches the spirit of this obligation.

A number of women chose to end their marriages when their husbands took second wives or mistresses.[14] They did not regard a decision to take another "wife" against their wishes as Islamic. On the contrary, "This has nothing to do with Islam. This is oppression." Polygamy is not just an individual burden, but it creates conflicts throughout the community; "Multiple marriages . . . are problems for the community as a whole, and for men also." While it is possible to include a clause in the *nikah* that precludes the husband from taking another wife without the permission of his first wife—some contemporary *nikah* templates include this as an option—it is relatively unusual, and I came across only two women who had included such a clause. Almost all of those women who eventually ended their marriages over the issue of polygamy had not anticipated that their husband would assert a "right" to take another wife and were shocked to discover this expectation.

Premarital Counseling

One of the ways in which prospective couples can discuss and perhaps agree on their shared understanding of how they will practice Islamic values in their marriage is through premarital counseling. Often each individual assumes a particular approach (for example, regarding polygamy, or work outside the home, or relations with in-laws) without canvassing the other partner. As one leading proponent of premarital counseling points out, "Most couples spend more time preparing for the wedding than they do preparing for the marriage."

In most cases where premarital counseling is offered it is conducted by the imam, although some mosques have introduced professional therapists and counselors to develop and lead these programs. The role of the imams in premarital counseling flows from their formal responsibility for oversight of the signing of the *nikah* when the couple makes their commitment to one another. Some mosques actually require some form of premarital counseling with the imam. There are vast differences in the type of programming offered, which in many cases comprises one brief meeting between the couple and the imam that focuses on the delivery of a "lesson" on Islamic rights and responsibilities. Beyond this, just a few imams use premarital counseling as an opportunity to focus on a discussion of the *nikah* and its terms, and a small number will encourage consideration of possible additions or amendments to the marriage contract. Only a very small number of respondents negotiated the precise terms of their *nikah* with their prospective spouse and still fewer reported being encouraged to do so by an imam. Some imams told me they felt awkward about raising specific issues—for example, rights to divorce—with a couple about to be wed. Other imams may feel ill qualified to conduct such a discussion, as well as reluctant to add to their workload with each couple.

Some imams who are uncomfortable customizing the *nikah* instead encourage the couple to default to the common law in the event of a disagreement.

While this will improve the wife's position in the event of the dissolution of the marriage (that is, she will have the same rights as her husband to ask for a divorce), day-to-day differences over their roles within the marriage and reasonable expectations regarding work, education and children are not the business of the courts and require an understanding between the couple. Negotiations before marriage over the terms of the commitment made in the *nikah* may be made more difficult by family and, for some women, pressure to accept their husbands' wishes. "It's just the *nikah*"—assuming its actual content to be symbolic only—is a familiar refrain (echoed by Fashia earlier in this chapter). Many women in this study who were eventually divorced would disagree. Several reflected that if they had discussed their respective rights at the time of their *nikah*, "his true colors would have come out."

Not one of the divorced men and women in this study participated in anything they understood as premarital counseling before scheduling their *nikah*. However, the widespread assumption that "it's just the *nikah*" may also mean that some couples see little reason to meet with the imam before their wedding. Imams and others who offer premarital counseling generally conceptualize it as preventative intervention, "enabling positive marital outcomes via counseling and preparation." The most common model, and perhaps the simplest to implement, is an educational one. The rationale is that if a young couple is educated about their responsibilities, they are more likely to live up to them—or at least, they cannot claim that they did not realize what they were getting themselves into. Many professionals working with Muslim families place great emphasis on the importance of education and information for women entering marriage, in order that they can be more assertive and confident about their rights in the relationship. Greater knowledge would allow women to refuse or resist unreasonable claims and expectations by their husbands, who falsely assert that their demand is based on Quranic principles or Islamic law. The importance of education is also frequently stressed in relation to marriages between Muslims and non-Muslims.

There are growing calls in the Muslim community for greater emphasis to be paid to the importance of premarital counseling in the development of the *nikah* and other shared understandings between the couple. This is often expressed in response to a rising level of marital breakdown within the Muslim community. As a result, a network of resources aimed at promoting and assisting with the development of both premarital and marital counseling is gradually emerging. One example is the Healthy Marriage Initiative, which in 2008 introduced the Healthy Marriage Community Covenant, asking imams to commit to at least three sessions of premarital counseling with a couple before conducting a *nikah*. Perhaps filling the service gaps, premarital counseling services advertise online and are offered by telephone, and questionnaires aimed at couples considering marriage can be found on the Internet.[15] In an innovative program offered at the Adams Centre in Virginia, participants explore personality types, attitudes towards money, sexuality, communication, issues in intercultural marriages and the influence of the extended family. One of the imams involved in this program told me: "This is becoming a science for us—we take this very seriously."

A significant challenge for premarital counseling in the Muslim community is whether families who are excited at the prospect of a "good" marriage will be willing to respond to signs of incompatibility before the *nikah* is signed—for example, when the couple discover in discussions with the imam that they have very different views about gender roles in marriage—and support the ending of an engagement. If the breaking off of an engagement continues to carry a social stigma—which it does in some communities— premarital counseling is unlikely to be very effective in either its preventative or educational function.

Foundations of Islamic Marriage and Family Life

The values and "rules" of Islamic marriage derive from both religious and cultural traditions. While there are differences over how such commitments are realized in practice, some core principles stand out. These include a lifelong commitment to marriage, the choice of a compatible partner (and all that assumes) and an arrangement of rights and duties in a heterosexual relationship. These principles are reflected in many different levels of adherence and practice. This is especially evident among those who were born or largely raised in North America, whose expectations and preferences are often shaped by that experience. The manner in which they relate to and integrate their faith into their married lives also reflects their personal preferences, personalities, aspirations and character. Just like any other couple, Muslim couples face the challenge of fitting together, via negotiation and accommodations, their different beliefs, values, cultures and personalities.

Many of the principles described here as central to Islamic marriage and family life—for example, the aspiration to a lifelong commitment—are also important to non-Muslim couples. They take on a particular meaning, however, within the traditions of Islam. Other principles can only really be understood in the context of Islam, for example, marriage as "completion" and Islamic ideas about obedience, authority and financial responsibility within marriage.

Marriage Is between a Man and a Woman

Marriage in Islam is exclusively concerned with heterosexual relationships. References in both the Qur'an and *hadith* prohibit sexual relationships between men, and a smaller number proscribe lesbian relationships.[16] Mainstream Muslim opinion condemns homosexual activity, and it is not known how many Muslim men and women are gay and lesbian. Some Muslim countries have enacted legislation punishing homosexuality with death.[17] There is increasing attention in Western countries to the resistance expressed by gay Muslims to a rhetoric that condemns their behavior as "a moral disorder."[18] One young Muslim woman regretfully explains in the Channel 4 documentary *Gay Muslims*, which aired in early 2006, "You can't be proud to be gay in Islam. It's an un-Islamic notion."

Contemporary Western scholarship on sexuality and Islam characterize Muslims as both antisexual (although this is contested by many Islamic scholars, who argue that sexual desire, including female desire, is explicitly permitted and encouraged in Islam)[19] and antihomosexual. According to Bouhdiba, "In Islam, male homosexuality stands for all the perversions and constitutes in a sense the depravity of depravities."[20] Nonetheless, there is some historical evidence that it was socially acceptable in some Muslim countries and Islamic cultures for older men to have sexual relationships with younger boys, in common with many other earlier cultures.[22] While gradual change in this area might be anticipated as homosexuality between consenting adults becomes increasingly accepted in mainstream sexual mores, especially in the West, at present only sexual desire as it exists between husband and wife is accepted by most Muslims as part of a harmonious relationship intended by God. Marriage in the following discussion is limited, therefore, to a contract between a man and a woman.

Marriage Is the Completion of the Individual

Marriage is widely regarded by Muslims as a positive and even necessary step in individual social and religious development. In a well-known *hadith* attributed to Bayhaqi,[23] the Prophet Mohammed says that "when a man marries, he has fulfilled half of his religion, so let him fear Allah regarding the remaining half." This expression—abbreviated to "marriage is half the religion"—appears frequently in advertisements for marriage seminars and lectures on Islamic marriage. Being unmarried is regarded as less than "complete." The implications of staying unmarried are especially negative for women: "The Muslim family system perceives a single woman as leading to *fitna* or social disorder."[24] This view is reflected in many of the comments of divorced women who told me that they were regarded by others as a dangerous threat to married men. Several convert women told me that they felt under pressure to marry—or to remarry, if they were divorced—as soon as possible.

Marriage in Islam is understood as the fulfillment of personal and spiritual development, "life-affirming rather than life-denying."[25] Marriage completes the individual, spiritually, practically and sexually. Spiritually, because marriage allows each spouse to draw closer to God. Practically, because the institution of the family—centred on a married man and woman and their children—is the principal unit of Islamic society. Sexually, because dating and sexual contact outside marriage are impermissible. Marriage is a means of regulating sexual desire and passion and requires faithfulness between a man and a woman. A man who is not married is instructed to restrain his desire until he is married.

> "Let those who find not the wherewithal for marriage keep themselves chaste, until Allah gives them means out of His grace."[26]

Sexual fidelity does not always mean faithfulness to a single woman on the part of her husband, because he may take more than one wife. The principle is that only once a woman is regarded as a wife in Islam are sexual relations with her permitted. This also means that until a marriage is ended Islamically, the wife remains sexually available to her husband. This sometimes becomes a critical point when Muslims couples divorce. A number of women told me that husbands continued to assert that they were still their sexual "property" after they had obtained a civil divorce, and until they were also Islamically divorced. Several male respondents repeated this assumption.

An emphasis on marriage as "completion" (as well as the general prohibition on sexual relations outside marriage) means that many young Muslims place significant pressure on themselves to find a marriage partner. Often their families ramp up this pressure. One young woman told me, "I had no real choice. Everyone—including my parents—was pressuring me to marry." A middle-aged man looked back with regret on his failed marriage and said, "I paid the price for doing what my parents wanted." The emphasis on marriage as socially desirable may result in hasty decision making, to the potential detriment of one or even both of the marriage partners.

> When Shanaz's parents divorced following her father's adultery, their status in their community was badly affected. Shanaz's mother was advised by her friends that it would be a good idea for Shanaz, her nineteen-year-old daughter, to be married as soon as possible in order to counter any social stigma against the family—the children of divorced parents are sometimes seen as unsuitable marriage partners.
>
> Shanaz initially resisted the suggestion that she should be married—this was not her plan for her immediate future, and she had wanted to continue with her education, which she realized would probably come to an end if she married. But in the end she gave in.

Shanaz was married to a man with whom she had had almost no pre-marital dialogue, but her family liked him and was relying on the marriage to salvage the family's reputation. Her husband quickly became physically abusive, but by this time Shanaz was already pregnant with their first child.

Choosing the "Right" Partner

There is both advice and encouragement aplenty available to young Muslims on how to choose a marriage partner. Muslim marriage guides, matchmaking services and websites abound. Conferences and community events regularly include marriage "bazaars," where singles can eye up potential candidates. Seminars on choosing the "right" partner are regularly offered to sold-out audiences. This focus on finding a partner illustrates the enduring belief that Islamic marriage is distinctive and critical to personal "completion."

The idea of romantic love—described by one popular text on marriage as an "excessive attachment to the loved one"[27]—is often portrayed by both religious scholars and marriage advisers as an inappropriate basis for choice of partner, since it is based "only" on feelings that will change or decline over time. The word most frequently associated with romantic love by Muslim marriage experts is "unrealistic."[28] Muslim marriage guides often scoff at the notion of romantic love, characterized as flighty and fickle, and contrast it with a more lasting and practical love that enables the endurance necessary for a lifelong commitment.

"Not a soppy, sentimental kind of romantic dream, but the sort of love which will roll up its sleeves and get stuck into the mess."[29]

This dichotomy between romantic love and "practical" love seems difficult to sustain, both conceptually and practically. A preoccupation with, and a glamorization of, romantic love is commonplace in both Western and Eastern traditions, and in both Muslim and non-Muslim cultures. Young Muslims are presented with competing paradigms of love and marriage. As they watch their non-Muslim friends dating and experimenting with relationships, they are surrounded by alternative visions of love. As one young man acknowledged to me, "Growing up with the influence of the media and the movies, it was very difficult." But models of romantic love are not limited to Westernized media or the behavior of their non-Muslim friends. A growing number of Muslim matchmaking websites emphasize the "heart connection" of potential clients, as do their testimonials ("I found my dream guy," "I met my soulmate here," "We have fallen in love"). Islam itself offers stories and models of love-based marriages. The Prophet Mohammed is described as having such great love for his first wife, Kajidha, that contrary to the custom of the times he did not take another wife during her lifetime and was heartbroken upon her death, refusing to marry again for three years.

Nonetheless, there is a clear thread of Islamic teaching in both older and contemporary marriage guides that disparages romantic love.[30] "Marriage is not a playground where the ego thoughtlessly pursues its vanities. . . . It is an institution that helps a man and a woman pursue the purpose of their creation: to glorify and worship God and to work, within the extent of our capabilities and resources, to make the world a better place for those we share it with and for those we will leave it to."[31] Some Muslim marriage guides go so far as to blame a belief in romantic love for marital breakdown and divorce.

This rejection of romantic love is related to the belief that marriage should enable each spouse to draw closer to God. A number of divorced men and women felt that their partner had impeded their relationship with God because they adopted a different approach to observance, or held a more shallow (in their opinion) faith. This allowed these individuals to feel that the marriage was not meant to continue. Drawing closer to God needs to be compatible with, and not clouded by, what one feels for one's spouse; marriage should be a source of religious and spiritual nourishment, and not just about attraction or personal connection between the two spouses. Ideally the spouses will grow together as believing Muslims.[32] One young woman told me that she chose her husband because "[he] would make me a better person and a *better Muslim*" (my italics). A therapist and marriage counselor explained to me that Muslims understand the primary relationship to be between the Creator (Allah) and the individual. Other relationships—between husband and wife, between parent and child—are very important, but they are always secondary to the relationship with God. As she explained it, "Marriage is two plus God, plus their extended families—but the primary relationship of each person is with God."

The idea that awareness of God is integral to the marriage commitment for believing Muslims, and that this offers a stronger foundation for marriage than "only" romantic love, is poorly understood. Some non-Muslims hold extremely negative views about "loveless" Islamic unions, which they associate with any form of arranged marriage. Sherene Razack describes a campaign to convince Norwegian Muslims to embrace "the virtues of romantic love," which simplistically equated arranged marriage with oppression and romantic love with personal freedom. The assumption was that persuading Muslims to "demand" romantic choices would "liberate" them from arranged marriage.[33]

Muslims face the same dilemmas in choosing a lifelong partner as non-Muslims when it comes to assessing what objectively identifiable commonalities—aside from feelings of love—are important to long-term compatibility. Religious compatibility—composed of so many complex cultural and often idiosyncratic elements—is often difficult to measure before the couple lives together, as the stories of many respondents attest. A well-known *hadith* describes four criteria a Muslim man should look for in a wife which are more easily appraised at a distance. These are wealth; the nobility of her family; beauty; and character (in Arabic, *din*, which includes religious devotion).[34] Non-Muslims have the advantage of longer periods of courtship during which they can get to know more about the other person. Because courtship is often restricted in Muslim families there may be more dependence on parental criteria, knowledge and approval. This constraint, along with the rejection of romantic love and the admonition to find a partner who will enhance one's relationship with God, sustains the belief among some young Muslims that a "match" arranged by their parents—rather than their own "love" choice—may be a better way to meet the Islamic ideal of marriage. Personal "romantic" choices made without parental consultation are sometimes offered as an explanation for a failed marriage; a number of divorced men and women who participated in this study reflected in hindsight that they wished that they had involved their parents more closely in their choice of spouse, and regretted not taking their advice more seriously.

Others agree to be married to their parents' choice of partner in order to meet their parents' expectations, and to avoid disappointing them. Research conducted in Norway by Anja Bredal suggests that young Muslims sometimes acquiesce to arranged marriage out of solidarity, angry at the way in which popular culture stigmatizes the Muslim community and their traditional practices. They may hold back their own reluctance about conforming to arranged marriage out of a fear of causing more grief for their family.[35] There are also some signs that parents and children in immigrant Muslim communities are beginning to renegotiate the terms of this traditional expectation. In a 2002 U.K. study, Yunus Samad and John Eade describe an increase in "co-operative traditional" marriages (where wider choice and more options are offered, but parental consent remains essential) in Pakistani and Bangladeshi communities.[36] For example, a couple may meet independently but then the man will go to the woman's family for approval; or the family may contact a young man in whom their daughter is interested via social networking and then bring him to meet their daughter in a family setting. Expectations surrounding parental approval are also affected by gender. A 1997 study in Britain found that arranged marriage was more common for young women than for young men; 49 percent of Muslim men between the ages of sixteen and thirty-four said that they needed parental approval for their choice of partner, whereas for women this figure rose to 67 percent.[37] Samad and Eade also observe that the increasing education of young women is altering these practices within families.

The extent to which parental choices are advised or insisted upon ultimately depends on the particular family and power relations both inside and outside it (community pressure may also be a factor). A number of respondents described initially resisting their parents' choice but ultimately giving in. Parental preferences—for example, for someone within the same ethnic group—are still regarded as "safe" by some young Muslims who want to make a lasting marriage and for whom it is important that their choice of partner satisfies their parents (in much the same way as any young person). As long as dating continues to be regarded as un-Islamic—at least outside the "marriage bazaar"[38] and the burgeoning number of online chat rooms—parental choice and approval will continue to be extremely important, in form if not always in practice. The problem is that the ability of parents to make "safe" choices for their children may be diminishing as their expectations change. One young woman, whose marriage lasted just two months, reflected:

> "I told my father it wouldn't work. His expectations were based on the norms at home (in this case, North Africa); mine are based on growing up here."

Problems appear to be common when one spouse grows up in North America and marries a (otherwise unknown) partner from overseas. Some among the older generation continue to see such a match as beneficial. Samad and Eade quote an older Pakistani man as saying: "If a boy from here marries a girl from back home, then that girl keeps that boy within the culture. And if he is not straight, meaning out of line as far as his cultural duties are concerned, she brings him within the culture."[39] It is not clear whether the same rationale is operating when young women raised in North America are matched to men from "back home."

> Raheela's parents brought a man from Pakistan to marry her shortly after she graduated from high school. Raheela tried to resist this choice. "Even during our engagement [and before her husband-to-be arrived in North America] I expressed doubts [to her parents] about our compatibility, but I was told, 'Your family knows what is best for you.'"

The objectives of Raheela's parents and others similarly motivated are to ensure that their child makes a "good" marriage that will endure. Sadly, this may often be the opposite of what actually occurs. Raheela, whose experience was typical of many respondents, was divorced after just two years. While there is no evidence that an arranged marriage is more likely to fail than any other, factors sometimes associated with arranged marriage in these communities—including differences in age and cultural upbringing—raise questions about compatibility. There are signs that these customs are being questioned not only by young people but also by their parents. In a number of cases in this study, when an arranged marriage did not worked out for an oldest sibling, the parents will take a different approach with subsequent siblings' marriages, allowing more independence and choice (see, for example. the story of Rabia, in chapter four).

A Lifelong Commitment

While Islam permits divorce, a widely quoted *hadith* describes divorce as "the most hated permitted thing."[40] Marriage is understood as a lifelong commitment that should only be set aside under exceptional circumstances. Of course, Muslims share this ideal with millions of other hopeful newlyweds: as one young Muslim woman put it, "You think that you're walking into a fairy tale."

The aspiration to a lifelong partnership means that those who choose to end their marriages always face disapproval and sometimes intense social opprobrium. Criticism of those who ended their marriages in divorce was always voiced, often stridently, when I presented the results of this study to hundreds of Muslims in mosques and community centres across North America. While such criticism did not explicitly target divorcées—and was made by both men and women audience members—cultural norms frequently "blame" women. Disapproval was frequently framed as a critique of younger Muslims by the older generation who felt that young married couples did not "try hard enough" to keep their marriages together. It was extremely unusual to hear anyone speak up against this accusation. The same sentiment is widely shared outside Muslim communities by older people who are alarmed at the rising level of divorce. The frequency of divorce is, in turn, shaping more tolerant attitudes among young Muslims. This generational change is illustrated by Zohra's story. Zohra saw her marriage as a commitment for life and struggled with the recognition that her husband had left her and her marriage was over. Her adult children saw it differently.

> Zohra had been married for twenty-five years and had eight children with her husband. Her husband had left her and their eight children four years earlier, and Zohra had not seen him since. He had stopped sending any financial support and moved to another country where he had taken another wife.
>
> Despite these facts, Zohra remains uncertain about asking for a divorce and ending her marriage. She told me that she feels guilty and ambivalent about reneging on the promise she made to remain married to her husband

for the rest of her life. She said that she worries about what her family and friends will think of her if she gives up this commitment.

Zohra's adult children expressed their impatience to me with their mother's reluctance to divorce their father. To them it is obvious that this is the right decision, but they also acknowledged that it would be very difficult for their mother, who had been raised to believe that marriage vows could not be broken.

At the end of our conversation, Zohra told me, "It is not easy to end something that has lasted this long. . . . Islam says 'give your brother seventy excuses.'"

A serious commitment to marriage for life, however motivated, inevitably affects decision making about staying married and the assessment of "reasons" for ending the marriage by both spouses as others—their family, their community—look on. A number of divorced men and women told me that what initially inhibited them from breaking their commitment was that they did not feel that they had "real"—sufficient, serious—reasons for divorce. One man whose marriage had been through some troubled times but had stayed with his wife told me, "In our case, there was 'no meat' to justify a divorce. I still felt like I was doing something wrong. It [ending the marriage] did not fit into reasons that felt OK to me." "Real" reasons are often understood as severe relationship dysfunctions such as adultery, physical or emotional abuse, or the failure of the husband to support the family. Stories from the life of the Prophet suggest that he permitted divorce in much broader circumstances, including personal unhappiness and a sense of incompatibility. But for many respondents, their personal sense of the commitment they made to their spouse and to God meant that they could only live with a decision to end that commitment if they could provide reasons that went beyond personal unhappiness; sometimes they regarded unhappiness as a personal sacrifice that should be endured and not used as an "excuse" to break their promise to marry for life. As one respondent put it, "Divorce is considered bad in Islam. . . . You don't say that word!" Chapter four explores what factors are critical to divorcées and divorcés in giving up on their goal of a life-long commitment.

Obedience and Authority

The notion of wifely obedience is a common one in many religious traditions, along with the parallel concept of husbandly authority. For example, many Christian wedding vows refer to a passage in Paul's letter to the Ephesians which exhorts wives to "submit to your husbands as to the Lord."[41] Despite this parallel history, there is a widespread perception among non-Muslims that marriage in Islam is uniquely unequal, and that Muslim women are effectively slaves owned by their husbands. Anja Bredal describes young immigrant Norwegian-Muslim girls being stopped by anxious strangers on the street and asked whether they had been forced into marriage.[42] In the debate over the exclusion of women wearing the *burkah* (a full-body cloak) or *niqab* (a face-covering veil) from public services in Quebec, Canada, many of those in favor of the proposed new law argued that it was necessary to protect *niqabi* from pressure and coercion from their husbands to dress this way.[43] The same argument was made to promote similar legislation in Belgium and France.[44] The assumption that *niqabi* are coerced into this style of dress exposes the lack of understanding of the reasons some Muslim women choose to wear the veil.

The widespread perception that Muslim women are universally oppressed by their husbands is compounded by the willingness of some Muslim men to lay claim to authority over their wives. For these men, wifely obedience appears to include the imposition of rules about everything—for example, how they are to be addressed, what household tasks are "obligatory" and what they should wear. This can extend to the most bizarre claims; one social worker told me about a client whose husband told her that "good Muslim women" did not wear panties. Another had been told by her husband that a Muslim woman is not permitted to call her husband by his first name. Several women described their husbands as acting as if they "owned" them once they had made their *nikah*. One described marriage for a Muslim woman as "handing your body into slavery." The most frequently cited Quranic verse regarding a husband's authority (in Arabic, *qiwama*) over his wife is variously translated. For example:

> "Men are the protectors and maintainers of women because God has given the one (more strength) than the other, and because men can support them from their means."
>
> "Men are in charge of women, because God has made one of them excel the other, and because they spend of their property (for the support of women)."

The conception of wifely obedience derives from the same verse, exhorting the wife to accept her husband's authority in return for his responsibility to take care of her practical needs. Contemporary scholars—as well as ordinary Muslims—constantly debate the meaning of "authority" and "obedience." For example, does authority allow a husband to order his wife to cook for him? Have sex with him? Remain in the house unless he permits her to leave it? Is wifely obedience owed to one's husband or only to God? Just what does the "bargain" of marriage permit and require? Boilerplate marriage contracts generally do not include any explicit reference to either authority or obedience. A few contemporary *nikah* boilerplates include clauses that address these issues concretely. For example, the New Marriage Contract of Egypt stipulates that the parties "cooperate in work and in caring for the affairs of the family, the home and the raising of the children" and that "the wife shall be entitled to exercise her right to education and to work outside the home." Other clauses make clear that both parties—and especially a working wife—have a responsibility to contribute financially to the household.[45] Another *nikah* template promoted by a number of Muslim organizations in the United Kingdom refers to "all prevailing social norms, etiquettes and local customs (implicit or explicit . . . which are not in contradiction of [*sic*] the Sharia'h."[46] This could be helpful for a woman wishing to assert her wish to return to school or to work in the face of her husband's opposition, but it is too vague to support a clear case.

Many modern-day scholars argue that an overtly patriarchal assumption of husbandly authority and wifely obedience is neither Islamic, nor an accurate interpretation of the primary sources. Several suggest that "obedience" is better understood as "co-operation," rather than submission to a husband's arbitrary will. Feminist scholar Azizah al-Hibri argues that this view is reflected in the nature of the marriage contract, which is a contract for companionship, not for "services."[47] Others point out that the husband's "authority" is derived solely from his sole financial support, which is no longer the reality for many modern Muslim families. Moreover, some assert, even the original context of man the provider only anticipated his authority where he possessed superior knowledge or experience; it did not justify the imposition of his will on his wife. This is contrary to the teachings of Islam, which consistently disapprove of coercion. These scholars argue that the concept of *nushuz*, or "disobedience," developed by some modern Islamic legal systems and used (for example) to limit the basis on which a woman may seek a divorce[48] should be limited to acts of resistance and hatred by the wife against her husband, rather than monitoring her everyday social behavior.[49] In light of these interpretations, the assertions of men who believe that they should be able to "control" their wives appear absurd.

Nonetheless this type of behavior is widely tolerated in cultural communities with conventions of male control over women which exploit the potential for interpreting *qiwama* in its most chauvinist manifestations. As Tariq Ramadan writes, "To believe that nothing in the message of Islam justifies discrimination against women is one thing; to say that they do not suffer any discrimination in Western (or Eastern) communities is another."[50] Moreover, the ideal of a "good Muslim wife" who is obedient to her husband continues to be promoted by some influential contemporary media and literary sources. Take this example from a popular website:

> "Listen to and obey him, for contentment brings peace of mind, and listening to and obeying one's husband pleases Allah. . . . Make sure that you smell good and look good; . . . prepare his food on time, and keep quiet when he is asleep, for raging hunger is like a burning flame, and disturbing his sleep will make him angry. . . . Never disobey any of his orders, for if you disclose any of his secrets you will never feel safe from his possible betrayal, and if you disobey him, his heart will be filled with hatred towards you."[51]

Continuing cultural biases against women and in favor of male power exist in both Muslim and non-Muslim communities. When similar assertions of power and authority are made by non-Muslim men, the roots of their particular justification may be less tangible than the contested concept of *qiwama*, but the effects are just as real.

By far the most common complaint among the female respondents about the expectation of "obedience" is in relation to household tasks. Some women—themselves working outside the home, and sometimes the sole wage-earner in the family—described themselves as "slaves" to these chores. A smaller number of women spoke about difficulty persuading their husbands to permit them to attend school, work outside the home or travel independently. Sexual relations is a less commonly cited but complex site of male/female power. The notion of a Muslim wife sexually enslaved to her husband is widely assumed in an Islamophobic culture. This is not just an empty stereotype: in classical jurisprudence, the general duty of obedience owed by the wife to her husband included the obligation to have sex with him. A duty to be sexually available to one's husband is still asserted by some contemporary scholars; one popular marriage guide cites the Maliki school as permitting a man to have sex with his wife up to eight times a day.[52] It is difficult to imagine that this is literally accepted by many modern Muslim couples, although an assumption of sexual "ownership" is pervasive. Stories told by the respondents in this study demonstrated that some Muslim men still assume that they have a unilateral "right" to sex with their wives, an assertion that their wives usually reject and resist. No modern-day Muslim legal system yet recognizes marital rape as an offence, assuming the right of the husband to have sexual access to his wife but disparaging overt coercion. Such reforms have been relatively recent in the United States also; the first U.S. state (South Carolina) to criminalize marital rape did so only in 1975[53] and the last one (North Carolina) as recently as 1993.[54] Many Muslim legal systems (for example, Malaysia's) inherited a marital rape exception from the common-law system of the British colonizers. Difficulty accepting the fact of rape within marriage is reflected in the attitudes of some North American imams; one told me that he counseled a woman, "Even if [your husband] rapes you, remember you have seven children with him."

In interviews with both men and women, whether lay people or professionals, I found a very open attitude towards discussing sexual relations, including the explicit appreciation of sex for pleasure and not only procreation (in contrast with some other religions such as Catholicism). Many women respondents described their sexual relations voluntarily and comfortably—for example, when sex was unsatisfactory or limited or awkward. A small number of those who had experienced domestic violence also described sexual abuse by their husbands. This is part of a recognized spectrum of intimate partner violence. Sexual violence is a common escalation of physical abuse over a prolonged period.[55] No one described the justification of sexual violence with reference to "Islamic" norms, but all these women experienced their husbands as behaving as if they "owned" their bodies. All the descriptions of oppressive sexual demands came from women who also described physical abuse; no others attributed their marital breakdown to unreasonable sexual demands.

Among the imams, who play an important part in the social construction of norms, there is a wide spectrum of attitudes regarding conventions of authority and obedience between husband and wife. Some imams fail to discourage, and even actively encourage, the worst possible assumptions about male privilege and control.

"If the woman is the problem in the relationship, then the man has the authority in Islam to correct his wife."

However, others are openly dismissive of the most patriarchal assumptions about "obedience." Some imams described their efforts to correct men who assumed that their wives should do all the cooking, cleaning and child care, even in families where the wife worked outside the home, and a few ridiculed this assumption.

"Where is it in the Qur'an that says that the woman must clean and cook? The Qur'an is about fairness, not about duty. . . . They confuse *shari'a* with cultural traditions that oppress women."

One imam described the belief among some Muslim men that they have the right to "control" their wives as "cultural baggage." A number of imams told me that the real problem is a lack of Islamic education for women, which allows chauvinistic misconceptions to continue unchallenged. How open these same imams are about these beliefs when they address public audiences of men is unknown. What is clear is that cultural and social norms exert more influence than Islamic jurisprudence or scholarly debate about the appropriate Islamic "exchange bargain" between husband and wife. Many respondents spoke about modeling their own marriage on that of their parents, and about bringing these expectations into their marriage. This often led to conflict when the values of the two families were very different.

> "My husband's family was more traditional [than my own] and placed a greater emphasis on obedience by women to men. His mother was more passive than my own by nature, and his brothers' wives came from overseas so they had lower expectations than she did of independence."

Disputes over male authority and female obedience sometimes focus on public behavior by the wife, and the extent to which the husband should be able to control her in the public sphere. This woman described the contrast between the expectations she had been raised with and those of her fiancé:

> "My father was and is comfortable talking to other people and my mother warned me always about knowing what my body language was saying and respecting myself, but this did not mean that I could not have a conversation with another man. . . . But [my fiancé] saw this as a sign of bad behavior in his intended wife."

Even when no overt constraints are imposed, male authority is sometimes exerted in a way that makes clear that women should not challenge or question the superior position of their husbands. This same assumption thwarts genuine negotiation. As one woman put it, "He had a different conception of what being a Muslim and a Muslim wife was to me—and of course he believed that the man should have his way with this." Conflict may be further exacerbated by the need to maintain public appearances, especially in cultural communities with entrenched assumptions about male authority over women.

> Zarinah's husband did not limit her educational and professional development. However, as an imam, he demanded that she accede to his authority in religious matters. Little by little, Zarinah felt that her husband began to claim this authority in other areas also, for example, his attitudes about the role and place of women. He resented her challenging his views and insisted that she accept his authority.

As her children were growing up and becoming more independent, Zarinah began to look for new personal goals. She enrolled in a doctoral program. As a longtime teacher in an Islamic school, she took on additional responsibilities as school principal. She also began to argue ever more frequently with her husband about his attitudes towards women and his assumption of male superiority. She asked him why if in Islam, men and women were considered equal—a principle he accepted—were women treated as second-class citizens, disparaged and put down within their own culture?

Zarinah's challenges to her husband's opinions did not fit with his assumptions about how an "obedient" wife should behave. He was embarrassed that his community saw his wife as failing to submit to his authority. He told Zarinah, "You will have to go back to keeping your mouth closed. It's OK for you to think [these ideas], but I don't want to hear about your opinions."

Financial Responsibilities

Islamic law requires the prospective husband to provide an adequate *mahr* or bridal gift (of an unspecified amount or value). Some women told me that they did not understand the significance of the *mahr* at the time that they were married, and hence did not negotiate in their own best interests, sometimes accepting a symbolic gift or a very minimal sum. In theory, this should have been prevented by the intervention of her *wali* on her behalf, but in some cases such advocacy failed to materialize. In classical Islamic law, the husband has sole financial responsibility for his wife and any children during the marriage. The wife retains her rights to property she owned in her own right before marriage, and to her own earnings once she is married. The idea of male financial responsibility is central to a classical Islamic understanding of family structure, deriving from his obligation to secure his family's security. As one Islamic scholar told me, "Everything else is ancillary to this." In return, the wife will accept her husband's authority over her and their family.

Today the classical principle is coming under significant pressure, and many Muslim couples do not subscribe to it. Islamic law allows for the modification of the *nikah* to reflect a different financial arrangement between the couple. Alternately, a couple may simply agree between themselves to adopt civil law principles such as community property. Nonetheless, the classical view continues to be reiterated in some contemporary writing about Muslim marriage[56] and is consistently referred to by many imams. It is still difficult for Muslim couples to present a different economic model to their community—for example, when the wife is a breadwinner, or the husband wants to stay home and take care of the children—because they are challenging not only the monetary model but also the gendered assumptions that underlie it. This places both spouses under pressure to conform to the traditional model. The expectation lingers that men should shoulder full responsibility for the family, and a man who cannot meet this obligation is sometimes seen as unmanly. "Where the woman is the breadwinner the marriage will not be seen as an Islamic marriage by the community." Of course, non-Muslim families with stay-at-home dads often face similar questions and biases.

A traditional economic model of family life is incompatible with societal changes taking place not only in North America, but also throughout much of the Muslim world. The rise in working women throughout the whole population means that women are increasingly accepted in Muslim families as a dual, primary or even sole breadwinner. Fifty-nine percent of Muslim women—higher than the number of women in the general population—reported having a job in a 2009 U.S. survey.[57] The wife is the primary wage-earner in a growing number of Muslim families, and in many other families both are income-earners. The female respondents in this study included doctors, researchers, lawyers, scientists and other professionals. Many women described working while their husbands went through school, or working during a period when their husband was unemployed. Some clearly welcomed their personal financial independence because it enabled them to make their own decision about staying in their marriage. However some women were clearly struggling with leaving behind the traditional assumption that their husband would be the financial provider, even where they earned significantly more than their husbands. One professional woman ordered to pay support to her husband told me, "I tried to tell the judge that it was not acceptable for me to pay spousal support in Islam, but he didn't listen." This challenge to traditional gender roles and responsibilities is especially problematic when the marriage breaks down and their arrangement becomes a matter of community knowledge.

> Umbrime had worked and supported the family in a professional position while her husband struggled with mental illness. While her husband continued to work periodically, there seemed to be little community disapproval. When the marriage broke down, the court assessed their incomes and ordered Umbrime to pay spousal support to her husband. Umbrime told me "This is considered totally un-Islamic." It was also very important to Umbrime that her husband pay her the *mahr*. To do otherwise, she said, would render him "pitiful" in the eyes of his community.
>
> The family put their heads together with an imam to work out how the order could be complied with. The imam came up with a solution: Umbrime's

parents would pay their *zagat* for the year to her ex-husband. This approximately covered the amount Umbrime was obliged to pay to her husband under the court order, after the *mahr* had been deducted. "This saved him from the shame of receiving money from his ex-wife—and was exactly the right decision for me. I could move on with my life."

Every imam I interviewed acknowledged that women frequently work outside the home after they married, but they adopt a variety of practical and jurisprudential approaches to the issue. The most traditional imams minimize the impact of working wives on the family structure and reiterate the classical expectation that "women are not responsible to give but to build—educate, feed, keep healthy—the children." They insist that the only basis on which the classical assumption of male financial responsibility can be overridden is if the wife voluntarily agrees to share her income and/or property with the family: She cannot be forced to do so. This is understood as a voluntary variation of the traditional balance of rights and obligations, which Islamic jurisprudence clearly permits.[58] In contrast, the efforts made by Umbrime's imam suggest that a husband who might need to rely on some financial support from his wife should be protected from shame. This approach seems at odds with the Quranic tradition; the Prophet's wife, Khadija, a businesswoman, at one time supported him financially.

Other imams take the mainstream scholarly view that changing social norms demand continuous adjustments, and that it is in the nature of *shari'a* to evolve a practice that reflects these changes.[59] These imams responded to Umbrime's story—which I described to them—by saying that they felt that it was unnecessary to devise this pretence (the more traditional imams were more sympathetic to the plan). The more progressive group saw Islam as fully compatible with working wives and understood resistance to this as cultural, not religious. "Either one is obliged to support the other. Let him or her spend from what he or she has." As one put it somewhat impatiently, "Why would the support of the wife for her husband be *haram*? In an Islamic marriage, the parties can agree to whatever they like, including for example that the woman should support the man."

The struggle for full acceptance of women as wage-earners and even the primary breadwinners in Muslim families illustrates the complexity of blending the traditional values and principles of Islam, which originated in a very different social and historical family structure, with contemporary family life. Open acknowledgement and discussion about the challenge this reality presents to the traditional model is still limited. One woman commented dryly that Umbrime's story shows that "women are still trying to protect the egos of men." Men whose wives work—and especially those who are unemployed themselves—may feel that they need to exert control over their wives in other ways, such as monitoring their relationships with work colleagues or demanding that they retain control of spending. The persistence of some ingrained beliefs about male authority and financial responsibility, held by both men and women, means that some have more trouble with this adjustment than others. This reinforces the observation that personal and cultural attitudes towards gender roles in marriage are far more significant in shaping contemporary norms than debates over the interpretation of Islamic law.

The Future of the *Nikah*

The continued widespread use of the *nikah* among North American Muslims affords it great potential as a practical vehicle that uses "law and legal awareness as an instrument of social change."[60] Growing numbers of Islamic organizations advocate the use of the *nikah* as a vehicle for the negotiation of marital values and expectations, arguing that its scope and utility for Muslim couples in twenty-first-century North America is unlimited. The experiences of men and women in this study who described mismatched expectations over authority, responsibility and autonomy within marriage illustrate the need for more advance discussions between couples over the form of the *nikah* if they wish to clearly rebut traditional expectations. Organizations promoting the use of the *nikah* urge women to read their boilerplate carefully in order to determine if they wish to propose alternative clauses or amendments to it before they sign on the dotted line. Some imams and Muslim lawyers continue to search for ways to draw up the *nikah* that will maximize the chances that a court will regard it as an enforceable contract in the future.

Many women respondents commented that imams should step up and take a stronger role in advising couples that the *nikah* can be amended. All those (small number of respondents) who included revised or additional clauses—for example, giving them an equal right to divorce or prohibiting polygamy—in their *nikah* regarded this as a wise decision. Others who did not regretted it in hindsight, but simply did not know enough at the time to ask for modifications to the boilerplate contract. And even with knowledge, many others do not ask to see their marriage contract because "at the time of tying the knot, a lot of importance is given to trust—trust our soon-to-be-husband, trust your parents."[61]

The *nikah* cannot anticipate and resolve every issue that will arise when a marriage begins to go wrong. However the widespread passivity that surrounds the use of a boilerplate, unstudied *nikah*, in contrast to a proactive approach that uses the marriage contract to shape and confirm shared understandings of the future, is thrown into sharp relief when couples encounter problems and disagreements about their rights and responsibilities, roles and expectations in a modern marriage.

4 STAYING MARRIED

The commitment to lifelong partnership is a central value for Muslim marriage, as it is for other major religions. Both Catholic and Protestant theologians understand marriage to be a lifelong union.[1] Hindus regard marriage as a lifetime commitment and the strongest social bond that can be made between a man and a woman.[2] Even among those religious groups that permit polygamy, such as the Fundamentalist Church of Jesus Christ of Latter-Day Saints,[3] marriage is still seen as a lifelong commitment that can only be broken in exceptional circumstances.

Aside from theological doctrine, it is natural to hope that the love expressed in a commitment to marriage will last forever. In reality, every married couple experiences problems—disagreements about roles and responsibilities within the marriage, struggles to communicate constructively and perhaps fundamental clashes of values about how to live their life together. Of course, not all conflicts are equal—some are transitory, some protracted, some resolved easily and others intractable, and some—where abuse and violence is involved—are particularly damaging and destructive. The most severe and prolonged conflicts force one or both spouses to re-examine their commitment to one another.

The stories told in this book for the most part describe marriages that did not endure—the study solicited participation from divorced men and women. Many others struggle without resolution in unhappy or dysfunctional relationships, perhaps resigning themselves to staying married or simply managing the conflict. For those who ended their marriages, the process of reflection and evaluation often took a long time, decades even. In a few cases that formed part of the study, a decision was made to stay in the marriage but uncertainty continued.

The stories illustrate the complexity of the decision-making process and the questions respondents asked themselves over and over. How long and how hard should they work at trying to keep their marriage intact, both practically and emotionally? Should they raise a conflict or stay silent, give voice to dissatisfaction or resign themselves to expecting less? How could they work on areas of disagreement or was there no room for negotiation? Who could they turn to for help? At what point had they tried long and hard enough?

This chapter focuses on how Muslim men and women live out their commitment to a lifelong partnership, and how they make decisions about whether or not to stay married. The intention is not to evaluate the wisdom of these decisions, nor to measure them in relation to the problems the spouses describe, but to identify the most important influences on their decision-making process. This chapter also examines the role of the imams and the extended family in reconciliation processes, and how respondents experienced these.

The Story of Baseem and Naja

I interviewed Baseem and Naja several times over the course of three years, during which time their relationship went through some highs and some lows. The escalation of conflict they describe, and the strategies they employed to try to resolve their differences, are in many ways typical of stories I heard from other newlyweds. The only part of their story that is less typical is their eventual recourse to a professional counselor.

When I first interviewed Baseem, he had been married to Naja for less than two years. His short marriage appeared to be as good as over. As he talked to me over tea, Baseem seemed utterly disconsolate.

His parents and his wife's family had arranged the marriage. Baseem really liked Naja's family, and he thought that his fiancée was very pretty and smart. In fact, he admitted that at first he was both thrilled and a little startled to find himself engaged to be married to such a beautiful girl, whom he had considered to be "out of his league."

However, in hindsight, Baseem recognized that he did not think as carefully as he should have about the decision to get married. Instead, he found himself "sleepwalking" into marriage. Once the engagement was announced, events—especially wedding planning—took over. "Once I had started on this road, I just kept walking—I never really made a decision." The couple learned little about each other and spent little time together before their wedding, focusing instead on planning for a big celebration with 700 guests. Naja reflected that during the buildup to the wedding "the material world took over. We got caught up in outer feelings, not inner feelings."

Conflict over how they would negotiate their life together broke out almost immediately after the *nikah*. Baseem and Naja were both bright and ambitious, both in school pursuing professional career goals. Their lives as newlyweds were completely different from that of their parents. It also began to become clear that the two families—albeit from the same cultural community—had very different expectations for the young couple.

Naja's family, whom Baseem had liked so much at first meeting, were turning out to be a lot more traditionally minded than his own. In many ways, and despite her commitment to her education and her career goals, Naja took a quite traditional approach to the marriage. She expected Baseem to take care of her (financially) and she of him (cooking and cleaning). She was very close to her family, and their opinions were very important to her. However, she was living a life very different from that of her mother or grandmother.

Baseem told his wife, "Have your own thoughts. Don't tell me what your mother thinks." This confused and upset Naja, whose reaction was, "But I have only my family to look up to." He wanted her to be a strong, independent woman; "I didn't want to come home to someone who wanted to do my laundry." For her part Naja felt that Baseem did not appreciate her and was not taking care of her as she expected a husband to do. The couple began to fight a lot.

An informal family intervention involving Baseem's mother and Naja's mother was unsuccessful, serving only to heighten the conflict and the differences between the two families. Even the idea of involving their parents (which was Naja's) turned into a conflict. Baseem thought that "this was turning this into a public event [but] . . . it was private." Naja took a more traditional approach and wanted the families involved. After the intervention, the arguments got worse. Naja moved out and spent a month at her parents' home. Baseem eventually came to get her, and they reunited. But their problems were not resolved, and the fights began again. Naja moved out and began to live alone. Now when they talked—which was rarely—they discussed divorce. Each was waiting for the other to take the initiative and file for divorce. But neither made a move. For six months, they were at a stalemate.

Naja turned for help to an imam who was well known locally for his sympathetic work with couples considering divorce. He had been Baseem's teacher years earlier, and they both felt comfortable with him. The imam asked them to come together to talk with him, and he wouldn't take no for an answer. Baseem was reluctant, but later he reflected, "The imam was very persistent. He kept calling me asking if I was coming to the meetings. I would call and cancel, but then he would call the next day and ask,

"When are you going to reschedule?" After a couple of meetings, the imam suggested to the young couple that they seek some professional counseling, and referred them to a trusted person.

We shall return to Baseem and Naja's story at the end of this chapter. Their experience illustrates the dilemmas facing young Muslim couples who find their relationships in crisis within a short time of their *nikah*. Neither was prepared for negotiating differences over how they imagined their life together. Having made a "forever" commitment, what should they do now, and how would they deal with the disappointment of their families and communities?

What Influences Decisions about Whether to Stay Married?

Each individual brings his or her own values—including hopes, expectations, fears, tolerances and goals—to an appraisal of the relationship. For Muslims, these values may be drawn from their understanding of religious laws as well as cultural expectations. However, deciding whether or not to stay married seems to be no clearer for Muslims than for anyone else.

The process of internal dialogue and external negotiation over staying married is difficult, unpredictable and complex. This study found no evidence of marriage being treated as an easily disposable commodity, shed at the first signs of "trouble." None of the divorced women and men in this study reached their decision easily, quickly or lightly. They describe confusion, disappointment, anger, hurt and fear for the future. They wanted to make every possible effort to enable the marriage to continue: "I needed to feel that I had tried everything I could to save my marriage, [therefore] that I had done nothing wrong." This appreciation is missing from some community dialogues over divorce, in which there is often an assumption (especially among the older generation, for whom divorce was rare) that young couples who divorce simply "don't try hard enough." Theories advanced for the decline in sustained commitment to marriage include a lack of strong role models, especially for young men; a culture of "wanting it all"; the overbearing influence of in-laws;[4] changing gender roles within the family; and a failure to grasp the mutual responsibilities of husband and wife in Islamic traditions. Whatever the cause of marriage breakdown, a decision to end a marriage is always accompanied by months and sometimes years of personal angst and introspection.

It is possible to identify a number of critical variables in the decision-making process from the experiences of the respondents. The first is the nature and extent of marital conflict. Conflicts that turn violent and abusive present very different

issues than those that relate to incompatible lifestyles or divergent religious practices, although any one of these may be a decisive factor in ending a marriage.
Detailed discussion of the causes of marital conflict, including domestic violence
and abuse, follows in the next chapter. A second critical variable for all respondents,
no matter what their level of religiosity, is their understanding of and orientation
towards the relevant religious laws. A third factor is the attitudes of their family
and immediate community, in particular their tolerance of divorce. Each of these
variables interacts with a fourth, the values and personality of the individual. The
respondents share many common values as Muslims—leading one to lament "I
cannot go to my Canadian friends to solve these problems . . . because they have
different values"—but they are also diverse individuals. Stereotypes of Muslims,
particularly Muslim women, often underestimate the diversity and the complexity
of the decision-making processes for each individual.

Each of these four variables (the nature of the conflict, religious laws, cultural
attitudes and individual decision making) operates at varying levels of consciousness. Sometimes respondents do not explicitly reference religious principles, yet
certain assumptions (such as the tolerance of Islam towards divorce) surface in
response to interview questions. Similarly, cultural values and attitudes are sometimes assumed and unspoken, and sometimes explicitly identified. Most individuals need to explain how they reached a decision about their marriage, including
how they assessed the situation, how they rationalized their options and how (if
at all) they reached emotional closure. Sometimes, one of these variables is crucial. For many more, it is the interaction among them that explains their decision-
making process.

Religious Law Regarding Divorce

Every respondent talked about how they understood the obligations of Islamic
law in relation to staying married and seeking divorce. Even those who did not
contemplate obtaining a religious divorce still talked about what their faith
taught about the ending of a marriage. The application of religious law to their
dilemma was on the minds of every respondent, including those who were critical
of how they saw it being applied, particularly to women. Many of these respondents pointed to a cultural overlay that often construes the law narrowly, blaming
women for a "failure" in marriage, and sometimes pressures them to stay married.
"I kept going [in an unhappy marriage] for years and years because that was how
I grew up—you are told, marriage is for life, whether good or bad, and you just
put up with it."

Some of these respondents asserted that a more tolerant approach is more
authentic to Islamic principles. One woman who faced enormous family resistance

when she was contemplating leaving her abusive husband put it simply: "If you look just at Islam, Islam would never have wanted me to suffer in this way. Islam is a beautiful religion—but the culture can turn it ugly and distort it." Those women who were clear that they had the right to end their marriage often cited the story of Jamilah. "My mother would not accept that my marriage needed to end. I told her the story of Jamilah and I told her, the religion is more important than the culture here."

Among those who are critical of a narrow interpretation of women's rights to divorce under religious law there is still a pervasive need to satisfy their own conscience, to feel confident that they had "done the right thing" as a Muslim. "When you believe in Islam—whether it is as a devout or a moderate believer—there is always a voice that asks you, 'Are you doing it right?'" Among those who were more traditionally religious the principal concern was whether they had a "good enough" reason to divorce. One woman considering whether or not to stay married told me, "I felt like I was doing something wrong. It [ending the marriage] did not fit into reasons that felt OK to me." Her husband felt the same way: "Religiously, I don't believe that we have a valid excuse to be divorced. I have not yelled at her or abused her." Some referenced their commitment to one another back to their *nikah*, which many understand as a sacred covenant binding a couple and their families together in the eyes of God. A promise to marry and remain married for life is made not only to one's spouse, but also to God. "It's not simply a matter of saying, 'it doesn't work,' because marriage is a promise for life." For these Muslims, contemplating the end of their marriage is seen as both a personal and a religious failure.

For some of the most religious individuals, the way they told their stories reflected an assumption that meeting their religious obligations requires personal suffering and sacrifice. Islam, in common with other religions, places a high value on acts of self-sacrifice and suggests that such sacrifice—etymologically, "to make sacred"—will be rewarded in an afterlife. Referring to the Old Testament story of Abraham who was asked by God to sacrifice his son, the Qur'an states, "We reward those who do right."[5] Embracing personal suffering—and avoiding, at least for now, the uncertainty and distress that will certainly follow a decision to end the marriage—may also reflect a desire to establish certainty in an uncertain world. For the most religious respondents, continuing to live with a spouse whom they no longer loved, or even enduring abuse, was also an important part of establishing the "serious reasons" they believed they needed to bring themselves within the law. Examples include a marriage of thirty years during which the husband had had continuous affairs; a marriage that lasted for ten years but which had been desperately unhappy from the first week; and a marriage of over twenty years that had been characterized by constant physical and verbal abuse (I talked with this woman for almost an hour before she acknowledged to me that she had been divorced four years earlier. Her shame was such that she still needed to hide her status as a divorced woman).

Whether the approach is conformist or critical, understanding of the religious law plays some part in decision making over remaining married for all North American Muslims. Another factor described by every respondent as significant in reaching their decision is the cultural norms of their family and community.

Cultural and Family Attitudes towards Divorce

Deciding whether or not to stay married becomes even more complex when family and community values are added to the mix. Dread of what others will think surrounds a decision to divorce. "When you divorce you not only divorce your spouse but also your friends and family." One imam told me that facing the judgment of one's family and community "is very scary. They have to decide if they have the emotional strength to go through the process, and this includes the possible rejection of their family." And while the responsibility of the imam is to share his interpretation of Islam rather than promote particular cultural practices, the normative expectations of the community often play a significant role in shaping the advice that he dispenses. In many cases, community members are "more familiar with their culture of divorce and marriage than with their Islamic rights and responsibilities."

The ending of a marriage is always a painful and distressing event, regardless of whether faith-based beliefs are involved. In an earlier study I conducted on divorce, a divorced man who did not follow any particular faith summed it up this way: "It [the divorce] was hell. It hurt me; it hurt my kids; it hurt my ex-wife; it hurt my parents, her parents."[6] While studies show that tolerance of divorce is increasing as divorce rates rise,[7] divorced people still often take on a sense of shame and failure, probably reflecting a universal disappointment with marriages that fail.[8] Some cultural and faith groups have historically strongly discouraged divorce and continue to frown on those who seek to end their marriages. In some Muslim cultural communities there is profound and deep-rooted resistance towards the ending of marriage—including the stigmatizing and social exclusion of divorced people, especially women. The stories of respondents in this study suggest that intolerance of divorce (and in particular of divorcées) is the most extreme in some South Asian communities. There is some evidence, although it is less consistent, of intolerant attitudes towards women who seek separation or divorce in some parts of the Arab community. The stigma attached to ending a marriage appears to be least negative—and the community most supportive—for women whose families come from African Muslim countries such as Somalia and Ethiopia, where a decision to end a marriage appears to be socially acceptable and does not attract widespread approbation or assume failure.

The differential impact of intolerance for divorce on women is striking, and acknowledged by women and men alike. The asymmetrical structure of Islamic divorce creates additional pressures: "When a woman is asking for *khula*, she is literally asking for permission, so their reasons are up for debate, and this becomes the business of the whole community." Women are widely regarded as responsible for keeping the family together, which means that "in any culture a divorced woman will not be looked upon favorably." The experiences described by Muslim women are familiar to women of other faiths and of none. Patriarchal values habitually assume that the woman in a broken marriage is "at fault" or culpable—whatever the circumstances, and including cases of abuse and violence, or where the divorce is initiated by the husband—and as a result women often pay a disproportionate price for a decision to end their marriage.

Respondents who faced the greatest intolerance frequently expressed frustration with the contradiction between the literal permissiveness of Islamic teaching on divorce, and the rigid, even authoritarian, approach of their communities towards keeping marriages intact. These communities police their own members using social sanctions. One woman described how her own research on Islamic law pointed her in one direction, but her family and community in another. "Divorce is seen as a failure. . . . I was looking at the problem and how to be divorced from a religious perspective, but culturally I met with a lot of resistance." Despite this recognition, it is inescapable that community attitudes are a potent factor in decision making. One's image in one's community is crucial to a sense of belonging, social status, social life and feelings of personal empowerment and safety. When individuals are new to North America, perhaps face language barriers and do not work outside the home there may be particular problems of social isolation and dependence on the marriage partner, who may sometimes also be their sponsor. For those who have grown up in North America there may be a fear of alienating one's family and cultural community. Increasingly experiencing hostility from the dominant culture, North American Muslims often find themselves members of highly cohesive—and sometimes rigid and defended—cultural and social groups. Instead of membership being positive and affirmative, it is often associated with a sense of alienation and defensiveness. "[Muslim communities in North America] do not have healthy social spaces in which to discuss and self-define—this makes them proud and rigid." This process of retrenching in the face of hostility affects even the most apparently socially integrated members of the community, who may feel that they need to show their loyalty to community norms by observing traditional marriage and divorce practices.

This environment, especially for individuals born and raised in North America but tied to an original community through their parents, produces conflicting feelings: on the one hand, intense loyalty to the community; on the other, a feeling of being constantly judged by it. Compliance with community norms becomes especially important, and upsetting widely held views—for example, by disclosing unhappiness or abuse in a marriage, or seeking divorce—comes at a price. Several respondents described the shock and even the anger of the community when their marital problems became known. In addition to coping with their own sadness and uncertainty in considering separation from their spouse, they must manage the cognitive dissonance of acting in a way that is contrary to values they have absorbed as a lifelong community member.

Anticipating the tenacity and impact of cultural norms and the negativity with which some communities regard any marital problem, let alone a decision to separate, women in particular frequently expressed a sense of hopelessness and even despair about contemplating the end of their marriage. They were constrained not only by a desire to do everything possible to save their marriage— reflecting a sense of individual responsibility—but also by the social stigma they would face. "It is the fear of what awaits you if you get divorced that actually keeps you in the relationship."

Community is often synonymous with family—but not always. Some respondents described their families taking their side against a hostile community, which made it much easier for them to ride out disapproval. For obvious reasons, families are often more sympathetic than the wider community. In other cases, the initial reactions of family members seemed to be shaped by the conservative norms of the surrounding community. One woman described going to her parents over and over to complain about her abusive husband.

> "I kept asking my father for a divorce. My mother kept sending me back. I felt like a prisoner, a slave, unloved, verbally abused and sometimes physically also. . . . My mother and sister told me that if I left my husband they would make sure that I was penniless. They did this because divorce is taboo and because in their minds I could not possibly leave a man who is a doctor, with social prestige and status."

Many young Muslims described to me the pain and sorrow they felt they had caused their parents when they ended their marriage. Bringing shame and embarrassment to their parents further compounded their own misery. The parents of some younger divorced women and men have watched their children grow up in a culture far more tolerant and accustomed to divorce than in their country of origin. Sometimes immigrant communities hold fast to values that are changing or have already changed in their countries of origin; many Muslim countries are now experiencing rising rates of divorce, but the migrant population may assume that the status quo remains the same as when they left.

Some respondents experienced initial pushback from their families when they announced that they wanted a divorce, but as they came to understand more about the nature of the conflict this usually turned to sympathy and support. Some women described how the experience of their marriage had fundamentally changed their family's attitudes and expectations regarding marriage, in some cases the way they approached the question of marriage for other siblings.

Rabia and her husband were married in her parents' native India. The families arranged the marriage. "Everything was decided for us, and we had a boilerplate *nikah*."

The couple set up home in North America, where Rabia had been born and raised. However, the couple quickly began to have marital problems. Rabia went to her parents to tell them that the marriage wasn't working, and that she wanted a divorce. Her parents were shocked, and initially unsympathetic. They were concerned about how the community would regard their family if she was divorced. They kept asking Rabia to try again. They insisted that the families meet in mediation to try to bring about a reconciliation. It was only when Rabia's husband came forward and agreed that the marriage wasn't working that her parents accepted there would be a divorce.

Rabia says that this experience has changed her parents' assumptions about marriage. She has now remarried. Her parents played a much smaller role in arranging her second marriage. They have also pulled back from arranging the marriages of her younger sisters. Further, "They dissuade their friends from doing the same for their daughters. They have learned from my experience that things are done differently here."

Individual Decision Making

Responses to conflict vary widely among members of any single social, cultural or religious group. Muslim men and women are diverse individuals, and their values, personalities, orientation to conflict and other preferences and tendencies play an important part in their decision making. For example, many respondents were forced to assess how much social disapproval they could tolerate if they went ahead with a decision to divorce. Some found a new circle of friends or switched to a different mosque; some stayed in their original community and stopped going to the mosque at all, enduring isolation and hoping for change; others moved their family to an entirely new location. The response of an individual to external hostility is a marker of their innate conflict style, as well as their personal resources. Typologies of personal conflict style have been developed by conflict theorists who suggest that each individual has a preferred response to conflict, at least in circumstances in which some variables are held constant—for example, conflicts at work, with family and friends, in unfamiliar settings and so on. One classic typology proposes five basic conflict orientations—avoidance, accommodation, negotiated compromise, interests-based negotiation and competition.[9]

These five approaches to conflict in general are reflected in a range of individual responses to marital conflict. Those who prefer avoidance—a common strategy for many of us—will often decide to continue to live with the conflict and not "make waves." One common avoidance strategy within a relationship is for these individuals to develop an independent life for themselves and minimize interaction with their spouse (sometimes described as an "isolation" strategy).[10] When this approach is taken, the marriage may endure for a long time but end once certain obligations are discharged, for example, when children leave home. A number of the older female respondents fit this pattern. Alternately, if accommodation is a preferred strategy the spouse will accept a particular behavior or the demands being made on them—perhaps because they continue to feel a strong bond of love to their spouse—rather than consciously avoid them. Those individuals who prefer accommodation are unlikely to develop a clear independent life and are less likely to seek divorce. In contrast, someone who adopts a strategy of negotiated compromise might ultimately agree to a pragmatic solution that "splits the difference"—for example, a wife under economic pressure to work might ask for more help with household tasks and childcare from her husband in return, or one spouse may propose to the other that they take turns in working and going to school. Interests-based negotiation requires a deeper analysis of the issues that are causing conflict and a sustained effort to understand the other's point of view, in order to develop a mutually acceptable balance between the interests of each. Both types of negotiation strategy suggest an engagement (in contrast to avoidance) between the couple in relation to their conflict; the difference is in how they conceptualize an outcome or solution. Finally, adopting a competitive approach implies confrontation and contesting. Those individuals who embrace this approach—or who eventually resort to it perhaps after trying out the other strategies—will often focus on a single dominant issue and demand a certain desired outcome, believing that their interests can only be met in this solution—perhaps that their spouse stops abusing alcohol or drugs, seeks help for anger management, or that domestic abuse ends. They may give their spouse an "ultimatum," and if they cannot meet it, the marriage may end.

Recourse to all five approaches is distributed among the respondents, with many using more than one strategy over the course of a long marriage. The type (and seriousness) of the conflict may affect choice of strategy (for example, smaller issues may be avoided, but serious and repeated conflicts are more likely to lead to negotiation or confrontation). Individual response may be habitual and engrained, or it may change over the course of the relationship, as past experience affects future choices. Personal conflict orientation is also critically affected by access to resources, which includes personal financial resources, levels of family support and responsibility for children and their particular needs (often determined by age, capacities and so on). Women (and men) considering ending their marriage often face economic constraints. Women are significantly more likely to have a reduced standard of living following divorce than men.[11] They may also face other obstacles—for example, who will take care of the children if a working mother decides to leave her husband? If she does not receive alimony, can she manage financially? Will her family help her? Men confront some of the same questions, and others as well. How do they adjust their relationships with young children if they leave them in the custody of the wife at the end of a marriage? Can they continue to play a role in raising these children? Or can they share custody (not part of Islamic tradition)? Can they afford to maintain two homes?

Faced with such questions, each individual must assess his or her personal commitment to staying married, or ending the relationship. He or she will ultimately reach the decision that is best for them personally, whether or not it makes sense to others. This is a high-stakes deliberation. And in the end, no matter how much advice the couple seeks, it is a deeply personal decision.

> "On the day of judgment I am responsible for myself and my own decisions. . . . I have to live Islam for myself—not what someone else told me to do."

Reconciliation

There is a strong tradition in Islam of reconciliation and peace-making that dovetails with a desire to avoid ending a marriage wherever possible. The Qur'an exhorts warring couples to try to reconcile and find peace, partly in the name of Islam's commitment to dialogue and peace building and specifically to enable their marriage partnership to continue wherever possible. Abu-Nimer writes, "Islam obligates its believers to seek peace in all of life's domains."[12] The Prophet exhorts wives who fear ill treatment by their husbands to "make peace between themselves. Peace is better."[13] Generally, the Qur'an and the *Sunnah* emphasize forgiveness, mercy, tolerance and patience in numerous verses, many suggesting future divine rewards for personal sacrifice in living out these virtues.[14] Conflicting spouses are encouraged to meet with family arbitrators—one chosen by each family—to try to avoid a breach.[15] Even if the couple does decide to divorce, the Qur'an stipulates that "it shall not be wrong for the two to set things peacefully to rights between themselves; for peace is best and selfishness is ever-present in human souls."[16]

Reconciliation between spouses is usually facilitated by family members, religious leaders and, occasionally, professional marriage counselors. All imams regard efforts at reconciliation in order to preserve the marriage to be their first responsibility when dealing with marital conflict. As one writer puts it, "Islam does legally allow divorce, but makes it morally and socially difficult."[17]

The Social Welfare Role of the Imam in North America

Imams are a critical reference point not only for religious matters but also for social, family and even economic issues for many Muslims. Families—not necessarily regular attendees at prayers—often turn to the mosque when they face a crisis. This highlights the differences between the role played by imams in North America, and their contemporary and historical role in Muslim countries which is largely confined to leading prayers. In North America, imams play an expanded social welfare role, which gives them greater power and influence. Many Muslims come to North America without their extended families, to whom they might ordinarily turn for this type of assistance and guidance. In turning instead to their religious leaders for help with family problems, Muslims are acting no differently than members of other religious groups, whose clergy have historically provided first-line counseling and welfare services for community members.[18]

Muslims' needs often go unmet by public services, which many Muslims regard as untrustworthy and suspect harbor discriminatory attitudes towards them or, at best, remain ignorant of the important values that motivate Muslims. In some cases, there is a real fear of making oneself vulnerable to an organization or individual outside one's own community. This problem has become much more intense since 9/11. One psychotherapist described to me how, after 9/11, social welfare agencies began to focus on Muslim families in New York schools. She described how this resulted in inappropriate interventions justified by inaccurate and stereotypical assumptions associating Muslim men with violent behaviors, and in some cases led to families leaving New York and returning to their countries of origin. In the face of this degree of religious and ethnic profiling, it is not surprising that Muslims are turning away from public services and towards the mosque. "The Imam in the West is expected to be a one-stop shop, a marriage counselor, prayer leader . . . "

Anyone who has spent time in a North American mosque knows that the imam's office is a focal point for conflict within families, between spouses and occasionally among unrelated community members. Although not for everyone, in the absence of other alternatives and despite the mosque's limited resources, many of those struggling with family and other conflicts and problems will turn to their imams for help. I have seen the pressure that some imams—and sometimes other mosque personnel—face on a daily basis from families and individuals seeking their assistance with everything including conflicts with teenagers, arguments between families and neighbors, disputes with landlords over rent, problems with obtaining welfare benefits, and marital issues. Often the room outside the imam's office is filled with people waiting to see him. On several occasions I was inside the imam's office conducting an interview when distraught individuals burst in and interrupted. On other occasions, the imam has taken an extended telephone call from a desperate person during an interview; at the end of the interview he will leave to pay a home visit or see this individual in his office. The scene is often chaotic, with more people looking for support and advice than there are available resources to handle them. As a practical matter, some imams have introduced screening procedures whereby a social worker or counselor will see an individual first.

Not all imams are willing to embrace an expanded social welfare role. Some remain at arms' length from their community. This distance is in some cases exacerbated by linguistic barriers; a few imams speak only Arabic, whereas many members of their community do not. A few reject the idea of working so closely with their members on everyday issues, preferring to see themselves as religious contemplatives and scholars. In contrast, a growing number of modern-day North American imams, especially younger ones, regard their assistance with family and social welfare issues to be a central part of their responsibility. The limited role that some imams accept as community counselors means that there is greater pressure on those who do step up to this task (including other mosque officials).

Many imams have little training to equip them for a social welfare role and fewer resources to assist them. Most imams do not have access to training designed specifically for them (which is just starting to emerge in a few major cities), nor the resources necessary to undertake it. Just one of the more than forty imams I interviewed had completed any formal training in counseling, although many expressed a strong interest in such training if it were available to them. Many imams talked about the importance of their developing some cultural knowledge of contemporary life in North America, without which they are far less effective and relevant to those who seek their help. As relative newcomers—most imams come to North America in their thirties or forties at the invitation of mosque trustees, having grown up and studied in an Islamic country—imams often find it difficult to connect individuals with other community agencies, assist them with navigating state services and benefits, or to relate to community politics and local issues important to their members.[19]

The Role of the Imam in Marriage Counseling and Reconciliation

It is commonplace for the imam in a North American mosque to be approached by one or both spouses, or their families, for advice about marital conflict and sometimes for direct intervention. Reconciliation is the motif of every imam with whom I spoke about marital conflict. Their focus is on preserving the marriage and keeping the couple together. All the imams I interviewed emphasized their role in reconciliation over any part they might play in dissolving marriages. Many were initially reluctant to acknowledge any role beyond counseling and the facilitation of reconciliation. It proved impossible to obtain any concrete numbers on divorces, and I stopped asking—the question seemed an affront. In some cases, moving on from the general topic of reconciliation to what happened in the case of a particular couple unable to reconcile was an awkward transition, punctuated by long silences, and requiring me to coax the conversation along gently.

One imam told me that he was so demoralized by the rising number of couples and individuals who came to him seeking divorce that he wanted to put a sign on his door that read, "No divorces, only marriages." Despite or perhaps because of their sadness over the rising number of broken marriages they see, many imams work very hard at facilitating reconciliation between couples. Some work very long hours, often meeting with families in their homes and scheduling meetings in the evenings to accommodate work schedules and childcare needs. For some, this work is highly motivating. One imam told me, "There are pleasing principles inside the Islamic tradition—it feels good to do something right. . . . Continuing the traditions gives energy to the family system. It's like a Duracell battery—it pushes me forward."

I asked every imam I interviewed why they thought individuals came to them for help with their marital problems, rather than going to lawyers, police, counselors or other service providers. They all told me that they hoped that their intervention would encourage some further and deeper spiritual reflection, although it was equally clear (and recognized by many imams) that by no means all respondents were really interested in this; many had already made their minds up that they wanted divorce and (as a woman) were entitled to ask for it. Many imams saw themselves as an alternative resource in the absence of their extended family, whom they may have left behind in their country of origin. A number of imams described the importance attached to "doing the right thing" by seeking religious guidance, even when the individual might not be traditionally observant. "They are afraid that they might make a mistake, Islamically. They wish to function Islamically and correctly in their family sphere." Many imams also point out that, unlike a lawyer or a counselor, their services are free. The importance of this for some families should not be underestimated. Aside from the obvious attraction of a free service, some hold suspicions that people who charge for their services cannot be genuinely committed to helping; this feeling is reflected in comments made about lawyers and counselors. Some imams suggest that another reason that people come to them is because they can offer a higher level of confidentiality: "People trust the imams with their secrets." Not all respondents shared this view.

Many imams contrast their commitment to reconciliation and healing with the value of public agencies, lawyers and the police, which are widely regarded as escalating conflict by promoting individual rights at the expense of the family. A constant theme was that Islam is more committed to reconciliation and forgiveness than Western institutions, which are perceived as encouraging demands for entitlements rather than a focus on obligations and duties. The strength of collectivism in Islamic cultures suggests that a purely individual focus might be "selfish" because it does not take into account the interests of the whole community. Taken to an extreme, this may be suggested as a reason not to use the American or Canadian legal system, pejoratively associated by some imams with Western secularism.

Less conservative and more widespread is the view that Muslims prefer a dispute resolution forum that understands and respects the fundamental values of Islam and avoids the damaging adversarial approach of some public agencies and courts. Some imams use this contrast to describe the unique role that they can play in family conflict:

> "I am able to extinguish a fire that is very dangerous. Imams are in a better position to contain a marital dispute than lawyers—who make their money out of conflict and divorce."

A minority of imams are only prepared to work on reconciliation, telling me that they do not "offer" divorces. This may mean that they would only do so under exceptional circumstances, or perhaps that they were uncomfortable disclosing that they ever sanctioned divorce. This seems to be at odds with the example of the Prophet, who approved divorce for women in a variety of circumstances. As one possible explanation, a number of respondents referred me to a *hadith* which says that the number of divorces allowed by a religious leader will be recorded and counted on the Last Day, when they must each be accounted for. In a similar vein, one community worker working with an imam to screen victims of domestic violence explained the "mindset" of the imam this way:

"The imam thinks that if they break the family apart, there will be the judgment of God [on them]. They will not break the family apart as easily as we think they should. . . . [describing how she takes photographs of victims at the hospital showing their injuries] The reason I do this is because of the culture of the imam. He wants to be absolved from the responsibility of breaking the marriage."

Some imams may take distance because they feel underqualified and ill prepared—"out of their depth"—to work with such contentious and emotional issues. Many social and community workers pointed out to me that some imams feel unfamiliar and uncomfortable with some of the typical problems that beset Muslim families living in the West—for example, parent/teen conflicts over independence, drug or alcohol use, or gang membership—problems which may not be well understood by an imam who most likely grew up in a Muslim country and came to North America later in life.

Domestic Violence and Reconciliation

An important barometer of the responsiveness of the imams to individual situations—when and how reconciliation might be appropriate, or even feasible—is the way they handle cases involving allegations of domestic violence. The strong emphasis on reconciliation means that some imams encourage spouses to stay together even where there is domestic abuse. In some instances, these imams are making a genuine expression of commitment to salvaging the relationship and accept that they would refer to other authorities if their efforts were unsuccessful—in other words, they want to give the marriage "one last chance." This approach may be welcomed or even invited by the couple themselves, if they believe that the behavior can be altered and the marriage saved. Several imams told me that they would consider reconciliation in domestic violence cases if the offending party (in each case this was the husband) took responsibility for what he had done; others spoke about referring batterers to anger management classes or men's groups. However, without proper training in recognizing the manifestations of family violence or its consequences, the best of intentions may sometimes lead to alarmingly naive tactics on the part of the imams. One imam told me that when he hears from a woman alleging domestic violence,

"I assess the threat. I talk to the husband. Often I go to the house and meet with them. I get them to promise me about future behavior. I cannot involve the police because I am not a party. There is a cultural stigma to involving the police. . . . The cases are not really that severe in terms of calling the police. The Muslim men who are abusive are not crazy or drunk—it is just something that happens momentarily, they are discussing something with their wife, and he gets angry and slaps her. It is not that he is going to kill her. Most of the time it is not physical abuse, it is just threats. But it is wrong to threaten them."

This statement suggests a lack of understanding of the role of the community in reporting alleged criminal behavior. It also minimizes the extent and the impact of various types of abuse. While the final sentence—which seems to be an after-thought—recognizes that threatening behavior is wrong, the remainder of the statement does not take this form of abuse seriously. The minimization of abuse, a rejection of recourse to outside authorities with enforcement powers, combined with this imam's insistence that reconciliation is always the preferred course, raise serious safety concerns. Another imam told me about a woman whom he advised to reconcile with her husband despite the fact that he had raped her, because she had seven children with him. It is inevitable that these attitudes discourage some women from seeking any kind of assistance from an imam in cases involving abuse or violence. Many social workers and related professionals in the Muslim community described experiences to me that either they, or their clients, had had with particular imams who have continued to press for reconciliation and discourage the woman from accessing other support agencies and resources, even in the face of substantial evidence of sustained domestic violence. Similarly, Samia Bano, in her review of cases heard by the U.K. Shari'a Council, found that some women who asked the council for divorce were asked to attend a reconciliation meeting with their husbands even though a restraining order was in effect.[20]

In contrast, other imams told me that "in domestic violence cases, there is no room for reconciliation." Instead, their protocol is to refer the woman to the police or to a shelter. Some imams are speaking out about domestic violence at Friday prayers, attending educational programs offered by local agencies, cooperating with Muslim social service agencies to raise awareness of domestic violence issues, and in some cases work alongside social workers in screening cases for signs of abuse or violence. The full spectrum of attitudes among imams towards women experiencing abuse is discussed in greater detail in chapter five.

Working with Women

Among those imams who offer marital counseling, some feel considerably more comfortable counseling men than women; a few refuse to see women in the absence of their husbands. This raises a host of practical difficulties, because in the majority of cases it is the wife who initiates a request for assistance. In some cases, the husband refuses to go to the imam with his wife because he does not feel that there is a problem. In other cases, for example when the conflict is over alcohol or drug use, domestic violence, and/or infidelity, the wife may feel that she needs to speak to the imam about these matters without her husband present. On the other hand, if the husband wishes to end the marriage and is unwilling to participate in counseling, the structure of Islamic law allows him to divorce her unilaterally, or he could take another wife. In some cases, the husband had already left his wife and children and moved on to another family; he was not interested in meeting with the imam. In contrast, if the wife wishes to divorce her husband, she must first obtain permission either from him or from another authoritative source—in North America this is usually an imam. Alternately, if the man does go to the imam, his word may be set above that of his wife. "He will dominate the process—he will get his story in first. This way the males get all the money and the property."

The disinclination—or discomfort—of some imams towards working with women is manifest in a number of ways. Some women respondents told me that they felt that the imam did not treat them with respect, appeared disinterested or cut them off when they tried to present their case. Others described being kept waiting for long periods of time despite having made an appointment and seeing men being given priority over them. Others were unable to make an appointment, and instead were turned away over and over again.

It is difficult to assess how far misogynist and chauvinistic attitudes explain the discomfort of some imams towards counseling women. Such attitudes towards women clearly exist among some Muslim clergy, in common with some clergy of other faiths. Most major religions reflect such biases both historically—for example, in the persecution of "witches" by Christian churches in the fifteenth and sixteenth centuries[21]—and in more permanent ideologies—for example, the virtual exclusion of women from positions of authority in most major religions, including but not limited to Islam. Explicitly chauvinistic and even misogynist attitudes rarely came through during my interviews with imams, although one might imagine that some self-censorship was taking place since they were being interviewed, usually in person, by a female. Among the exceptions was one imam who unabashedly explained to me that the Qur'an makes it clear that "man is above woman" and went on to explain that women are more emotionally fragile than men because they are affected by hormonal changes during menstruation; as a result, they must depend on men to maintain and protect them, and they cannot share the unilateral right of their husband to end the marriage.

Both women and imams offer a variety of explanations for the reluctance to offer sympathetic counsel and support to women experiencing marital conflict. Of course, those imams who will not give divorces will not entertain the idea of meeting with a woman whom they know in advance wants to talk about obtaining a divorce from her husband. Imams who take this highly restrictive approach towards divorce are generally known by reputation among women in their community, and women rarely approach them unless they are desperate and have no other recourse. Among imams who will consider giving divorces there is sometimes a concern that spending time alone with a woman in confidential counseling will contravene a social and, for some, religious norm (there is a *hadith* that says that when an unmarried man and a woman are alone together, Satan is in the room). However, the most significant factor in avoiding working with women appears to be a fear of male backlash if the imam is seen to be taking the side of a wife against the wishes of her husband. I have heard a number of stories of imams being threatened—sometimes physically, for example, "stay away from my wife"—by husbands after counseling their wives, in particular when the wife is seeking permission to divorce. They may also risk anger from other male community members, some of whom may hold positions within the mosque—for example, as a member of the board of trustees, usually dominated by men—and have influence over both the security of their employment position and their authority in the community. As a result, some imams, in the words of a marriage counselor working with Muslim women, "are dropping the ball here. They are reluctant because there is no Islamic court [to give them legitimacy]." But she continued, "I used to feel angry with the imams, but now I feel compassionate. How much personal risk do they want to take?"

Male anger against imams whom they see as interfering with their authority is illustrated by the quasi-permanent demonstration on the sidewalk opposite the head offices of the U.K. Shari'a Council in West London, which since 1985 has offered Muslim women the opportunity to petition for divorce to a panel of imams and senior scholars. Indignant Muslim men hold up handwritten signs expressing their discontent at their wives being permitted to divorce them. When I asked about the demonstration, the registrar of the council responded with a chuckle, "It needs to be uncomfortable for the men." Not all imams are this principled.

Rehana went to her imam—on the urging of her grown children—to ask for his help after enduring almost forty years of infidelity on the part of her husband. Rehana had repeatedly asked him to give up his affairs, but he would not. His womanizing was widely known in her community.

The imam told Rehana that he couldn't get involved. Her husband, a successful businessman, was a significant figure in the community, and he had given a lot of money over the years to the mosque. He had also received a prominent community recognition award, and the imam did not want to upset him.

When her imam would not help her, Rehana went to a lawyer and eventually divorced her husband. Once she was divorced, her imam came to her house and congratulated her. Rehana reflected, "He was thinking about the mosque and not the people of the mosque—but how can you get people to come to the mosque unless you think about the people?"

Many Muslim professionals working with families and couples are vocal in their criticism of imams who do not work sympathetically with women. "Imams hide under the mask that it is not right to destroy the family—but really the man is already destroying the family—and the imam does not want to deal with it and make the women continue to live in these situations." This attitude is frequently attributed to cultural influences; a social worker in an Arab neighborhood commented that "imams come from countries where women have to endure violence at home—they just have to put up with it. This is a part of Arab culture." Some imams join in the criticism of those who are not open to listening to the troubles of both men and women. One pointed out that when imams do not offer a sympathetic ear, they effectively "drive" people into relying on the legal system, thereby weakening the sense of community among Muslims.

Process and Practice

There are many differences in the ways imams attempt to realize their goal of reconciliation, and in the time and energy they devote to this work. Their efforts reflect a wide variety of beliefs and practices—both about their role and the potential effectiveness of any intervention. Most imams learn on the job. Lacking formal training, some give more time and thought to developing their own processes and principles for practice than others. Several imams mentioned listening and ensuring a balance of airtime between a man and woman who meet together as important skills in facilitating a dialogue between disputants. Many referred to the importance of maintaining impartiality and learning how to hear both sides fully: "I learned that we cannot hurry the process." Sometimes, couples settled matters for themselves, if given enough time.

Some imams were eager to describe the sorts of questions they ask couples, including "Did you have any good days with each other? What were these like?" and "Do you really imagine that one of you is 100 percent to blame?" Another told me that he asks both parties to make a list of three items they would like to change about the other. They then review both lists to see if there is any common ground. Another described his approach as follows:

"My first course is . . . to touch every part of their conscience. In most cases it is miscommunication, or a difference in their expectations."

Procedurally, most imams will ask both spouses to participate in a discussion aimed at resolving the conflict and facilitating their reconciliation. "God desires peace and we try to effect peace." The extent of the effort made by the imam to bring the recalcitrant party—usually the husband—into counseling varies widely. Some imams put considerable energy into this task, for example calling the husband's family or sending a registered letter to his last known address. Some adopt a standard procedure, allowing a certain period of time—anything from three months to one year—for a response, or sending a letter out three times before concluding that there will be no response. If the husband remains unresponsive to the imam, the imam may proceed to take explicit "next steps" towards releasing the wife from her *nikah*. In some cases, the imam seems to be affronted at the husband's unresponsiveness to him and at this point will become far more sympathetic towards the wife.

Other imams are less proactive, doing little or nothing to place pressure on the husband to attend counseling with his wife. Some women who were unable to persuade their husbands to attend a meeting with the imam—or when the husband was unresponsive to the imam's solicitation—were then told that there was nothing further that the imam could do for them. Others describe being told to go home and speak to their husbands about coming with them to counseling, advice they considered impractical (dangerous even) without some clear sign of support from the imam and perhaps some pressure from the imam to encourage her husband to attend. One woman told the imam that her husband was physically abusing her, and the imam told her she must tell her husband to come and talk to him. The imam made no effort to contact her husband himself. This woman told me, "Of course, I was too afraid to tell my husband that I had spoken to the imam about our marriage."

Imams take many different approaches to involving the extended family in reconciliation discussions. Sometimes the families are already involved; some respondents described family meetings as a natural first step before they contacted the mosque. Family meetings may involve the spouses and their families, or sometimes just the male relatives on both sides in the absence of the spouses. Because many Muslims believe that the support of the extended family is critical to the success of the marriage they are often closely involved in any reconciliation efforts. Some imams routinely involve the extended family—and in particular the father or other male relatives of the wife—in any dialogue about reconciliation. One imam described his role in dealing with marital conflict as managing "two tribes," not just the husband and wife. In some cases, one or the other family wants a divorce but not the couple themselves. In others, one or both families are working desperately to keep the marriage intact. Several imams observed that additional problems are sometimes created by the "interference" of the extended families, and so prefer to take a case-by-case approach.

> "Involving families is a double-edge sword—if I know that a family can make a positive contribution then I will include them; if I think they are not progressively minded then I do not want to include them."

The influence of the extended family on one or the other side on the outcome of reconciliation efforts may be critical to the outcome. A number of women identified the point at which their husband's family turned away from working on reconciliation with a listening ear to both parties, towards supporting their son, as a decisive moment. Salma's story illustrates the impact of her husband's family's attitude, as well as a somewhat typical progression in reconciliation efforts from family meetings to working with the imam, but in this case, to no avail.

> Salma met her husband when they were both students. After they married, she saw his attitude towards her change. Her husband came from a family more traditional than her own, and he now began to try to restrict her behavior and choices in ways she had not anticipated.
>
> After a period spent studying together overseas, Salma and her husband returned to North America and moved in with his parents. The problems escalated. As they began to argue more and more about restrictions on her, Salma and her husband brought in their respective families to help them to resolve their marital problems.
>
> A number of family meetings were held to discuss the issues that had arisen between them. On one occasion her husband's father walked out of the family meeting—he seemed to be losing patience. Next the couple turned to the imam who had married them a year earlier. After a long meeting convened by the imam that included members of both families as well as Salma and her husband, they made an agreement that seemed to address their problems. They had worked really hard, meeting throughout the evening and until the early hours of the morning, but they seemed to have a way forward.
>
> Members of both families signed the final agreement, which set out the issues the couple would work on as they continued in their marriage. Salma and her husband also agreed to return to the imam if there were any further problems.

Then Salma found out that her husband's family had talked privately with the imam before the meeting had taken place. This discovery made her question their good faith in the reconciliation process they had just completed. She began to suspect that they had decided that they wanted their son to divorce her.

Over the next month, Salma continued to live with her husband in his parents' house, and they both tried to observe the agreement they had made with the imam. However, Salma felt that there was no longer any interest on the part of her husband's family in making the marriage work. Following an argument just a few weeks later, her father-in-law packed Salma's suitcase and brought her back to her parents' house against her wishes.

Salma and her husband talked about the agreement and how they wanted to carry on with their marriage. They agreed that what was most important was that any decision about the future of the marriage would be made jointly by both of them, and not decided for them by their families. Once again, Salma agreed to move back in with her husband and his family.

Just two weeks later, Salma's husband decided that the marriage was over. His family behaved as if she was no longer of any consequence to them. She pleaded with her husband—"Why do it this way? We can end it but not this way"—but he ignored her pleas, packed her suitcase and took her back to her parents' home. He threw her possessions onto her parents' front porch and left without speaking to them.

Salma was distraught over the break-up. She felt that her husband had been encouraged by his family to behave this way and to break his commitment to their agreement. The next day she called the imam who had been working with them and asked him to contact her husband's family. They did not respond at all for a long time. Then her father-in-law called the imam and told him that he had washed his hands of the marriage.

As in Salma's case, some imams will draft up agreements following counseling. Written agreements are intended to keep the marriage working by clarifying the expectations of each partner and attempting to avoid future disputes—for example, by including undertakings about the use of money, the cessation of another relationship, or agreements over participation in education, payment on a family debt, or more equal distribution of household tasks. At times these agreements—which are sometimes committed to writing and signed by both parties—include an undertaking to return to the imam or another arbitrator in the event of future conflicts. As Salma's story shows, the most important element of a written agreement is good faith.

Reconciliation Experiences

Many imams told me that they managed to resolve most of the marital conflicts that they saw. There is no way of confirming this claim. Few imams track cases after they leave their offices, and it seems unlikely that those who are dissatisfied with their reconciliation experience will return, instead taking their request for divorce to a court or a lawyer. Since this was a study of divorce, most of those who volunteered to participate did not reconcile. Many, however, had reached a point of "no return" by the time they went to the imam and were already determined to end their marriages (seeking help too late is a phenomenon widely noted by marriage counselors and mediators).[22] Certainly some imams are able to work through conflicts with couples—especially if they come early enough for reconciliation to still be possible. How do respondents themselves evaluate their experience of working with an imam on marital counseling and reconciliation? And how far does the reconciliation process assist them in weighing the four factors described earlier—religious obligation, cultural norms, the particular nature of the conflict, and their individual needs—in reaching a decision about staying married?

At their best, reconciliation processes are a positive reinforcement of the importance of marriage vows, as well as a practical way of addressing problems.

Faraji has been married for twenty-three years and has been in marriage counseling with his wife and their imam for the past three years. Going to the imam was his wife's idea. Originally Faraji thought that the marriage was over, but now he believes that with work, it may be possible for them to continue as a couple. He is both surprised and pleased at how helpful the counseling process has been to both him and his wife. "It is because of the imam's efforts that we are still married. He has shown me why it is important to consider reconciliation. I am not giving up—the imam has given me reason to think it through and work it out."

Faraji now hopes that the counseling process will enable this marriage to continue. Asked about the expectations of his family and community to stay married, Faraji's response is that his family's opposition ("it is frowned upon") to divorce certainly created some pressure on him to make the marriage work and avoid a divorce. However, he believes that these expectations helped him to stay committed to the reconciliation process, which is now paying off. "It's not so much pressure, so much as I want to live up to my community's expectations of me. No one is going to force me to stay with my wife—they want me to try, and so I will try."

Others who did not eventually reconcile—such as Salma, whose story was recounted earlier—nonetheless understood the advice and facilitation offered by the imam as a genuine effort to help. Some men and women praised the understanding of the imam whom they consulted and the effectiveness with which he listened to both sides. One woman described the balance struck by the imam with whom she and her husband worked between exploring reconciliation on the one hand, and on the other really listening to what she and her husband said that they needed.

> "The imam was very respectful—he asked first if there was a possibility of reconciliation. . . . He used gentle questioning to find out what was happening . . . . In a horrible time for me, he confirmed how wonderful it is to be part of this community. He was a big support to me."

Other respondents spoke of the comfort that they felt knowing that the imam would observe Islamic values in counseling them. One described it as "counseling from a spiritual perspective. . . . I knew he [he imam] would not be finger-pointing, like lawyers are, but would be neutral . . . and he would attempt reconciliation." The meaning of "neutral" here contrasts a lawyer's advocacy for one side with the work of the imam with both parties. Imams apply Islamic values to their understanding of the conflict—this is why many respondents chose to go to them in the first place—and so are not "neutral" in that sense.

In other cases, a tension existed between a sense of obligation on the part of the respondent to accept the imam's desire to try to effect reconciliation, and his or her need for the imam to recognize that the marriage was over.

Sana felt that she had reached a decision that she had to end her marriage by the time she went to the imam. However, the imam pushed for reconciliation. While Sana would have preferred not to, she attended three or four reconciliation meetings convened by the imam—sometimes lasting late into the night—with her husband. "I was patient, I accepted the process . . . even though I was frustrated and I knew I wanted a divorce right away." She continued to feel that it was her responsibility to put effort into some reconciliation—although "in my head and my heart I did not believe that this could work."

After three months and a series of meetings Sana felt that the imam was finally beginning to listen to her when she said—as she had all along—that she wanted a divorce. Eventually, the imam gave them permission to divorce.

For both Sana and Faraji, their participation in the reconciliation process was a way of acknowledging the factors that were important to them in deciding whether to stay married. In Sana's case, it was primarily a matter of religious principle. For Faraji, it was important that he behaved honorably in the eyes of his community.

At worst, efforts at effecting reconciliation are experienced as a constraint on considering any other options, including divorce. Some respondents were extremely critical of the imam's efforts, describing the focus on reconciliation as controlling, insensitive and failing to give recognition to their personal circumstances. Several women expressed frustration with the assumption of the imam with whom they worked that "it would make [the woman] happiest to be back with my husband." Some women who had already spent years trying to repair their marriages—including intervention by family members and recourse to marriage counseling—were unable to persuade the imam to accept that they had made their best efforts at reconciliation and were required to go through another set of meetings which they felt had no purpose. Others complained that their interests were largely overlooked in the reconciliation process, especially when they ended up being "represented" by a male family member who would speak "for" her.

> "I felt alone and confused. There were too many people involved, and everyone had their opinion of the situation. . . . My treatment was also of little importance. My exhaustion gave way to my father representing me."

A number of women respondents complained that the reconciliation process is unsympathetic towards them—and may reflect an assumption that the wife is "to blame"—and biased in favor of their husbands. This view was reinforced by some social workers. One woman described her imam's perspective as follows: "A woman should ignore their [*sic*] husband's shortcomings and in return, things will somehow settle back into its place." Several imams explicitly recognized this problem. One told me, "Some imams are doing harm; they are siding with the men," but added, "These imams, they develop a clear reputation in the community." Similarly, women who are ready to leave abusive relationships do not seek out imams who are known to minimize or disregard domestic violence. Other women told me that they would not contemplate seeking help from an imam for more practical reasons: because they would feel uncomfortable talking to the imam about intimate issues or because they do not know the imam as well (if at all) as their husbands do. Their husbands are more likely than they are to hold a formal position within the mosque.

Marriage Counseling by Other Professionals

Islam teaches that good mental health—which enables wise decisions about critical life choices, like whether or not to stay married—requires a reconciliation between one's spiritual and physical selves. The Qur'an exhorts Muslims to be "patient in tribulation and adversity and times of stress—such are the God-fearing."[23] In common with other religious faiths, Islam assumes that the physical self is subject to the influence of worldly forces and selfish desires, and that Muslims should try to overcome or control these impulses by achieving a strong, calm inner peace through a close relationship with God. The process of spiritual and mental development is a journey that ultimately leads to a state of "peaceful self."[24] Muslims are not constrained from using a variety of means to enhance their mental health; on the contrary, this would seem to be their responsibility.

Nonetheless, resistance to professional counseling has deep cultural roots in Muslim communities. It is often assumed—and preferred—that the family should resolve its own problems rather than looking for help "outside." In some parts of the Muslim community counseling services are regarded as shameful and embarrassing, "back-door initiatives." In those few mosques where resort to counseling is strongly encouraged, it is usually the result of the imam's leadership. A group of Muslim therapists with whom I met one evening all agreed on the problem: "Muslims therapists are not generally used by their own community—they are regarded with suspicion."

There are numerous elements to this resistance, which appears to be cultural rather than religious in character. One is skepticism about paying for services (in comparison with the imams, who are free). The prevailing belief, as one put it, is that "someone offering advice (for free) does it because he cares, it comes from the heart, rather than as a professional service." There are also concerns about confidentiality and others in the community "hearing about" their problems, coupled with a general lack of understanding about the confidentiality obligations of professional counselors. Gender may also play a role in hesitation to use counselors; as one woman told me, her husband considered it "unmanly to open up to someone."

There is a similar reluctance among some Muslims to use non-Muslim counselors, exacerbated by the concern that they will not be able to relate to the experiences and values of Muslims. Of the three respondents who used a non-Muslim counselor, two were completely satisfied, but one felt that the counselor could not understand his perspective. His assessment was that the counselor was "divorced from our religion and culture, and so could not offer any value." Worse, some North American Muslims are afraid of being misunderstood, stereotyped and, worst of all, penalized by non-Muslim professionals. One woman told me that her fear about going to a non-Muslim therapist was that "once they see my husband's appearance and hear his obviously Middle-Eastern–sounding name, they'll jump to the conclusion that he's a chauvinist pig, based on their stereotypes of Arabs and Muslims."

How Individuals Decide: Four Case Studies

The strong bias among Muslim men and women in favor of staying married is sustained by a combination of religious principles, cultural beliefs and personal circumstances. The innumerable layers of complexity surrounding this decision mean that no tidy generalizations are possible about the ways in which Muslim couples—whether they are religious or more secular, childless or with kids, and whichever ethnic community they identify with—handle the challenge of marital conflict. The personal context of each marriage is unique, and this matters as much as whether or not the individual is traditionally religious. As Talal Asad observes, the way that people balance their obligations and their aspirations "is a complicated business involving disciplines and traditions of reading, personal habits, and temperament, as well as the perceived demands of particular social situations."[25]

To complete this chapter, I have chosen four stories that illustrate the confluence of religion, culture and individualism in reaching a decision over staying married. Three of these stories ended in divorce, and one in reconciliation. Each storyteller took a different route to finding his or her way through marital problems, choosing a different process. None of these four cases involved domestic violence or abuse, because of the distinctive concerns and issues raised by such conflicts.

> Mary came to North America from North Africa as a teenager. She married her partner—against the wishes of her family—once she was settled in North America. They were married for five years and had one child.
>
> Mary realized almost immediately after their marriage that she and her husband were very different. As time went by, their lifestyles became increasingly incompatible. When Mary decided that she needed to end the marriage, she went to her extended family for help. She did not go to an imam for counseling or other assistance; she did not know any local imams well, and in any case she was reluctant to share her personal problems with a relative stranger.
>
> Instead, Mary called her father-in-law and asked him to put pressure on his son to agree to the divorce. The divorce was agreed between the families. There was no need for a legal procedure because Mary and her

husband were married with a *nikah* only. The whole matter was kept within the family, and she did not have to give any public explanation of why she was ending her marriage.

Mary grew up believing it is always possible to make a mistake and change one's mind. The ending of her marriage was "relatively painless" and straightforward for her and widely accepted in her community.

Kareema had no family to turn to in North America. Her process for working through her decision over whether to stay married or not was quite different from Mary's.

Kareema came to North America from Syria. She had been married for twenty years and had four children with her husband. For many of the last ten years, her husband had lived and worked in the United Arab Emirates (UAE) while Kareema and their children lived in North America. About five years ago, he took another wife in the UAE and stopped supporting Kareema and his children in North America.

Kareema believed that she must obey her husband and fulfill all her responsibilities as a wife. As a religious person, she understood marriage to be a promise made between herself, her husband and Allah. She must not break these commitments unless there is no other possible course for her.

Kareema spoke to her husband frequently by phone, trying to salvage the marriage. She prayed for guidance from God. Her husband refused to consider reconciliation or moving back to live with his family in North America, or even to support them financially. Finally she asked him, "How can I give you all your rights as your wife, when I'm not taking any of my own rights that Islam gave me?" She asked the imam to contact her husband and ask him to give her a religious divorce.

The next story—told by Ambreen's daughter—describes a different set of competing influences and pressures. For many years, Ambreen understood her religious obligations as prohibiting divorce and had none of the sense of reciprocity that led Kareema to eventually ask for a divorce. Unlike Mary, the community surrounding Ambreen was unsympathetic to her plight.

Ambreen came to the United States from India as a newly married young adult. Her three children were all born in the United States. At the time of our interview, Ambreen had been divorced for several years. Her marriage had lasted for more than thirty years.

Ambreen's daughter told me that as the oldest child both her parents confided in her. They each told her of their unhappiness in the marriage. "You could see that they hated each other." She knew from many private conversations with her mother that "the problems were there right from the beginning."

When Ambreen turned to her family for help, she was told by her sisters and mother to "deal with it and keep your mouth shut." So Ambreen stayed in the marriage, despite her husband's public relationship with another woman. Everyone knew that this woman was his mistress. However, the marriage struggled on. Their daughter told me: "They both had emotional problems which they hid behind a mask of religion."

When the youngest of their three children turned eighteen, Ambreen's husband asked her for a divorce. Ambreen resisted the idea for several years. She wanted to stay married to her husband even though he had caused her such deep unhappiness for so many years; she saw it as her religious duty. Moreover, her social standing depended on her marital status. Her mother and sisters insisted that she stay married.

Ambreen's husband continued to press for a divorce, and she finally agreed. In the aftermath of the divorce, Ambreen found that she is not so unusual in her community; she has met many other women who have ended their marriages. She has also discovered that others among her generation have been hiding similar problems for many years, holding fast to their commitment to marriage for life despite great unhappiness and marital conflict. Moreover, other women in her social circle are now coming forward with stories similar to her own and asking their husbands for divorce.

The ending of her commitment to her husband was a huge adjustment for Ambreen. As an older South Asian woman she was raised to believe—and encouraged in this belief by her own family—that it is unacceptable to end a marriage.

Finally, let us return to the story of Baseem and Naja:

I met Baseem again almost eighteen months after I had first interviewed him. At that time he had told me that he thought that his marriage was "on the rocks." Then Baseem appeared at a talk I was giving about the research study in his local community, and he brought his wife, Naja, with him. The smiles on their faces as they walked into the room together said it all. Baseem wrote to me later. He explained that they had both worked with a Muslim marriage counselor, recommended by the imam they had gone to earlier. He praised the commitment of the imam and the counselor to helping them work things out. He and Naja agreed to do another interview with me.

After months of working with the counselor, Baseem and Naja appeared to have reached a clear understanding of the differences in the way they had each imagined married life. They could see where each had imposed their expectations on the other. Now they needed to agree on what their shared expectations should be. They had also agreed that they needed to work on their problems without the intervention of their families, and told me that this was proving to be a good decision.

Both Baseem and Naja talked about how their consciences had troubled them when they were considering divorce. Naja described a dream she had had about facing Allah and having to justify a decision to ask Baseem for a divorce. Naja said that she realized that if she were to look for a new husband, it would be someone with exactly the same qualities of character that Baseem had. So surely they must be able to work out their conflicts?

Baseem and Naja continue to work with the counselor. Today they describe themselves as happy to be married to one another but still working on their expectations and hopes for their marriage. As they say, it's an ongoing project.

5 MARITAL CONFLICTS AND ABUSE

In their interviews, respondents disclosed many of the conflicts and tensions that they had experienced in their marriages. While I did not ask direct questions about the causes of their marital conflict—the study was framed as focusing on process choices (their recourse to Islamic marriage and divorce) and I was careful not to intrude into personal and potentially sensitive territory—virtually every respondent volunteered this information, some at length, in the course of telling her or his story. This chapter looks at the themes that emerged in this data, offering a window into common and recurrent conflicts between Muslim couples.

The most frequently repeated of these themes is conflict over gender roles within the marriage and, specifically, what is expected of a good Muslim wife/ husband? Gender relations dominate the balance of power and authority within the relationship and raise many of the same issues (for example, of "obedience" and "authority") discussed in relation to Muslim marriage in chapter three. The disputes described by the respondents are in many ways a reflection of broader societal changes in the social and economic roles of women, both inside and outside the family, but they are played out in unique ways inside North American Muslim families. In many cases this became an overt conflict centring on the woman's role and responsibilities as a Muslim wife, including (for example) work outside the home, household chores, schooling, as well as general freedoms and public behaviors. These conflicts tend to become especially disruptive when there is a strong contrast between the values and expectations of a young couple and those of their parents and/or in-laws. Almost all the marriages explored in this study struggled with some aspect of this transition. A second set of conflicts derives from and relates to the particular structure of Muslim family life and its traditions. These include recourse to arranged or semi-arranged marriages; the continuing relationship between the spouses and their extended families; and the taking of a second wife. There were also conflicts over differences between the spouses over their approach to religious practice. A third set of conflicts involves violence and abuse. In a quarter of the marriages that ended in divorce, physical—and to a lesser extent, emotional—abuse was described as the cause of the breakdown. All these accounts of abuse came from women, and represent one in three of all female respondents. The issues that arise in these cases are often related to the other themes, but because the conflict is expressed very differently—using aggression and sometimes violence—and raise different imperatives regarding assistance and safety, these cases are presented and analyzed in a separate section.

Many of the marriages in the study experienced conflict in more than one of these three battlegrounds. Often, it was the interaction between different elements of struggle between the couple—rather than the individual elements quantitatively—that most completely described their conflict, which in most of these cases could not be resolved.

Many of these themes in this chapter seem universal to all or at least many couples, no matter what their religion or culture. At the same time, each of the individual narratives is shaped and colored by their immediate family and community culture, which provide the critical context for both the causes and the management of their conflict. In almost every case this cultural context has three distinct elements or identities: Muslim, North American and (in varying degrees of distance or closeness) a Muslim country overseas. This chapter asks whether Muslim couples in North America understand and address these conflicts any differently than other couples. Do any of these themes have special meaning and significance for Muslim couples, or are they simply struggling with the same challenges—economic, emotional, social—that confront many partnerships in North America? Do the principles of Muslim marriage as the respondents understand them affect how they understand and address these types of conflicts? Do the opinions of their families affect their judgment? Does a distinctive North American Islamic identity emerge from the ways that respondents—particularly those born and raised in the United States or Canada—organize their marital relations and manage their conflicts? The stories presented here attempt to tease out some answers to these questions.

Expectations over Gender Roles and Authority

The most common theme in marital conflict was a mismatch between the expectations of husband and wife about various aspects of family life. The expectations that each spouse brings to the marital relationship—expectations that usually reflect family norms and cultural traditions—are critical to both the scope, and the difficulty, of the subsequent negotiation between them. The institution of the family is central to Islamic values and culture, and many respondents reflected a strong feeling of pressure to get marital roles and norms "right"—to conform to the image of the "perfect Muslim family." But there are many diverse understandings among North American Muslims about what that idealized family life looks like and the relative rights and responsibilities of men and women, as Sadia was shocked to discover.

> Sadia was married in a big community ceremony. "People saw us as the 'perfect couple,' the 'it' couple." The marriage also fell apart in public; her husband took another wife whom he pursued very publicly several years after his marriage to Sadia. The problems in the marriage had started right away—Sadia's husband was first physically violent towards her on their honeymoon.
>
> When Sadia eventually went to a lawyer about a divorce, the reaction from her friends and community implied that she was betraying this image of perfect family life. "The women said, 'Forgive him, men will be men.' They told me, 'Why do you have to be so seddity?'"[1]
>
> Ten years later, Sadia reflected, "I kept asking myself—how could so many bad things happen in a marriage like mine, that looked so perfect—did I deserve it? It rocked me to my core. I felt, 'Look, I did what you all told me to do—I was a virgin, I waited for sex, and this is what I got—a horrible public breakup from an abusive man.'"

Given the assumption that marriage between Muslims (especially from similar cultural backgrounds) will maximize the synchronicity of values between the couple, it is startling to see how often spouses have quite different views on questions of family life and gender roles within marriage. Admittedly, being Muslim and growing up in North America is very different from being Muslim and growing up in Pakistan or Syria or Somalia. In this study, these so-called transcontinental marriages often faltered. But so did marriages where both spouses were Muslim who grew up in similar cultural environments. Frequently differences in expectations are fundamental—such as Sadia's assumption that her husband would be monogamous—and are unanticipated, coming as a complete surprise to both partners. Mismatched expectations often became a power struggle between the spouses, and with a frequent default to a claim of male superiority. Many women challenged this default, sometimes by relying on their own family traditions, and sometimes by asserting their personal values.

Mismatched expectations covered a wide spectrum of issues relating to the organization of family life. Sometimes the ensuing conflicts related to practical questions such as who would work outside the home, who would attend school, and who would do household chores. For example, would both spouses work outside the home and, if so, who would be responsible for cooking, cleaning and, if applicable, childcare? Sometimes the difference in values related to how the family would organize its economic affairs—for example, would the couple merge their earnings in a joint bank account or would they keep them separate? Would they send money home (overseas?) to a relative or support a relative living in North America? Would both husband and wife share economic responsibility for the household, or would the husband carry primary financial responsibility (as Islamic family law assumes) for the family? Another common area of mismatched expectations related to the future relationships between the spouses and their extended families—for example, should the couple live with the husband's parents? How much time would the couple spend with their parents and in-laws? How influential would the mother-in-law be on her son's behavior and choices in his new family?[2]

Most respondents attribute differences between themselves and their spouses to the ways in which each grew up, and the degree to which each family is more "traditional" or more "contemporary" in outlook. Many respondents expected that their own marriage would look very similar to that of their parents, despite the many structural and social differences between the generations. Obviously, how well this approach works depends on the degree of similarity between the values and expectations of the two families. When expectations differ between a couple, the extent to which they can address these by independent negotiation, or perhaps with the help of a trusted adviser—rather than calling in aid their family customs on either side—appears to be critical to their ability to problem-solve, rather than remaining fixed in competing positions which mirror their own family traditions and practices. Several stories in this study demonstrated that couples who develop their own approaches to how they organize their married and family lives do better in resolving conflicts between them than those who cannot separate their own choices and decisions from those of their extended family and are accustomed to looking to an authority figure (usually a parent) for guidance regarding rights and permissions. Many other respondents offered this observation in hindsight, after their marriage had ended. The limited family role models available to many young North American Muslims exacerbates the extent and intensity of conflicts over norms and roles in marriage and homemaking. Most respondents acknowledged that their only role model was their mother or father, who may have grown up quite differently from them, or occasionally their siblings.

Seeing conflicts through the lens of their own families values either legitimized or challenged the assumptions now made by their spouses. Sarah told me that when she married her husband, "I would cook for him and his brother and live like a maid. . . . I did what I saw in my culture, what I saw my brothers' wives do, I did that." In contrast, Maghabeen could not square the expectations her husband appeared to have of her with her own family norms.

> Maghabeen met Hamid while they were both graduate students. She married him a few years later, against the wishes of her family.
>
> Although both had come to North America from similar regions of Pakistan, it quickly became clear to Maghabeen that their families were very different. Her family had encouraged Maghabeen and her three sisters to go to university, and all three were pursuing professional careers. Despite the fact that he met her while studying, her husband appeared to have a different idea of the value of education and work for Maghabeen.
>
> In the months after her marriage, Maghabeen found that Hamid was increasingly restricting and monitoring her movements. He accused her of having an affair at work, and harassed her about her relationships with her work colleagues. He told her that she should stop working outside the home. He accused her of "not respecting her culture."
>
> Maghabeen found this assertion confusing and disturbing. She asked her husband, if her sisters in Pakistan could work (they were both doctors) why could she not work? She told Hamid that she would call one of her sisters in Pakistan and ask her opinion. She wrote an email to her sister and asked: "Does your husband allow you to work? To have friends? To go out on your own?" Her sister replied yes to all these questions.
>
> Maghabeen decided that there was no reason that she should accept these restrictions from her husband. But Hamid would not back down and eventually the marriage ended.

The mismatched expectations described by so many respondents were aggravated by one or more of three critical factors: the power dynamics within the relationship; the impact of societal changes in gender roles and especially in the public participation of women; and generational changes and adjustments.

Relationship Power and Authority

Embedded in all relationship conflicts is a struggle over power and authority.[3] Typically, disputes over appropriate family roles and norms in these heterosexual marriages begin as specific conflicts over (for example) how much assistance the wife should expect with household chores and cooking or how much money to send to a family member overseas, and transition into more serious arguments over who has the power and authority within the relationship to make this determination. In some of the conflicts described in this chapter, the consequence is the abuse of power in the form of physical violence or emotional abuse by one or the other spouse. In others, taking a different arc, the dispute serves as a natural channel for working through unresolved issues about the balance of power between the couple.

Relationship struggles between heterosexual couples—both Muslim and non-Muslim—are frequently characterized by patriarchal assumptions, in the most extreme cases understanding marriage as an unequal relationship in which the man has authority and the woman should do his bidding. These assertions of male power are often justified by some kind of biological explanation—varying between cultures but with common themes—which explains male authority as the "natural" consequence of superior physical strength and/or emotional stability. Manifestations of power flowing from this emphasis on physical strength and the assertion of psychological superiority include control over decision making, authoritative knowledge and assessment, and elevated social responsibility. The universality of conflicts around power and authority, and especially in relation to gender, reflects the entrenched patriarchy of many religions, providing an explanation for the exclusion of women from positions of authority in many, including Catholicism and Islam.[4]

There is a pervasive public view in the West that Islam is uniquely associated with male privilege and that Muslim marriages epitomize authoritative male behavior and female submission. Muslim women raised to believe that their husbands (and formerly their fathers) should and do hold the power in the marital relationship—and in particular where this is misunderstood as a religious obligation—are especially vulnerable to this assumption. Inside marriage, Islam is sometimes used as a justification for chauvinist behaviors, with women being told that if they advance an opinion or argue a course (or decision or public behavior) other than that preferred by their husbands, they are behaving "un-Islamically." Sometimes these disputes reflect genuine differences of belief —for example, arguments between the couple over what is appropriate dress for a Muslim woman. In other cases disputes appear entirely disingenuous and simply a means of asserting power and authority—for example, the assertion of one man that his Muslim wife was not permitted to call him by his first name or that women are required in Islam to undertake all housework and cooking. Characterizing male power and female obedience as religiously proscribed is a potent weapon; as Dena Hassouneh-Phillips concludes in her study of marriage practices among American Muslim women, "Women tended to comply with the expectation that they obey their husbands when they believed it was a religious duty."[5] A traditional reading of *qiwama* (husbandly authority)—promoted by some imams and religious scholars, as well as some popular Islamic media[6]—reinforces non-Muslim stereotypes about the inequality of power relations within Muslim families.

The unjust and oppressive assertion of male power can and is frequently challenged on religious grounds. Many scholars point out that the Qur'an introduced women's rights, including rights to property, financial support and free choice of a marriage partner, which in the context of the seventh century were significant inroads on male privilege. Feminist Muslim scholars have developed a strong voice and a growing body of literature that presents twenty-first-century Islam as fully compatible with and supportive of women's rights and equality with men.[7] Regardless, in contracting for marriage in their *nikah*, many Muslim women accept (at least in form) some version of the concept of *qiwama*. A more progressive understanding of *qiwama* is that it provides the frame for a mutual bargain made between husband and wife, and that the terms of this bargain are different now than they were in the seventh century (when men typically provided financial security and women took care of the home). Today the "bargain" could include both partners working outside the home—removing the source of the traditional authority of the husband—or another arrangement which engages both spouses in household responsibilities.[8]

For some women respondents, there was a constant nagging fear that they were behaving un-Islamically, even as their heads and their hearts told them otherwise. One woman told me, "When my husband told me not to do certain things, I would wonder whether I really was a 'good Muslim woman'—but the other side of me knew that really Islam did permit me to be more independent than my husband allowed." Reda came to a similar conclusion.

Reda knew that her husband's behavior—his need to control her movements, his relationships with other women, his drinking—was un-Islamic and wrong, but she still felt trapped by his demands that she behave as a "good Muslim wife."

Reda became increasingly confused about what it meant to be a Muslim. "The way I have practiced [Islam] all my life is through fear—it stops you doing lots of things (like drinking, and dating). On the one hand I need some time anyways to take care of myself—but I feel like I will get punished if I do those things."

Reda faced a dilemma experienced by many other Muslim women who believe that they are entitled to be treated better—equally, and with respect—but (like Sadia, in the first story in this chapter) found that their husband's behavior was widely tolerated by their community. This made it extremely difficult for them to feel confident or safe in going to others for support.

When a marriage is based on an assumption that authority rests with the husband, many other consequences flow. Disputes over family finances—control over money and spending—often relate to conceptions of a role either as the "breadwinner" (assumed to control spending) or the primary "homemaker" (usually the recipient of an allowance). Questions of authority balanced with responsibility arise again when women take on additional roles outside the home, but are expected to manage these additional new tasks as well as their previous responsibilities with little or no assistance from their male partners. Of course, authority may not always equal power—for example, a working husband may delegate power to his wife to control the household budget—but in many cases authority (derived from traditions, culture or religious views) is combined with the power to make and impose a decision about how matters are managed. Women respondents cited numerous examples of the assumptive assertion of male power that left little or no space for dialogue, including decisions over having children, relocating, disposing of shared property and the wife attending school or working outside the home.

At its worst, the assertion of power and authority leads to violence and abuse. Most conflicts over power and authority inside marriage do not end in violence, but all abusive relationships turn on issues of power and control. When one partner is willing to use violence or abuse as a means of controlling his or her partner, it may be manifested as physical or sexual violence, emotional and verbal abuse, or all the above. While many of the issues surrounding mismatched expectations, and some of those relating to the balance of power and authority between spouses, are susceptible to dialogue and resolution over time, the same assumption cannot be made when there is family violence. An abused spouse has a far lower tolerance for dialogue—which may be distorted by intimidation on one part and fear on the other—and often little willingness and ability to engage in counseling and efforts at reconciliation. Disputes over power and authority that become violent are dealt with in the final part of this chapter.

Societal Changes in Gender Roles

Changing expectations of the "proper" role of a Muslim husband and wife relect rapid and far-reaching changes in societal norms surrounding gender roles. Couples inevitably understand their own relationships in the light of contemporary social norms, especially those of their own community. The scope of what is imaginable, possible and appropriate for women—especially in relation to work and education—has changed dramatically in the last half century. Young Muslim women growing up in North America increasingly expect that they will continue with their education after high school, and many aspire to professional careers. For more recent immigrant women whose families are relatively socially mobile in their country of origin there is a similar expectation that they will be fully

educated and seek professional work. In either case, there is a parallel expectation that these educational and work goals will somehow be combined with marriage and raising a family—values which remain relatively unchanged.

The emergence of feminism as an organizing principle for women to challenge their traditionally passive role in marriage and assert a right to equal treatment in education and work runs like a lightning rod through a historical
accounting of change over the last fifty years. Although associated by Muslims—
often negatively—with the West, feminism has emerged in both North America
and many of the countries of origin of those participating in this study.[9] While
many of the signs of real advances remain ambiguous—plenty of evidence still
exists of enduring inequality in the workplace, differential expectations and treatment of boys and girls in many families, and pervasive patriarchy—the participation of women in public life, including education and work, has changed
dramatically. These changes have occurred over the past half century in North
America, and more recently in some Muslim countries.

In 1964, Betty Friedan wrote of married women's lives that "career is a problem, education is a problem, . . . even the admission of women's intelligence and
individuality is a problem."[10] It was widely assumed that the sole purpose of a
woman's life was to look after her husband and her home, and to raise their children. The 1950s saw the age at which American girls and women got married
younger and younger (by the end of the decade, the average age at marriage was
twenty and still dropping).[11] Middle-class women were living the "suburban
dream" as housewives—yet many of these materially privileged women experienced a pervasive sense of discontent and lack of fulfillment. Despite having won
formal legal privileges such as the right to vote and to hold property many years
earlier, North American women who were not under economic pressure to work
were expected to support their husbands and adopt a homemaker role. Moreover,
they were expected to want to fill this role, although many, silently, found that
they did not. A 1976 Gallup survey[12] reported that 76 percent of American
women described their highest goal for a fulfilled life was marriage and children,
with just 32 percent saying they would like to combine family life with a full-time
job.[13] In 1980 just 17 percent of women questioned in a Louis Harris poll said
they would prefer full-time over part-time work, and in 1984 only 29 percent of
married women held full-time jobs.[14] The stubbornly low value placed on women
working outside the home, assumed to be an economic necessity rather than a
personal choice, further affected the types of work seen as appropriate for
women—part time rather than full time, unskilled rather than professional.

Times have changed. In a 2009 survey, 58 percent of women in the general U.S.
population reported having a job; among Muslim women, the figure was 59 percent.[15]
While economic necessity is often the driver for women seeking work outside the

home and women are still often ghettoized in poorly paid work, behind these figures lies a seismic shift in the way in which women's role as wives, mothers and workers is conceptualized and widely accepted. The number of women working in the United States is about to exceed the number of men employed in the workforce—partly a result of recessionary forces but nonetheless a milestone.[16] Improved access to higher education also means that increasing numbers of women achieve professional status. To give one among innumerable examples of this change (from my own professional context as a law professor), in the 1950s just 4 percent of law school entrants were female; by the 1990s, the numbers of men and women in law school classrooms were almost equal.[17] At odds with the widespread perception among non-Muslims that women are held back from education and work, one in three working Muslim women now hold professional positions (for example, doctors, lawyers, teachers, bankers), higher than that of the general U.S. female population and close to the 35 percent figure reported by Muslim men.[18]

Whereas some parts of the Muslim world continue to deny girls and women access to education and work, in many Muslim countries there is evidence of the enhanced public participation of women and girls, as well as measurable shifts in attitude. This increased participation is important for my study because it means that some Muslim women and their families arrive in North America having already expanded their expectations as a result of their experiences in their country of origin; at the least, they experience no conflict between trends in their country of origin and those in North America. For example, in Egypt, following the 1952 revolution, the percentage of women among university undergraduates had doubled by 1986, to 32 percent.[19] Further education generally correlates with an older age upon marriage and, as Fatima Mernissi points out in her seminal study of gender relations in Moroccan society, "disturbs the traditional sexual identity reference points and sex roles in Muslim countries, which are obsessed with virginity [by proscribing dating] and childbearing [which takes place later for educated women]."[20] Even in Iran, where conformity to traditional gender roles is still widely expected in business and government, the segregation of education following revolutionary Islamization has encouraged more conservative families to send their daughters to school and to university, where 60 percent of students are now women. As one journalist reporting on this phenomenal rise commented, "Iranian women are using university studies as a way to leave home, postpone marriage, and generally earn greater freedom and social respect.[21] Although vast gender discrepancies still exist—for example, just 20 percent of the workforce in the Middle East and Africa is comprised of women, and the proportion of women who are illiterate remains approximately twice that of men in most North African and Middle Eastern countries—a rise in female education especially at the secondary level is part of a global trend.[22]

Reflecting the exceptionally well-educated demographic of the Muslim community in North America, Muslims are the second (after American Jews) most highly educated religious group surveyed by Gallup in 2002, with 40 percent saying they have at least a college degree, compared to 29 percent of all Americans.[23] Muslim women are statistically as likely as their male counterparts to say they have a college degree or higher education.[24] The educational demographic of my sample reflected these high levels of education among North American Muslims, with a large number of respondents holding both undergraduate degrees and professional qualifications. Although respondents were not asked directly about their work or occupation, more than one-third of female participants referred to their work either in the context of telling me their story, or (less often) as a factor in their marital conflict. Their stories also illustrate how the development of their working—and often professional—lives is more closely related to changing economic conditions than to changes in religious doctrine or belief. Some work because they have clear goals for their own self-fulfillment and personal satisfaction, others because their families need the income. None of these women regarded their working lives as incompatible in any way with their beliefs and Islamic values. As one Muslim feminist scholar points out, "The basic determinant for the role of women in a society is not religion, which can be interpreted to support whatever is necessary in society, but the economic and political situation."[25]

Changes in female public participation inevitably mean changes in private life and family ordering. Many families, both Muslim and non-Muslim, experience tensions and sometimes overt conflicts—both practical and principled—as a result of the expanding role of women outside the home. The influx of women into both further education and the workplace has resulted in increasing "inter-role" conflict—conflict between one's family role and work role and responsibilities. More and more women combine family responsibilities with work, and look to their male partners to change their expectations of how much they will contribute to the running of the household and childcare. Research suggests that the readjustment of roles within marriage has not kept pace with the enlarging role of women as workers as well as homemakers, and the consequence is more conflict at home.[26] Some examples of how these tensions played out in the stories of the respondents follow below.

Generational Changes

As expectations of power and role relations between men and women have shifted over the past fifty years, a gap has opened up between the experiences and attitudes of the last two generations. Young women who have come of age in developed countries postfeminism often lead very different lives from those of their own mothers and grandmothers; young men have different expectations of the type of relationship they hope for with their spouse than their fathers and grandfathers. Younger respondents in this study are often trying to develop new models for family life that are quite different from those of their parents' generation, and for which they rarely have family role models.

Muslim or non-Muslim, members of Generation X[27] share similar experiences as they struggle with questions of identity, work and gender, whatever their religious or cultural backgrounds, including those with no religious affiliation at all. They also share core values, including a desire for a work-life balance and individualistic goals for self-realization. This is counterintuitive for older women who now watch their Generation X daughters asserting, "Me too." One female Muslim academic described this to me as the "Burger King syndrome," by which she meant (pejoratively) the means for instant access to the satisfaction of one's needs. Whereas their parents (either "Builders" [those born between 1922 and 1943] or, more likely, "Baby Boomers" [those born between 1944 and 1960]) were more focused on "climbing the ladder" at a particular job in order to achieve stability and improved status, Generation X'ers are looking for flexibility and mobility. These contrasting values about work in turn reflect different conceptions of gender roles within marriage: The ladder-climbing loyalty of the Baby Boomers was only possible with either paid housekeeping and childcare, or a wife at home.

Modern Muslim couples are developing marriage partnerships that embrace many values that their parents would not recognize—for example, husbands undertaking child care and household tasks, wives acting as primary breadwinners, a general desire for mobility and flexibility, a balance between professional and family time, and perhaps a willingness to subordinate professional advancement to lifestyle choices. Generational conflicts are especially profound between couples who are born and grow up in North America and an older generation that arrived as adults. Even understanding the forces that create conflict between spouses over gender roles is to some extent generational: How does one understand a conflict that one never had?[28] How does one relate to a lifestyle value that one never had?

Regardless, older family members often get drawn into these conflicts, weighing in with an opinion, especially in those families where the role and authority of the extended family remain strong. Many respondents described the playing out of conflicts over gender roles in which each spouse turned to their own family for moral reinforcement. These disputes rarely found a happy ending. The differences in lifestyle and values between the members of Generation X and their parents often mean that the arguments marshalled by the older generation—even if they might support a particular case, such as whether or not the wife should work outside the home, or take primary care of children—are rarely commensurate with those of their adult children. In subsequent generations, one might anticipate new and further generational conflicts over alternative family structures.

Conflicts

Mismatched expectations, fueled and fanned by advances in the public role of women, barely held in check by entrenched notions of male power and authority and challenged by a new generation of Muslims born and raised in North America, produce a range of overt conflicts. Sometimes these conflicts are challenging to the relationship but are manageable when each spouse recognizes the need to adapt and adjust. The underlying question in each personal story is how rapidly, and at what cost, are these couples able to renegotiate their individual and shared responsibilities and their expectations of one another, in order to save their marriage?

Working Wives

Despite sweeping changes in attitudes towards women working and accessing higher education, some Muslim women continue to experience constraints on their access to both education and work. These women want to further their education and develop a professional career but find the personal ambition and independence associated with these goals become a source of conflict between them and their spouses. Other women find that they are expected to work in order to support their family economically, yet their husbands still expect them to shoulder the burden of household chores and childcare. As one female respondent—married for thirty years, during which she had raised six children and worked outside the home—told me resentfully, "I always did both the female and the male jobs." When conflict breaks out over the rights and responsibilities of working wives, it is usually manifested as a struggle over the adjustment of traditional gender roles inside the marriage.

> Harith and his wife Ameena were each born and raised in North America and are members of a small and close-knit Muslim community. Harith described his wife as very "Westernised"—she was continuing with her education and anticipating a future career—and yet in other ways, very traditional.
>
> After their marriage, the couple moved into a home close to the school that Ameena attended. As a result, Harith had a long commute to work, sixty miles each way. Harith felt that because he had a longer day

than his wife, she should take on more of the household chores than him. Disagreed, arguing that they should shoulder the same burden. She emphasized the importance of them each taking an equal share of the chores, if they were to be equal partners.

Ameena came from a wealthy, traditional family. She told Harith that she expected him to take care of her financially, as her father had done. Harith was confused and perplexed by this. He was already committing all his financial means to the marriage and had expected that when his wife finished school, she would find a job, and as a modern couple they would both contribute financially to their household and eventually to their family. He had trouble understanding what she meant by "equality" in their marriage, and neither seemed able to explain to the other what it might look like.

Harith and Ameena struggled for the next twelve months with a growing sense of confusion about what their appropriate expectations of one another should be. This created great resentment between them, which they were unable to resolve in counseling. Eventually they decided to divorce.

In other work-related conflicts we can see the impact of traditional attitudes towards the social segregation of women. Some women described their husbands as deeply suspicious about their activities at work—even when they were expected or even required to work outside the home—and especially about their relationships with male colleagues. Shireene described how her husband would frequently turn up at her workplace and call her names in front of her colleagues. Out of work for long periods, her husband would monitor her movements between home and work, timing her drive home and interrogating her if he thought that she had not driven directly home. This led to constant fights. The next story illustrates a similar conflict over control and independence.

Shanaz's career took off after her children were born. Her husband, Amir, worked away from home, and she became accustomed to juggling work and childcare. However, when Amir returned from overseas to live full time with the family they began to fight. Amir became physically abusive and worried that Shanaz would reveal this behavior to those with whom she worked. He began to constantly ask her to tell him where she was going and with whom she was working and wanted to accompany her on work assignments.

Matters came to a head when Shanaz began to work with a particular male colleague of whom Amir became very suspicious. One day when

Shanaz was scheduled to drive to a work assignment with this colleague, Amir again insisted that he accompany her. Shanaz said, "Something snapped inside me—I could not stand him trying to control me anymore." She refused to take Amir with her and drove to the meeting alone, having arranged to meet her colleague there. Amir followed her and when she reached her destination jumped out and began physically assaulting her colleague, calling him anti-Semitic names and accusing him of sleeping with Shanaz.

Shanaz and Amir separated shortly after this incident. Shanaz reflected that she is still treated with suspicion in her community about her relationships with her male colleagues, and she feels very isolated.

Going to School

Many women described their continuing desire for access to education once they were married. In a few cases, women described what they saw as a choice—between staying married or getting an education.

Rubina was married at seventeen in a union arranged by her parents in Pakistan. She returned to North America with her new husband and started a family. Rubina constantly raised with her husband her desire to continue her education, which had ended when she left high school at sixteen, but each time he refused to consider it, suggesting instead that she have another baby. When her marriage ended after thirteen years, Rubina negotiated for her husband to pay her college fees. She described her graduation from college as "a symbol of my freedom. I should have done it years ago."

In most cases, women managed to remain in or go to school with little or no overt resistance from their husbands, but the harder, long-term adjustment was over roles within the marriage. Some women told me that they thought that their husbands tolerated their continued schooling as long as they continued to run the household. Another woman described how her husband and the wider community blamed her "Western education" for their marital conflict, illustrating the confluence of fears over women's extended education (this woman had obtained two graduate degrees) and fears over the influence of "Western" ideas. Whereas denial of access to education is rarely the sole reason for ending a marriage—it is more typically combined with other active constraints or passive disapprovals regarding working outside the home, earning an independent income or establishing collegial workplace relationships—it is often experienced by women who have since divorced and completed an education as a motif for the problems they experienced within marriage. Many will return to school when their marriage ends.

> When she was first married, Madiha aspired to become a lawyer, but her husband told her there was no point to her going to school, since she would be staying home and taking care of their children. He suggested that if she wanted to go to school, she should take his classes for him, registering under his name and completing his assignments for him.
>
> When I spoke to her three years later, Madiha was in the process of divorcing her husband, who had become physically abusive towards her. She told me that she felt that it would be very difficult for her to recover, emotionally, from the relationship but that she will "use the pain to finish school and achieve the dreams that no one wanted me to accomplish."

General Freedoms

A small but significant number of women described what they saw as a shift in their husband's attitudes towards them following their engagement or marriage, and increasing assertions of control over their behavior. Most were genuinely shocked and completely unprepared for this and the conflicts that it produced. One woman reflected on the moment that she realized that she had married a man whose values and expectations diverged dramatically from her own. "This was a completely different plane of existence than I live on. The weight of my mistake just fell on me, right there."

Many of these women understood efforts to control them in relation to even the most trivial matters as assertions of male power. One woman told me that the continuous conflicts she experienced with her husband from just a few weeks into their marriage—"we disagreed on everything, how to clean the house, selling my car"—were because "he wanted to always feel like 'the man' in the relationship." A few women described efforts to keep them indoors and socially isolated as a means of control, often accompanied by extreme jealousy of any other relationship. This constraint was especially harsh for those women who were recent arrivals to North America and had no existing social networks. One young mother who came to live in an urban suburb from her native Lebanon told me that she was cut off from the world by her husband—"He controlled me like the TV with the remote." One woman described her husband's efforts to cut her off from contact with her own family members. Other women talked about feeling disregarded or ignored, "treated like a second class citizen, always belittling me." One woman poignantly remarked, "He [my husband] wanted me to cancel myself." These are all manifestations of emotional control.

Only a small number of these women understood their husband's behavior to have anything to do with an asserted religious principle—for example, complaints about modest dress. Many of the restrictions imposed seemed to have nothing to do with widely accepted religious norms, and the storyteller recognized this. One woman, born and raised in North America, described her Pakistani husband forbidding her to drive. A social worker told me that she had a woman client whose husband had told her that Muslim women did not wear panties. Other women could not square their husband's own lack of religious observance with their demand that they behave in a traditionally observant way.

> "My husband was not at all religious—that is, he did not pray—but he was obsessed with whether I was dressed modestly, whether I was seeing other men, and became more and more opposed to my working outside the home."

Many of these women were highly skeptical about their husband's idea of "Islamic" norms within marriage; "Men often believe in certain ideas but they are not Islamic!" Despite this, religious justification can be a highly effective disguise for the social and sexual control of women. Challenging something framed as a "religious" obligation is far more difficult and risky than standing up against perspectives grounded in personal opinion, political ideology or historical tradition. Even when the wife did not accept the constraint imposed on her as a religious principle, she still had to deal with her family who were often inclined to counsel submission to her husband. Acquiescence to unchallengeable "religious" norms may mean that other explanations for the behavior—for example, mental health problems, addictions and other influences on male behavior—are overlooked. The confluence of so-called religious justifications with the patriarchal cultural norms of some North American Muslim communities can create a dangerous situation where it discourages family or other outside intervention. In the next story, the family did eventually intervene but delayed until matters had reached a crisis point.

> Baheera came to live in North America with her husband Dawar several months after their wedding in Pakistan. She wanted to live with her family here (an aunt and uncle), but Dawar would not agree to it, and instead they moved into a tiny basement flat with his brother. Baheera felt embarrassed by the lack of privacy both for the couple and for herself. Her husband restricted her comings and goings and insisted that she cook and clean for himself and her brother. He also became physically abusive towards Baheera.

Baheera tried to maintain contact with her family members living in North America, but Dawar cut her off from all social and family ties, including her aunt and uncle and a neighbor whom she had befriended. She sometimes spoke by phone to her aunt, who asked about her well being, but did not feel she could tell her the truth about her situation.

Finally, Baheera's aunt came to visit her in the basement apartment and saw how she was living. She was disturbed at what she saw but did not at this point say anything to Baheera's husband or otherwise intervene. However, Dawar clearly believed that her family might now involve themselves and learn more about his treatment of Baheera. He woke her in the middle of the night and told her, "We are going back to Pakistan." Baheera recalls in great embarrassment that he took her to the airport in her pajamas. "I was crying for a quarter to call my auntie, to tell her I was leaving." Baheera spoke to her uncle and told him what was happening.

Baheera and Dawar flew back to Pakistan, but her uncle alerted family members there who met them at the Karachi airport. Her family took Baheera from her husband and would not let her return to him. This was the end of her marriage.

Conflicts Reflecting Islamic Traditions
Arranged Marriages

A growing literature documents the practice of arranged marriage and its cultural roots and motivations. Generally, choice of a marriage partner within one's own social, religious or cultural group is driven by a desire to maintain cohesive group boundaries, and it is widely assumed that a choice within one's own group will strengthen both the group and the marriage itself. Marriage within one's own community is extremely common across all ethnic groups and especially within the South Asian community,[29] where arranged marriage seems to continue to be most common.

Changes are apparent in the norms surrounding partner choice for contemporary Muslims in the West. There is an emerging debate over the differences between, for example, "arranged marriage," sometimes described as "co-operative traditional" marriage where there is some personal choice but parental consent remains essential,[30] and "forced" marriage, widely regarded as coercive. The line between these two constructs is not always clear, as the comments of many respondents demonstrate; a desire to satisfy parental and community expectations may negate or overwhelm aspirations to personal choice. Parents and other family members are often regarded as critical players in the negotiation over choice of partner, and younger people frequently acquiesce to their preferences in order to show solidarity with the community discourse, holding back their reluctance and unease in fear of causing disappointment to their family.[31] These emotions and torn loyalties are clear from the stories of decisions to marry a person recommended by one's family (see chapter three). As one young woman, now divorced, told me, "I was young [at the time of the arranged marriage] and not assertive. My parents thought they were doing the right thing for me, linking me up with someone who was successful—I did not want to disappoint them." This sense of obligation is reinforced by socialization patterns that, for girls in particular, often include conforming to parental choice of partner.

> Manal was married by arrangement at the age of eighteen to a man seventeen years her senior. While her husband, like herself, had grown up in North America, the strangeness of being married to an older person whom she did not know or choose for herself was overwhelming for her, and the marriage quickly failed.
>
> Looking back, Manal felt like she had no real choice in the matter. "I told my father it wouldn't work, but they [her mother and father] encouraged me to do it. Their expectations are based on the norms at home [Somalia], mine are based on growing up here."

While there is no empirical evidence suggesting that these marriages are more likely to fail,[32] the desires to meet parental expectations and satisfy community norms sometimes combine to produce the type of "sleepwalking" into marriage described by Baseem in chapter four. Differences in age and birthplace appear to significantly contribute to couples' difficulties in settling on a shared set of values for negotiating their intimate relationships and future family life—for example, marriages arranged between one spouse who is born and raised in North America, and one who comes from overseas to be married and live in North America. Described as transcontinental marriages, these arrangements attract the most vocal criticism inside those communities that continue to practice arranged marriage. The spouse coming from outside North America faces many challenges, not only adjusting to a different language and perhaps finding employment but also a social and cultural adjustment that they may either embrace, or firmly reject. Establishing marriage expectations, including premarital counseling and negotiation over the *nikah*, are even more difficult when the spouses will not meet until shortly before their wedding day. Aisha and Raheela were both married to men who came to North America from overseas. Both experienced almost immediate conflict with their spouses and their different ideas about the role they were expected to play as "traditional" Muslim wives. Aisha was born in North America. Her husband came from Lebanon where he was raised in a village which was very traditional. Aisha told me, "I really tried to adapt, but it just did not work. He wanted me to be submissive." Raheela, who grew up in North America, made a similar point:

> "As a traditional man who had grown up in Pakistan, my husband expected me to make all the compromises. And there is still an assumption in my community that younger girls are easily moulded."

In several cases the North American partner and his or her family acted as sponsors for the other party to obtain rights of residency in the United States or Canada. While sponsorship is a critical part of the arrangement, the responsibility of sponsorship may overshadow other issues in the marital relationship. One respondent told me that as a sponsor for her spouse, she felt obliged to remain married to him at least until he gained permanent residency status, even though the marriage was, in effect, already over. Since residency rights are inevitably tied to economic opportunity, this possible consequence of an arranged marriage is open to exploitation. Khalid—who came to North America from Pakistan as a baby—bitterly described his marriage to a young woman from Pakistan as follows:

> "We had our *nikah* in Pakistan. . . . I sponsored [my wife] to live in the United States. She arrived eighteen months later. Just three months later, she asked me for a divorce—over the phone, while she was visiting relatives. She had already cleaned out the safe. The whole motivation was for her to get legal residency."

There is growing criticism within the Muslim community of arranged marriages, and in particular of transcontinental marriages. "The traditional way of choosing a spouse is not working in the community." Many people observed to me anecdotally that they were seeing a steep rise in the number of short arranged marriages between one partner born and raised in North America and another coming from overseas, an observation that is borne out by this study. One leading Islamic scholar commented:

> "When people go outside the country to find a marriage partner they often have very different expectations. Families do this to hold on to cultural traditions, but the two people are not really compatible."

A Pakistani-American man, now married to an American convert, told me that in his first, unhappy marriage, "I paid the price for doing what my parents wanted.

I did this because I grew up in Pakistan. But I tell my own kids [born in North America]—you should make your own picks [of a marriage partner]. If I don't like it, it's tough luck for me." The contrary impulse, noted by a number of respondents, is to continue with a commitment to arranged marriages because of a concern with social image. The same man quoted above put it bluntly: "They don't care for their kids as much as they care for social status in their marriage." It remains to be seen which of these two impulses will come to dominate in North American Muslim communities.

Cross-Cultural/Convert Marriages

Almost 20 percent of the sample were marriages where one partner was a convert to Islam, or where both spouses were born and raised as Muslims but were born in different parts of the Islamic world. By "cross-cultural" I am including here marriage between a man and a woman who have different countries of origin, even if they are in the same region; marriages between men and women from different regions (for example, South Asian, Middle East, North Africa); and marriages between those born into a Muslim family and converts.

I noticed that whenever I first raised the topic of rising divorce rates with imams and community leaders, their first reference was almost always to cross-cultural marriages, which are widely assumed to explain most instances of marital conflict. This may be wishful thinking. My study produced no evidence that these partnerships are inherently more conflictual than others, or necessarily less enduring and more likely to end in divorce. Three of the cross-cultural marriages in my sample had lasted for more than fifteen years. It is possible that transcontinental marriages, discussed above, which are not widely understood as "cross-cultural" within the community—indeed, they are seen as consolidating cultural ties—may contain more seeds of conflict than conventionally described "cross-cultural" marriages. Again, the outcome appears to depend ultimately on the flexibility and willingness of the individual spouses to accommodate one another, and perhaps the tolerance and support of their families.

The types of conflicts present in cross-cultural marriages are to a large extent no different than those that arise between Muslims who share the same cultural background. In common with couples who share the same cultural background, most issues for cross-cultural couples arose as a result of mismatched expectations, disputes over appropriate gender roles, and the sharing of power and authority in the relationship. However, in some of these marriages, a particular belief—held by one spouse and rejected by the other—may present an unresolvable dispute.

Najat was born in Afghanistan but was raised and educated in North America. Her husband was born and raised in Egypt. They began to argue shortly after their marriage about whether they would circumcise their children. This is customary in Egypt, but not in Najat's culture. Her husband was unyielding on this point, and Najat was shocked. For Najat, their differences on this one issue represented a chasm of deeper differences between them.

Of course, irreconcilable differences over divergent beliefs may also arise between couples of the same cultural background. One Pakistani woman described her (Pakistani) husband's desire to marry their daughters to his nephews. This woman took her daughters and left for North America.

Conflicts may also arise from different cultural norms regarding communication and tolerance for fights. One male respondent told me that his American convert wife (he was Indian) behaved in ways that were alien to him coming from another culture, including talking casually about divorce and having heated arguments. "To me it was foreign to bring up divorce, and to yell so much." Some cross-cultural marriages also encounter significant differences in the spouses' approach to religious practice. Rema—a Pakistani woman formerly married to a Saudi man—found that her husband followed the *shari'a* practiced in Saudi Arabia, which led to many conflicts between them.

> "He wants to follow the Saudi version of *shari'a* which would have me return the children to him. But I do not follow or agree with the *shari'a* of Saudi Arabia. It is not the real *shari'a*. I have my own sense of *shari'a*. . . . The Prophet did not want women to be treated unfairly. The *shari'a* is not oppressive to women. The Saudi version is a misinterpretation of the true *shari'a*."

In a few cases, a cross-cultural marriage was never approved or accepted by the family of one of the spouses. These particular partnerships seemed to be doomed from the outset. Managing family tensions around their choice of marriage partner places Muslim sons and daughters in a difficult place as they try to balance their feelings for their chosen partner with the importance they place on the support and involvement of their family. When they face problems inside the relationship, they may avoid turning to their families for advice and support, as so many Muslim couples do, for fear of their disapproval or even active efforts to end the relationship. As a result they miss out on potentially valuable resources to assist and support them. If they do turn to their families for help, they may encounter a very different set of values about staying married than if they had married a partner whom their parents had approved.

Eyaad met his (Catholic Asian-American) future spouse in high school. Eyaad told me, "We fell in love and I could not resist her. We had no choice but to be married." However, Eyaad knew that they were in for a rough ride with their families. Although his parents gave him permission to marry, he knew they were not happy. His wife's family thought he was an "Arab terrorist."

When the young couple began having problems, Eyaad went to his family for advice. "I found that my family were immediately pro-divorce—this was not the help I had hoped for or wanted!"

Marriages between a Muslim man and a convert woman manifest some unique conflicts that appear to flow from a real or perceived power imbalance. The husband may lay claim to being a "real" Muslim and uses this "advantage" to criticize his wife. There is a sense of powerlessness among some converts as a result of their shorter association with Islam; they feel that they simply cannot know as much or as well as their spouse. One convert told me that she avoided consulting with an imam about her marriage because she was concerned that she might be taken advantage of because she knew less than other Muslims about Islamic law and her own obligations. In an interesting twist, some female converts told me that they felt that they were more committed to the pure observance of their faith than their husband, because they carried no cultural baggage which might distort or obscure how they practiced their faith.

Diana's story illustrates many of these dynamics. It also hints at the fact that while some conflicts may be framed through religious or cultural differences, the conflict may be more about personal incompatibility.

Diana converted to Islam while she was a university student. She met and married her Muslim husband overseas. She then sponsored him to come to North America.

From the outset, Diana recognized that her husband—Hadad, a Syrian Sunni—came from a very different culture than her own. She knew that it would take patience and perseverance for them to be able to understand one another well enough to live together in North America. Once Hadad arrived, she quickly discovered that he had a very different idea of what it meant to be a Muslim—and in particular what it meant to be a "good Muslim wife"—than she did. Hadad asserted that as the man in the relationship, his view must prevail. Raised and educated in North America, Diana was not inclined to accept this point of view.

Hadad regarded his Arab culture as the touchstone of a "real" Islamic lifestyle. Highly observant, Diana saw herself as a part of an evolving

North American Muslim culture which is not specific to any one Islamic culture. Hadad told her that her conception of an American Islam was nonsense. He accused Diana of simply adopting Western thinking and told her, "I'm Arab and I think like a Muslim—and you're [North American] and you dress like a Muslim but you don't think like a Muslim." If Diana argued with Hadad, "He would accuse me of being a Westerner. He had no idea of a Western Muslim identity."

Hadad told her that he wanted their children to be brought up "Arab and Muslim." Diana responded that while she obviously wished to raise their children as Muslims, she could not raise them as Arab—instead she imagined that they would together raise their children as North American Muslims.

When Diana suggested that they go together to speak with their imam about these issues, Hadad refused to go, He told her, "Unlike you, I already know all about the Qur'an." At this point Diana felt that their disagreements had gone "beyond culture. . . . I felt that he wanted to change my whole personality."

Relations with In-Laws

It is traditional within Muslim cultures to maintain a strong bond between a married couple and both of their families. In some cases, this may mean sharing a home with one or the other's parents, at least for an initial period. There may be an expectation of financial assistance, either from parents to their child and spouse, or vice versa. The parents of each spouse may expect to be consulted over major decisions, and often will assume to act as role models for their son or daughter in their new family configuration. As expectations, life experiences and values change from one generation to the next, this connection may become a source of conflict rather than a source of support and strength. Worse, differences between the spouses themselves may be further accentuated by differences between the two families.

Samana Siddiqui cites conflicts with in-laws as the number-one reason that Muslim marriages fail.[33] Sometimes the relationship between mother-in-law and daughter-in-law is a particular point of tension, with each believing that they should play the dominant role in the husband's life. In some Muslim cultures the mother-in-law customarily retains significant power and authority over her son—and therefore her new daughter-in-law. In the most traditional configuration, a newly married woman is expected to submit to the will and authority of her mother-in-law on a range of matters, even in her own household (the same obeisance is not expected of the husband in relation to his wife's mother). It is not difficult to imagine the struggle over independence for the new couple that this norm can create. Typical battlegrounds are personal privacy within a shared household and decision making without parental oversight. "In a traditional marriage, the mother-in-law is one of the greatest obstacles to conjugal intimacy."[34] The couple may find they have different expectations of the continuing closeness of the mother-son relationship, as Reda (whose story is also told earlier in this chapter) discovered.

> Reda was concerned about the relationship between her mother-in-law and her husband. They seemed to regularly join forces to criticize her. They would often leave the room on family occasions and talk together behind closed doors, sometimes for hours. Her husband even gave his mother their joint savings to hide in her bedroom. When Reda tried to raise her concerns about this and other aspects of her husband's behavior, he was violent and abusive towards her. When Reda tried to raise this with her mother-in-law, she refused to discuss it with her.

Adultery and Second Wives

One in seven of the respondents described adultery or conflict over a second wife as the most significant reason for ending their marriage. The frequency with which this issue arose suggests that it may also be a common source of conflict between couples that stay married. Such conflicts are usually described from the perspective of the first wife, although in a few cases male respondents told me that their wife's unwillingness to agree to their taking a second wife was a reason for ending the marriage. It is notable that in more than half of the cases involving marital infidelity the female storyteller did not talk about a "second wife" but instead characterized the behavior as adultery, the same term that would be applied by non-Muslims with no tradition of polygamy. This frames the problem very differently than if polygamy were an accepted practice.

The classical law understands the concept of marital fidelity very differently for men and women. The Qur'an permits men to take up to four wives—who can then be sexual partners—provided that they treat them equally.[35] Women may have only one sexual partner. This legal inequality is reflected in social norms. For example, it is quite common for women to cite their husband's adultery or second marriage as a source of marital conflict, whereas the suggestion of female infidelity arises relatively infrequently. But when it does, it is toxic. Furthermore, when women become aware of an extramarital relationship, their family and community sometimes pressure them to accept or at least "keep quiet" about this behavior.

> Rehana was married at fifteen, and almost immediately her husband—nine years older than her—began to pursue other women and have affairs. At one time he was sexually involved with the best friend of their daughter.
>
> Rehana asked her husband many times to give up his relationships with other women, but he always refused. She put up with this behavior for forty years before asking for a divorce. When she finally took this step, her friends told her, "Rehana, you took it for forty years, your husband is a person of wealth and means, why could you not have taken it for longer?"
>
> Rehana went to her imam on several occasions, but he also refused to help her. Eventually she went to a lawyer and obtained a civil divorce.

Some women spend years in denial about their husband's philandering. Ambreen (whose story is told in chapter four) knew of her husband's relationship with another woman—whom he set up in a separate household, where he lived much of the time—for many years but persisted in keeping up the fiction that she was simply a "maid" her husband needed to take care of him in his other house. Ambreen's denial reflects the deep humiliation and sadness that so many of these women experience, often over many years. Their responses range from resignation and embarrassment, to resentment and anger, as the next story shows.

> When Rushkana married her husband Khalid, he told her that he was divorced from his first wife, with whom he had two children. Rushkana accepted Khalid's continuing responsibilities to his first family, but believed that he was free to marry her. She committed herself to working full time in Khalid's business. When he decided to establish a mosque and become an imam, she backed him in that project also.
>
> Six years after their marriage, she discovered that her husband had recently fathered another child with his former wife. Another year later, there was another baby. This time, Rushkana was forced to admit to herself that Khalid had been lying to her that his relationship with his first wife was over. However, he refused to talk to her about it.
>
> Rushkana hired a lawyer. When her husband still refused to discuss the matter with her, she applied for a dissolution of their marriage—only to discover that her husband had never legally divorced his first wife. Rushkana was shattered to discover that in the eyes of the law they were not legally married.

Far more common than bigamous relationships are cases where the husband has married another woman with a *nikah*, but without legally registering the marriage. For the wives left behind, of course, this is just as heartbreaking and demeaning. Two of the women whose stories were told in chapter four—Zohra and Kareema—found that their husbands had already created a new family system for themselves before they had engaged in a discussion of any marital problems or a formal separation. When Aini found herself in this situation, she was fortunate to find two imams who were prepared to strongly advise her husband against taking a second wife. The experiences of other respondents suggest that the overwhelming majority received a less sympathetic audience. The outcome, however, was the same - the intervention of the imams was to no avail.

Aini had been married for eighteen years when her husband became involved with another woman. He wanted to marry her. Aini and her husband turned to their imam for counseling.

"[The imam] talked to my husband about his behavior—he tried to straighten him out. He said it was not permitted in Islam to marry four wives simply to satisfy lust—and that taking multiple wives was just a historical matter."

However, Aini's husband continued in his determination to marry his mistress. Aini asked another imam who knew them both well to talk to him, confident that he would also try to discourage him. But once again the imam's advice had no effect. A few months later, Aini's husband married his mistress overseas.

While there has been a historical pattern of tolerance of male infidelity within many communities, Muslim women are beginning to take a firmer stand over extramarital affairs and any remaining assumptions that their husbands may always take another wife. One indication is the fact more than half the cases in which marital infidelity was an issue it was described by the first wife as adultery, rather than a dispute over a second wife, suggesting that North American Muslim women are not making the same assumptions as their own mothers and grandmothers that men are entitled to go outside their first marriage to take another partner. Some North American Muslim men share their perspective, speaking out against multiple marriages in contemporary society. There is some evidence that assumptions regarding polygamy are unraveling in Muslim countries and belong to an earlier, and different, socioeconomic structure; and that polygamy has never really been widely accepted (although it is clearly still practiced) among North American Muslims who wish to integrate into mainstream society. If these women found their views reflected by their imams—which with the exception of the story of Aini, was not the experience of most women in this study—this would offer an important opportunity for a re-examination of the place of polygamy in contemporary Muslim communities in North America. It would also increase the chances that couples would be encouraged to discuss this issue before their *nikah* and perhaps choose to include a clause clarifying the question of polygamy.

Conflicts over Religious Practice

Differences over religious practice and religiosity were the cause of marital conflict for one in four respondents, with a further 10 percent citing differences over whether they should handle their divorce using religious or American legal principles. While religious differences were rarely the only cause of incompatibility between the couple, disputes that reflected the spouses' contrasting religious beliefs and practices were common. While religious practice here may be a placeholder for other differences—personality, approaches to gender roles within marriage, or expectations of marriage generally—how the partners frame these disputes is different than in non-Muslim marriages.

Conflicts of this nature were fought over both form and substance. In some instances, one spouse held different views over the proper form of religious observance: for example, appropriate dress for women, or prayer obligations. Rema, whose story is told above, found her Saudi husband's view of *shari'a* to be completely different from her own (her family came from Syria, while Rema was born in the United States). Far more common were cases where one spouse questioned the sincerity and depth of the other's real commitment to their faith; for example, "He was more religious than me in form, but not in substance or lifestyle." A number of women complained about a double standard, where (according to the wife) her husband did not conform to Islamic principles (prayer, abstinence from drinking, extramarital affairs) but would nonetheless require or prohibit certain behaviors by his wife (for example, "modest" public dress, communication with other men at work or working outside the home at all). The women who told these stories did not consider their husbands to be religious in anything other than form, or to be making an authentic religious argument; "He was using Islam in his own way—he was manipulating and making things work for him." A few women said that they initially conformed to these demands but no longer believed them to be Islamically justified but instead a means of maintaining male privilege. An interesting and parallel conflict described by a small number of men was that their wives said that they wanted independence and equality, yet continued to insist that they had the right to be financially supported by their husband. Harith—whose story is told earlier in this chapter—felt that his wife "manipulated religious principles" by demanding both financial support and independence.

Some of these respondents also complained that what they considered to be their spouse's lack of genuine religious commitment—either in form or substance—interfered with their own spiritual development and well being. Some, like this woman, felt that "my marriage got in the way of my faith." Disputes over religious practice between Muslim couples carry powerful symbolism. As one woman put it, "It's hard to confront someone who questions whether you are a good Muslim." This admonition goes to feelings of self-worth, and can significantly undermine mutual respect. One male respondent told me that as a result of their differences—he was a formalist, his wife more spiritual and private in her faith—"I looked down on her religious practices." In some marriages between a convert and a Muslim-born spouse there was an additional layer of conflict with the latter arguing that the convert spouse had different (and implicitly less Islamic) "instincts" in their religious and lifestyle practices. For example, "He went against Islamic law because he was not raised as a Muslim, and this [system] was not part of his instincts, like [sic] it is for me." For some converts this adds to their sense of being treated as a "second-class" Muslim.

Religious issues often came to the forefront when a couple began to consider divorce. This is discussed in detail in chapter six.

Domestic Violence and Emotional Abuse

One in four of the respondents in this study described domestic violence. All these accounts of abuse came from women and represent one in three of all female respondents. This does not mean that there are no issues of violence and abuse initiated by women against male partners—simply that there were no examples of this in this study. However, one study estimates that women are ten times more likely than men to experience domestic violence.[36] Almost all these cases involved allegations of physical violence—including hitting, punching and rape. A much smaller group described emotional or verbal abuse, including instances where a husband repeatedly told his wife that he intended to unilaterally divorce her, take away their children or take another wife.[37]

For these women, continuous abuse over a sustained period of time is the most significant factor in their decision to end their marriage. They usually describe verbal abuse that escalates over time to physical violence and sometimes forced sex. Hamdi's story is typical of this pattern.

Hamdi made her own choice of husband and was supported in this by her family. She thought that Karim seemed like a decent person. Since Karim was still in school, Hamdi was the main breadwinner for the family for the first two years after they were married. When Karim finished school and found a good job, they relocated to a new city. Everything looked good for them.

Then Karim began to be verbally abusive towards her, shouting at her and calling her names. By this time Hamdi was pregnant, and she had quit her job when they relocated for Karim's new work. Hamdi said that Karim did not like the fact that she was no longer earning. The verbal abuse became worse and worse, and eventually he became physically abusive as well, hitting and kicking her.

Hamdi told Karim that she did not feel safe with him and wanted some intervention, either from their families or their imam. He responded, "No one can tell me what to do," and the violence continued. After the birth of her child, Hamdi took the baby and fled to her family's home.

Some of these women were also afraid for the safety of their children, although all the violence reported to me was directed at women and not at children, who were sometimes witnesses to verbal and physical abuse. Perhaps unsurprisingly, given the constraints placed on alcohol and drug use by Islam, violence appeared to be only occasionally related to excessive drinking or substance abuse.[38] In the general population, while there are indications of heavy alcohol and drug use among men who assault their wives, there is no clear evidence that alcohol and drug use is a causal factor in domestic violence.[39]

Abuse within marriage is "an unacknowledged epidemic"[40] in North America. The real extent of domestic violence is notoriously difficult to calculate because information is often hidden or withheld—out of shame and embarrassment—and underreported to police and other authorities. Research suggests that a woman is assaulted or beaten by her intimate partner every eighteen seconds in the United States.[41] The U.S. Federal Bureau of Investigation estimates that almost 30 percent of the 2.5 million women who are victims of an act of violence every year in the United States experience domestic violence by a spouse or boyfriend, and that male partners beat 3–4 million women every year.[42] There is no data to suggest that levels of partner abuse are higher in Muslim families than in others, although reportage is notoriously unreliable. One study conducted in Dearborn, Michigan (where a significant amount of the data for this study was collected), found between 18 and 20 percent of Muslims reporting domestic abuse.[43] A similar low-volume qualitative survey conducted by the North American Council for Muslim Women in 1993 found that 10 percent of Muslim women and children experience domestic violence (including offences against children such as incest). These comparators suggest that the experience of domestic violence among one in three of the women who participated in this study of divorce is consistent with estimates for the frequency of wife abuse within the general population.

There is just one verse in the Qur'an that relates to domestic violence, and its interpretation is a source of enduring controversy.

> "Men shall take full care of women with the bounties which God has bestowed more abundantly on the former than on the latter, and with what they may spend out of their possessions. And the righteous women are the truly devout ones, who guard the intimacy which God has [ordained to be] guarded. And as for those women whose ill-will you have reason to fear, admonish them [first]; then leave them alone in bed; then beat them; and if thereupon they pay you heed, do not seek to harm them."[44]

There is a voluminous literature debating the meaning of "beat", or "tap," or "hit," as it is sometimes translated. Some of the literature proposes that any physical assault on the wife by her husband must not leave a mark (suggesting hitting a wife with a *miswak,* a small, soft fibrous twig) and should not be on the face but on other parts of her body, an interpretation which clearly condones the act of assault.[45] Other scholars argue that the Arabic word used in the original text (from the root *"darb"*) actually means "to separate from" and that the form of admonishment is better translated as withdrawing sex.[46] This interpretation is controversial. Many other scholars argue that this single verse should be understood in the context of the frequent admonitions in the Qur'an to treat wives with kindness and respect and that the Prophet Muhammad never hit women;[47] in one instance, he is reported to have discouraged a woman from marrying a man who was notorious for beating his wives.[48] They argue that in the context of the seventh century, this verse suggests a more moderated approach to wife assault than would have been the prevailing cultural norm.

This verse continues to be called in aid to bolster an assertion that Islam condones wife beating. The underlying problem is that whatever interpretation, however ambiguous or definitive, is given to this single verse, religious dogma (from any religious tradition) can be used to justify particular actions that may or may not be a part of that religious faith, in order to maintain the power and privilege of an individual or group. The use of claimed religious proscriptions to control a partner and justify violence is especially prevalent in cultural and religious communities that historically privilege male power and authority.

> "Throughout history, religious beliefs, traditions and teachings have been used both to justify and to denounce the use of violence against women.

When religious teachings are used to justify domestic violence, they become a tool by which batterers assume and maintain power and control over their partners. . . . Some interpretations of religious texts and teachings imply that husbands have absolute authority over obedient and submissive wives."[49]

In this way religious values—or any other belief or ideology—may be called in aid to support and justify violent behaviors that are based in patriarchy and assumptions of male control. When a man hits a woman, quibbles over the interpretation of religious texts are far less important than the patriarchal belief systems that sustain male violence against women. None of the women who described domestic violence in their marriages believed that their husbands had a religious "right" to beat them, and none told me that their batterer actually quoted religious dogma in defense of his right to use violence. Nonetheless, religious issues—usually the assertion by the husband that his wife was behaving un-Islamically—often lit the fuse for abuse. Other researchers have noted that men may justify their abuse by telling their wives that she is a "bad Muslim" and hence deserves this ill treatment.[50] This is an extraordinarily potent insult, described by one researcher as "spiritual abuse."[51] "The use of [religious] teachings to justify abusive behavior and the imbalance of power within a relationship can also further contribute to the feelings of guilt and self-blame many victims experience as a result of the abuse."[52] Self-blame and negation of the self is a commonly experienced consequence of domestic violence by all women,[53] and an accusation of being a "bad Muslim woman" feeds into this.

A short time into their marriage, Maya's husband became first verbally, and then physically, abusive towards her. He berated her about her dress (which he claimed was immodest, although she was always covered and wore *hijab*) and her relationships with her male work colleagues. He told her that she was becoming "too American" and should instead become "more Pakistani." He threatened to kill her and told her how he would cut up her body.

Maya did not believe that her husband had any kind of "religious right" to assault her. However, she was estranged from her family—who had disapproved of her marriage—and having given her virginity to her husband, she felt that she had no choice but to stay with him now.

One night Maya's husband hit her so hard in the eye that he smashed her contact lens to pieces. She was in a lot of pain, but he forced her to have sex with him. He acted as if it was his right, despite the terrible injury he had just caused her. The next day, he took her to the emergency room, although she did not tell the doctors what had caused the injury. Maya cried for hours and hours after they returned home. The violence and the claims that Maya was "a bad Muslim" continued.

Like Maya, the women who described an experience of domestic violence to me saw their abuser as trading on a cultural expectation of male dominance that meant that he could rely on community tolerance of his behavior (just a few reported their spouse's fear of being reported to others). In practical terms, their anticipation of the response of other family and community members to whom they might tell their story of abuse obviously affects their decision about remaining in the marriage, or reporting the violence. What some discover when they turn to others in the community is that "the message given . . . is to be patient and accept."[54] In this way, their assessment of their best course of action is critically affected by cultural—specifically, family and community tolerance of wife abuse—rather than religious norms. In some cases, women reported that the absence of physical violence in a marriage was considered to be a positive attribute, rather than a basic expectation; one woman reported being told by her friends when she talked about her desire to end her marriage (she knew that her husband was cheating on her with other women), "But he doesn't hit you, he is a good man." Nasreen's story illustrates the difficulties some women experience in persuading their families to take their concerns over their safety seriously.

> Shortly after they were married, Nasreen's husband "threatened me and put a fist to my face." Distraught and afraid, Nasreen swallowed a bottle of sleeping pills. Her father and father-in-law took her to the hospital, where an argument broke out between them over what the couple's fight was about.
>
> On her release from the hospital, Nasreen did not want to go back to her husband—she was afraid for her safety—but her parents pressured her. Her husband's family saw her as a "whistle blower."
>
> Nasreen went back to her husband, but the fights—and her fears—continued. She turned for help to a counsellor at the hospital, whom she had met when she was admitted. "I wasn't sure when I didn't have the support of my family if this was for real or not. When I heard from my counselor, 'We have to figure out an escape route for you,' it made me feel better."
>
> The next time threats from her husband began, Nasreen called her father, and he came and took her away. Now her family took the problem seriously. Eventually Nasreen obtained a restraining order against her husband.

Patriarchy is pervasive across cultures, but in some Muslim communities it appears to take an especially rigid form.[55] This raises the critical question of whether domestic violence is differentially embedded in and supported by Islamic culture and (asserted) religious principles. Media reporting—which rarely distinguishes between religious and cultural values—frequently suggests that there is an inherent tendency to violence among Muslim men. This may be a reflection of the tendency to ascribe the actions of a minority—especially a minority widely feared and vilified—to their inherent cultural or religious beliefs where these are distinct from, and unfamiliar to, those of the mainstream. Political scientist Mahmood Mamdani points out that Muslim men who assault their wives commit the same violent acts as non-Muslim men who assault their wives; however, the framing of such events tends to attribute Muslim family violence to culture, but non-Muslim family violence to deviant behaviors. Mamdani calls this "culture talk."[56] The consequence is, "The assumption that in *our* culture [referring to non-Muslim cultures], violence is an exception so we must investigate the perpetrator's psyche or life experience, while in *their* culture [Muslim culture] violence is the norm, so what is relevant is their entire culture or religion" (italics in original).[57] The stereotype here is the triangle of "The imperiled Muslim woman, the dangerous Muslim man, and the civilized European."[58] These stereotypes are clear in reportage of wife assault in popular media. When Aasiya Hassan was brutally murdered by her husband Muzzammil in Buffalo in 2009, media coverage constantly referenced Muzzammil's Muslim heritage, the fact that the Hassans ran a Muslim television station, and the fact that Aasiya was decapitated. In the same week a white American man also murdered his wife by decapitating her, but that story never mentioned their culture or (Christian) faith.[59]

Another explanation for the association between domestic violence and Muslim families is recent reportage of incidents of so-called honor-based violence (HBV). Socially constructed notions of "honor" relate to family, social status and power; "honor" codes have appeared throughout history in all cultures and are not limited to Muslim cultures. Honor codes operate both explicitly and implicitly in communities in which they act as a means of social control, specifically male control of women. In some Muslim families "honor" is related to the sexual control of women (in particular their virginity). Although HBV is widely condemned by the Muslim community, the concept of "honor" may be used to justify violence against women and girls when they behave outside the sexual and social norms determined by men in their community—for example, dating before marriage or marrying a non-Muslim.[60] An honor code may also silence women who would otherwise report domestic violence to the police or other authorities (hospitals, shelters).[61] A focus on HBV has led to public debate over a special category of "cultural crimes," an idea dismissed by the Canadian federal government.[62] Many in the Muslim community have strenuously rejected the assumption of "honor" as a uniquely "Islamic" justification of male violence against women, pointing out that these are violent criminal acts no matter what their supposed "justification" and calling for such crimes to be treated in the same way for all perpetrators.[63]

The common cause of violence reported by women in this study was their husband's assumption of control over them, fueled by anger over alleged "wrongs" (one woman described her husband becoming violent if she "laughed too loud"; others described fights over rejected cooking, failing to keep the house sufficiently clean and tidy, and any mention of association with male colleagues at work), and not an appeal to religion or a breach of any "honor" code. These women provided ample evidence of the impact of patriarchal norms on their ability to seek help. As Zareena Grewal writes, "Culture alone does not cause violence; however the effects of violence are always cultural, as are the conditions that allow abuse to persist."[64] Many women who suffered abuse offered examples of the ways in which their husbands' behavior was tolerated—by turning a blind eye, or discouraging the wife to seek outside help—by their cultural communities. Abusers in all communities and cultures will always exploit power, acquiescence and silence. The willingness in some parts of the Muslim community to accept particular interpretations of male authority and privilege may make some Muslim women especially vulnerable to male violence. Writing about the experiences of South Asian Muslim communities in the United Kingdom, Zahira Latif notes that "the role of the family and the community is pivotal in reducing, perhaps even preventing, domestic violence."[65]

As a consequence, barriers to reporting domestic violence seem to be even more complex and acute in the Muslim community than they are for other women suffering abuse. Women frequently report advice from imams and family members to avoid contacting the authorities or involving the police. This is framed as their duty to the family and the community, in part because of the cultural significance placed on staying married. Some women spoke about their families—especially female relatives, including mothers, mothers-in-law and aunts—placing pressure on them to stay silent. Norms that discourage women from seeking help for abuse include a desire to avoid family shame and preserve "face."

> "You cannot bring in Americans to a situation like this. This would be an embarrassment to both families, the cops would not understand your culture or your traditions and it would become too Americanised. This would be 'fad-de-ha' [an embarrassment]."

An emphasis on collectivist values and harmony and a disdain for "selfish" individualism means that calling the police may be regarded as an assertion of selfish interests that is disloyal to the community—a particularly well-defended norm in a time of public hostility towards Muslims. As a result of the combination of these factors, "the system offers resistance,"[66] that is, to involving external authorities in accessing services and resources for abused women. This problem is significantly compounded by a well-documented[67] fear—heightened significantly since 9/11—of encountering hostile, discriminatory or, at best, uninformed attitudes about Islam.

The attitude of religious leaders to whom women turn for help is critical to establishing community standards regarding domestic violence and the tolerance of male violence against women. Unfortunately, imams manifest a wide spectrum of attitudes towards domestic violence and Islam and serve to exacerbate confusion and ambiguity over the teaching of Islam regarding marital violence. Some imams are clear in their condemnation—one described "zero tolerance" for domestic violence—and several work hard to raise awareness. One told me, "When I find a case of domestic violence in my community, I bring it to the light instead of keeping it hidden. Wife-beating is un-Islamic. It is critical to hold men accountable for this." However, other imams have a far more limited and less critical understanding of male violence towards their wives. Several talked about differentiating their approach depending upon the "severity" of the abuse, the "tolerance" of the wife and whether or not the abuse was "life-threatening." A number of social workers told me that most imams did not recognize the existence or the impact of emotional abuse.

Women respondents tell many different stories about the response they received from imams to whom they disclosed their victimization. A number described imams who minimized the reported assaults. The underlying theme here is that husband-on-wife violence is "normal" and "no big deal." As one imam told me with a shrug, "He raised his hand, she opened her mouth—maybe she deserved it." Women who had suffered domestic abuse over many years—including women whose husbands had convictions against them for violence or were the subject of restraining orders—reported being told to "go home and pray" to God for his guidance and help in maintaining their marriage. Some imams include advice to abused women such as trying to look more attractive, or to cook better meals for their husbands. Behind this advice was sometimes an implication that the woman who reported domestic abuse was not to be believed. One woman went to her imam after suffering years of physical abuse at the hands of her husband, attacks so violent that she had needed medical attention. Despite this, the imam did not take her seriously and sided with her husband.

"I had told the imam that among the reasons I wanted a divorce was that X had threatened to kill me. After talking with X personally, the imam called me back to say, 'This man couldn't kill a chicken.'"

Some imams actively discourage women suffering abuse from contacting or appealing for assistance to outside agencies, including police, refuges and the courts, suggesting that it is somehow "un-Islamic." Even when there is no explicit discouragement, there is a feeling of helpless passivity surrounding these imams. One imam told me, "There is a stigma to go to the court and to take their husbands to the police. . . . They [the husbands] will chastise her by the way they will treat her later on." He went on, "Some Muslims think that the police are infidels." Even among those imams who have publicly condemned domestic violence, suspicion of the authorities—presumably communicated to those who seek their advice—lingers. "Muslims have far greater trust in an imam than a lawyer or the police. . . . When the police get involved this causes more delays in reconciliation" (assuming reconciliation always to be the best outcome). Numerous social workers and related professionals in the Muslim community described to me experiences that either they, or their clients, have had with particular imams when there has been continuing pressure for reconciliation and discouragement from accessing other support agencies and resources seen as "un-Islamic" and too rights-based—even in the face of substantial evidence of prolonged domestic violence. Women face a battle not only with their violent spouse but also with their community if they report the abuse. Ruksana Ayyub, writing about the South Asian community in the United Kingdom, notes that "violence in marriage is generally condemned but when it does happen the religious community gives no clear consequences for the violent behavior. Furthermore, the religious community condemns any woman who seeks legal protection from an abusive spouse."[68]

Other imams are clear about their responsibility to involve the police in cases of abuse and routinely contact the authorities when they hear an allegation of abuse. They anticipate and explicitly counter any misapprehension that it is disloyal or "un-Islamic" to involve outside authorities. This group appears as yet to be smaller than those imams who either discourage or tacitly reject outside assistance, but there are signs that they are becoming increasingly vocal in their criticism of other imams, in some cases taking steps to lobby others to publicly condemn wife abuse. One told me bluntly: "The imams who are anti-police should ask themselves, what do I do when someone breaks into my home? The system is there, and it should be used—it may have issues, but this is the law." Some of these activist imams are working with Muslim organizations to call attention to the barriers that exist for some women in notifying the police and other agencies of their plight, arguing that a perceived or actual cultural gap between Muslim women experiencing domestic violence and the outside world exacerbates their reluctance to talk about the problem and access appropriate resources. There are a number of committed campaigners against domestic violence within the North American Muslim community. The Islamic Society of North America has recently established a Domestic Violence Forum that acknowledges "Muslim institutions and organizations that have been silent too long on the topic."[69] The Peaceful Families project, an organization of the North American Council for Muslim Women, aims to raise consciousness and empower leaders within Muslim organizations and mosques to stand up and take the risk of acknowledging and condemning domestic violence.[70] Interfaith organizations are also doing important work on raising awareness of domestic violence and encouraging women to speak out: for example, the Interfaith Domestic Violence Coalition convened by Jewish Women International and the Faith Trust Institute, which works with all religious groups to end sexual and domestic violence.

Shireene's story illustrates the complex and multiple barriers that exist for Muslim women seeking outside help to escape domestic abuse.

Shireene had suffered abuse at the hands of her husband for many years when she finally went to her imam for help. He told her, "You must be patient." The imam said her husband must come and see him himself, but he made no effort to contact him. Shireene was too afraid to tell her husband that she had spoken to the imam about her marriage.

Shireene continued to endure the abuse. She found that she could not talk to her family about her husband's violent behavior, so instead she withdrew from them. Within her community, Shireene said, it is always assumed that it is the woman who is to blame. She did not go to any other imams for help, assuming they would all have the same attitude.

After one violent incident, her husband threw her out of the house. Her Muslim neighbors told her not to call the police, telling Shireene, "You are the criminal if you call the police." But this time—finally—she did call the police. They saw the bruises on her body. The police proceeded to charge her husband, but Shireene was too afraid to give evidence against him. Because she refused to co-operate, the charges were dropped.

Couples of all faiths—and those of no faith—experience many of the causes of conflict in Muslim marriages. Nonetheless, as the data on domestic violence shows most starkly, the experience and sometimes the resolution of the conflict may be different for Muslim men and women, framed by distinctive cultural expectations about family life. Some of the stories told in this chapter reflect the struggle of traditional values about marriage and family life—which often relate only loosely to religious principles but are frequently associated with an "Islamic" way of life—to adapt to contemporary conditions. Life in the West has changed dramatically, especially for women, in the last fifty years. In Muslim families, the search for appropriate Islamic rules and norms to give certainty to roles and responsibilities in the face of dramatic social change adds a further dimension to the challenges of adaptation and transition.

Muslim communities in North America are at a critical point in their transition from their countries of origin to life in the West. The evolution of a Western Islamic identity, which reflects religious and cultural beliefs, the joint impulses of generational and societal change, as well as an emerging (and highly diverse) sense of what it means to live as a Muslim in North America, is as yet unfinished. This lack of a coalesced Muslim identity further challenges the already complex renegotiation of gender roles between husband and wife when one or both spouses seeks an "Islamic path" which balances Islam with the cultural context.

6 GETTING DIVORCED

Historically, divorce has been limited in Muslim countries by both law and social expectations. Despite the fact that Islam explicitly permits divorce, legal restrictions on women's access to divorce exist in many Muslim countries and are especially pronounced in South Asia, reflecting both the stricter jurisprudence of the Hanifi school applied in the *shari'a* courts there and an intense social stigma against divorced women. Generally, Muslim countries have a lower rate of divorce than other countries at a similar stage of development. For example, the divorce rate in India, a majority Hindu country, is three times the rate of neighboring Pakistan.[1] Many Muslim countries have gradually introduced reforms to family law that enable women as well as men to exercise their right to divorce, but the practice remains inconsistent. Throughout the Middle East, while reforms to classical Islamic family law have been slow, divorce is becoming increasingly common; one recent study estimates the divorce rate in Kuwait at over 25 percent, 38 percent in Qatar and as high as 46 percent in the UAE.[2] In Africa and North Africa, divorce appears to be relatively socially acceptable, and informal marriage and divorce systems are widely practiced.[3] Similar degrees of permissiveness and tolerance are apparent in these same cultural groups once they reach North America. The most conservative norms regarding divorce, and (in this study) examples of the most pronounced social disapproval of divorced women, are seen in South Asian communities.

Divorce appeared to carry little stigma in the Prophet's community. While the Qur'an tells Muslims that divorce is "the most hated permitted thing,"[4] there are other Quranic verses which treat divorce not only as permissible, when the spouses cannot live happily together, but also somewhat unexceptional. The process of divorce is explained in some detail in more than twenty Quranic verses. Women's rights to divorce are also acknowledged; "They [women] have rights similar to those [of men] over them in a just manner."[5] The *hadith*s of Jamilah and of Barira, both described in chapter two, suggest that, in the words of one Muslim scholar, "divorce was much more accepted at the time of the Prophet than our community remembers." As one imam put it, "Divorce . . . is as simple as not being attracted to a man. But no one follows that!" Another imam who described the Jamilah *hadith* asked me rhetorically, "So then what is the problem with divorce?" At the same time, divorce is neither welcomed nor desired; as one religious leader expressed it to me, "The door [to divorce] is not locked, but it is not wide open either. It is important not to get into a panic situation thinking that the door is locked forever."

While no recent studies exist of the rate of divorce among North American Muslims—census figures do not break down divorce along religious or cultural lines—there is a widespread belief among Muslims that divorce has substantially increased in the last twenty years. According to a 1992–2002 study conducted by Dr. Ilyas Ba-Yunus, the overall divorce rate among Muslims in North America over the previous ten years stood at 32 percent compared with a rate of 51 percent in the general population.[6] If these figures are accurate, the rate of divorce in the Muslim community remains lower than the general North American population, but it is far higher than in most Muslim countries and appears to be creeping closer to the American norm. The Ba-Yunus study is the only quantitative study of Muslim divorce in North America I could find, and the demographics of its sample are very different from those of this study, reflecting several trajectories of change. For example, Ba-Yunus found that 78 percent of women in his survey had only a high school education,[7] whereas in this study almost all the female respondents were educated to a college level or above. Although Ba-Yunus also found problems with transnational marriages,[8] he found divorce to be lowest in the youngest age group. In contrast, this study found the highest number of divorces (and shortest marriages) among younger people.

What both studies share in common is the observation that the divorce rate in the North American Muslim community is rising sharply. For many families, and especially those originating from South Asia where divorce was rare a generation ago, this is a huge change. Every imam, therapist and social worker whom I asked about the divorce rate in their communities believed that it was rising significantly. Of particular concern are divorce rates among younger people. An online survey conducted for an Islamic organization in 2009 found that one-third of the marriages which ended in divorce lasted five years or less.[9] In my study more than half the marriages that ended in divorce lasted five years or less, with 23 percent lasting less than one year. While these are both small-volume studies, the high number of short marriages may be related to particular problems with some transcontinental marriages, discussed earlier. Within the general population in the United States, the median length of a first marriage that ends in divorce is just under eight years.[10]

Deciding to Divorce

Deciding to seek a divorce is a difficult and often frightening step. Most respondents were clear about the point at which they arrived at this decision. Many wavered for some time, trying to make the marriage work. I was told repeatedly that it is an Islamic responsibility to make every possible effort to save a marriage. "I did try hard because this is an Islamic principle." For most, the decision to move towards divorce required some support from friends and family—and the willingness to ask for it. Both Fatima and Alia eventually reached a point of "no return" when their minds were made up. Their stories offer contrasting routes out of a marriage—one relying on family and Muslim friends, and the other supported by non-Muslim friends and work colleagues

> Fatima knew that she had made a mistake in marrying her husband within the first year of her marriage. Part of her distance from her husband was her feeling that he was not committed to his faith in the way that she was; she thought that he sometimes behaved in ways that she described as "un-Islamic." Bottom line, her husband was not the man she thought he was.
>
> Fatima had been raised to believe that marriage was for life, and she was embarrassed to admit to a problem. First she talked to some of her Muslim women friends and to her mother. They asked, "Is he abusing you?" Her answer was no. They also asked, "Is he taking care of you?" She acknowledged that, yes, for practical purposes he was. Her mother and friends dismissed her concerns; "You're not going to find anyone better. What's the problem?"
>
> However, Fatima became increasingly unhappy. Her husband got a new job and was away from home a lot traveling for business. His two children from a previous marriage moved in with them, and Fatima now found herself responsible for them full time.
>
> On their tenth wedding anniversary, Fatima told her husband about her unhappiness and asked for a divorce. He agreed to give her the *talaq*.
>
> The next day Fatima called her father and told him about her decision to divorce. She expected him to be angry, but he told her, "What I pray for is whatever works in your life that Allah should give you, and whatever is bad He shall remove."
>
> Fatima and her husband were divorced amicably, using a mediator to reach an agreement based on Islamic principles.

Alia struggled for eight years in an abusive marriage, with the level of violence gradually increasing. She had married in North America against the wishes of her family, who remained in Pakistan, and she did not feel she could go to them with these problems.

Alia's husband told her that she was "fat," and so she joined a tennis club. She saw this as a way to make new friends. She was socially isolated because her husband guarded her jealously.

One day at the club, she "told one of my tennis buddies about the problems in my marriage. She suggested I consider divorce. I was furious. I had always harbored a prejudicial view of divorced people. I saw choosing not to accept, cope or compromise as a personal weakness and had an attitude that a divorced person must have been unreasonable in their expectations and with their spouse. . . . I was shocked at the suggestion."

But gradually Alia became more accustomed to the idea. The abuse was getting worse. She went to see a divorce lawyer, who she also met through the tennis club. She felt exhilarated after consulting with the lawyer because she realized that she could free herself. But she was still trying to give the marriage another chance to work—and the violence continued.

Finally Alia moved out of the matrimonial home. Her boss at work helped her move. Eight months later she filed for divorce.

Combining Islamic Divorce with Civil Divorce

Fatima and Alia obtained both a civil divorce and a religious divorce. Both women felt that they needed an Islamic divorce in order to release them from their *nikah*. This allowed them to feel that they were released from their marriage vows in the eyes of God and that they had met their Islamic obligations. Just like the *nikah*, Islamic divorce is a system of private ordering, running parallel to, but outside of, the formal system of laws and courts. As such it has no legal effect. All the divorced men and women interviewed for this study who were legally married in North America (or whose overseas marriages were recognized in Canada or the United States) had also obtained, or were in the process of obtaining, a civil divorce in the courts. The only exceptions were those marriages that had not been legally registered in the first place. For these couples an Islamic divorce was sufficient because they had no legal relationship to dissolve. While individual needs varied, generally a civil divorce was considered necessary in addition to a religious divorce in order to formalize the arrangement, resolve contentious issues and secure access to formal enforcement mechanisms. Imams, who understand that North American courts do not recognize Islamic divorce, promote the practice of obtaining both a religious and a legal divorce. As one imam put it, this enables a divorced person to feel that "I have satisfied my Lord and I have satisfied the court." Some go so far as to require that a civil decree be obtained before they will approve a religious divorce.

The use of Islamic divorce as complimentary to rather than as a substitute for legal divorce for couples who are also legally married-the vast majority of marriages in this study—challenges the widespread public misconception that North American Muslims who seek a religious divorce are choosing it "over" state divorce; in fact, most Muslims understand each system to have a particular purpose and meaning. As one respondent put it, "The common law allowed me to feel practically and cognitively divorced; the Islamic process allowed me to feel spiritually divorced." However, respondents consistently described their religious divorce as the more psychologically meaningful process, enabling them to really "feel" divorced. Religious approval was especially critical for women, who otherwise felt restricted in their freedom to move forward emotionally and to consider new relationships.

Mona married her husband in Kuwait, and ten years later the family immigrated to North America. She filed for divorce in the United States after seventeen years of marriage.

Despite her lawyer's reassurances, the civil divorce did not feel like closure for Mona. She understood it as "simply legal papers to ensure that the girls [her three daughters] could be with me." Mona's friends told her that a legal divorce from a court would not be accepted as a religious divorce. Her [ex-] husband said he did not recognize this divorce, and that she was still his wife—and he told their children this. Mona turned to her parents, who lived in Egypt, for advice. They made enquiries and told her that her civil divorce would be accepted at their mosque as the equivalent of a religious divorce. But Mona still felt unsettled.

"I wanted to clear my conscience with God. This was the only way I could see the possibility of remarriage. Otherwise there would be a doubt inside me that I was still married. I wanted to be clear. I came to [North America] to start a new life and I wanted to be clear from the past."

A year later, Mona asked a Muslim arbitrator to give her a divorce. Over the next six months, she worked with the arbitrator and her husband (via e-mail and phone calls), and eventually they both signed an agreement to divorce.

"There was a doubt inside me about whether I was divorced. If I am married to someone am I committing adultery? So I had to remove this doubt."

Many respondents described a strong attachment to their right, as citizens, to access the legal institutions of the state, but they also expressed their commitment to secure religious permission for divorce. They expected to be able to use both the formal family law system and an informal religious process. None saw their participation in these parallel processes as diminishing their sense of citizenship; on the contrary, they understood their approach as an expression of both an Islamic and a citizenship identity.

Islamic Divorce as Informal Private Ordering

Islamic divorce is a classic example of a system of private ordering, with its own rules, processes and norms. Such informal systems, which are neither legally binding nor recognized by the state as legal processes, exist within families, communities and even workplaces. They set the standard for expected behavior, reward conformity to those values and punish digressions by (for example) social exclusion and shunning. Some private ordering systems are particular to a faith community, as in this case. Other examples of similar faith-based systems include the private mediation system developed by the National Conciliation and Arbitration Boards of the Ismaili Muslim Community[11] and private conflict resolution within the Mennonite church.[12]

Informal systems often operate "beneath the radar" and are frequently unknown to those outside that community. Media reporting of Islamic divorce processes in Ontario (2003–2005) and the United Kingdom (2008) set off a firestorm that resulted in part from shock and surprise among non-Muslims who had no prior knowledge of this informal system. The absence of formal recordkeeping or central standard-setting, typical for a private ordering system, also means that Muslims attending different mosques and dealing with different imams are largely uninformed about the practices of others. When I spoke at community meetings I was asked frequently about divorce practices in other cities and regions. Local variations in the practice of the imams and incremental changes—for example, the emergence of panels of imams to adjudicate on divorce—neither engage nor affect the whole system and may be largely unknown outside a particular locality. Lacking any formal, central monitoring of divorce practices, Muslim women have developed informal networks to share their personal experiences with local imams. They collect and share information about which imams are likely to be more, or less, sympathetic to a woman who seeks a divorce, and their attitudes towards domestic violence, working women and other important issues.

Private ordering systems may have as great, or an even greater, impact on the lives of those who choose to use them as those that emanate from the state-sanctioned system, especially if they represent meaningful principles and processes not available in the other system. Private informal systems depend on the commitment of those who use them—rather than the state—for their authority and legitimacy.[13] Use of the *nikah* ceremony and recourse to religious permission for divorce among Muslims reinforces their sense of shared identity and social cohesion and perpetuates continuing attachment to these processes.

Informal systems are often sustained by oral history rather than formalized as written rules or procedures, which means that there may be many different practices and understandings. The folk knowledge that emerged in interviews offers many examples. One woman related that her uncle had told her that, because her husband had not slept in her bed for three nights, she was automatically divorced. Another told me that if a woman is speaking to her husband and he turns his back on her, this provides grounds for the wife to divorce him. In a time of rapid social change, many variations can emerge, unrestricted by formal decision making or oversight. This allows for flexibility and perhaps more individualized help for those who turn to such systems; but it can also mean marked inconsistencies and unfairness.

How Informal Systems Affect Data Analysis

Although Islamic marriage and divorce in North America manifest some of the features of law—for example, these are processes that many Muslims accepted as legitimate, and reflect some basic norms which are applied to the context of each case by third parties who are widely regarded as having some authority in these matters—they have no fixed structure or procedures. While there are boilerplate *nikah*s, a Muslim wedding ceremony in North America will reflect individual and family culture, rather than a single uniform process. Even more so, the process of Islamic divorce has a few consistent features (described later), but it largely depends on who is seeking divorce and who is facilitating it. Variations exist in how the process unfolds, and there is no common, defining ritual or ceremony. In this way, Islamic divorce is a social-psychological phenomenon rooted not in a single or particular process or formally recognized outcome, but in the collective (and diverse) imaginations of those Muslim men and women for whom it is culturally and spiritually important.

This reality had important implications for fact-gathering in this study. Because Islamic divorce does not have any fixed or required characteristics, the personal accounts provided to me in interviews cannot be held up against an agreed template of what "is" or "is not" a "real" or "authentic" religious divorce. In the absence of a single recognizable procedure and set of norms, neither the facts nor the process characteristics of each case are determinative of outcome. Far more significant in relation to outcome—that is, whether divorce is agreed or permitted—is the attitude of the imam and, in some cases, the persistence of the supplicant.

No standard or widely used documentation (unlike that for the *nikah*) or central authority approving religious divorces exists. Instead, whether or not an individual obtains approval for religious divorce and release from their marriage vows is a matter of individual judgment and perception. Some respondents felt satis-fied that, having consulted with an imam and then going on to secure a civil divorce, they were divorced both legally and Islamically. Others did not feel this way, even though they may have taken exactly the same steps. In the absence of any external means of identifying a "real" Islamic divorce, I must rely here on whether the respondent believes and asserts that he or she has obtained a religious divorce. The only measurement of "evidence" for the religious divorce, whatever form it takes, is that it must be sufficient to satisfy the respondents and their families that their marriages have been dissolved in the eyes of God.

Why Is Religious Divorce Important, and to Whom?

By no means all North American Muslims seek religious approval for divorce. Just how many do is unknown. A small number—5 percent—of divorces or divorcees rejected the idea of consultation with an imam and were clear that they did not want an Islamic divorce. However, the size of this group may be skewed by the fact that the study solicited respondents who would speak about their experience of religious divorce; one would expect this figure to be higher in the general Muslim population.

What the study does show is that desire for religious divorce is both wide-spread and common among Muslims in North America. The study was able to identify many individuals for whom religious approval for divorce was very important. Each person interviewed knew of others who had sought religious divorce. The demographics of those seeking Islamic divorce are diverse, in-cluding members of the South Asian community (approximately half the sample), those whose families came originally from the Middle East (almost 30 percent), and 10 percent identified as African (primarily from North Africa and the Horn of Africa). Six percent were African American. Three percent were Caucasian converts to Islam. One-quarter of the sample was born in North America, one in four came to North America as a young child and roughly one-half as an adult, usually to study. The sample is a very highly edu-cated group, with one in two possessing a professional qualification and/or a graduate degree (75 percent of men and 41 percent of women). Almost all the remainder had a college or university degree (25 percent of men and 53 percent of women). Just three women had only a high school education (some returned to school following their divorce).

Muslims have a number of overlapping and multidimensional motivations for seeking an Islamic divorce, which are reflected in the way respondents tackled the task and the procedures they sought. For example, those who understood it as their religious obligation to obtain permission for divorce were generally more persistent in their efforts, despite innumerable setbacks, and more exacting in their needs for particular process rituals and outcomes. Those living a relatively secular lifestyle often met their needs with a more perfunctory, simple procedure, for example by the husband simply pronouncing *talaq* in a private conversation with his wife, or at the end of a civil court hearing, or obtaining a paper from the imam that they can show to their families stating that they are divorced.

Four broad motivations emerge from the data, which are very similar to those described for using a *nikah* for marriage in chapter three. For many respondents, motivations fell into more than one of these four broad categories.

Religious Obligation

For some respondents, obtaining an Islamic divorce is clearly and strongly related to meeting their religious obligations. This means that religious divorce is understood as a mandatory step, rather than as a weighing of alternatives: "It is not a matter of choice." For a Muslim who understands *shari'a* to govern every choice she or he makes, the application of Islamic principles to the ending of her or his marriage is "obvious." "Everything I do is according to what God tells us in the Qur'an. It was common sense for me to go to the imam, and I could not imagine any other way."

Individuals who are motivated by a strong sense of religious duty often go to great lengths to obtain religious approval for divorce. One male respondent who had a lengthy negotiation with his wife's family over securing religious approval told me, "I needed God's forgiveness in this." Some women spent months, even years, returning over and over to the same imam or going between different imams in order to obtain a "blessing" for their decision to divorce. I describe this second approach as "imam shopping." Some respondents had approached up to four imams in different mosques in their efforts to secure permission, and others had returned continuously to one imam over a period of up to a year. Their persistence—in the face of multiple obstacles, including unsympathetic imams and uncooperative husbands—is a confirmation of their need for religious permission for divorce.

> "It [Islamic divorce] settles . . . all the gaps. . . . They [women seeking religious divorce] have done everything that they could do in their faith, and they have something from an imam or religious scholar that says that they have done everything they could have done [to repair their marriage], and they are free and clear."

The most observant respondents want to follow what they understand as *shari'a* in as many aspects of their life as possible, including what they believe to be the correct procedure to ensure that they have a valid religious divorce. Nasreen went to extraordinary lengths to ensure that she was properly divorced and to remove any trace of ambiguity that her divorce was valid in the eyes of God.

> Nasreen's husband—who had already moved out some months earlier—left her a voice mail giving her a triple *talaq*. Nasreen regarded her marriage as a contract between herself, her husband and God, and she needed to know if this contract was broken or not. "Am I still a wife? I had to find out what the [Islamic] law says." Her conviction that her relationship with her husband was over was only a part of it. She also needed to know that they were divorced in the eyes of God.
>
> Nasreen spent several months soliciting scholarly opinions on the validity of the voice mail *talaq*. She approached local religious scholars for an opinion and also reviewed information available on the Internet. She was no longer with her husband, and in all practical respects the relationship was over—but she still needed to know that she was released from her *nikah*. Once she had established to her satisfaction that she was properly divorced according to Islamic law, she went to a lawyer and filed for a civil decree.
>
> Nasreen knew that she wanted a legal divorce because as a professional woman born and raised in North America, she wanted both the formal documentation and the protections it provided to her. But first she had to feel sure that she was divorced in the eyes of God. "If it was over I did not have to keep working on my marriage. . . . I knew that I was abiding by the laws that I believe come from God."

For Nasreen and others like her, the focus is on meeting obligations rather than seeking entitlements. This narrative understands "rights" not as access to legally protected entitlements (for example, spousal support, asset distribution, child support) but as the blessing of God and the support of one's community following a recognized religious divorce. Access to this "right" flows from the discharge of obligations, including reconciliation, family consultation and permission. As Seyyed Nasr writes, "Our rights derive from fulfilling our responsibilities towards Him [God] and obeying His will."[14] Despite the emphasis on fulfilling obligations and the difficult path to secure permission, women consistently described Islamic divorce to me as their "right."

For some women, Islamic divorce may include accepting financial outcomes that are disadvantageous to them and their children. Although many imams and couples negotiate different arrangements, classical Islamic law does not provide spousal support after the first three months of separation beyond the payment of the *mahr* and does not treat spousal assets as shared. Some women told me that they were not interested in asking for anything other than what they understood themselves to be religiously entitled to, because "God's standard of fairness is above any biased human standard of fairness." Although many women are willing to ask the court for common law remedies when they feel they are not being treated fairly by their ex-husband, the most devout commence divorce, at least, with a commitment to only Islamic outcomes. Accepting limited financial support may for some individuals be the final step in discharging their obligations, requiring some measure of self-sacrifice to enable them to be released from their *nikah*, in full satisfaction of their conscience.

The determination with which some women respondents pursued religious divorce as their "right" is striking. The primary goal of this group is to do everything necessary to satisfy God that they worked hard at their marriage, that they have now followed the correct steps to release themselves from their *nikah*. Once they are religiously divorced, they are free to consider remarriage. The focus is on taking personal responsibility for the moral order of one's life. This is internalized not as a legal compulsion but as a personal matter between the individual and God.[15]

Islamic Identity

For other respondents, Islam represents a tradition of social and community living rather than a formal set of religious obligations. One imam described this group as "the 'in-between people,' who are proud of their identity as Muslims and [want] to do this appropriately and Islamically." One way of understanding this motivation is that the connection to Islam is more significant in establishing identity for these individuals than their formal obeisance to God. A religious scholar expressed this impulse as follows:

"To retain that [Islamic] identity, it is often necessary to . . . accept the traditions, because of the need to be part of that identity space. . . . Many Muslims reject the religious commitment but retain the cultural commitments."

The "in-between people" are not traditionally religious—and would often tell me this over and over—but they definitely *feel* Muslim. Their Islamic identity offers them meaning and connection to others via both personal intimacy (for example, with a spouse) and community. It also offers them the opportunity for some autonomy within which to develop their personal values and beliefs. It feels completely natural for these individuals to integrate as a relatively secular modern family into North American culture yet to continue to practice some critical rituals, usually associated with times of crisis and personal transition. For example, they might hold a *nikah* party followed by a wedding with Western music, clothing and food. They might seek a religious divorce in addition to a civil decree "because my mother wanted me to get one," and they have a niggling feeling that they want one too.

The imams recognize that many of those who come to them for religious divorce are not traditionally observant. Their understanding is that these individuals are looking for affirmation that they have "done the right thing" Islamically. For example:

> "[When there are] life-altering things people choose to do things Islamically."
> "Even if they are secular [Muslims], they don't want to mess with sensitive family issues . . . they want to do it right."

There is also a need to satisfy one's conscience.

> "A desire for spiritual peace is universal . . . every human being is looking to satisfy their conscience."
> "[People are seeking] . . . an affirmation that they don't need to feel guilty."

This does not mean that these Muslims are "merely" cultural in their commitment to Islam, or entirely secular in their lifestyle. Each integrates his or her religious values and faith-based beliefs in a different way, and Islam plays many different roles in their lives—but it clearly plays a role. For many, it was important to describe their sense of a personal and private relationship with God, despite their acknowledgement that they were not "traditionally" religious. As one put it, "I am not religious, but I am God-fearing." This internal spirituality is at the heart of Islamic teaching—a private submission to God (a "yes" to God[16]) rather than the observance of particular religious rituals.

> "Religion is just a set of rules and regulation and practices. It can lead to spiritual enlightenment but not necessarily—in many cases it is an inhibitor. Spirituality is a person's relationship to the creative force and a person's connection to the whole universe."

This understanding of religion as a private inner spirituality is resonant of a wider trend towards faith as a personal experience rather than a publicly expressed ritual practiced with multiple others.[17] At the same time, many respondents emphasized the importance of processes like Islamic marriage and divorce to reinforce the bond among members of their community and their connection to their country of origin—retaining their distinctiveness from North American culture while at the same time finding their place within that culture. The opportunity to retain one's original cultural identity may enable fuller integration into a new one, because it allows for the actual creation of a sense of "belonging" and the evolution of a new, multicultural identity.

Many men and women who are committed to meeting both Islamic and North American cultural expectations experience these as parallel loyalties. These are not traditionally religious individuals—nor would they describe themselves as such— but they are identify strongly as Muslim. They will use the courts, but many will also seek out a private ritual that satisfies their family, their community, and themselves that they are "really" divorced. The burden for actively seeking permission falls on women because of the structure of Islamic family law. Many of these women do not conform to the stereotype of someone who is highly observant and traditional, or perhaps socially isolated and subject to family control. Highly educated, professional and often relatively secular women nonetheless feel the need to obtain religious approval for divorce. Reflecting this reality, one social worker commented, "[Many women] get caught between the imams and their ideas and the courts and their downsides. It is not simply that ignorant women go to the imams and liberated women go to the courts—the situation is much more complex than that."

Finding Closure

An important aspect of what motivates all Muslims who seek an Islamic divorce, however religious or secular they might be, is the need for closure. Closure enables individuals to accept their new, unmarried status and to move on with their lives. It may be connected to a sense of religious duty, or to a more private spiritual need; for others, it may be a psychological need for an appropriate ritual of closure.

A critical dimension of closure for Muslim women is the possibility of remarriage. In order to be free to remarry, or even to consider other relationships, many Muslim women need something that represents religious approval. Similar constraints do not apply to their husbands:

> "As a married woman, you cannot entertain other suitors. I needed to be free. . . . It is my right to be free. Men do not have to be as free, because they can marry more than one wife."

The commitment not to engage in another relationship until properly released from a previous one is faith based, not legally motivated. The same sense of constraint applies to women married by *nikah* only (and therefore legally free to marry). One young woman—who was married with a *nikah* only and therefore technically free to consider marriage—told me that even socializing with a man other than her husband felt inappropriate until she had a religious divorce, "I had coffee with a man and it felt wrong!" For this young woman and others there is a strong feeling that they are unable to move on to new relationships without obtaining approval that releases them from their *nikah* promises. Both observant and more secular women described the same need for closure. For many it was a matter of completing the circle: "If you come in by the Islamic door, you should leave by the Islamic door." Or, as another male respondent put it, "Otherwise . . . why have a *nikah*, why not just have a legal marriage?"

Some of those who did not achieve a satisfying Islamic divorce continued to feel uncomfortable about the outcome:

> "It still bothers me. I would have had more closure if I had had an Islamic divorce. The wedding was based on Islamic law. Where is Islamic law here in what happened to me?"

Others needed closure with their family or wider community of friends. "It is difficult to reach closure when you are being told, 'We don't think you are really divorced.'" A number of women were concerned that without a religious divorce, their spouse would continue to behave as if they were still married; as one woman expressed it, "In his mind, I would still be his wife." Finding closure in the acceptance of one's ex-spouse that the marriage is over was more than an abstract problem for several female respondents. In one case, a man continued harassing his wife five years after their civil divorce, insisting that they were still married.

Practical Considerations

Finally, practical reasons—self-interested rather than cultural, psychological or religious in nature—complete the explanation for why some North American Muslims seek a religious divorce. Respondents placed less emphasis on these factors—perhaps because they were not as altruistic—than the other motivations they described, but they were came up frequently in interviews. The most commonly mentioned practical considerations relate to timing and costs. In Islam the waiting period between the decision to divorce and the finalizing of the dissolution may be as short as three months (the *iddat*). In contrast, most common law jurisdictions require a period of physical separation, usually six months to one year, before a petition for divorce can be brought. Lower costs are associated with obtaining a religious divorce (the services of the imam are free in virtually all cases) followed by filing for uncontested civil divorce, a process that can often be managed without the assistance of a lawyer. Some respondents said that they hoped that an Islamic divorce facilitated by an imam would reduce the costs of hiring separate lawyers and fighting a protracted legal battle (much the same motivation that drives the growing trend of "kitchen-table" divorces[18]). Sometimes this strategy was successful; in other cases the couple argued over the consequences of divorce and ended up in court.

How Does Religious Divorce Take Place?

Media coverage of so-called Islamic arbitration suggests the imams preside over formal "court-like" hearings over divorce, including, for example, an oral hearing, the weighing of evidence and a written decision. This is a misapprehension. In the vast majority of cases, the process followed bears little or no resemblance to a formal arbitration. Instead it is a highly informal and idiosyncratic process, albeit with some common features which are described below. Instead of a courtroom, the venue is usually the imam's office or the home of one or the other spouse's family. There is no formal presentation of evidence, the parties are not legally represented, there is rarely a written agreement to arbitrate, and no record of the proceedings (other than, in some cases, a record of the outcome). The closest that an Islamic divorce as it is presently conducted in North America comes to a formalized arbitration model is when a panel of imams consults over whether to approve a divorce.[19] In these instances the deliberations adopt a paper review process rather than an oral hearing. Such panels are still relatively unusual, although they appear to be on the increase.

The vast majority of Islamic divorces in North America continue to be handled by individual imams. Each develops his own procedure and exercises his personal discretion and judgment when asked to approve a divorce. Some characteristic features emerge from the descriptions provided by the respondents.

Recourse to a Third Party

Imams oversee most religious divorces. Occasionally a religious scholar or, in a few cases, a self-styled Muslim arbitrator plays the imam's role. I came across two such arbitrators and one scholar who assisted couples in understanding Islamic law regarding divorce. Islamic law does not require a third party to preside over divorce if the spouses can mutually agree and understand the required procedure (see below). Alternately, a woman can ask her husband (or perhaps his family) for a divorce, and if he is agreeable—or, more controversially, if he is ill-treating her she may not require his formal permission—she has no need of recourse to a third party. "If a woman knows her rights she does not need the imam." However, a third party facilitated or adjudicated more than 90 percent of the religious divorces described by the respondents, and in 95 percent of those cases the third-party role was played by an individual imam or panel of imams. In the following discussion I shall generally refer to the third party as an imam.

Imams describe their role in the divorce process in a variety of different ways. Some understand themselves as adjudicators, providing an expert opinion on the correct interpretation of the Islamic law in a particular case. These imams will often ask the parties to sign a document agreeing to accept their decision before they provide it. Such an agreement is probably unenforceable since the courts would regard it as a contract with a religious purpose, but it brings a degree of gravit as to the process. In practice, conforming with a decision or the advice rendered by the imam is a matter of personal choice, but most parties accept it—they are there to take the counsel of their religious leader. Other imams say that while they will encourage the parties to reach an agreed solution—for example, when the husband agrees to the wife's request for divorce—they are ready to evaluate the proper course of action and impose a decision if no agreement is possible. When asked about their authority to render such a decision, most imams sidestepped the question by suggesting that it was not their opinion, but rather their "best reading" of God's advice—therefore the authority lies in Islamic law and *shari'a*, not with them. One told me: "This is not about taking sides but about taking the side of God." Another described his role as "articulat[ing] the Islamic position in order that the husband and wife will then decide for themselves based on this advice." Given the authoritative position of the imam and the fact that he is sought out for his expertise, it is likely that respondents will regard taking his "guidance" as obligatory.

Other imams view their role as a mediator or facilitator of a difficult discussion in a search for mutual understanding and agreement. These imams tend to devote more time to working with couples and individuals and consider marital counseling, reconciliation, and advice regarding divorce to be an important part of their vocation. Some are eager to extend their skills through formal training, as well as to empower the parties with whom they work.

> "The imam and the courts should not just listen to the people blaming one another, they should give them tools to deal with the situation."

One respondent described effective listening by the imam with whom she and her husband worked:

> "I felt very supported. I felt open enough, without fear, to say what was on my mind, no fear of being misunderstood."

Some imams will not offer assistance with divorce at all, limiting their role to marital counseling (and a few will not offer counseling either and appear uncomfortable with meeting with women alone). These imams will generally redirect an enquiry about divorce to a lawyer. There is remarkably little evidence of any organized system of cooperation between (for example) local Muslim lawyers practicing family law and the mosque, which seem to operate in quite separate spheres within the community. Referrals are only occasionally made by an imam to a specific lawyer.

Initiating the Process

Most imams agree that the wife usually approaches them alone for advice and assistance with divorce. This is the consequence of the need for the wife to seek permission for divorce, in contrast to her husband's right to divorce her unilaterally. One imam suggested that about 90 percent of his divorce cases begin in this way, and in many cases, the husband never participates. This means that many of the descriptions of the process provided by respondents are confined to the experience of the single supplicant, who is almost always the woman (there are a few cases in the sample of men who approached the imam but could not persuade their wives to come with them).

Imams take a variety of approaches to try to engage the other spouse in the process, just as they do when trying to convene reconciliation discussions. Some are more proactive than others. Sometimes the imam will manage to persuade a reluctant husband to come to a meeting, either by calling him or sending him a letter. This step in the procedure is often critical to the outcome, since some imams will refuse to approve divorce unless they have first spoken with both sides. Characteristically, initial meetings focus on the possibility of reconciliation (see chapter four).

Permission for Divorce

Many imams restrict their role in marital dissolution to agreeing to (or refusing) divorce *simpliciter*, and will not discuss any other practical consequences of divorce. Whether or not they get involved in financial and other negotiations, some imams require that a civil decree be obtained first—as one put it, "for clarity." Some respondents complain that this approach means that they do not gain the advantage of shorter waiting periods for an Islamic divorce. Other imams will issue a religious divorce without a civil decree, but in all cases imams appear to emphasize the importance of also obtaining a legal divorce, especially in relation to enforcement of any agreements.

Not all imams provide written documentation regarding religious divorce, although it appears that more and more are developing their own forms for this purpose. Some of the imams I interviewed appeared to keep no records of divorces they had approved and provided nothing in writing to the parties either. However, with the rising number of divorce requests, and mindful of the controversial nature of some of their decisions, it may become increasingly common for them to keep records, and for the parties to ask for written documentation that they can show to their families or spouse. Respondents contemplating returning to live in their country of origin were especially concerned about obtaining documentation attesting to their religious divorce to enable them to be regarded as single in those countries. In addition, some women needed evidence of a religiously approved divorce in order to acquire their own passport for travel purposes (for example, Iranian women, who when married are prohibited from traveling except with their husbands).

The Consequences of Divorce

Of the imams I interviewed, approximately half consider their role to be finished once approval for religious divorce has been agreed (or refused). They do not attempt to fashion any subsequent agreements on the practical consequences of divorce—for example, questions of child support, alimony, property division, the care and support of any children, payment of the *mahr* and so on. Some imams express discomfort with convening this discussion, preferring to send parties to a lawyer or the local family court, especially (but not only) when the matter is contentious: "I don't get into that." This imam made a point brought up by many others, that since he cannot enforce any outcomes he proposes, he would rather leave it to the courts:

> "Muslims of America cannot enforce the law. . . . In this country the only one who can enforce is someone authorized by the law of this land which would be a judge."

Many respondents described securing a religious divorce without any attendant discussion over financial or any other issues, or at most, a discussion over the payment (or not) of the *mahr*. In such cases, including those in which both parties worked together with the imam to draw up a divorce document, questions of ongoing support (alimony) and the division of property were not addressed. In some instances this is because the imam preferred that the parties take these issues to a lawyer. In a some cases, the silence of the imam on the urgent question of the future practical consequences of the divorce—especially for a woman without means, or with the care of children—appears uncaring and even negligent.

> Sandra worked through her divorce with her husband and their family members on both sides. A meeting of both families resulted in an agreement that she should keep her *mahr*, because of her husband's ill treatment of her (he was physically abusive).
>
> Sandra went to the imam after this meeting in order to get a formal authorization for the divorce. She found the imam difficult to communicate with. He did not speak good English, her first language, and she felt that he was unsympathetic towards her. "I felt like he was trying to be sure my ex's rights were taken care of, rather than seeing how awful my situation was."
>
> She asked the imam to adjudicate on the question of alimony. He told her, "You left the house; that's your problem." So she asked for financial support until the divorce was final—during the *iddat*—but the imam was not supportive on this point either. She asked the imam to help them to resolve the question of their wedding expenses a year earlier, which she had paid for. But, again, he was not interested in discussing this. He did not offer any advice on resolving these financial issues with her husband.
>
> Sandra was very critical of the way the imam played his role. "An imam should set out what my rights are—but he did not recognize them at all. He should have recognized that I deserved maintenance without me having to argue for it. . . . Justice is a huge part of Islam and this imam did not play this card well."

In contrast, other imams include discussion of some or all of the consequences of divorce as a regular part of their protocol. Some attempt to draw up a detailed understanding regarding support, children, property and other issues consequent on divorce. Occasionally a lawyer is brought in at the point that the couple is ready to draft their agreement; in other cases, the imam writes up the agreement and they both sign it. In some cases where the couple did not work with an imam, or where they only worked on the permission for divorce with the imam, they made an agreement based on Islamic principles with the assistance of a lawyer.

Such an agreement, however developed, can be submitted to a court as a consent order in an application for uncontested divorce. Despite the general prohibition on enforcing a contract with a "religious purpose," it seems that these agreements are usually approved by the family court without demur, provided they do not make explicit reference to religious principles. Some imams understand the need to ensure that the language used is sufficiently religion-neutral—for example, no references to Allah or the use of Arabic terms such as *mahr* - to ensure that the court will approve the agreement.

Imam- and Forum-Shopping

Variations in practice and outcome mean that "imam-shopping" is widespread and well known to imams, social workers and Muslims seeking divorce. "If the imam refuses, then you can go to a different imam. There are hundreds of imams . . . to choose from!" This is not so simple for women who have no means to travel beyond their local community and cannot find a sympathetic imam close at hand. Some women will go from imam to imam soliciting help and advice, eventually achieving the outcome they want—but sometimes not.

> Lina had been married less than two years and had two young children when her husband began to use drugs and became physically violent towards her. A new immigrant with no family to turn to, Lina went to the local imams for help. She told her story to four different imams, asking for permission to divorce her husband. She wanted to return with her children to live with her family in her native Lebanon but was afraid to do so without first releasing herself from her marriage.
>
> None of the imams Lina approached would give her a divorce, despite the fact that her husband had criminal convictions for drugs offenses, and that Lina had obtained a restraining order against him. Each imam told her that she needed her husband's permission to divorce, which her husband refused to give. Lina's husband told one imam that he would agree to a divorce if his wife—who had permanent residency status in the United States—first applied for a Green Card for him. This imam suggested to Lina that this would be an appropriate price for her to pay to obtain a divorce. Lina refused.
>
> When I met with her, Lina was unsure what she would do next. However, she was determined to find a way out of her marriage and certain that Islamic law allowed her to divorce. She told me, "I have my rights. [Islamic law requires] a husband must be good to me, or leave me by myself. God will defend me, not the imams."

Imam-shopping occasionally results in spouses obtaining conflicting opinions about the permissibility of divorce from different imams, sometimes from North American imams and sometimes from imams from their countries of origin, which pit the families against each other. There is also some evidence of forum-shopping, where a husband will compare opinions—usually focusing on monetary consequences—not only among different imams but also between a religious and a legal divorce by obtaining a legal opinion on the likely outcome in the courts. Unsurprisingly, many imams express distaste at this approach—"They should be trying to please God, not themselves,"; "You cannot play with Islam this way"—and some will refuse to give advice at all when they are aware that the individual is "shopping around."

Approaches to Religious Divorce: Five Narratives

While each individual experience is unique, and there are many variations in process, the respondents' descriptions of divorce—excluding the 4 percent of cases in which the parties reconciled, and another 7 percent in which the parties were still contemplating divorce but had not yet taken any concrete steps towards it—fit within one of five broad narratives.

A Dialogue Process

Closest to the spirit of descriptions of divorce in the Qur'an, some religious divorces are the result of the husband and wife working together to come up with an agreed outcome that is consistent with their Islamic values. In these cases both husband and wife accept that the marriage is over and rely on the teachings in the Qur'an that permit divorce in order to release one another from their *nikah* promises. The Qur'an exhorts men who wish to divorce using their unilateral right of *talaq* to treat their wives justly and with kindness. It contemplates a period during which the spouses will cease sexual relations and consider their joint future (the *iddat*). At this point (usually three menstruation periods to ensure that the woman is not pregnant) they may reconcile or they may part on terms that are fair and respectful.[20]

Slightly more than one-quarter—26 percent of respondents—secured a mutual agreement to divorce following dialogue and negotiation with their spouse. Not all these divorces were amicable. Often one spouse initiated the divorce discussion, with the other accepting but far from welcoming the outcome. In some cases, the parties were able to agree that they would divorce, but some unresolved issues—for example, property distribution and support—ended up before the courts. Nonetheless, these divorces are distinguished by the fact that both husband and wife participated in the decision to divorce. Some couples are careful to observe the formalities set out in the Qur'an, for example the period of the *iddat*, and they are often attentive to managing the consequences of divorce in an

Islamic way (for example, by each spouse retaining their own property and/or by paying the *mahr*). Others are content to use American or Canadian law to determine the outcome once they have reached an agreement to divorce in Islam.

Respondents who used a dialogue approach may be overrepresented in the sample. These individuals may have felt more at ease sharing their stories with me because they were easier to talk about than high-conflict experiences. They may also have achieved more closure, having worked through the process with their spouse. The very high educational demographic of the sample may also mean that many of my respondents were well informed about their duties and rights in Islamic law, giving them the means for dialogue.

The dialogue cases offer an important contemporary model for the Muslim community because they reflect many of the Qur'anic principles, while at the same time developing modern, Islamic outcomes for divorce (for example, the recognition of women's work or shared custody arrangements). Slightly more than half of these divorces had recourse to a third party, usually an imam, with the remainder completing whatever ritual they deemed necessary either by themselves or with the assistance of other family members (again suggesting a high level of knowledge). When the parties went together to an imam, they typically worked through a period of counseling (usually exploring reconciliation) before reaching an agreement on divorce. In most cases this was formally accomplished using *talaq*. The use of *talaq* in this way represents the simplest method of ending the marriage when there is acceptance on both sides, enabling both parties to take responsibility for the end of the marriage and the wife to retain her *mahr*. There is some suggestion that it may be less socially embarrassing for the divorce to be accomplished by *talaq*—*khula* may be seen as the rejection of the husband by the wife and may also usher in arguments over whether or not the wife retains her *mahr*.[21] By contrast, *talaq,* while the formal right of the husband, is the most straightforward route to ending a marriage when both parties agree (it may also be used oppressively, as described below). One woman had a clear plan in place once her husband agreed, at her request, to divorce her. "I told him to go to the mosque and talk to the imam. I said he should bring two witnesses, and then call me and give me the *talaq*. And that is what he did." The mechanism of *talaq* may also be preferred because it allows for the possibility of reconciliation up until its third and final pronouncement.

For those parties who did not use a third party to facilitate their divorce, the husband simply utters the *talaq*—"I divorce you"—and the divorce is complete (after the third pronouncement). "If a woman knows her rights she does not need the imam"; "we do not need any blessing." Some women told me that they avoided going to the imam because they did not feel comfortable with his intervention and preferred to work things out directly with their spouse. A few respondents (or their families) still sought documentation from the imam once the divorce had been agreed between them.

> Umair and his wife were in agreement that their marriage was at an end. He described their mutual decision as "intuitive and internal." They sought out an Islamic mediator, someone whom they both trusted, to help them complete their divorce.
>
> Umair and his wife observed some elements of an Islamic divorce process which were symbolic to them. These included the advice of a knowledgeable third party regarding their Islamic obligations, and the pronouncement (in Arabic) of "I divorce you."
>
> Umair explained that it was important to him to behave in accordance with both his values and his faith. For him, this meant that he and his wife should treat one another fairly, and as equals.
>
> Following their Islamic divorce, Umair and his wife submitted a divorce agreement to the court based on the law of the jurisdiction in which they lived.

Whether or not they have finalized the divorce with a third party, the couple typically works out the consequences of divorce with outside advice. This may take the form of a family discussion, consultation with an imam, or by jointly retaining a lawyer—sometimes, but not always, a Muslim lawyer. When the outcomes were agreed, couples applied Islamic principles in varying ways. In a few cases, this stage of negotiation proves more difficult, and one or more issues are taken to a court for adjudication. These issues are discussed in detail in chapter seven.

Unilateral Talaq

The most painful stories I heard were of an entirely unexpected *talaq*, when the wife is taken by surprise to be pronounced "divorced" by her husband. When *talaq* is used in this way, there is no dialogue or negotiation between the couple or an agreement to use *talaq* for divorce as the simplest approach. Instead, *talaq* is used to strip a woman of her marital status without her consent and sometimes (when the husband has already gone to the imam) without her knowledge. Many respondents—including some imams—described unilateral *talaq* as an "abuse" of "privilege." One woman whose husband used a unilateral pronouncement of *talaq* to divorce her told me that he had often used these words in anger to her during their marriage and that this was not what Islam intended. "When Muslim men abuse women with the inappropriate and unthinking use of words *talaq*, they should know better—this is not a law for their convenience—this is not a law for them to abuse. Muslim men have very limited knowledge and information about the meaning of this right and of women's rights." Nonetheless, she considered herself to be divorced having been given *talaq* three times.

In an effort to reduce unilateral divorce and the avoidance of responsibilities, many Muslim countries now require registration of an intention to pronounce *talaq* and notice to the wife.[22] Other countries require registration of all *talaqs*— for example, Iran and Malaysia—which acts as a deterrent to impulsive unilateral divorces and rules out *talaq* when the husband is intoxicated or enraged. In a few modern Islamic legal systems, such as that of Ethiopia, unilateral *talaq* has been abolished altogether. So when North American Muslim men exercise unilateral *talaq* without giving their wives notice or consulting with them, they are deploying a privilege that is no longer available to Muslim men in many Islamic countries. This provides an important context for the efforts of the imams to informally regulate and moderate this practice.

The sample contains just eight accounts (7 percent) of divorce effected by unilateral *talaq*, and half of these were overseas divorces. Drawing on what I have been told by imams and social and community workers, this figure is probably a significant underestimation of how often Muslim women in North America are dismissed by their husbands in this way, sometimes with the passive or even active support of an imam. Although two of the North American accounts of unilateral *talaq* came from men (one of whom gave his wife *talaq* in anger, but she eventually filed for divorce, and the other who gave *talaq* to his wife over the phone), I did not expect many men who had acted in this way to come forward voluntarily for an interview. Their wives may also feel that their story of rejection is too personal to share.

One young woman who shared her story with me painted a horrifying picture of the abuse of *talaq*, with, in this case, connivance by an imam.

> After thirteen years of marriage and five children, Pouran's husband left her and began to live with another woman. Pouran was called to the mosque by the imam and given a paper, signed by her husband and the imam, saying that her husband was divorcing her.
>
> Pouran had not spoken to her husband for many months, and the first she knew about a divorce was when she was handed a written paper (in Arabic). It said that her husband would pay $1,000 a month towards Pouran's *mahr* (which was $20,000) and towards payments on their home, and a further $500 a month for child support.
>
> The imam told Pouran that she must sign this paper also. When Pouran expressed shock, the imam told her, "You aren't the first one to get

a divorce and you won't be the last." He said that her husband had a right to divorce her and that the paper showed that he would make payments to Pouran and her children.

When I met Pouran several months later, she told me that no payments had been made. She had been back to the imam to complain, but he asked her, "What do you expect me to do?"

Pouran could not make payments on their home or their car. She could not afford to hire a lawyer to take her husband to court for support. "All I have is Medicaid and food stamps."

Pouran had appealed to her family for help, but they had been unable to persuade her husband to pay support. Pouran had tried to talk to him herself, but "he doesn't listen. . . . He treats me as powerless because I have no money."

Some Muslim women believe that the vast majority of imams—just like the imam in Pouran's story—are willing to promote unilateral *talaq* and are untroubled by the consequences. My interviews with imams suggested a different, more nuanced picture. None of the more than forty imams I asked about the use of *talaq* seemed entirely comfortable with its use, and most gave me complex and involved answers. The largest number felt that they had no option but to facilitate such divorces, because of the classical right to unilateral divorce: "If he is insisting on it, we have no choice." What distinguished these imams from one another was how obstructive they were prepared to be to frustrate unilateral *talaq*, or ameliorate its consequences. The most proactive of imams talk about using *talaq* only as a "last resort." Strategies to discourage *talaq* include urging a period of reflection or "cooling off"; suggesting that the wife come in for a discussion; picking up on a technicality, for example, rejecting the *talaq*'s validity if it was delivered in anger or if the wrong words were used, or even advising that there is insufficient reason to pronounce *talaq*. Only a few imams offered an explicit justification for unilateral *talaq*, arguing that the husband's financial obligation makes divorce more consequential for men than for women and in just a few instances asserting that the "more emotional" nature of women means that they should not be able to divorce their husbands without permission.

A still larger problem with the use of unilateral *talaq* is that many men proceed without coming to the imam for advice—and, perhaps, discouragement—at all. There is no requirement for third party approval, and many men know it. The only practical constraint, beyond the arguments described above, may be the requirement of witnesses. Shia jurisprudence requires *talaq* to be pronounced in the presence of two witnesses,[23] although there is no such requirement for Sunni Muslims. In the absence of Islamic courts, some Muslim men in North America regard the exercise of *talaq* to be their private and unlimited entitlement. The consequence may be abandonment, when the husband walks away from his wife and their children, sometimes immediately starting a new family, asserting that Islam affords him the right to both unilaterally determine divorce and to take another wife. At minimum, the failure to seek third party counsel about the appropriate use of *talaq* may create confusion and uncertainty, as in the case of one man who continued to sleep with his wife after giving her *talaq*. I also came across several cases where a non-Muslim lawyer was complicit in the exercise of unilateral *talaq*, telling the "divorced" wife that her husband had divorced her Islamically and advising her (inaccurately) that he owed her no further obligations.

A small number of imams go further than simply discouraging the *talaq*. "Islam hates the *talaq*. We try to prevent the *talaq*." Some are developing arguments that they believe allow them to advise men that unilateral *talaq* is no longer effective in Islamic law. The reasoning is that the Qur'an envisages dialogue and negotiation over divorce, not the imposition of the decision of one spouse on the other, and the abuse of *talaq* by some Muslim men has invalidated its use. One imam told me,

> "Originally when man's relationship with God was strong there was no harm in giving this right to the husband. But it has been abused, and now there are equal rights between husband and wife in relation to initiating divorce."

Disputes over the efficacy of unilateral *talaq*—allegedly completed overseas—are starting to appear in the domestic legal system. I interviewed four women whose husbands are contesting an application by the wife for divorce in the United States, arguing that the couple was already divorced by *talaq* in an overseas country. The husband's claim is that this prior divorce, which he argues should be recognized under the principle of comity, absolves him from further financial responsibilities towards his ex-spouse. When an alleged unilateral *talaq* is being used to reduce or even eliminate any financial responsibility on the husband's part for his wife and perhaps children as well, this is an obvious abuse. Each of the women in these four cases told a similar story of deception on the part of their spouse.

Sheeba and her husband returned to their native Pakistan for a vacation with their two young sons. When they arrived at the airport in Karachi, Sheeba's husband suggested that she and the boys spend the night at her family home, saying that he would meet her again the following morning. Sheeba noticed that he was separating their luggage; she told me that she wondered at the time why he was doing this if they were to meet again in the morning.

The next morning Sheeba did not hear from her husband. She called the hotel where he had stayed the night before, but the staff told her that he had checked out. That night a divorce paper—stating *talaq*—was delivered to her family house from the court office. Over the next few days, Sheeba was unable to locate her husband. His family would not tell her where he was.

Sheeba told me that although her husband had been acting "strangely" in the weeks before their trip to Pakistan, there had been no discussion about any problem he had with their marriage. She later learned that her husband had been moving and hiding money and assets during this time, presumably in preparation for the divorce he was planning.

Unable to persuade her husband to speak with her, Sheeba eventually returned to the United States with her sons. She found that everything had been sold—her home, her car and her possessions. Penniless and without legal status in the United States, Sheeba was helped by friends and by a refugee organization which helped her to obtain asylum.

Sheeba is now a doctor at a major hospital. Her sons are both in high school and doing well. She still feels a lack of closure over her divorce. Although her friends assure her that she is free to remarry, she does not feel the same way. As she says, the divorce was effected without her knowledge or agreement. "It's a man's world. He was using Islam in his own way—he was manipulating and making things work for him."

The incremental development of case law in this area, and other respondent experiences, are described in chapter eight.

Wife-Initiated Divorce

The most common storylines in the sample—accounting for more than one-third (36 percent) of the database—describe a divorce that is initiated by the wife, sometimes with the begrudging agreement of the husband but with no joint dialogue, negotiations or other evidence of mutuality. The proportion of wife-initiated divorces is significant, indicating that more and more Muslim women are making crucial decisions involving marriage and divorce on their own. My results are similar to those of a 2009 survey on divorce for SoundVision, an Islamic foundation, which reported an even higher percentage—64 percent—of female respondents initiating the divorce process.[24]

As outlined in chapter two, Islam allows for the release of a wife from her marriage in two ways. The most straightforward—described as *khula*—is with the consent of her husband upon payment of compensation, usually the relinquishment of any deferred *mahr* and the return of any marriage gifts. Or, in the absence of the husband's agreement, divorce can be effected by the ruling of a judicial third party. Known as *faskh*, this is normally the purview of an Islamic court but in North America is sometimes offered by imams. Because of a widely reported cultural stigma attached to a man being asked for divorce by his wife, where the possibility of *faskh* exists the husband may be more motivated to accept the inevitable and give his wife *talaq*.

Both *khula* and *faskh* are understood and applied in a variety of ways in Islamic jurisprudence. Some jurists—and some Islamic legal systems—require the husband's consent in every case for *khula*, while others argue that only some forms of *khula*—divorce because of mutual aversion, or *mubaraa*—require permission. This uncertainty is reflected in the multiple approaches towards giving *khula* adopted by North American imams. There are also debates in Islamic jurisprudence over when it is necessary for a woman asking for *khula* to return or forfeit her *mahr*. These same debates are played out in the variable practice of the imams in North America.

The five schools of Islamic jurisprudence present somewhat different grounds for *faskh*, ranging from long-term abandonment to cruelty and ill treatment. These are reflected in a number of significant variations among modern Islamic legal systems: for example, in the Philippines, *faskh* is awarded in cases of lunacy, impotence or disease;[25] in Ethiopia, for desertion, adultery, abandonment or other "serious causes."[26] Some Islamic legal systems now recognize simple incompatibility as grounds for *faskh*.[27] To add to the confusion, some systems—notably Egypt and Pakistan—describe judicial annulment as "judicial *khula*."

It is not surprising therefore that the terms *khula* and *faskh* were often understood inconsistently—interchangeably even—in interviews with imams and especially with other respondents. Only 6 percent described their divorces as annulments, although some instances of *khula* would probably be more accurately characterized as *faskh* (that is, secured without the husband's permission). When the husband is brought into discussions with the imam and, albeit reluctantly, agrees to divorce, the process looks more like *khula*. When the husband is unwilling to participate in any way, and his refusal to agree is effectively overruled by an imam, the process looks more like *faskh*. Some imams say that a husband must not "unreasonably withhold" permission for divorce from his wife, referring to Quranic verses which encourage fairness and kindness; this further blurs the distinction between *khula* and *faskh*. Because of the looseness with which these terms are used, this section analyzes all divorces requested and pushed through by the wife, whether these are described as *khula* or *faskh*.

For women seeking divorce, the most immediate practical issue is the circumstances under which an imam will agree to act without the consent of her

husband. Few North American imams are conversant with the complex jurisprudential debates over divorce, or with a single argument in any depth, which
means that the approach of an individual imam is less likely to rest on a particular interpretation of Islamic law (their knowledge is often limited to a selection
of supportive principles) and more likely to reflect their personal opinions and
underlying values about women's rights, and a woman's role in the family system.
This variation in practice is so pronounced that where a woman lives and to
whom she has access for advice is often critical to whether or not she can obtain
a religious divorce (and depending on how far afield she is able to "imam-shop").

The many different understandings of *khula* and *faskh* in Islamic law mean
that a reason can be found to deny or approve a divorce under almost any circumstances. "In practice, the concept of *khula* is wide enough to accommodate
all kinds of reasons" (my italics). Another imam told me, "If a wife wants *khula*
and doesn't want to stay with her husband then she doesn't have to." Characteristic of claims to wide-ranging personal discretion, another imam told me,
"The reasons given by the schools for allowing *khula* are guidelines only; they
are not in the Qur'an and we are not bound by them". This imam understood
this as allowing him broad discretion in considering "reasons" to dispense with
the husband's consent to divorce. A number of imams gave me a simple explanation for their openness to *khula* divorce: Islam does not force a woman to
stay with her husband against her will. As one put it, "It is better to have pain
today than to live in hell forever." The motivation of imams who adopt a wide
interpretation of the conditions necessary for *khula* or *faskh* is clear: it is "to
prevent the suffering of women." Some of these imams will take some proactive
steps to bring the husband in for a discussion. One imam told me that he routinely made three attempts to contact the woman's husband, and if he were
unsuccessful he would award an annulment. Another stipulated six months,
another one year.

At the other end of the spectrum, a minority of imams told me that they did
not see themselves as having any authority to intervene without the husband's consent. This group may be underrepresented in the sample; imams who are unwilling
to consider a role in granting divorce or who feel conflicted about it are probably
less likely to want to talk to a researcher about their practice. Some imams will take
no action if the wife cannot produce her husband for a discussion—even when he
has already abandoned the family for a new wife or is violent. Some imams simply
tell women to go home and pray, work harder at their marriage and give the problems more time to resolve. This may mean that women return over and over again
to the same imam, putting their case for divorce. Some imams will only agree to
give a religious divorce once the wife has obtained a civil decree. Willingness to
give a divorce at this stage may reflect the imam's knowledge of the *fatwa* that

states that a civil decree is equivalent to a religious divorce (see chapter eight) or may simply represent his acceptance of civil authority. Imams who are opposed to divorce regard it as a threat to the stability of the Muslim family and take an especially negative view when it is the wife who is pressing for divorce. One imam told me that a woman who asked for divorce without what he described as "good reasons" was "destroying the dream." Even when there is a general acceptance of divorce as a reality, there may be extreme reluctance to facilitate it. Such reluctance may be the result of a personal antipathy towards involvement in marriage dissolution. Again, some imams are simply more comfortable than others in substituting their own judgement for that of a violent or errant husband. Most commonly, the imam's approach will reflect the norms of his community. Some imams express a well-grounded fear of community backlash if they appear to be overly "liberal" in granting divorce against the wishes of the husband, a fear most apparent in communities with more conservative attitudes towards divorce. Even in communities that are more liberal, and with a solid body of legal scholarship on the right of women to be released from their marriage under a range of circumstances, the fear of social opprobrium affects decision makers, who depend upon influential male members of the mosque for their position and status.

Imams who are prepared to give women permission for divorce in the absence of their husband's consent must still find a rationale to support each decision. Many talk about the need to find a "good reason," not just a whimsical complaint, as well as facts that substantiate the woman's request. Just how these facts are interpreted and what information is understood to be significant reflects their underlying orientation. For example, how individual imams respond to allegations of domestic violence made by women seeking divorce will reflect (among other factors) the credibility they attach to the stories they are told, their tolerance of aggressive male behavior and their views on the rights and duties of a Muslim wife. Many imams insist that any form of abuse or violence constitutes grounds for divorce. Others appear to distinguish between "acceptable" and "unacceptable" domestic violence. One imam told me, "Domestic violence depends on [its] severity. If the husband is threatening her life, they must be separated. . . . The Qur'an teaches a system of discipline but not to leave any mark on a woman."[28] Others talk about factoring in the "tolerance and forbearance" of the individual, an attitude which assumes that a certain amount of abuse is acceptable. Some women describe imams telling them to go home and "try again," having heard their description of domestic abuse, or respond with expressions such as "I've heard worse." Behind this casual attitude lies a resistance to acknowledging any fissures in Islamic family life and a determination to maintain a myth of happy Muslim families. Other imams and arbitrators who take domestic violence seriously see this as avoiding responsibility by denying the ugly reality.

When an imam does agree to give a divorce to a woman without her husband's permission or agreement, there is still the issue of the *mahr*. Strictly speaking, *khula* requires the return of any *mahr* already paid, along with any wedding gifts; Jamilah, for example, was asked to return to her husband the orchard that he had given her as a wedding gift in order to secure a divorce. Alternately, if the *mahr* has been deferred, it will now be forfeited. Many imams understand this rule to apply only when there is no fault on the part of the husband—as in the Jamilah story— and will order a *mahr* to be paid (or retained) if the reason for the divorce is the husband's ill treatment of his wife. A number of respondents pointed out that the wife's obligation to strike a bargain is sometimes used by her husband to escape what would otherwise be his obligation to pay a deferred *mahr*. Men sometimes pressure their wives to ask for *khula* instead of pronouncing *talaq*, because that way they can demand the return of the *mahr* or refuse to pay any deferred *mahr*. Or when the husband wants to resist a divorce, he may make financial demands on his wife to return a *mahr* or other "gifts," which effectively constrain her from seeking *khula*. For the same reason some imams told me that they discouraged a large *mahr* at the time the *nikah* is signed, because it might make it more difficult for a woman to secure her release from the marriage.

Here, too, imams' practices vary widely. Consistent with the reasoning above, some told me that they would order the payment of the *mahr* when the man was "at fault" in the divorce. Other imams appear to routinely ask women to return the *mahr* whatever the circumstances of the divorce. One woman, having finally secured a civil divorce from her alcoholic husband, was told by her imam that she must forfeit her $50,000 *mahr* if he was to give her a religious divorce. Some of the proposed "bargains" look more like blackmail; take, for example, the story of Lina, related earlier in this chapter, who was told by an imam that he would give her a divorce if she agreed to her husband's demand that she first apply for a Green Card on his behalf.

Ruskshana—who went "imam-shopping"—found a range of opinions on the status of her *mahr*.

Ruskshana and her husband were unhappy from the very start of their arranged marriage. Within a short time, they were fighting constantly, and Ruskshana's husband began to be verbally abusive and to throw things at her. The couple separated, and Ruskshana filed for a civil divorce.

Ruskshana went to her mosque and talked to the imam. He told her, "I can give you *khula*—but the problem is that your *mahr* was really high, and you will have to pay this back to your husband if you are to get *khula*."

Ruskshana went to another imam whom she knew, and he gave her a different opinion. He told her that she could give some of the *mahr* back if she felt generous, but really she did not need to because her husband had treated her badly and had not maintained her for three months, forcing her to use her *mahr* for their expenses.

A third imam whom she consulted gave her the same advice, and so she adopted this course. She told me that it was important for her to get this clarified. "I wanted to keep my bases clean. If I owed him money Islamically, I would pay it—I wanted to verify that I was in the clear."

Some women told me that the issue of the *mahr* never came up in their discussions with the imam and that no effort was made to enforce this promise. For some of these women, the overwhelming priority was to secure a divorce. They told me that they were unconcerned about their *mahr*; they just wanted out of their marriage.

> "Although it was my right to do so, I had no respect left for the guy and I was not going to fight him for money. I also wanted him to be a dad for his daughter and if I went after him for money that would have been ruined."

Other women see the payment of the *mahr* as a moral issue, the fulfillment of a sacred pledge. They will continue to fight for their *mahr*, with varying degrees of success. Occasionally, these women find an ally in an imam who pressures the husband to pay them the *mahr*—but these are the exceptions. Most imams take the view that "there is only so much you can really do, except to appeal to his [the husband's] better senses and his sense of religious obligation."

Failure to Obtain a Religious Divorce

Not everyone who seeks a religious divorce will obtain one. One in five (20 percent) of those who wanted what they understood as a clear and authoritative release from their *nikah* vows did not achieve this. This number includes those who never found an imam who would give them permission to divorce, and others who did not want to involve an imam, but instead tried, without success, to engage their spouse in a mutually agreed process. The one in five figure also includes a small number of individuals who despite being advised that their civil divorce was the equivalent of religious approval according to a recent fatwa[29] could not accept this and were left feeling that they were not properly divorced in Islam.

The most frequently cited reason for failure to obtain a religious divorce was a lack of cooperation by the other spouse. For women, failure to obtain a religious divorce usually meant that they were unable to find an imam who would agree to grant them a divorce without the participation or cooperation of their husband. Without the support of an imam, they relied, unsuccessfully, on family and moral suasion to persuade their husband to agree to a religious divorce. Some women who were unable to obtain religious approval for divorce instead went directly to the court for a legally binding outcome. These women felt they had no other recourse because their husbands were unwilling to follow what they understood to be Islamic principles in negotiating their divorce.

There are two possible perspectives on the failure of these women to obtain a religious divorce. One is that it is the consequence of the imams' unwillingness to recognize women's legitimate rights to divorce, perhaps because of lack of interest or concern (the women described the imam as being "too busy," "not interested," or telling them that "this was between me and my spouse, [that] he would not get involved"), because of an unwillingness to be placed in the position of facilitating divorces, and/or the fear of a negative reaction from the husband's family or the wider community if they approved a divorce. An alternate explanation, most commonly offered by imams, is that they do not have the authority to give divorce in the absence of the husband's permission or that there is no basis in Islamic law for a divorce in a particular case.

The majority of these stories of failure to obtain religious divorce came from women, who unlike their husbands cannot act alone in pronouncing themselves to be divorced; however a few men also described how their aspiration to a mutually agreed divorce using Islamic principles was turned down by their wives. Although they could have divorced their wives unilaterally using *talaq*, some male respondents wanted their spouse to participate in a process with them and the imam.

> When David and his wife agreed to end their marriage (both had plans to remarry), David found that they had very different ideas about how to carry out their divorce. David wanted both a civil and a religious divorce. His first proposal to his wife was that they use a single lawyer to file for a legal divorce and submit a consent order based on their discussions with a knowledgeable imam or scholar; that way they could use Islamic principles to resolve any disputes. But David's wife preferred to rely on her legal rights in relation to custody and the division of property. She told David that "her only protector" was the law. The consent agreement she came up with was based on the civil law, not on Islam (for example, it referred to a period in which they "co-habited" before marriage and assumed that their assets were shared).
>
> Unhappy with these terms, David took advice from an imam and also from an Islamic scholar. His wife refused to talk to the imam with him.

She obtained another opinion from a different scholar who came to a different conclusion than the opinion David had obtained.

At the time of our interview, David had hired his own lawyer and was making a new proposal to his wife based on Islamic principles. He was resigned to the fact that they would now use the court system to negotiate their divorce, and that this would not feel like a religious divorce for him. David had taken it for granted that his wife would want to use Islamic principles in their divorce, and her resistance took him by surprise.

Some respondents continued to feel a lack of closure, even many years after their marriage was ended by civil decree, because they had not obtained religious approval for their divorce. Others felt that having made a genuine effort, and having been rebuffed either by their spouse, the imam or both, they were no longer concerned about religious permission; in fact, the experience had soured them on the idea.

Deqa wanted a religious divorce as well as a legal decree. "I thought, we got married Islamically, so let our departure from each other be Islamic and blessed." This way she would feel that she had fulfilled all her responsibilities. "Everything is clean, and as a wife my responsibility would end." However, despite obtaining an opinion that she had a right to divorce from an Islamic scholar, her husband refused to cooperate.

The relationship between Deqa and her husband deteriorated further after he refused to cooperate with a religious divorce. They began to fight over money and other assets. Eventually Deqa obtained a civil divorce. "By this time, I felt divorced. I just cannot think about an Islamic divorce any more."

No Interest in a Religious Divorce

Finally, a small group (5 percent) did not seek a religious divorce and were content to rely exclusively on the legal process. Since the study solicited the experiences of those who had sought religious divorce this number is certainly an underrepresentation of this group. Small as this group is, the reasons given by these respondents (all of whom are female) are likely to be reflected in the wider population. The dominant theme is a fear of being taken advantage of, resulting in a poor financial outcome. Some of these women did not want to go to an imam because they believed that they would not be fairly treated or would be pressured to stay married; or that the problem was beyond the skills of the imam: "This is not something that the imam could handle. It is too messy, and he doesn't want to get involved." Two of these women had distanced themselves from their faith following abusive marriages and a disillusionment with Islam; "I associate Islam with everything I suffered in that culture." Most of these women believed that if they went to an imam for divorce, they would receive only their *mahr* and no further property distribution or support. Whatever their particular views on ongoing support or property distribution, around half of the imams I interviewed would not discuss any type of property or financial settlement, preferring to leave the individual or the couple to resolve these issues themselves (usually in the courts). The experience of the respondents with divorce outcomes is discussed in detail in chapter seven.

The Future of Islamic Divorce in North America

It is clear that for some Muslim men and women it is very important to obtain a religious divorce alongside a civil decree. Those seeking religious approval are extremely diverse across a range of variables. They include individual men and women who are both traditionally observant and more secular and represent all classes and levels of education, as well as individuals who are both new to and established in North America. Religious divorce is seen as a meaningful personal and spiritual process that is sought in addition to—not as a substitute for—civil divorce. Respondents do not see any contradiction between their desire for religious divorce and their need for a civil decree to formalize their divorce (and sometimes to resolve contentious issues).

Many respondents—some of whom educated themselves in the course of their experience of seeking religious divorce—talked about women's lack of knowledge of their Islamic rights. For example, some married women are unaware that they have a right to ask for *khula* in Islamic law, and that there is at least an argument to be made in some cases that they should not forfeit their *mahr.* A number of women emphasized the importance of women approaching the imams assertively, and with a good working knowledge of their rights in Islam. However, even with this knowledge, some women fail to obtain religious permission for their divorce. Some even cautioned that the imams appeared to be less sympathetic if they presented themselves as assertive and knowledgeable, perhaps seeing them as challenging their authority and their (often limited) knowledge of Islamic law.

I asked each divorced Muslim in my study how they would advise a friend or family member who needed help with marital conflict and divorce. Their responses were as varied as their personal experiences. Several women who went to a lawyer after first speaking with an imam compared the advice they received from the lawyer—which they characterized as more practical and sympathetic—with the reaction of the imam to their situation. These experiences are in contrast to the pervasive belief among many respondents that lawyers are likely to escalate and protract conflict. Tellingly, a number of women were clear that they would not advise another woman to go to the imam if they could find a way to obtain a religious divorce without their intervention: "They [the imams] are in the same old rut, saying the same old thing—don't get divorced." Even among those who had a good experience with their imam, there was caution in recommending this course to another: "I want to be careful because there are some quacks and some fanatics out there."

The emergence of regional panels comprising imams from a number of local mosques that offer divorces to women by *faskh* or annulment is a constructive step towards a more consistent and fair process. The collective expertise of such panels is a counter to the criticism that any single imam is insufficiently knowledgeable and authoritative to give annulments of marriage. Panels also offer safety in numbers for those imams concerned about community backlash and allow individual imams who are uncomfortable giving divorces to refer individuals to another resource. Systematic recordkeeping by panels enables women's advocates, especially domestic violence activists, to scrutinize decisions and develop empirical data on which to base critique and proposals for reform. The establishment of panels could lead to more training for panel members, which could include counseling and mediation skills as well as substantive education on Islamic family law.

At present, panels are still relatively rare, and the majority of religious divorces are handled by individual imams. As an informal system of private ordering which operates without consistent rules or procedures, Islamic divorce is largely dependent upon the discretion and opinions of individual imams. This leads to a number of problems, including unequal access for women who need permission for divorce and a range of approaches to marital conflicts including, most worryingly, some significant minimizing of domestic violence. Some Muslim women do not receive the support, protection and assistance that they hope for when they approach their imam for help with these conflicts, and especially when they ask for divorce. Whether or not they receive the help they are seeking depends largely on geography—the wide variation in practice among the imams means that where you live and whom you talk to is critical to your experience. It is critical that the Muslim community address issues of unequal access, inconsistent decision making and inadequate responses to marital violence. Aside from these challenges, a persistent concern exists that allowing private ordering for divorce may result in both monetary and non-monetary outcomes that are less than fair for vulnerable individuals. What difference does the choice of Islamic divorce make to individual outcomes? The next chapter addresses this question.

7 THE CONSEQUENCES OF DIVORCE

The ending of a marriage, and transition to divorce, is a time of profound and sometimes traumatic change. There are many practical challenges: financial security, perhaps financial viability, in the face of reduced income; possible relocation; decisions about returning to work or school; and all aspects of planning for the future as a single person. Monetary challenges in particular may cause distress, adding further strain to the emotional and psychological adjustments that all divorced men and women must make. When children are involved, newly single parents must address their needs as well as their own.

Accepting the reality of divorce may take place on three different levels, each raising unique challenges. One is behavioral adjustment (acting differently; for example, living separately and receiving support). A second is emotional (feeling differently; for example, getting over the loss of a companion and beginning to think about new relationships); and a third is cognitive (thinking differently; for example, understanding oneself as a single person).[1] All three dimensions of acceptance are important in order for a divorced person to move forward confidently and tackle the transition he or she faces. Each offers a framework for exploring the consequences of divorce and their impact on the respondents.

Faith may impact each of the three dimensions. Acting differently may mean adopting a different pattern or extent of observance, perhaps joining or leaving a spiritual community. Thinking differently may require the resolution of any tensions experienced between faith—and a belief in lifelong marriage—and a decision to divorce. An individual may feel closer to God as a consequence of so much stress and hardship—or further away. Many respondents expressed a need to be at peace with God and their decision (feeling differently). A critical question for this chapter is whether Muslim men and women experience these three elements of the transition from marriage to divorce any differently than non-Muslim couples—and whether they choose or prioritize different outcomes in order to achieve closure.

Newly divorced persons often struggle to come to terms with their status and to persuade their families and communities to accept them in their newly single persona.. The stories told here describe the informal negotiations that respondents engaged in with those whose approval and support they needed in order to pull their lives back together—their family members, their children, their friends and sometimes their religious community. These negotiations always reflect the prevailing cultural norms of that group, and it is clear that some communities are far more tolerant of divorce than others. On a personal level, these narratives describe how individual men and women make sense of their experience and their disappointment about the failure of their marriage. Divorce often provokes a reevaluation of core beliefs and values and a questioning of choices made in good faith but which did not bring the happiness that was hoped for. Some respondent reflections suggest this type of reassessment, which becomes part of the process of transition and adjustment. For most people, however, managing stress and trauma takes the form of conservation and maintenance—of relationships, of emotions—rather than transformation.[2]

Muslim couples in this study adopted many different approaches to drawing on classical Islamic law to develop what they felt were just and stable financial and legal arrangements in the aftermath of divorce. These outcomes have implications for support, property division and the care of any children post-divorce. A relatively small group held fast to the Islamic model and felt compromised by any settlement that did not conform with it; for example, women may reject extended spousal support or property division if they believe that this goes beyond their entitlement in Islam which they generally understand to be limited to a deferred *mahr* and support during the three-month period of the *iddat*. Far more women and men, however, preferred a selective approach in which they incorporated some Islamic principles into their divorce outcomes by agreement but brought contentious matters to a family court for adjudication—in which case they were obliged to accept civil law outcomes (and, in most cases, had no difficulty doing so). Some imams explicitly encouraged divorcing couples to adopt the civil law framework, and some couples chose to do so. For example, while Islam has no concept of blended property following marriage, some modern Muslim couples prefer to assume that they have blended their worldly goods upon marriage, in keeping with civil law regimes which either assume joint ownership ("community property") or consider all goods acquired either individually or jointly during the marriage to be marital property and subject to some form of equalization upon divorce. Historically, Islamic law has provided for a limited period of spousal support and assumes that it is only payable in one direction—from the husband to the wife. Again, there are many examples in this chapter of couples who preferred to organize their post-divorce finances differently, sometimes closer to the equalization model that prevails in modern family law. Child support is payable in Islam, and many imams use the child support guidelines in their jurisdiction to advise on appropriate levels of payment. In a few cases shared custody of children was negotiated, despite the fact that there is no principle of joint custody in Islamic law. The extent to which couples reaching agreement followed the Islamic law, and the degree to which they used civil law principles in their negotiations, varies widely. The picture that emerges from this study is of a blend of Islamic and civil law outcomes.

Each aspect of divorce consequences affects the others. Women who face adverse social consequences may be more likely to give up their claim to payment of a deferred *mahr*, or resign themselves to a limited property division; a few others are galvanized to seek a more just outcome by the negative attitudes of their community. Some of those most emotionally affected by their divorce could not find the energy to fight for support or other financial outcomes, preferring to bring their marriage to an end and move on as quickly as possible. Other respondents, most often women with sole responsibility for young children, cannot afford to give up on support and other practical outcomes, no matter how socially or spiritually distressed they are. Many variables shape these experiences—including family and community attitudes, assumptions about gender roles and responsibility within the family system, levels of religiosity, and comfort and experience with North American institutions, including courts. Once again, the influence of the imams—especially where there is little extended family to assist—is extremely important in setting expectations and norms for divorce consequences.

This chapter analyzes the stories told by the respondents about the social, legal-financial, and spiritual consequences of their divorces. The dataset includes 104 marriages, of which 93 ended in divorce. Eleven of these divorces were adjudicated by an overseas court in a Muslim country, despite the fact that one or both parties reside primarily in North America. These divorces raise special issues and are discussed in chapter eight. This chapter concentrates on the outcomes of the eighty-two divorces that took place in North America.

Social Consequences

The cultural pressure experienced by some men and women to stay married may translate into social stigma and even exclusion once the divorce has taken place and becomes open knowledge.

> Sanzia divorced her husband by civil decree after nine years of marriage and found herself ostracized by her community. Whereas her father was very supportive of her decision, and her mother slowly came to accept it,

Sanzia's friends and acquaintances remained very critical about her decision to divorce. In an effort to appease some of this criticism, Sanzia sought a religious divorce because, "I lived in a conservative community and [without a separate religious divorce] they still regarded me as a married woman."

However, things did not improve after she had obtained a religious divorce. Sanzia found that she and her three young children were being "boycotted" by the community. "Suddenly, my children had no invitations to sleepovers or birthday parties."

Sanzia eventually moved to a new community with her children. Her reflection: "When you divorce, you do not only divorce your spouse, but also your friends."

This degree of social opprobrium is acknowledged not only by divorced men and women but also by many of the imams and social workers who work with them. Some divorces result in long-term and even permanent family rifts. Sanzia was gratified by the acceptance and support of her father and mother, despite the "cold shoulder" she received from her community. Sometimes a divorced woman finds herself isolated from her family as well, and her divorce is never spoken about openly. Such an intolerant reaction may be explained in part by the relative newness of divorce as a phenomenon in the Muslim community. One woman told me, "I was the first person in my family to divorce. I have twenty-one aunts and no one had ever got divorced before."

Sometimes the initial response of the immediate family anticipates the reaction of the wider community to news of a divorce, and may reflect and reinforce these intolerant attitudes. The public nature of a failed marriage in a community that prizes stable family relationships is a potent source of shame and loss of face that some families will go to great lengths to avoid. There is sometimes an effort to distance other family members from the assumed shame, and a concern about protecting their personal reputations against the types of aspersions cast on the "transgressor." "Community members who are aware of the 'shaming' incident must be reassured of the 'worthiness' of the family." This is sometimes accomplished by rejecting the transgressor. Similar responses to family crises can be seen in other communities (for example, young, pregnant, unmarried women who were routinely "sent away" until they had delivered their babies[3]). A divorce—like a pregnancy outside of marriage or a marriage outside of a closed religious and ethnic group—strikes at core assumptions of morality and respectability within the culture. Intolerance and even rejection may become normative and understood as a means of strengthening these moral values.

In family life, many of these moral values are underpinned by patriarchal and chauvinistic beliefs. Crossing religious and ethnic differences, there is a pervasive belief that wives are primarily responsible for making the marriage work and carry a disproportionate burden of shame when it does not. In any community where women are seen as primarily responsible for the happiness of their families—and their husbands primarily responsible for meeting the family's material needs—they are liable to be blamed in the event that their marriage ends in conflict and acrimony. This attitude was described by social workers as particularly widespread and prevalent by in the South Asian community where "There are cultural assumptions about blaming the woman for the failure of the marriage."

Divorced women are often seen as both aberrant and a danger to others who wish to keep their families together. They are stereotyped as sexual predators looking for a new husband. Women without husbands are sometimes seen as threatening. "My friends started becoming protective of their husbands; they were afraid of me!" Being single and unmarried is an undesirable status in many Muslim cultures, because of the emphasis placed on marriage as completion: "The mosque looks down on both divorced and single women." However, as this female respondent went on to explain, single women have not yet "failed" at marriage, and thus the greater stigma is reserved for divorced women. Some men express reservations about marriage with a divorced woman, assuming that they are unsuitable for remarriage. Some divorced women articulate a similar fear that they will be unable to find a new partner. "Divorced women are still seen as desperate enough to settle for any man. . . . Even well-educated people still adopt this attitude. There is a saying in my culture, 'You never ask a man whose daughter has been divorced to mediate a dispute'—that is, they are not highly regarded." This prejudice is not confined to Islamic culture; the Gospel of Matthew quotes Jesus as equating sex with a divorced woman with adultery.[4]

> Anticipating these judgments on her, Sarah wept throughout her interview. Sarah was devastated by the ending of her eight-month-old marriage. This was despite the fact that during the short time she had lived with her husband—first in Pakistan and then in North America—she had endured physical abuse and social isolation.
>
> Nonetheless, Sarah was filled with a deep sense of shame that she could not make her marriage work. Staying first in her mother's home in Pakistan, she didn't want to see anyone, describing herself as "so ashamed." She returned to North America because of her concern for her mother's social embarrassment; as long as Sarah remained in her mother's home "she had to answer for me to everyone." Sarah lived with another family member in

North America for a year before she faced the need for a divorce from her husband and began to consider the rest of her life.

Many of the women in the study expressed the same types of fears and anticipated exclusion and isolation. Over time, most were accepted and reintegrated into their families and community. For these women, their worst fears were not realized; however, "The fear of what awaits you if you get divorced actually keeps you in the relationship." A number of women talked about discovering that their decision to divorce was no longer unusual, that there were growing numbers of divorced women in their community and even at their mosque. "There are lots of women who have been through the same experience—there are lots of other divorced women in the world. And almost all of them are successful in their lives." This woman and several others also mentioned that they had received many proposals of marriage; in fact, several had remarried by the time I interviewed them. Another woman reflected on the challenge of living a fulfilled and social life after divorce: "Being happy and being divorced challenges other people's stereotypes. I don't want to be seen as a trailblazer—but I have realized . . . that it is possible to find a compassionate way through this." Significantly, while some women were still distressed to talk about the circumstances of their divorce, and feared what their future would look like, none seemed regretful about their decision. "The ending of my marriage gave me space and freedom. Like I was a canary and someone opened the gate for me." These statements are resonant of descriptions given by non-Muslims when they are released from a marital relationship that has felt oppressive and limiting.

Spiritual Consequences

I asked each divorced person to describe to me what, if any, impact their divorce had had on their faith. A small number told me that there was really no impact at all, for a variety of reasons. Some did not regard themselves as especially religious in the first place. Others felt confident that there was no tension between their faith and their decision to divorce and experienced no "cognitive dissonance" as one woman put it. She continued: "My faith and my decision ran in tandem." Others drew a clear distinction between matters of the human heart and relationship issues—and matters of faith. For example:

"I no longer blame the religious part of this for the marriage ending—it was the human relationship that went wrong."

"What hurt and harm was done to me was done by an individual, not by the religion."

Other respondents could not as easily separate their emotions about divorce from their feelings about their faith and described one of two outcomes. The overwhelming majority told me that the trials they faced in ending their marriage brought them closer to God and strengthened their faith. Typically respondents described how their faith helped them to cope with their emotional distress and uncertainty, an observation noted by researchers.[5]

> "The hardship of the separation and the loss made me pray with more awareness and gave me a higher awareness and more of a reliance on God."

Others spoke about praying for guidance and finding peace through their decision, difficult though it was.

> "It was a hard choice, but at the same time, I then felt whole religiously."

Urooj drew inspiration from the life of the Prophet.

> Urooj was married at sixteen in her home country. In the first month of her marriage she went to her parents and begged them to let her come home. Her husband was already beating her. Her parents told Urooj that she must stay with her husband. She returned to him and remained for eighteen years, despite suffering constant physical abuse.
>
> Urooj had three daughters. She went back to school in her home country and eventually became a family lawyer there. She sometimes represented women who sought divorce and saw one of her clients murdered by her ex-husband as she came out of the court with her divorce decree. Urooj could not imagine trying to divorce her husband.
>
> This changed when her husband began to arrange for their daughters to be married to his nephews. This was the final straw. Urooj decided that she could no longer stay in her marriage. She left her husband and brought her daughters with her to North America. Today she is a successful professional woman living permanently in North America.
>
> "My faith gave me the strength to make the decision to leave. I thought about how the Prophet made the decision to leave Mecca and go to Medina—he made it there as a leader. So I thought, yes, I can leave and go to [North America] and make it there."

Some respondents described a qualitative difference in the way they related to their faith after the traumatic experience of divorce, bringing them "closer to God" and to "a higher level of spirituality." Some described how they felt better able to practice their faith following their separation from a spouse for whom it was less important. Some respondents whose families were unsupportive described instead turning to God. "Every single family member was against me. It is important to be able to turn to . . . whatever it is you call God." Forgiveness was also important to some, and for this man it brought him back to his faith:

> "Doing these bad things gave me a reason to get close to God and ask his forgiveness. And I know that he has forgiven me."

A number of divorcées talked about their greater consciousness as Muslim women following their divorce. Some women felt a higher calling to work for others and for justice as a result of their own experience. Researching and understanding their Islamic rights brought them greater self-confidence and a sense of personal security. When they experienced chauvinistic attitudes, some fought back with renewed energy and knowledge.

> "For a successful woman it is especially hard to accept that they are failing in the home—society programs successful women to feel that they cannot fail [there] . . . women have internalized these cultural assumptions. . . . Women need to know their rights and also reflect on their position and roles. As a Muslim woman, I feel that my faith has given me strength and flexibility to maneuver—I have used it to survive."

A far smaller number told me that their experiences of marriage and divorce— and, in particular, the negative and unsupportive responses of their family and community—shook the tenets of their faith. While less common than those who found spiritual strength or renewal, these experiences were often life-changing. One woman talked about the day she looked in the mirror and took off her *hijab* because she was no longer willing to keep up the appearance of "a happy Muslim family." This woman eventually returned to her faith, but for Rubina her experiences in her marriage and her struggle to leave drove her away from Islam for good.

> Rubina was married at seventeen in an arranged marriage after her parents discovered that she had fallen in love with a non-Muslim boy. Her husband was a doctor and significantly older than her. The marriage was seen as a good social match, but Rubina was very unhappy. Her husband treated her badly. She told me, "I felt unloved and abused."
>
> Rubina became very depressed. She struggled on in the marriage—she had two children—but constantly sought a way out. Her family was horrified

at the idea that she might leave her husband and told her that if she did so she would be "penniless," that they would not help her.

After Rubina made two suicide attempts, her family finally accepted that she had to leave her husband and agreed to help her financially. By then, the damage was done. She has remained estranged from her South Asian culture and her faith.

"I believe in God, but I do not think of myself as a Muslim. Now I associate Islam with everything I suffered in that culture. Even [where I live] I stay away from the [South Asian] culture because they look down on you when they know you are divorced. They look at me like I am a second-class citizen."

Rubina recognized that it was cultural interpretations of Islam that had kept her imprisoned in her marriage for so many years. Many others made this point:

"Mostly Muslims who feel bad about divorce do so because other people project this onto them—it is not about their own faith connection."

But for Rubina the damage was done. She could no longer feel any sense of comfort or security with her faith.

Legal-Financial Outcomes

If it were possible to make a direct comparison of the financial (support, property division, child support, payment of the *mahr*) and legal (child custody and access, and the use of court orders to enforce and collect financial agreements) consequences of divorce between Muslim and non-Muslim couples it would provide a simple answer to the question posed at the start of this chapter—whether Muslim couples choose different divorce outcomes than non-Muslim couples. The question is important because of frequently expressed concerns about Muslim women, in particular, "doing worse" using an Islamic system for negotiating the consequences of divorce than they would using the civil law system.

However, both the question and the assumptions that underlie it are flawed, and the reality more nuanced. First, drawing supposedly objective conclusions about "better" or "worse" outcomes obscures the complexities of these decision-making processes for individuals. Money and property are by no means all that matters to divorcing couples. Some respondents were preoccupied with managing the social and spiritual outcomes of their decision to divorce, rather than asserting any particular financial or legal entitlement. Many spoke about the importance of their choice to move on with their lives, instead of continuing to fight over money, property and so on. Others saw themselves striking a bargain in which they gave up a financial claim in exchange for ending an unhappy relationship. Striking these priorities in the course of divorce negotiations is not an experience unique to Muslim couples. The subjective nature of divorce is a reminder that the evaluation of outcomes is always more complex than a mathematical formula, and will reflect both personal and cultural values.

The original question further assumes that Muslim men and women choose (or, as the concern is often articulated, are coerced into) exclusively Islamic outcomes, and that these outcomes are different in every way from civil law approaches to divorce settlements. In fact, this study shows that neither assumption is correct. While there are some important differences between Islamic and civil law approaches to post-divorce finances and other arrangements—described below—there are also a number of strong similarities. Second, the picture that emerges from data collected on the financial and legal outcomes of divorce for Muslim couples reveals relatively few arrangements that adopt exclusively (classical) Islamic outcomes. Most agreements reached between Muslim couples reflect both Islamic and civil law principles; and where the issues require adjudication, civil law principles are accepted.

The privatization of family law—moving deal-making out of the courts and into the hands of individuals and sometimes their advisers—means that in many cases both Muslim and non-Muslim couples negotiate financial and legal outcomes in the form of a "kitchen-table divorce," based on their own sense of fairness and expediency, yet "in the shadow of the law."[6] As long as there is informed consent, adults can agree financial outcomes between themselves, whether or not they meet the formal legal standard; the exception is child support, which cannot be waived by agreement. A kitchen-table agreement may be submitted to the courts and turned into a consent order. Consent orders are not usually in the public domain, but those respondents who reached agreement with their ex-spouse in this way—sometimes with the help of an imam—often shared with me the terms of that agreement.

Many of the divorced men and women in this study sought and obtained approval for their religious divorce from an imam but then brought claims for support and other issues (for example, the division of property and the custody of children) to the courts, which determined the outcome using civil law principles, not Islamic ones. Some couples negotiated their own, Islamic version of a kitchen-table agreement (sometimes with the help of an imam) which they submitted to the courts as a consent order. And when they cannot reach an agreement, Muslim couples—just like non-Muslims—turn to the court for the adjudication of any issues which they cannot resolve between themselves. The result is that whether via a consent order or an adjudicated outcome, most Muslim couples end up with financial and legal outcomes which are a blend of both Islamic and civil law principles.

Understanding the differences between the Islamic principles that Muslim couples may draw on and those applied by the courts allows us to recognize when, and how, the principles of both systems are combined in the eventual outcome of any case. Interviews with imams revealed many different interpretations of Islamic law as well as their influence on final decisions about legal and financial outcomes. Note that only approximately half of the imams appear to give specific advice on divorce consequences under Islamic law, with the remainder limiting their intervention to approving the religious divorce (or not).

Spousal Support

In contemporary North America, theories of spousal support are constantly evolving, and a full or even partial review is not possible here. When the marriage is shorter, and childless, the courts will sometimes limit support and may propose a "clean break,"[7] which aims to promote the economic self-sufficiency of each partner. In longer marriages, the courts will consider compensatory approaches— for example, compensating a stay-at-home wife for lost economic opportunities[8]—as well as ways to equalize future income between the spouses (by awarding support to the lower-earning partner).

These resolutions are very different to the model of post-divorce support in classical Islamic law. There, the responsibility of the husband to financially support his wife lasts only during the period of *iddat*, or the "waiting period" following divorce.[9] Because the original purpose of the *iddat* was to ensure that there was no pregnancy, it usually lasts for just three menstrual cycles. This limit on post-divorce financial obligations on the husband's part reflects the structure of family systems in the seventh-century economy. "The husband originally was given the most rights because he also had the greater responsibilities—for example, taking care of his wife's parents and his wife's sisters." Some scholars continue to argue for this approach: "By discontinuing maintenance after the *iddat* period for the divorcee ... Islam has, in fact, rendered a great favor on her freeing her permanently ... from economic dependence on her ex-husband."[10] Many women would strongly disagree with this perspective, but some of the imams hold to the traditional view and continue to assert that the limited obligation to pay support to an ex-wife must be understood "in the context of a larger family picture—the man carries responsibility for tuition fees [i.e., child support], for the paternal grandparents, and for the payment of the *mahr*."

Aside from the *iddat* period, the major element of post-divorce support in a classical Islamic model is the payment of a deferred *mahr*, as promised in the *nikah.* Some scholars suggest that payment of a deferred *mahr* could substitute for a lump-sum payment, similar to that sometimes awarded by the courts (especially in shorter marriages without children when the court is looking for a "clean break"). "The *sadaq* [or *mahr*] offers the woman a clearly defined property or amount of money she could rely upon after the divorce, without the need for further negotiations."[11] While this is the intention, securing payment of a deferred *mahr* in contemporary North America is far from straightforward or automatic. In this study slightly lessthan half of the divorced women to whom a deferred *mahr* was promised received it in part or in full at the time of the divorce, or (in the case of longer marriages) received court-ordered support that they understood as a substitute for the *mahr*. As the previous chapter described, some imams advise women that they have to forego their claim to *mahr* if they initiate the divorce. The courts continue to hesitate to enforce this promise as part of a prenuptial contract, a fact that appears to be widely known among husbands who want to avoid payment. Without the backing of either the imam or the courts, the *mahr* often goes unpaid. Some women told me that they could not face the fight—with their husband, with his family or with the court—of asking for their *mahr*. A further problem with understanding the *mahr* as commensurable with a court-ordered support payment is that sometimes the *mahr*—which is described in the marriage contract—has a minimal or insignificant value (different cultural practices exist), and it is never adjusted for inflation, so by the time of a divorce it may no longer reflect a fair and realistic amount for the wife.

The lack of formal recognition given to the *mahr* leads to a further difficulty: how to fairly combine it with a court-ordered payment. It would be possible to assess a paid *mahr* as a "set-off," which can be deducted from further support, either ordered or agreed (or even factored into a property division, if the *mahr* is treated as an element of marital property). I came across just one family court judge, herself a Muslim, who told me that she regularly deducts a paid-up *mahr* from the total of any spousal support she orders. Sometimes the husband will ask her for a copy of the court-agreed property settlement in order to show this to his imam to "offset" the *mahr*. There is no authority in law for this approach, and this judge was clear that this is her personal and idiosyncratic approach.

Some imams are clear that the classical view on spousal support is simply outdated. "Islamic family law is based on assumptions that do not exist here in North America—for example the notion that if a man and woman get divorced, her family—her male relatives—would take care of her, so that she is not on the street. But as immigrants and first-generation Muslims we often do not have a clan, or family networks here." Aware that the traditional principles no longer reflect the economic and social reality of the place of women in the family and the workplace—"these principles are now challenged constantly in

Muslim communities"—many imams are searching for more appropriate alternatives. Some argue that in the event of divorce the husband can be required to compensate his wife for years of housework and child care. While this is not a widely recognized or practiced principle, some imams use it as additional leverage to pressure a husband whom they felt should be more generous in his financial provision for his ex-wife. Other imams will justify pressing for extended spousal support with the many admonitions in the Qur'an to the husband to be kind and generous to their wives in the event of divorce.[12]

Some imams and scholars argue that the obligation to pay the *mahr* combined with an expanded notion of spousal support mean that "Islamic family law principles come very close to the same result as [civil] law on dividing the assets. This is achieved by . . . giving back to the woman the value of the work they put into the household, or the money [earnings] they put into the household during the marriage." This statement may be true given particular conditions, for example, a large and fully paid *mahr*, an agreement to compensate a stay-at-home wife for housework and child care, or when reimbursement of earnings throughout the marriage (for example, selling the matrimonial home or dividing savings) works out at an approximate equalization of assets between the couple. These conditions are rarely realized in practice.

However this argument may be academic since many of the divorces in the study did not adhere to the strict Islamic law on financial consequences. A number of imams and divorced people described agreements to me that included spousal support paid by the husband beyond the *iddat*—sometimes over a limited period of time, or provided as payment of rent, or for school, and voluntarily assumed as a moral obligation. An important factor in making such an agreement is the knowledge that in the event of a dispute the courts can order payment, and that most states and provinces require a measure of income equalization after divorce. Problematic for some Muslim men and women is the idea that spousal support should flow in both directions, that is, from wife to husband when she is the more financially comfortable and secure party. Most men and women told me that they were obliged to obey the law of the land and had no difficulty accepting court orders—in either direction—when they could not reach an agreement. A very few were offended by the contradiction they saw between their religious rights and obligations and the court's order. Such a position appears to be self-serving for women, but here it is cast —by a professional woman who was ordered by the court to pay support to her ex-husband—as a violation of religious and personal norms.

> "I tried to tell the judge that it was not acceptable for me to pay spousal support in Islam, but he didn't listen—he did not care about Islam."

A number of younger women were comfortable with taking some responsibility for financial support (of both their children and their ex-spouse) after divorce because they were the primary breadwinners. It is clear from Islamic jurisprudence—and reinforced by the comments of many imams—that a wife may voluntarily assume support, using the same principle of consensual variation that allows for the development of original contractual clauses in a *nikah*. As two younger and well-educated imams put it to me, "Whether or not this is Qur'anic, this is Islamic." Another described the Islamic principle as follows:

"If she is poor, he spends on her—if he is poor then she spends on him."

But in practice "Many Muslims will resist any changes to this [classical Islamic] paradigm." Even when the wife is the primary breadwinner, some couples struggle with transferring financial responsibility after divorce from the husband to the wife, or assuming a shared responsibility. Umbrime's story, also referred to in chapter three, is an example of an effort to present an acceptable compromise to the community.

Umbrime was her family's primary breadwinner when she and her husband agreed to divorce. Her husband was suffering from a mental illness and was unable to work regularly. As a professional working wife, Umbrime was advised that the court would likely order her to pay spousal support to her husband.

She and her parents turned to their imam for a solution. He proposed that her parents pay their charitable contribution (*zagat*) for the year directly to their daughter's ex-husband. This amount would be approximate to the annual support that their daughter would be required to pay by the court, minus the amount of the *mahr* that her husband owed her. This solution "saved him from the shame of receiving such a payment from his ex-wife."

A number of imams to whom I recounted this story told me that they felt that such a solution was unnecessary because a woman may voluntarily agree to support her husband. They understood the arrangement to be necessary to satisfy cultural misgivings, not religious or legal principles. Moreover, some of those I asked to comment on Umbrime's story regretted that this type of problem solving reinforces the impression that Islam is opposed to fairness between the spouses: "A commitment to what is seen as tradition [in this case] is in fact abusing the image of Islam."

Property Division

Another critical difference between Islamic family law and family law as it is applied by the courts in the United States and Canada relates to matrimonial property. In Islam, spouses retain their own property when they marry. In some jurisdictions (including Canada and nine U.S. states), the financial resources and assets of both partners are treated as merged at the time of marriage (described as "community property"), although specified items may be excluded. In others, property acquired during a marriage either individually or jointly is considered to be marital property and will usually be equalized upon divorce.

Again, the historical context is important in understanding the origins of the Islamic rule. In seventh-century Arabia, the Islamic law was seen as a means of giving women financial independence from their husbands by overcoming the pre-Islamic (and post-Christian) assumption that both she and her goods became the property of her husband upon marriage. The concept of equalization of marital property in the civil law system protects women who do not have independent earnings and/or assets, for example, women who have stayed home to raise children while their husbands progressed a career. In contrast, the separate property regime of Islamic law is advantageous (especially when combined with the limits on spousal support in the classical law) for women who have their own income and/or property, but extremely disadvantageous to women without personal property or income.

The contrast between the Islamic and the civil law approach to matrimonial property and its division means that some women do better under one system, and some under the other, depending on their individual circumstances. Women who are independent earners and/or have significant independent property and assets do better in Islamic law because they will retain 100 percent of what they brought into the marriage. On the other hand, women who do not have independent earnings and/or property are rendered dependent upon the voluntary support of their husbands. Such women will do better financially in the civil law system (assuming that they can enforce any court orders). Despite the high levels of education of many women in the study, a significant number did not work outside the home during the years that they were raising children and some only returned to school after their children had left home. Aside from issues of fairness, these women often needed to share in property resources in order to support their family following divorce.

In practice, many modern Muslim couples have an expectation of sharing assets and resources both during their marriage and if they come to resolve the financial consequences of divorce. This arrangement may be formally incorporated in their *nikah*, or more commonly simply an understanding between them. A number of respondents told me that because they had been born and raised in North America it was natural for them to assume the principle of community property. In practice, many of those in shorter marriages have little or no shared property that needed dividing in any case. The advice that imams give divorcing couples on this issue is, as usual, divergent. Some will encourage couples to divide their property according to civil law principles, if it fits their personal circumstances. There is limitless potential for flexibility in such arrangements within Islam. One such imam described his approach this way:

> "To me, it is obvious that in a committed marriage the husband and wife would pool their resources. But this is not required of them Islamically."

Other imams do not discuss property division with divorcing couples at all, and if it comes up, refer them to a lawyer. In this respect as in many others, communication between imams and family lawyers is at best minimal and often nonexistent: "It's like the right arm is not connected to the left arm."

Support, Care and Custody of Children

Financial support of children of a marriage until they reach adulthood is a clear responsibility in Islamic law, just as it is in civil law. Following the same pattern as spousal support, historically this obligation has only been applied to the father. Again, a mother may voluntarily assume responsibility for child support, just as she can for spousal support. The obligation only attaches to biological offspring, whereas in Canada and the United States support may be extended to "children of the family."[13]

Some imams encourage couples to agree child support using the child support guidelines applied in their jurisdiction (a number of imams kept this document in their desk drawer and pulled it out to show me during an interview). Others are far less proactive, and some never broach the issue of child support— or any other financial consequences of divorce—leaving the parties to negotiate between themselves or seek recourse to the courts. Even if they do little to facilitate this, there is a widespread assumption among the imams that child support is payable either voluntarily or by court order.

In contrast to the similarities between Islamic law and civil law in relation to the basic obligation to support children, at first glance there are dramatic differences between each system in relation to the custody of minor children. Family courts in the United States and Canada apply a universal—albeit highly subjective—standard for determining contested custody: "the best interests of the child."[14] State legislatures in the United States and the federal government in Canada delineate relevant factors including the health and safety of the child; preserving the status quo; emotional ties; and the mental and physical health of the child.[15] In many jurisdictions, joint or shared custody is a default position to ensure that children maintain relationships with both parents.[16] In civil law, custody has historically been awarded to the mother in the event of a dispute. This pattern has changed and the outcomes of contested cases are now approximately 50/50.[17] In contrast, classical Islamic law assumes that custody lies with the father once the child has reached a certain age (different for boys and for girls, similar to an earlier civil law standard), although a variety of arrangements may be made for the care of the child. Generally fathers have formal custody of their sons from around the age of seven, while girls stay with their mothers until they are teenagers or, sometimes, until they are married.[18] Remarriage by the mother impacts custody; classical Islamic law states that girls cannot be raised by their stepfathers. Remarriage by the father does not affect custody.

Over the four years of the study and among the eighty-two cases I examined in which divorce took place in North America I found just one case in which a child was removed from a mother against her will and given to the father. To my surprise, this one exception was not the result of an imam applying classical Islamic law but an order made by a North American court removing custody from a very young postpartum mother, following an agreement that she made with her husband's family.

Bita (whose story is also referred to in chapter three) met her husband while she was a high school student, and they were married in a *nikah* before she had graduated. Bita realized her mistake almost immediately— her husband was emotionally abusive—but found that she was pregnant. She turned to her family who helped her complete high school and stay healthy.

While she was pregnant, her husband continually told her that Islamic law would give custody of the child to him. Her parents suggested that it would be better for the child if Bita allowed her husband's family to raise him or her; they could not help her raise the child herself. Before her baby was born, Bita agreed to give up custody of the baby to her husband's family.

Three weeks after the baby was born, Bita attended a court hearing about custody to formalize the agreement. "My husband was afraid that I would change my mind about giving up my baby. But I was still in shock from the birth." Bita told me that she was on the stand for "one minute." Her husband told the court that they were not legally married (they had a *nikah* only). Bita does not remember being represented by counsel and had no one to negotiate on her behalf. The court approved the agreement and gave sole custody of their child to her husband, with access one day a week awarded to Bita.

At the time of our interview, Bita's son had just turned nine years old. He is well adjusted to his family. Bita has only ever had weekly access to him, despite asking her husband many times to allow her more time with her son. Instead, he always told her to get a lawyer and fight it out in court. Bita's past experience meant that she could never face doing that.

Bita is now a research scientist at a major North American university. She is still haunted by her experience.

I also interviewed four women who had lost custody of their children under Islamic law, but all four were orders made by courts in Muslim countries overseas.

When I questioned the imams about how they advised parents on custody, they were all adamant that they emphasized the "best interests" principle, which they saw as consistent with Islamic values of flexibility, responsiveness to context and fairness (this is the standard now applied by the courts in some Islamic countries).[19] Each played down the importance of the classical law and instead emphasized contemporary cultural values about raising children. I probed each imam further on this point, asking for example how they managed the potential separation of siblings at differing ages under Islamic law. (There is a presumption against separating siblings in the United States and in Canada that is taken into account in assessing "best interests."[20]) The imams told me that they would not separate siblings unless it met the "best interests" standard. Since this standard is highly subjective, it is possible, likely even, that some apply considerations (for example, levels of observance or the presence of desired role models) that would not be considered relevant by the courts. Of course, family court judges may also apply subjective values to the interpretation of "best interests." Moreover, many imams described criteria that appear similar to those applied by the courts, for example:

"In order to try to find out what is in the child's best interests, I would . . . consider what type of person these individuals are. If the child is old enough, I would try to speak to the child—they may be young and inno- cent but they are also the most honest."

"In Islam they say that the kids should stay with mom until they are seven, but I think it is different for every case. Islam is fair, and we have to look at the whole situation too."

"What do I do if a father demands his son at age seven? Well, he must have developed a relationship to do this. It's usually done only to get back at the wife. If I see this is happening, I shall make a decision in the best interests of the child."

This last imam recommends joint custody, despite the fact that there is no such concept in Islamic law.

"Children need both parents, unless one is in prison or in a serious situation. I always recommend joint custody to the court."

A number of imams talked about consulting the child, also in keeping with contemporary practice in family courts in North America.

In common with the classical principles of spousal support and property division, Islamic law regarding child custody is a product of a particular historical period with its attendant social assumptions, one of which is that children would be raised by female relatives—if not a mother, then by aunts or grandmothers. There is widespread consensus among the imams that in the absence of an extended female family network, many Muslim men are either unable or unwilling to take care of their young children and will not ask for custody.

"The subtext to the religious rulings about custody is the assumption that there is an extended family involved who will help to raise the children, that it is a whole family responsibility. . . . Here in North America rarely if ever would custody [rules] be applied in their literal sense because the considerations underlying them are not fulfilled."

None of the imams could describe a custody dispute that they personally adjudicated or otherwise resolved. "I have never seen a case where the father insists that they want custody of the children; this is always worked out between the couple." Although there may be some reticence to talk about their role in disputes over children, it seems clear that when the imams encounter a fierce conflict over custody they will refer the parties to a lawyer or to the courts. Some of the more proactive imams will help parents to resolve child custody and access issues at an earlier stage, and some will assist divorced couples with supervised access sessions held at the mosque.

While my conclusion is that the imams generally do not advise or apply classical Islamic law on child custody, many women express a real fear that the Islamic principles may be used to leverage other—for example, financial—negotiations. Both Muslim and non-Muslim couples sometimes dispute custody, or threaten to deny access, as a tactic in divorce negotiations.[21] In a few of the cases in the sample, there was evidence that the husband (who probably had no real intention of taking custodial responsibility) used such a threat to his advantage. In two instances, this threat led the wife to accept a compromised financial outcome in return for holding on to her children. A number of the imams acknowledged this strategy.

"Husbands often say, 'hand me over your children and then I will give you the divorce.'"

The potency of the threat is based on a widespread fear—also assumed by the wider population—that Muslim men who demand custody of their children will be assisted by imams and the men's families. Najat certainly believed this to be the case and made her decision to abort her baby accordingly.

Najat married her husband after just two meetings. They had met at university, and the year after graduation he asked her to marry him. She said no several times but eventually accepted him. She was impressed with his intelligence. What's more, all her friends were getting married. She describes herself as "really naive." Against the wishes of her family, she married him.

Almost immediately they began to argue. Her husband was Arab and Najat was not, and back in his home country where the marriage took place "he completely changed. . . . I was an outsider, not an Arab. He could take control."

The couple returned to North America immediately after the wedding. Najat found out that she was pregnant. But the marriage was already in crisis. "I was emotional during the pregnancy, and he was already withdrawing from me; it was very hard." In her second trimester, Najat's husband threatened to divorce her and told her that he could take the child. Najat was horrified and believed that she would eventually lose custody to him.

Najat was torn over what to do. "I had fallen in love with the baby and I cried and cried. But at the same time I was afraid of being in a custody battle with my husband." She went on: "I stopped loving and caring about the baby. I began to research Islamic websites and the question of abortion."[22]

Najat told her mother that she was having some bleeding. She went to the clinic and had an abortion. It was an ugly experience. Afterwards, she told her family that she had had a miscarriage. And that she wanted a divorce.

Recognition of Marriage

A final issue that may be relevant to different divorce outcomes for Muslim and non-Muslim couples is the recognition of their relationship in law. A Muslim couple married overseas in a legal ceremony is regarded as married for the purposes of Canadian and U.S. law, under the principle of comity. However, when a Muslim couple marries in North America using a *nikah* only and does not register their marriage with the legal authorities (approximately 5 percent of the cases in the sample), a court will not recognize the union. This was what happened to Bita when her husband's family represented her as not married to their son when they asked the court to approve their agreement to take custody of her baby.

Obviously if their marriage is not recognized by a court, a couple cannot obtain a legal divorce. If the couple is not treated as legally married, the court will approach the consequences of the ending of the marriage differently. Child support may still be payable on production of evidence of paternity. Furthermore, a court-ordered financial settlement between the spouses—for example, a lump-sum payment or ongoing alimony—is still possible when there is an enforceable cohabitation agreement. In the United States such payments are described as palimony, and the legal principle was established by the *Marvin* case in 1976.[23] However, I did not come across any Muslim couples who made such an agreement. Among the small group who did not obtain a legal license there was an assumption that they were (Islamically) married and not "merely" cohabitants. In Canada, a couple married with a *nikah* only could in theory present their relationship as "common law"; all Canadian provinces make provision for treating common law relationships of a certain length and nature (usually a minimum of two or three years in length, and where housing and finances are shared) in the same way as a legal marriage for the purposes of property division and spousal support.[24] It is a moot point whether a Muslim couple married Islamically would be willing to be treated as a "common law" couple rather than as formally married, since Islam forbids them from living together outside marriage. Myine and Amira, whose stories were described in chapter three, were each married with only a *nikah*, but both were entitled to claim rights as a common-law spouse in the jurisdiction in which they lived. Myine negotiated a satisfactory financial settlement with her husband. Amira did not and was left destitute, but she was uncomfortable asserting an entitlement as a common law spouse. In a jurisdiction which does not recognize common law marriage, monetary claims between an "unmarried" Muslim couple (in the absence of a cohabitation agreement) will be treated as a private debt, rather than part of a family obligation, which can create significant unfairness.

Rushkana met her husband when he was married to his first wife, and began to work for him in his business. A few years later, telling Rushkana that he was now divorced, he proposed to her. They were Islamically married and lived together as man and wife for twelve years before Rushkana discovered that his relationship with his first wife had continued; in fact, her husband continued to have children with his first wife. She asked for a divorce.

The court did not recognize Rushkana's marriage nor her claim for a share of her husband's assets. Her husband agreed to a religious divorce, and the secretary of her mosque advised Rushkana that she could consider the marriage over.

This was not enough for Rushkana. Having worked alongside her husband in their business for so many years, she wanted her share of the assets. Her husband made her an offer of $10,000, which she rejected as insufficient. "It is not enough for me because we have not resolved the financial issues. I am entitled to maintenance and division of the assets."

Rushkana continued to work with a lawyer to try to persuade a court to recognize her marriage and make an order on community property. She realized that it was a difficult argument to make, but "the rights of women in these cases need to be acknowledged, established in case law. This is especially important for women who have children; they need protection and financial support."

Further unfairness is caused by the fact that Rushkana's husband could not be prosecuted for bigamy because he was not legally married to her, only to his first wife. Rushkana's case and others suggest a need for an organized legal advocacy campaign on behalf of women who suffer injustice as a result of Islamic processes that they understand as binding commitments but are not recognized by the courts.

Outcomes of Religious Divorce: Three Narratives

An analysis of the legal and financial outcomes of divorce produced three contrasting narratives. The two most prevalent—looking for a "clean break" and asking for an eventual release—reflect the length of the marriage and the issues at stake. In a much smaller group of cases (of varying lengths) the narrative theme is a preference for only those outcomes which are considered "Islamic."

Looking for a "Clean Break"

Slightly more than half of the marriages in the study lasted for less than five years. Shorter marriages are increasingly commonplace in the general population as well; a 2002 U.S. study suggests that the median length of a first marriage that ends in divorce is just under eight years and of a second marriage about seven.[25] Of the shorter marriages, 90 percent were childless. A significant number of these unions were arranged, by the families often bringing one spouse (typically the husband) from the family's country of origin to be married to a wife born and raised in North America. In some cases, the couple had barely started living together before realizing that they were incompatible.

Without children to support, and in many cases little joint property, these marriages are usually simpler to unravel than those that last longer and produce children. A "clean break" approach has been widely developed in U.S. case law,[26] and to a lesser extent in Canada.[27] The rationale is that in a shorter marriage there should be an emphasis on spousal self-sufficiency following divorce rather than a "pension for life." In both the United States and Canada, time-limited support or single lump-sum payments are common in these cases, especially for marriages of five years or less.

Many respondents in shorter marriages without children sought a "clean break" with few continuing obligations on either side. Even so, there is almost always a reliance on the relationship that may cause a sense of grievance or unfairness: for example, when one spouse has worked to put the other through school, when one or the other has relocated (even from overseas) at some personal cost or when there has been joint investment in a home, a car or other goods. In some of the shorter marriages one spouse remained responsible for sponsoring the residence of the other even after the marriage was (in effect) over. The most frequently cited conflict was the retrieval of personal possessions, and there was rarely any significant shared property. Some respondents asked an imam or the police for assistance in retrieving their belongings, or requested that the extended family intervene. A few even began court proceedings, but most took the view of this woman.

> "I considered fighting over what I had left with him that I did not get back—but I thought that the amount of money it would cost me to go to court would be worth more than my belongings—plus I did not want to have to be in a room with him."

Few spouses were looking for ongoing spousal support following these shorter marriages. Almost all observed the requirement of the *iddat* (the maintenance of the wife by the husband for around three months). In a shorter marriage dissolved by the court using civil law principles, the expectation would also be for a relatively short period of support, although this presumption might be affected by other factors, including lost economic opportunities as a result of the marriage, each party's present ability to be economically self-sufficient and their individual needs.

A majority of women in these shorter marriages abandoned any effort to obtain payment of their *mahr*, either sooner or later. Only one-third of those married for up to five years who had a deferred *mahr* in their *nikah* received it in full, in part or some equivalent in-kind payment. Despite the fact that women often had very strong feelings about their right to the *mahr*, many gave up their claim when they found that they were unable to persuade their husband (or his family) to pay. Sometimes their husbands were reluctant to pay the full *mahr* when the marriage was short, and especially when the woman had taken the initiative on divorce (which they did in most of these shorter marriages). Some were clearly influenced by their knowledge that a court was unlikely to enforce a payment to the *mahr*, giving them the upper hand in any negotiations (in my study, the husband won all but one of the contests fought out in court over the payment of the *mahr*). Some women told me that they did not pursue their *mahr* because their husbands did not have the money to pay it; when a marriage ends after a short time, there is often no financial plan in place to enable the husband to pay the deferred *mahr*. In a few cases, the *mahr* was paid in installments over time after the marriage ended, or equivalence was given in the form of a car, or a contribution towards school tuition fees.

About one in five women in this group gave up their claim on the advice of an imam because they initiated the divorce (*khula*). This is despite the fact that the Islamic law is not clear on this point, and advice varies among imams. One woman was told that she must forfeit her *mahr* because she "refused to drop out of school and reconcile with my husband." One woman who described her husband as violent and abusive towards her said that the imam she consulted still told her that she was not entitled to her *mahr*; "you left the house, that's your problem." She described her "deep disappointment" in the imam's response. "He [the imam] should have recognized that I deserved support without me having to argue for it." Some imams simply assume that in every instance when the woman initiates the divorce she must forfeit her *mahr*, and will not even discuss the issue of payment of the *mahr* in these circumstances, even when there has been domestic violence or other abusive behavior by the husband. This approach undermines the integrity of the promises made in the *nikah*.

Rightly or wrongly, many women appear to willingly accept a trade of their *mahr* for their freedom. For some, this acceptance was eased by their need to ensure that they had met what they understood to be their obligations; as one woman told me, "I wanted to keep my bases clean. If I owed him money Islami-cally, I would pay it—I wanted to verify that I was in the clear." Other women who gave up their *mahr* said that they did not want to take on the struggle of the fight. "My mental peace and freedom are more important than money"; "More than anything I want a divorce, not money." Some women gave up their *mahr* even in the face of advice to the contrary. "My father said that . . . I was still enti-tled to my *mahr*. But honestly I didn't want it; I just wanted to get the hell out of there." These women did not understand themselves to be giving up their *mahr* as a matter of principle—many told me that they continued to believe that their husbands had neglected their religious duty by failing to pay—but because of the difficulty in obtaining it.

Less than 10 percent of couples in these shorter marriages had children. In each case, the children remained with the mother. Also, in every case, if child support was not paid voluntarily the woman applied to the court for an order (and subsequent variations). Obtaining a court order was not a panacea for the problems of obtaining such support voluntarily (many women told me that they still did not receive regular payments), but another strategy that some women chose to try. None of the respondents who went to court reported any tension between their actions and their beliefs. In fact, some saw going to the courts as an appropriate, Islamic way to resolve a conflict.

> "We believe that [civil] law should apply to the ending of our marriage because this is the law of the land and this is the ethical way to do this. I stayed home to care for the child and so I should receive support. . . . This was for me very Islamic—to protect the woman's rights rather than to say that we have to be true to the letter of the law. It is a religious obligation to be fair."

About one in three of these shorter marriages proceeded through divorce by mutual agreement and dialogue and managed to negotiate an outcome accept-able to both spouses which often reflected a combination of both Islamic and civil law principles. The next case illustrates how a young professional couple—with a young child—managed to formulate an outcome that for them felt fair, Islamic and practical.

> Khalid and his wife separated shortly after the birth of their son, just one year into their marriage. They agreed that they needed a divorce, but struggled with whom to consult about the divorce outcomes. Even-tually, both retained counsel but also asked advice of mutual friends. The agreement they reached included observing the *iddat* and the full

payment of the *mahr*. At her request, Khalid gave his wife a notarized statement of *talaq*.

Khalid also agreed to pay child support according to the jurisdiction's payment guidelines and one year of spousal support to his ex-wife. Khalid told me, "Spousal support for one year would probably not have been payable Islamically, because she was living with her parents—but this was OK with me." It was very important to him to retain contact with his son, and maintaining a good relationship with his ex-wife was critical to this.

The couple had some conflict over access in the early years—Khalid's ex-wife took custody of their son—but they have resolved these issues over time, and seven years on, Khalid has regular contact with his son and a good relationship with his ex-wife.

Asking for an Eventual Release

Longer marriages usually require a more complex unraveling of family and financial affairs. In the sample, 31 percent of marriages lasted between five and fifteen years, and 17 percent more than fifteen years. A number of these longer marriages took place in a Muslim country overseas, often when the wives were still teenagers. These women typically came to North America with their husbands shortly after their marriage, settling down and having children over the next couple of decades. The majority of these women did not work outside the home during this time and instead took care of the children and the household. In some cases one or both spouses appear to have been unhappy for many years, but faced what they felt were insuperable obstacles to divorce.

One woman told me that just one week into her marriage (she was sixteen) she went to her parents and asked to be released from her commitment. "They were not sympathetic. . . . I was unhappy, but then perhaps I was too young to know what unhappiness was?" She stayed married for almost twenty years before seeking a divorce. Along with many others this woman faced both family opposition and social stigma, first by complaining about her marriage and ultimately by leaving it. Many waited until their children were older before asking for a divorce. A few women I interviewed were still undecided about seeking a divorce even after many years of abandonment. One woman with eight children whose husband had not provided for them for four years was still debating with herself whether it was right for her to ask for a divorce. She knew what she would do—she was confident that her imam would give her a divorce—but added, "It is hard for me to finally decide [about a divorce] until I see him face to face." Since her husband had remarried twice and was now living in another country, it seemed unlikely that that was going to happen.

There are striking similarities in the approach and experiences of those who described a divorce after a marriage of five years or more. First, these cases are more likely to go directly to court and the parties more likely to ask for an imposed adjudication using civil law principles than in shorter marriages. All but one of the marriages that lasted fifteen years or more was resolved in court; in that case, the woman's husband told her that if she pursued support, "I will kill you." In around one-third of the marriages that lasted between five and fifteen years an agreement was worked out by consent (for example, based on an agreement facilitated by the imam) and submitted to the court; the remainder were contentious and resolved only by a court. Another difference in the pattern of dissolution for longer marriages was the role of the imam or other religious adviser. The imam's role was often relatively insignificant compared with the part he plays in dissolving shorter marriages. Most of the women in longer marriages described approaching one, or sometimes several, imams earlier in their marriage, sometimes on numerous occasions and being treated unsympathetically. Several told me that the imam advised them to return to an abusive husband and "be patient." Another asked her imam to release her from her marriage when it became clear that her husband was having multiple affairs, but he refused to help her. Another woman began the process of seeking a religious divorce by meeting with her imam and her husband but felt that the imam believed her husband's allegations that she had been unfaithful to him (this woman worked outside the home, and her husband was jealous of her male colleagues). It seems that once these women had finally made their minds up that they wanted a divorce, often having waited for many years, they no longer believed an imam could help them and instead went directly to court.

For some women, their recourse to court reflected their concern that they might be taken advantage of in a negotiation by their more worldly-wise husbands, who had often been the sole earner and controller of the household's finances (a similar concern exists for some older non-Muslim women). Three men whose marriages ended after more than fifteen years described their wives insisting on resolving the divorce in court, rather than cooperating in a religious divorce with an imam. These women evidently believed that they were more likely to secure fairness and to protect their interests by going to court than by returning to the imam—whose permission for divorce they may have already secured—for a negotiation over divorce consequences.

> "When you go to court, you have rules, they are written down. When you go to the sheikh, he does not have rules, he does not follow the Book [the Qur'an]."

"I felt that I needed and wanted state protection. . . . You have to in any circumstances know your rights. . . . For me knowing my rights means having a representative in the court who knows my rights."

After many years of marriage and, in some cases, years of housework and child care with no independent source of income, resolving the economic position of these women following divorce is typically more complex than for their younger counterparts whose marriages have been shorter and childless. Their frequent recourse to the courts to resolve the legal and financial consequences of divorce supports the theory that these women recognize the importance of a legally enforceable outcome that reflects their contribution to the marriage. Some began (perhaps many years earlier) with the aspiration of negotiating Islamic outcomes for their divorce, but in the absence of what they considered to be a fair offer they went to court and accepted a civil law resolution. These women see themselves as "doing the best they can" to meet their Islamic obligations. Many expressed a strong sense of entitlement to a reasonable financial settlement. Their experience may have brought them to a different perspective on this than their family and friends; women who received court-ordered spousal support after very long marriages frequently described being censored by others as "un-Islamic," but they faced down the criticism.

Ambreen (whose story is also told in chapter four) agreed to a divorce from her husband after many years of unhappiness. Her husband, Rajul, had maintained another home and a second wife for twenty years, a fact well known in the community. Ambreen had begged Rajul to give up his other wife, but he always refused. Finally, when their children were grown, he proposed divorce, and she reluctantly agreed.

Rajul proposed a religious divorce only; he wanted to avoid resolving their financial affairs in court. He claimed that this was to save them all money; he told her "the lawyers will cheat you." Rajul argued that the concept of shared matrimonial property was un-Islamic. This approach to their finances clearly advantaged him: "If you avoid the American court system, the financial stuff stays the way it is, which is that he controls everything."

Ambreen refused to accept this arrangement. She told Rajul, "Either divorce me or don't, I don't want this 'in limbo' arrangement." So Rajul agreed to a legal divorce, which meant that he had to accept that his wife of forty years would get half of their shared property, and ongoing alimony.

Despite criticism from her friends, Ambreen "happily" accepted support, although there is no provision for this in Islamic law. She didn't really need the money—she used it to do some home renovations—but she felt that she was entitled to it. It had been a long marriage. She had also agreed to give up any future claims his children might have on his property. She also did some research and satisfied herself that her court divorce with consent was the equivalent of an Islamic divorce.

Some women—like Ambreen—saw spousal support as an alternative to receiving their *mahr*, and did not expect to keep both. The likelihood of women receiving a deferred *mahr* after divorce is somewhat higher among those who have been married longer. In this study the figure rises from around one in three for those married for five years or less, to almost one in two for those married more than five years, and rising to just over 50 percent for those married longer than fifteen years. These figures include women who told me that they understood their court-ordered support as inclusive of the *mahr* where this was outstanding. Women who contested the *mahr* in court had a similar experience to those in shorter marriages: they were almost always unsuccessful. Those women who did not receive their *mahr* in any form often held on to an enduring sense of injustice. They experienced this both personally, and as an affront to their faith. The way they saw it, by refusing to fulfill their *nikah* promise, their husbands knowingly acted in a manner inconsistent with Islam. Of course, as one woman put it, "An Islamic contract does not hold much weight for someone who does not practice Islam." Nonetheless, faced with a choice between staying married or giving up their *mahr*, women "do the best they can—the rules of necessity kick in."

Of course, access to a court-ordered outcome does not guarantee that payment will be made. These women faced the same problems with default that others do. As well, some were deterred from asking for some aspects of their entitlement either because of their difficulties with using the system ("the judge told me to go to another building to claim child support, but I never went"), their husbands' lack of resources ("I knew he had no means to pay") or, in a few cases, the difficulty of resolving conflicts over overseas property.

Seeking only "Islamic" Outcomes

"Even if the law . . . gives me more—like rights of women—I prefer always to go to the *shari'a*. I refer everything to what pleases Allah. I want to guarantee what will be waiting for me [in the afterlife]. I do not want to sacrifice my afterlife for something small in this life."

In contrast to those individuals who first pursued Islamic terms for their marriage dissolution but gave up when they found their spouse to be uncooperative, the imam unsympathetic, or any offer unreasonable, a much smaller group continued to embrace only Islamic outcomes. While these women constituted a very small group (less than 5 percent of the sample), they held very strong views. The woman quoted above had been abandoned—with their four children—by her husband several years before I met her. He had moved overseas and remarried. They had been married for twenty years. She was ready to ask for a divorce but insisted that she would not seek spousal support since she was not entitled to it in Islam—only child support—and that she would forego her *mahr* because she had initiated the divorce. In turning away other possibilities such as extended spousal support or property division, these highly religious women sometimes frustrated their legal representatives. In the event that court-ordered support is ordered, they also want to avoid "double-dipping."

> The wife of an imam who counsels women with marital problems told me the story of a woman who came to her husband for advice after a court had awarded her 50 percent of the matrimonial assets, a sum of $70,000. She asked him, "Am I entitled to this money Islamically?" She had already been paid her *mahr*, which was a comparable amount. The imam advised her that she was not entitled to keep both her *mahr* and the 50 percent award (while other imams may hold different opinions on this point, this was his advice). The woman returned the $70,000 to her husband. When I expressed some surprise, the counselor told me, "The goal is not to obey a man, however much we may love him—we do it for God."

For these individuals, acting fairly and acting Islamically blur together in their decisions about a divorce settlement. In some instances what feels right appears to be primarily about a sense of personal fairness and achieving spiritual peace of mind. The goal of pleasing God is merged into a sense of moral and ethical behavior.

> Lubna was married for seven years when she and her husband finally agreed to divorce. They had no children. They had been discussing divorce for some time—her husband had wanted a divorce many years earlier— but Lubna proposed that they give the marriage another chance.
>
> When they did finally agree to end the marriage, Lubna felt that it was fair to assess their financial settlement based on what it would have cost for them to divorce after a much shorter marriage. She told me that she preferred to take less than 50 percent of her marital assets and property because "divorce must be just." She had persuaded her husband to stay married for longer than he wanted, and he should not have to pay more as a result. As well, Lubna told me, his father was now dead, and he needed to support his female relatives.

Lubna did not tell her family about the settlement, which she and her husband agreed between themselves. She recognized that her family may regard it as unequal. However, Lubna reflected that her priorities were different from those of her family in this situation. "They see money as more important than peace of mind."

These women did not see themselves as accepting a "lesser" outcome. While many accepted a lower financial settlement than they may have been entitled to at civil law, they were assertive about what they saw as due to them Islamically (their *mahr*, the *iddat*, child support, fair treatment). They placed their immediate financial settlement within a much larger context—their future in God's hands.

Umaima and her husband had marital problems almost immediately after their marriage, and after eighteen months they separated. Umaima told her husband that she wanted a divorce, "and it became clear that I had to do it Islamically."

Umaima's husband told her that because she had initiated the divorce, she could not regain the earnings and property that she had contributed to their short marriage. There was no *mahr*. Umaima was relieved that she did not have to fight her husband over the *mahr*, but she did want some of her own money back. They had bought a home together, and she had contributed both capital and mortgage payments. She simply wanted enough money to be able to start up again. She felt that this would be an Islamic outcome because it would be fair.

Umaima and her husband each hired lawyers. Umaima's lawyer told her that she was entitled to half their matrimonial home. Her lawyer argued that they should go to trial, but Umaima refused to take this route.

"Muslims believe that the ultimate provider is God, and this is particularly important when it comes to monetary income. God will provide. Whatever is due to me will come."

But "at the same time I was not prepared to walk away with zero." She and her husband eventually worked out a settlement with the help of an imam. Umaima got a settlement of $20,000, and her husband retained ownership of the home. This amount was neither 50 percent of the assets nor the value of what she had contributed. When she told her lawyer that she would accept this settlement, he was frustrated and told her, "Do what you have to do." Umaima just wanted it over. "This is the most hated permitted thing—you don't want any more drama." She also had a moral clarity about her decision.

"At the end of the day the ultimate judge for what we were doing was God. . . . Whatever I need will come to me, and he will ultimately be punished for not being fair. The second part is that I walk away with dignity. . . . To take it to court would have given him a lot more satisfaction, whereas he is really accountable to God."

Conclusions

The financial and legal outcomes of divorce for Muslims in this sample often look similar to those reached by non-Muslim couples, either because they ask for and accept an adjudicated outcome, or because an agreement made between them reflects civil law as well as Islamic principles. Most couples make some initial effort to agree outcomes that are consistent with Islamic law and principles. These may be very specific (for example, observing the *iddat* or paying the *mahr*) or they may be generalized as a fair and just—"Islamic"—outcome. Some of these agreements, perhaps anticipating future conflict, accept civil law outcomes on a voluntary basis or blend together Islamic and civil law outcomes.

Muslim couples—just like non-Muslims—often face the dilemma of agreeing to a less-than-perfect post-divorce arrangement negotiated between themselves, or asking a court to make a decision for them. There appear to be few inhibitions on Muslims using the courts to resolve contentious issues, especially in longer marriages where financial issues are more complex and critical. Having tried and failed to obtain a more conventional "Islamic" arrangement, many women who have wanted to end their marriage for many years are very comfortable with seeking and accepting a court-imposed outcome, and the courts are used by those who are strictly observant as well as those who are less formally religious. Only a very small group (all women) told me that they would reject any outcome that went "beyond" what they understood as their entitlement in Islam.

The impact of divorce on personal beliefs and spirituality—at least over the long term, once the initial shock has passed—appears to be limited. Almost all the respondents told me that they had little or no difficulty reconciling their faith—however practiced—with divorce, at least once they had reached this decision. Many women became increasingly confident as they read and researched their rights in Islam to divorce, and increasingly critical of the ignorance and negativity that they sometimes heard from their families and friends about divorce in Islam. Most relied on their faith to sustain them in this confidence, and many remarked that this experience had brought them closer to God and more committed to their faith. Just a few said that their experience had driven them away from Islam.

While the financial, legal and spiritual consequences of divorce take some different forms for Muslim men and women, the greatest contrast between the experiences of Muslim and non-Muslim couples lies in the social consequences of divorce, particularly for women. A stigma against divorce continues in some non-Muslim communities also, along with a lingering, generalized societal disapproval of divorcées (especially when there are children, who are seen as harmed by divorce). Even so, Muslim women sometimes face social consequences which are much more adverse and long lasting than they would be for most non-Muslims in contemporary North America. The continuing assumption in some Islamic cultures that women are to blame for the failure of a marriage runs through attitudes towards marriage (and respective roles and responsibilities), and results in the differential social treatment of divorcées. A more balanced and equitable approach is critical not only to address the disproportionately negative impact on women, but also to enable Muslim communities to squarely face the reality of divorce and all its consequences.

8 LEGAL ISSUES FOR ISLAMIC MARRIAGE AND DIVORCE

The practice of Islamic marriage and divorce in North America raises a multitude of legal questions that reflect the uncertain, disputed, quasi-legal space within which these traditions continue. Should the courts recognize an Islamic divorce? An Islamic marriage ceremony conducted without a legal license? Are the promises made in the *nikah* an enforceable contract in American or Canadian law? We know from chapter seven that many Muslims have recourse to both the Islamic principles and traditions that are meaningful to them and their families, and the family courts in their state or province. What is the relationship between these two systems?

Generally, neither Islamic marriage nor divorce has any legal effect in North America. Both procedures require a further legal element—in the case of a wedding, obtaining a marriage license for that jurisdiction, and for divorce, a civil legal decree—in order to be legally effective. If a Muslim couple chooses to marry using a *nikah*, or to divorce with the assistance of a religious adviser, these actions are forms of private ordering which have no formal legal status. Despite this, many would argue that the public justice system should try to support the genuine intentions and expectations of families whatever their religion or culture and "allow individuals to express and maintain their identity and beliefs in the setting of their family relationships."[1] At the same time courts confront the question of how far to acknowledge customs of marriage and divorce that may look quite different to the Judeo-Christian traditions that are entrenched in the legal system. They may also be asked to assess whether religious and cultural choices such as Muslim marriage and divorce adequately protect vulnerable parties.

The overarching question is how to find a balance between providing fundamental rights to all and respecting diverse traditions and beliefs. This is a difficult balance to strike in simple or universal terms, as the personal stories in this book illustrate. This chapter describes the approaches adopted by courts in both Canada and the United States to Islamic laws and traditions, and the political context which frames these decisions.

Islam as the "Other" System

Legal rules about the relative roles, rights and responsibilities of spouses and their children reflect innate values about the appropriate way to structure and run a family. In the United States and Canada many aspects of family law are rooted in Judeo-Christian traditions and beliefs about family life. These include the concept of monogamy, the prohibition of marriage between those related in certain ways, and the age at which marriage may be legally contracted. They extend to the appropriate role of parents in selecting a partner for their children, and the relationship between the two families when a couple marries. Historically, Protestant traditions have dominated the development of divorce laws in North America, beginning with a notion of "fault" which is still reflected in many popular beliefs (although no longer in law) about "justice" in the ending of a marriage. Custody determinations have historically favored the mother, although a modern "father's rights" movement is intent on redressing the balance. There is an assumption that marriage (or divorce) means a merging of at least some of the spouses' individual property (the rules vary between common law and "community property" jurisdictions), which is then divided in the event of divorce using some form of equitable distribution.

While many people no longer associate any of these assumptions or principles with a religious belief system, so entrenched are they in our assumptions about marriage and divorce, in fact none of these principles is normative for Muslim legal systems. Islam has no concept of matrimonial property, a very different approach to spousal support after divorce, and different traditions regarding child custody. Historically, some Muslim societies have practiced polygamy and in some cases have developed different expectations about appropriate family relationships surrounding marriage (for example, marriage between cousins). While many of the respondents in this study clearly rejected some or even all of these ideas in favor of the family law model that they had grown up with in North America, many are aware of some dissonance between the norms of the two systems. Islamic law and norms become the "Other" in a system which makes many contrary assumptions. As Pascale Fournier writes, "When claims to universality go unchallenged, minority people's cultures are measured against unstated norms and become the abnormal, the Other."[2]

This chapter first discusses the three main areas of contention that arise in the relationship between state law and Islamic traditions referred to (figuratively if not literally) as Islamic family law. The first and most straightforward relates to the legal standing of the process of Islamic marriage and divorce in North America. A second and more complex set of issues surrounds the recognition of agreements reached between spouses in relation to either marriage—that is, prenuptial-type agreements regarding the resolution of future disputes—or divorce, for example, a negotiated or mediated agreement on divorce consequences. Much of the work of the family courts now relates to recognizing and enforcing negotiated agreements—formalized as "consent orders"—made between a couple at the end of their marriage. In principle, one might expect any freely contracted agreement to be treated the same way by the courts whether it is made by a Muslim couple, a couple with another shared faith, or a couple with no faith. In practice, different considerations apply that reflect general concern over the enforcement of agreements that are "religious" in nature, and particular concerns about enforcing "Islamic" agreements. A third and final category of contentious cases concerns the recognition of marriages and divorces that take place in a Muslim country. Legal marriages conducted overseas are recognized in North America—but the matter of divorce, by nature conflictual, raises different and harder questions. Does an overseas divorce absolve a husband from further obligations towards his wife and children who reside in North America? Can a court in Canada or the United States modify a divorce order made in a Muslim country? These cases may rely on the principle of "comity" to recognize as legally valid a procedure conducted according to the rules of another jurisdiction. Recognition may be denied when the court is concerned about the procedure or its outcome. Do the courts approach marriage and divorce formalized in Islamic countries—the broader "Other"—any differently from unions created or dissolved in countries with legal systems that look more like our own?

Providing the context for these legal questions is what we know about how Muslims in North America relate to and use the family law system. Some of this data—for example, the fact that Islamic divorce is sought in addition to and not as a substitute for a civil divorce decree—has already been discussed. Here I shall take a further and deeper look at the relationship between Muslims and the legal system, examining not only whether they use the courts but also how they feel about those experiences, and how they understand the relationship between court orders and their Islamic rights and responsibilities.

Why Are These Questions Important?

What may appear at first glance to be somewhat narrow and theoretical questions about the efficacy of Islamic law in a non-Muslim jurisdiction have become highly emotive political issues in the aftermath of 9/11. The relationship between private Islamic systems and public systems of justice has become a symbol of Muslim/non-Muslim relations in North America, emblematic of thorny questions of multiculturalism and accommodation in both Canada and the United States. "*Sharia* law" as it is often described in popular media, is widely seen as the means by which Muslims will aggressively impose their values and beliefs on others. Many Americans regard Islam as a threat, and there is significant public fear, sometimes expressed as hostility, towards Islamic traditions and beliefs practiced in the public gaze. The constant conflation of "*sharia* law" with so-called Islamic penal sanctions results in a natural assumption that *sharia* is harmful to Americans and represents the thin end of the wedge—a precursor to Islamic ambitions to take over American legal and political systems.

There is a little knowledge or understanding among non-Muslims regarding the substance of Islamic family law traditions. All minority communities—whether faith-based, ethnic or otherwise culturally distinct from the dominant group—maintain some informal and customary processes that are symbols of their shared heritage, for example, how to marry, welcome new members (children, in-laws), and how to commemorate the end of a life. The practice of Islamic marriage and divorce is assumed to be more threatening to a majority way of life and the rule of law than similar informal practices among other groups. Even though some religious groups have offered their members quasi-adjudicative services—again, mostly confined to family matters—for many years, the focus of controversy over alternative processes is clearly on Islam.

A number of jurisdictions in Canada and courts in the United States recognize the outcomes of religious arbitrations such as those conducted by the Jewish Bet Din and Christian ecclesiastical "courts" under state and provincial arbitration acts often modeled on the Uniform Arbitration Act.[3] In the United States the Federal Arbitration Act (FAA)[4] recognizes and enforces the outcomes of religious arbitrations.[5] Some states incorporate FAA provisions into their law or provide their own process to empower the courts to both review and enforce the outcome of a family dispute which is freely and voluntarily referred to private arbitration using an agreed set of principles (for example, New York State[6] and Florida[7]). The Ontario Arbitration Act in force at the time of the "*sharia* debate" (2003–2005) recognized religious arbitration—however, these laws had not impinged on the public consciousness until their application to Islamic divorce procedures became public. In fact, the Ontario Act had never been used to review or enforce an Islamic arbitration, whereas more than a dozen cases had been brought in relation to decisions of the Jewish Bet Din.[8] The Bet Din were swept up in the moral panic generated as Ontario removed recognition of all religious arbitrations from its arbitration statute in the wake of the controversy.[9] Evidently the fear excited by the idea of Islamic principles being legitimated by the courts in their review of arbitral decisions exceeded any concerns about removing recognition from other religious groups. British Columbia[10] and Nova Scotia[11] continue to recognize, review and enforce decisions from religious arbitrations.

The Oklahoma Referendum

Public controversy over the relationship of the courts to Islamic law burst into new prominence in 2010 with the introduction of a proposed constitutional amendment in Oklahoma to "forbid courts from considering either international law or *shari'a* law in deciding cases."[12] The Oklahoma referendum offers a striking example of the level of public anxiety about a "takeover" of the legal system by Islamists and illustrates many of the inaccuracies, misunderstandings and fears that characterize the debate. It comes on the heels of the controversies in Ontario and the United Kingdom (discussed in chapter one) which were similarly framed as the encroachment of "*shari'a* law" principles on the rule of law. In the process, complex legal and theological issues are reduced to simple slogans. When the Archbishop of Canterbury, Dr. Rowan Williams, intervened in this debate in a scholarly speech proposing a system that could accommodate both compliance with state law and respect for the private observance of "God's law" he was widely reported as "calling for" the imposition of *shari'a* law. As a result, many Americans appear to believe that courts in the United Kingdom already apply *shari'a*. In fact, the Shari'a Council of the United Kingdom referred to by Williams is a registered charity offering marriage and divorce services, and its decisions have no legal status.

Dubbed the "Save Our State" amendment, SQN755 was sponsored by former Republican Oklahoma state representative Rex Duncan. Duncan has a history of anti-Islamic sentiment, once expressed by the public refusal of the gift of a Qur'an. He described the amendment as a "preemptive strike" necessary to "remove a cancer."[13] Although, when questioned, he could not point to an example of Oklahoma courts applying *shari'a* law principles, Duncan maintained that "it's not just a danger. It's a reality."[14] The amendment passed by a 70 percent majority in November 2010.

The singling out of Islamic law raised immediate questions about its compatibility with the constitutional commitment to respect freedom of religion. A few days later, Muneer Awad, executive director of the Oklahoma chapter of the Council on American-Islamic Relations, filed a lawsuit alleging that the amendment violated the First Amendment's Establishment Clause that prohibits government from establishing a "national" religion or preferring one religion over another. Federal court judge Vicky Miles-Lagrange of the Oklahoma Western District issued a preliminary injunction, stating that the amendment "fosters an excessive government entanglement with religion." Miles-Lagrange wrote in her judgment that the amendment amounted to an attack on Islam and thus an attack on religious freedom. "While the defendants contend that the amendment is merely a choice of law provision that bans state courts from applying the law of other nations and cultures, regardless of what faith they may be based on, if any, the actual language of the amendment reasonably, and perhaps more reasonably, may be viewed as specifically singling out Sharia Law, conveying a message of disapproval of plaintiff's faith." It is expected that the plaintiff will apply for a permanent injunction. An appeal by the Oklahoma attorney general on the Lagrange ruling is pending.[15]

The Public Debate

The debate surrounding the amendment and Justice Miles-Lagrange's judgment illustrates many of the misconceptions and misapprehensions that run through current political and legal narratives regarding Islamic law and the courts. First, there is confusion over the nature of *shari'a* itself, and its role in Islam. Justice Miles-Lagrange agreed with Awad that *shari'a* is "not actually 'law' but is religious traditions that provide guidance to plaintiff and other Muslims regarding the exercise of their faith." The assumption of the amendment is that there is a specific body of laws constituting *shari'a*—a single code that Muslims universally agree upon—that American courts may be in danger of applying. In practice, there is no such code and instead "There is a [different] *shari'a* for every Muslim" The conflation of *shari'a* with criminal regimes in a few (widely regarded as aberrant) parts of the Muslim world further obscures the reality that the practice of *shari'a* for the vast majority of American Muslims is focused on family matters, primarily marriage and divorce.

In a climate of bias and fear, the ambitions of Muslims to promote Islamic law are grossly distorted. A second widespread belief promulgated by the campaign for the Oklahoma amendment, which recurs throughout the wider public debate, is that Muslim citizens desire the imposition and enforcement of "*shari'a* law" in North America.[16] There is a further implication that eventually *shari'a* will come to be applied to non-Muslims also. These assertions are made by an organized network of individual bloggers, scholars and activists as well as foundations that provide financial support. The so-called anti-*shari'a* movement has become a focus of sloganeering and campaigning for some politicians, who believe that they can establish their "credentials" by talking up this imagined threat and the need to resist it. The Oklahoma amendment was the first of a growing number of similar endeavors in other more than a dozen other U.S. states, most of which are using a version of the original amendment, and which are supported by online materials, videos and instructions on drafting such an amendment and organizing support. A 2011 study by the Center for American Progress describes the co-ordination of an effort "to rouse public fears by consistently vilifying the Islamic faith and asserting the existence of an Islamic conspiracy to destroy 'American values,'" which is sustained by an infrastructure of anti-Muslim information and misinformation.[17]

Data from respondents in this study and public statements by Muslim leaders reveal virtually no interest in or support for the formal legal recognition of Islamic family law. This study finds that Muslims understand their private choices of Muslim marriage and divorce processes as separate from the formal legal system. None of the 212 respondents—including many imams, legal scholars, Muslim lawyers and others working in the legal system—suggested that the courts should directly apply Islamic law to Muslims (or non-Muslims). Certainly a significant number of imams, as informal arbitrators, looked with envy at the "coercive power [which] lies with the State"; some recourse to legal enforcement would give them greater authority when, for example, they advise a husband that he should pay the *mahr* to his wife or make child support payments. As many acknowledged, "Moral and faith authority does not work all the time." However, this desire for greater authority does not translate into advocacy for either a court applying Islamic law, or a separate Islamic system with the force of law. Just three of the forty-two imams and third parties interviewed for this study advocated a separate, legally competent, Islamic tribunal, and one of these was the original advocate of Islamic tribunals in Ontario. Even he acknowledged that a separate system would be appropriate only for "a small number of cases" and that Canadian law would always trump Islamic law in the event of any conflict. Another well-known Canadian imam who had been described by the news media as supporting the proposal for Muslim tribunals in Ontario told me that he did not support such an idea, and instead articulated his position as follows:

> "[It is important] to give people comfort based on their beliefs. Canadian civil courts are not a part of Islamic beliefs—but as citizens we have to obey the Canadian laws. The Canadian laws always override the *shari'a*. But as a part of their religious freedom they will also use the Islamic law."

A number of other imams spoke out against the idea of a separate Islamic tribunal system, arguing that the goal should be integration, not competing systems. One imam pointed out the importance of maintaining the same standards for all: "It would be better to integrate elements of Islamic family law into the court system than to have a separate *shari'a* court.... This would be safer for both men and women." However, he also acknowledged, in a sentiment widely expressed, that as a Muslim he felt that "the court system needs to be less

Christian [and] accommodate the needs of the Muslim community." The sense that there is inadequate respect for or acknowledgement of Islamic norms in the courts is often a part of the experience of many respondents who do end up in court, discussed later in this chapter.

Respondents' widespread use of the legal system—formalizing marriage via a license, applying for a civil divorce decree as well as a religious divorce, and resorting to court for contentious matters—undermines the further assumption that support for Islamic marriage and divorce reflects an antagonism towards local laws and norms. Using a *nikah* for marriage or an imam for divorce does not mean that these men and women are rejecting the state legal system, but supplementing it with their own customs and traditions. I found no evidence for the contrary proposition, voiced by proponents of the Oklahoma amendment and others, that Muslim Americans do not want anything to do with the courts (see also the section "How Muslims Use the Courts" later in this chapter).

How American Courts Relate to Other Legal Systems

The Oklahoma amendment "forbids courts from considering or using Sharia Law." The courts in both the United States and Canada are permitted to refer to the laws and principles of other countries when necessary to apply the proper application of local law. When a court must determine, for example, whether a particular religious practice is protected under the First Amendment (or in Canada, under the Canadian Charter of Rights and Freedoms), they must refer to the relevant religious laws. In her judgment, Justice Miles-Lagrange offers the example of the protection of First Amendment rights for Muslim prisoners by giving them with access to *halal* food. Without reference to the Islamic law that regulates the eating of meat it would be impossible for the courts to know about, and protect, this right. Referring to Islamic law does not mean that the court applies these rules, either to Muslim prisoners or others, by requiring them to eat *halal* meat— but rather that its application of American law is informed by the rules of another system.

Another reason for American courts to refer to the laws of other legal systems is to determine the validity of an agreement or order that is made in another jurisdiction. Choice of law provisions allows courts to invite parties to choose a legal framework for the resolution of trans-state and transnational disputes over contract and tort, usually an issue only for commercial entities doing business across state or national boundaries. As well, both Canada and the United States adopt the principle of "comity" or legal reciprocity[18] to enable interaction with other systems where an individual may have previously resided. For example, an American couple who divorce in the United Kingdom and obtain an order there for financial support and custody would not expect to be treated as if they were still married by an American court, or to have that order reopened without good reason (for example, a significant change of circumstances). The basic premise of comity is that a procedure that follows the rules of one jurisdiction will be recognized as legally valid in a second jurisdiction. If courts in Oklahoma were to follow the amendment forbidding them from "considering or using *Shari'a* law," they would unable to honor the long-established tradition of allowing commercial parties to nominate the "proper law" that shall be applied in the case of any dispute, if the system chosen was either *shari'a* in general, or the law of a Muslim country. Similarly they would be unable to apply comity because they would be unable to determine the legal efficacy of marriages and divorces that take place in countries that have an Islamic family law system.

Although comity is a long established legal principle, "it remains remarkably vague."[19] Its application to cases of Islamic marriage and divorce conducted in Muslim countries is discussed in detail later in this chapter.

Islamic Marriage and Divorce Procedures

Couples who marry in North America are recognized as legally married if they have registered have their marriage with the legal authorities in the state or province in which they are wed. Marriages that are contracted in North America with a *nikah* only are not *prima facie* legal marriages in the United States and Canada. However, when the parties want a religious ceremony, it is facilitated by the authorization many jurisdictions provide to religious officials to solemnize marriages, effectively acting as a state agent for the formalities (for example, securing a signed marriage license).[20]

Legal traditions in both the United States and Canada favor the recognition of marriages that are genuinely contracted, even when they do not comply with all the formalities of solemnization.[21] This results in some, although somewhat inconsistent, flexibility in recognizing a religious marriage ceremony. For example, in *Persaud v. Balram*,[22] a New York State court found that a Hindu marriage ceremony with more than 100 guests but no legal registration of the marriage was nonetheless a valid marriage. An Ontario case, *Ayoub v. Osman*,[23] found that notwithstanding the absence of a license, a ceremony conducted "according to Muslim custom" and officiated by an imam fell within the provisions of s.31 of Ontario's Marriage Act because the parties considered themselves married. In these ways, efforts are made to address defects in the procedure adopted in order to recognize the reality of marriage and avoid unfairness (for example, the husband in *Persaud* sought to deny the marriage and avoid paying the *sadaq* or *mahr*). Other cases, however, take a stricter approach. For example, the judge in *Ahmed v. Canada* refused to recognize an Islamic marriage which took place by telephone between the groom (who was seeking a tax credit for alimony payments to his "ex-wife") in Toronto and the bride in Kenya, and which was never registered with the Ontario authorities.[24]

The assumption that a *nikah* alone does not constitute a legal marriage creates potential unfairness when a marriage ends and there is no clear recourse for securing a fair monetary settlement. Rema's story, told in chapter six, illustrates these dangers. In some jurisdictions, rights similar to those of spouses can be acquired by individuals who successfully claim "common law marriage" because of the length and nature of their relationship, but the stories of Myine and Ambreem in the same chapter demonstrate the difficulties this route presents for Muslim women. In any case, most U.S. states do not recognize a common law status for extramarital relationships.

The fact that an Islamic divorce is not a legal divorce in North America was widely understood among the respondents, and none reported that they believed themselves to be legally divorced unless they had also obtained a civil decree. However, visitors to the study website regularly asked this question, suggesting that by no means all Muslims who obtain a religious divorce before a civil decree appreciate this. All the imams told me that they made it clear to couples that their divorce would not be legally valid unless they also obtained a civil decree. More complex issues arise when a divorce is allegedly lawfully completed in a Muslim country, which bars or limits an application for financial relief in North America. This is discussed further below.

Islamic Marriage and Divorce Agreements

Although an Islamic marriage or divorce has no legal effect, an agreement made between the spouses may be enforceable as a legal contract. Promises made in a *nikah*—for example, a promise to pay a *mahr* or a wedding dowry—or in a divorce or separation agreement—for example, a promise to divide property in a particular way, or an undertaking regarding the upbringing of minor children—are capable of having legal effect if they have been properly formalized. In both form and intent, the Islamic marriage contract or *nikah* reads like a prenuptial agreement in which the spouses anticipate particular outcomes in the event that their marriage comes to an end. Courts in both Canada[25] and the United States[26] (although historically not in the United Kingdom[27]) enforce written prenuptial agreements, although there are some important limitations—for example, provisions on financial outcomes are generally enforceable but provisions relating to the care and custody of children are not. In the United States, the Uniform Pre-Marital Agreement Act[28] sets out basic procedural requirements (for example, the agreement must be in writing and there must be full disclosure of financial information) that have been adopted by many states. Some states have gone further—for example, Minnesota requires that the premarital agreement is witnessed[29] and California requires the parties to have independent legal advice.[30] The Uniform Act also allows the court to inquire into the fairness of the agreement by assessing voluntariness, the adequacy of disclosure of financial and property obligations, and the overall fairness of the agreement. However, when a premarital contract is litigated, "the burden [is] on the party seeking to escape the effect of the agreement to show that there [are] grounds for setting it aside."[31]

The same question of recognition and enforcement by a court applies to agreements made in the course of an Islamic divorce. In reaching their own agreement on the terms of their divorce, Muslim couples are behaving no differently than non-Muslim couples who increasingly prefer to negotiate the consequences of the ending of their marriage, often without legal representation, in so-called kitchen-table divorces. Relatively few divorcing couples now fight it out in divorce court with lawyers on either side.[32] If they are successful in reaching an agreement with their spouse this may be submitted to the court for approval as a consent order. In form, this is no different than a Muslim couple that is separating or divorcing making an agreement, perhaps drawing on Islamic principles, to resolve financial and property issues and make arrangements for any minor children. Private alternatives such as family mediation and arbitration are increasingly used to help effect such agreements; Muslim couples may turn to their imam or a religious scholar to act as mediator or arbitrator. The intervention of the court in privately negotiated divorce and separation agreements brought forward as consent orders is limited. There are some important requirements—namely provision for any minor children, which the courts will generally review—but otherwise most judges prefer not to meddle in a freely negotiated separation or divorce agreement, no matter what financial arrangement the couple chooses to make.[33] The judge's review is usually directed at ascertaining voluntariness, rather than reviewing the substance of the agreement.

In practice, court review of both premarital and divorce agreements that incorporate or refer to Islamic family law principles takes a significantly more rigorous course than the recognition of marriage and divorce contracts that make no reference to an alternative system of laws or religious principles. The legal principles governing the requirements of a binding contract are the same for all couples, but the degree of scrutiny varies. When the courts are concerned that the contract is a "religious agreement," they may review the agreement applying both public policy and fairness considerations (leading some imams and others to draft agreements that avoid explicit reference to Islamic principles).

Many cases attack recognition and enforceability on more than one of these grounds, and there is considerable overlap in the arguments. First, however, the court must be satisfied that a potentially enforceable contract has been made.

General Contractual Requirements

Any contract must comply with the requirements of the Statute of Frauds in order for a court to recognize and enforce it. Both a *nikah* and an Islamic divorce agreement are subject to these conditions.[34] First, the contract must be in writing (*Nassin v. Nassin*[35]). There must be evidence of a "meeting of the minds"—the parties to the contract must have clearly understood what they were agreeing to and share a common understanding of the meaning of the promises they have made. There must be no duress or coercion, although as the case law demonstrates this is a highly subjective measure. There must be "consideration" for each promise made—generally when a husband promises to pay a *mahr*, his wife's consideration in exchange for this promise is her agreement to marry.[36] Finally, the agreement must not be vague or ambiguous, which would raise difficulties in enforcing it.[37]

In practice, the interpretation of each of these requirements allows for significant discretion on the part of the court in finding a "meeting of the minds." In a California case, the fact that the husband was attempting to rely on a $30 *mahr* to avoid dividing a $3 million estate with his wife obviously influenced the court's eventual decision that the contract was too vague and uncertain to be enforced. The judge's rationale was that "an agreement whose only substantive term in any language is that the marriage has been made in accordance with 'Islamic law' is hopelessly uncertain as to its terms and conditions." Other cases reflect the judge's unfamiliarity with Muslim customs in marriage procedures. In a 2010 case in Washington State,[38] the judge refused to enforce a *mahr* promise because the *nikah* was reviewed by the groom just before the marriage ceremony, and he did not speak the language in which the *nikah* was drafted. This seems a reasonable safeguard to ensure voluntariness and informed consent. In this cultural context, however, different expectations probably apply. The groom in this case acknowledged that he was adopting a wedding format customary in his (Afghani) culture, and he would have anticipated that the *nikah* included a *mahr* (stipulated therein as $20,000).[39] It is also customary for the signing of the *nikah* to take place shortly before the wedding ceremony, and a boilerplate is often used (see chapter three). In a 2008 Ohio case the court concluded that the contract was made under duress because the signing ceremony was rushed, and the groom was "embarrassed and stressed" because the guests were already arriving.[40] In contrast, in *Khanis v. Noormohamed*,[41] an Ontario court ordered a husband to pay his wife a $20,000 *mahr* on top of other financial settlements ordered by the court and refused to accept his argument that he agreed to this under duress, telling him that he had had six years to complain about it before the marriage ended and the parties separated.

A related issue is access to independent legal advice. While the Uniform Pre-marital Act does not make independent legal advice a requirement for a valid pre-nuptial agreement, some states have added this stipulation. Case law in both the United States and Canada frequently stipulates that there should be access to inde-pendent legal advice.[42] In one case,[43] the court refused to limit spousal support to an amount stipulated in the *mahr* because at the time the wife signed the *nikah*, she had no knowledge of her future husband's financial circumstances, nor did she have independent legal advice. While it may be advisable for a variety of reasons for a wife to seek legal advice regarding both her *nikah* and the amount of the *mahr*, none of the female respondents in this study described seeking or receiving such advice, and such a suggestion would face numerous cultural barriers (in many cultural contexts this would be regarded at best as discourteous and inappropriate and at worst, suggests a mistrust of the other family). Regardless of this reality, (unfortunately not recognized by the courts), access to independent legal advice is an important protection for vulnerable people before they make a legally enforce-able commitment. These cases well illustrate the difficulty of balancing respect for established customs with providing protection against obligations which are less than freely and fully understood and accepted.

Public Policy Considerations

Further to the requirements of the Statute of Frauds and any additional statutory criteria, a court may determine whether or not a contract is compatible with "public policy," usually described as public morals or the established interests of society. This is a notoriously ambiguous and inconsistent category for judicial review—once described as "a very delicate and undefined power"[44]—and fre-quently reflects the judge's moral evaluation of the issues. "Public policy" here usually refers to a contracting standard that "the community as a whole has already adopted either formally by law or tacitly by its general course of corporate life."[45] When the court considers that this standard would be violated by the en-forcement of the contract it may refuse to recognize it.

Which aspects of the family law system can be bargained away as part of a premarital or divorce agreement without offending public policy? The only sig-nificant substantive limitation placed on premarital agreements relates to agreements regarding minor children; adults can consent to bargain away any part of their own financial interests. In a 2010 New York case,[46] the wife argued that a prenuptial agreement "overreached" when it excluded her from any share of the resulting income from her husband's graduate education and a new busi-ness he had started. The court found that she had voluntarily signed the agreement (in fact, it had been her parents' idea), and although under the circumstances the agreement was disadvantageous to her, it was nonetheless enforceable. The standard of fairness set by the courts for either a prenuptial agreement or agreements made upon separation or divorce is whether the substance of the agreement is "unconscionable." This is more than simply giving up entitlements; there may be good reasons to prefer to be generous, or simply to avoid further conflict. Instead, the agreement must be such as to "shock the conscience and confound the judgment of any [person] of common sense."[47] This is in keeping with a *laissez-faire* approach which promotes freedom of contract.

Is there any reason to treat a Muslim couple differently in relation to either a marriage contract or a divorce agreement? The most challenging question is whether "fairness" or "unconscionability" is culturally determined. Is it inevitable that the standard of what is understood as fair and reasonable within the context of any agreement is filtered through a cultural prism? If so, should the courts take cultural and religious expectations into consideration in determining what is "reasonable"? In *Langille v. Dossa*,[48] decided by a Canadian court, a Muslim father and a non-Muslim mother had agreed upon their separation that their daughter would live with her mother who would raise her as a Muslim. When the mother realized that this would place restrictions on her lifestyle that were unacceptable to her—for example, her ex-husband demanded that as an unmarried woman she not invite men to her home—she applied, successfully, to vary the terms of the custody order. The court's ruling implies that it would have been unfair to restrict the mother's right to make decisions about guests in her home.

The most consistent source of differing (cultural, religious) perspectives on what constitutes "fairness" between the spouses identified by respondents in this study was in relation to financial support (rather than property division or child custody, which were relatively less contentious) following divorce. This is also the area in which there was occasionally the greatest distance between the legal advice offered and some respondents' sense of appropriate outcomes. Several women respondents told me that when they advised their lawyer that they did not wish to pursue financial support that would fall outside what they understood to be their entitlement in Islam—for example, when a woman refused spousal support in favor of payment of a *mahr* or rejected the concept of community (blended) property and subsequent equalization—they were faced with consternation and discomfort and were sometimes pressured to change their minds. Obviously, legal representatives must ensure that their clients have full legal information before they choose to waive any rights, and many counsel were probably not previously aware of the differences between financial support in an Islamic and a civil law system. A measurable difference between legal advice and preferred options—when a family client rejects his or her lawyer's advice in favor of an outcome that feels better or fairer to them—is not limited to Muslim couples, as studies of collaborative family law and family mediation have shown.[49]

The lingering question is whether there is (and whether there should be) any more resistance to a Muslim woman deciding to refuse an entitlement because of her religious belief, than to a person wishing to avoid a protracted conflict with their spouse or offer a generous settlement for emotional reasons.

"Religious Contracts"

The courts have historically avoided enforcing "religious" agreements that require them to understand a religious doctrine in order to appraise its "public policy" impact. The courts are not in the business of evaluating religious principles, whether or not these are framed as "law." In the United States, the court's approach to religious questions is governed by the Establishment Clause, which prohibits the "establishment of religion."[50] This restricts the court from assessing procedural or substantive fairness in a religious contract. The result is the so-called prohibition doctrine[51] that holds that only "religion-neutral" agreements can be recognized and enforced by the courts. The problem with the prohibition doctrine is that it may prevent a court from enforcing an otherwise voluntary and legitimate contractual agreement simply because it is made by a religious body, or persons applying religious principles. This can lead to manifest injustice when an agreement—to pay a *mahr*, to organize property division between spouses using Islamic principles, or a promise to agree to a religious divorce—has been relied upon by one party. One writer summarizes this dilemma as follows:

> "Denying enforcement of a marital agreement signed by two individuals in a religious context might infringe on their free exercise rights, but interpreting and enforcing such an agreement on the basis of religious law verges dangerously on an establishment of religion."[52]

The courts have developed a number of approaches to avoid this injustice and promote freedom of contract.[53] This includes the "neutral principles approach," which allows the courts to adjudicate even in "religiously underscored cases" where it is possible to make a decision by applying "secular law without examining religion."[54] This approach has enabled some scattered instances where a court has recognized the *nikah* as an enforceable contract, treating "its secular terms . . . as a contractual obligation, notwithstanding that it was entered into as part of a religious ceremony."[55]

The difficulty of scrutinizing an agreement which is based upon an unfamiliar religious doctrine, and separating out its "religious" and "secular" elements, makes the courts nervous about enforcing any contract in which there is a suggestion of religious intent. The result is that despite the fact that Islamic law understands the *nikah* as a contract, and not as a religious sacrament, in most cases the courts will refuse to recognize its terms on the grounds that this is a contract "for a religious purpose."[56] In a 2007 Ohio case, the judge described the *mahr* in the following terms: "The obligation to pay $25,000 is rooted in a religious practice, the dowry is considered a religious act, not a legal contract."[57]

There is no equivalent to the Establishment Clause in Canada, but historically there has been a similar reticence to enforce religious contracts for the same reasons—that is, the state wishes to avoid the appearance of promoting or endorsing a particular religion. Similar problems arise when one side reneges on a genuine expectation which is couched in terms of a "religious obligation." This approach has been modified somewhat by the Supreme Court of Canada, which ruled in an important 2007 case[58] that an agreement in which a Jewish man promised his wife a Jewish divorce (or *get*) was enforceable. The reasoning adopted is similar to the "neutral principles approach." Writing for the majority, Madame Justice Abella said, "We are not dealing with judicial review of doctrinal religious principles, such as whether a particular *get* is valid. Nor are we required to speculate on what the rabbinical court would do. The promise by Mr. Marcovitz to remove the religious barriers to remarriage by providing a *get* was negotiated between two consenting adults, each represented by counsel, as part of a voluntary exchange of commitments intended to have legally enforceable consequences."[59] As Madame Justice Abella noted, the courts in Canada have previously adjudicated agreements made among members of another religious group—the Hutterite community—when "civil or property rights are engaged."[60] A different and creative approach—using statute rather than case law—adopted by the state of New York has the same intent as the reasoning in *Marcovitz*. Domestic Relations Law 253[61] requires a husband to remove any barriers to remarriage when he divorces his wife (provided the marriage is legal in that jurisdiction).

The American and the Canadian case law in this area highlights the difficulty of both defining and then separating "religion" from judicial consideration of obligations undertaken in a variety of cultural and social circumstances. The overlap between a "religious" obligation and family and community expectations, so obvious in conventions around Islamic marriage and divorce, means that what distinguishes a so-called "religious contract" from a private agreement which should have legal force is far from clear. This dilemma reflects the changing nature of religious practice in private life and the increasingly subjective and informal forms it takes.

On a practical level, Muslim women seeking to enforce the *mahr* have been encouraged by some recent decisions in both Canada and the United States. A series of British Columbian cases have upheld claims for payment of the *mahr*.[62]

In one, the judge commented, "Our law continues to evolve in a manner which acknowledges cultural diversity. Attempts are made to be respectful of traditions which define various groups who live in a multicultural community. Nothing in the evidence before me satisfies me that it would be unfair to uphold the provisions of an agreement entered into by these parties in contemplation of their marriage." In a 2010 Ontario case[63] the court treated the *nikah* as a legally enforceable contract and deducted the amount of the *mahr* ($60,000) from monies already taken by the wife from the couple's bank account, ordering her to only refund the balance. There was no legal marriage—both parties had other partners—and the court treated it as a simple monetary dispute between two adults, arising from an enforceable contract. In the United States, courts have occasionally used the "neutral principles" approach to enforce the secular obligations of the *mahr* despite the religious context in which the contract was made.[64] Most recently a *mahr* promise was enforced in a New Jersey case[65] where the judge asked, "Why should a contract for the promise to pay money be less of a contract just because it was entered into at the time of an Islamic marriage settlement?" and concluded that "this is nothing more and nothing less than a simple contract between two consenting adults. It does not contravene any statute or interests of society."[66]

It remains to be seen whether the reasoning in *Marcovitz* can be extended to applications in Canadian courts to enforce the *mahr*. In the absence of an authoritative higher court judgment, the law in this area is still developing, resulting in significant uncertainty for women attempting to rely on promises made in their *nikah*. Muslim lawyers and imams have responded by developing standard forms for marriage contracts that conscientiously avoid any reference to God or religion, with *mahr* undertakings framed as simple promissory notes. Several imams told me that they took care to remove any religious references from those agreements to avoid possible problems. There are signs of greater openness to jurisprudence that allows courts to recognize and enforce so-called secular obligations flowing from a religious act such as Muslim marriage or divorce, but the case law is patchy and inconsistent. The same observation could be made of judicial knowledge of Islamic law. In the handful of cases where the courts have engaged with the religious principles underlying Muslim marriage and divorce, judicial decisions reflect a superficial level of understanding. In a 1988 California case the court decided that it could not enforce a promise to pay a *mahr* because it could mean that the wife was "profiteering by divorce." The court evidently had no knowledge of the relative positions of husband and wife in relation to financial obligations in Islamic law. Equally alarming is a 2010 decision of the New Jersey Court of Appeals[67] which ordered the wife to return her *mahr* to her ex-husband on the grounds that her "fault" in causing the end of the marriage would require it to be returned in Islamic law. The court accepted the testimony of a single Islamic law expert to this effect, failing to recognize the highly contentious nature of this issue in Islamic jurisprudence. These cases illustrate the further difficulty of moving beyond the "religion-neutral" approach where the judiciary is largely unfamiliar with Islamic legal principles and procedural customs, still inevitably framed as the "Other."

Recognition of Islamic Marriage and Divorce Conducted Overseas

North American courts recognize marriages and divorces that take place in Muslim countries when they have been conducted in accordance with the formalities of that jurisdiction. The premise behind the doctrine of legal comity is that there should be some degree of reciprocal recognition among countries in order to maintain the stability of family and business relationships.

Recognition of overseas marriages is relatively straightforward. In the United States, a certificate of marriage from an overseas jurisdiction is recognized as long as that country is a signatory to the Hague Convention on the Celebration and Recognition of the Validity of Marriages.[68] In Canada, any marriage legally conducted in any overseas country will be recognized; the only exception (sometimes relevant to Muslim families) appears to be polygamous marriages.[69] The recognition of overseas divorce is more complex, and there are some important conditions. One or the other spouse must be able to show that they have a permanent home in that country. Evidence of residency (as it is described in Canada[70]) or domicile (in U.S. law) may include owning property, opening a bank account, voting or attending school. Under Canadian law this residence must have been maintained at least one year before the divorce, and there must be "a real and substantial connection with the foreign jurisdiction where the divorce was granted."[71] In practice, a court can often determine the fate of an application for legal recognition of an overseas divorce by the degree of rigor it applies to the claim of residence/domicile, which may reflect the comfort of the court with the particular jurisdiction for which comity is claimed. One counsel experienced in this area of practice described it as follows: "If we have real doubts about what is going on, we are going to put a higher threshold on what residence actually requires. For example, with identical facts the judge may find no real and substantial connection in Afghanistan because they do not like the facts, but they will apply the test differently in the United Kingdom. . . . The feeling is 'they are not like us, do we really want to support what they are doing?'"

In addition, public policy requires that reasonable notice of the divorce must have been given to both parties[72] that the divorce must be "genuine"[73], must not have been obtained by fraud, and must not offend against widely held "public morals".[74] If any of these conditions is not met, the court may refuse to recognize the divorce despite the fact that it complied with legal requirements in that jurisdiction. For example, in a case where an Egyptian man took another wife before his divorce (permitted under Egyptian law), it was held to be contrary to public policy and a Maryland court refused to recognize the divorce.[75] In Pakistan there is a requirement of notice for a divorce application, but if it is missing the court will still order a divorce and fine the applicant.[76] The absence of notice and "due process" means that this divorce is unlikely to be recognized in the United States or Canada.

Nawal came to the United States from Pakistan with her husband, Farid, ten years ago. In 2005, Farid returned to Pakistan where he married another woman whom he then brought back to the United States as his employee. Nawal only discovered this marriage a year later, when Farid asked her for a divorce. He coerced Nawal into signing a paper which asked for divorce as *khula*. She believes that he was afraid that otherwise she would ask him for a divorce in the United States on the grounds of his adultery.

Nonetheless, the relationship continued until 2009, when Nawal filed for divorce in a U.S. court. Farid contested the divorce—and Nawal's application for support—and presented the court with the paper he had coerced her into signing four years earlier and a divorce decree from Pakistan dated 2008.

After her first court hearing Nawal told me, "I never knew about this *khula* deed [the court decree of divorce] nor did my parents or relatives in Pakistan. I never received a note from the Union Council [the Pakistani court] either. I found out about all of this only in court. He is trying to prove that the *khula* deed from Pakistan is valid so that I won't get anything from his assets. If the American court accepts this *khula* deed, which is actually a fraud, all my daughters and I will get is child support. . . . I don't have a job and my daughters are young. We have no other source of income. My husband is a wealthy businessman."

Eventually Nawal's counsel won an order to dismiss the husband's purported foreign divorce. The judgment expressed the court's skepticism over her husband's claim to "domicile" in Pakistan, suggesting that while he traveled there periodically on business he did not reside there, and may have had another intention in seeking a divorce there rather than in the United States. The judge also referred to "an established principle of general jurisprudence, that no court will proceed to the adjudication of a matter involving conflicting rights and interests, until all persons directly concerned in the event have been actually or constructively notified of the pendency of the proceeding, and given reasonable opportunity to appear and be heard." He concluded that due process considerations had not been met here and would not recognize the overseas divorce.

Where an overseas divorce is recognized, it generally excludes the jurisdiction of North American court in relation to ancillary matters such as property division and support.[77] Nawal's case was one of four similar cases I came across. In each case, the wife contacted me and told me that her application for divorce and support in the United States had been met by an argument that she and her husband were already divorced in an overseas jurisdiction, and that the question of financial settlement (usually unresolved or minimal in the first "divorce") could not be reopened. The women had no knowledge of the overseas divorce until they brought their own application for divorce in the United States. Nawal's case is the only one of these four cases in which the claim for comity was denied, allowing her to proceed with her own claim for a divorce and a fair settlement. The three other women plaintiffs continue their legal struggle, facing diminishing financial resources and, often, a lack of knowledge and experience with Islamic law issues in their legal counsel. One of their (non-Muslim) legal counsel remarked to me, "Twenty-two years of practice and I am still amazed at what comes next." Some jurisprudence is developing to extend the denial of comity to cases where when the foreign divorce results in what appears to be a blatantly inequitable distribution of assets, or perhaps no orders for property division or spousal support at all. Here the courts will again rely on "public policy" considerations to refuse comity. For example, in considering whether to recognize a Pakistani divorce in which the absence of any agreement regarding the wife's share of matrimonial property meant that she had no claim at all, a Maryland court found this outcome to be "repugnant to public policy."[78]

When an overseas court makes a ruling on custody, any challenge is restricted by the Hague Convention on the Civil Aspects of International Child Abduction, which creates an international legal mechanism requiring contracting countries to return children who have been removed or not returned in violation of a custody order.[79] This convention solidifies the general deference for foreign judgments unless there is a complete departure from recognized principles ("best interests") for determining child custody. In a New Mexico case the court declined to second-guess the English court's ruling on custody: "The English family court's interpretation of its own domestic law is . . . entitled to our deference."[80] In another leading case, the court concluded that there was no basis on which to reject a Pakistani court's ruling on custody. "If the only difference between the custody laws of Maryland and Pakistan is that Pakistani courts apply a paternal preference the way Maryland courts once applied a maternal preference, the Pakistani order is entitled to comity."[81]

The application of the doctrine of comity to overseas divorces once again raises the dilemma of how to balance individual freedoms to engage in Islamic marriage and divorce procedures with safeguarding core rights and responsibilities as these are understood by North American courts.[82] On the one hand, reliance on comity may be critical to protecting a spouse who would otherwise be denied a legal status by her husband, where it would be unfair to deny such recognition for technical reasons (for example, a minor procedural defect in the marriage in the country in which it took place). On the other hand, comity may be used to escape financial obligations that would otherwise accrue in the United States or Canada following divorce (as in Nawal's case and the three other women I interviewed). There are practical and conceptual difficulties in assessing the merits of any individual case, including a general lack of knowledge about Islamic legal systems and Muslim culture, and in determining the facts of a dispute that occurred at least partially in another country and progressed through another legal system. The following case illustrates many of these dilemmas.

In *Jahangiri-Mavaneh v. Taheri-Zengekani*,[83] the parties were married in Iran, and a year later the husband—already a Canadian citizen—sponsored his wife to immigrate to Canada. However, less than six months later, the couple separated following an argument. The wife was sent back to Iran—apparently against her wishes—to live with her husband's family.

A divorce took place in Iran three years later. The circumstances of the divorce were contested, but the husband claimed that he paid a $30,000 *mahr*. There were no children. The following year, the wife returned to Canada as a landed immigrant. She then applied to a Canadian court for financial support as a spouse, claiming that the divorce in Iran was invalid.

Many practical matters were in dispute. What were the circumstances of the overseas divorce, and was the wife given notice? Was a monetary settlement paid? Was the wife's legal residence at the time Iran (as the husband claimed) or was this a fiction to facilitate the divorce (the wife's lawyer argued that being sent to Iran against her will did not constitute residence). In short, was the husband being unfairly asked to pay "again" for his divorce settlement, or was the wife treated in a way that would be contrary to public policy in Canada, allowing the court to refuse to recognize the Iranian divorce and reopen the question of support?

At first, the court recognized the Iranian divorce under the principles of comity, and the husband's motion to dismiss his wife's divorce application was successful. However, the Court of Appeal—pointing to "the absence of any evidence from anyone on the respondent's side who had personal knowledge of the facts in dispute"—overturned the decision. The parties evidently settled, since no further litigation took place.

It seems appropriate that the standard for overriding a legal divorce (or marriage) properly conducted in another country should be high, limited to evidence of fraud, deception or other egregious unfairness. The functionality and reciprocity of international law depends on respect among different legal systems. Reciprocity demands similar standards of system integrity, but cannot require the same norms or legal principles. .

American Muslims and the Courts:
Parallel Loyalties, Separate Systems

An examination of the legal issues raised by Islamic marriage and divorce is incomplete without asking how North American Muslims relate to and utilize the family court system. Almost every respondent who used Islamic marriage and divorce processes also sought a formal legal ratification of their decision. With the exception of a very small number of cases where reliance on a *nikah* only was in part the result of a general reluctance to use the state system, none of these respondents understood their recourse to Islamic marriage and divorce as a rejection of state institutional systems like marriage licensing or family courts For them this is not an either/or choice. Many North American Muslims marry with both a *nikah* and a civil license, and a significant number seek a religious divorce as well as (often before) applying for a civil decree. Informal dispute resolution processes like Muslim marriage and divorce are a feature of many minority communities who wish to maintain their own traditions and customs and an important element of community cohesion and "the community experiencing a sense of humanity." At the same time many respondents also described a strong attachment to their right to access formal legal institutions. When respondents used the word "right" or "rights" in interviews, they applied it to both their Islamic rights and their state or legal rights. The respondents also described their commitment to their Islamic culture by doing what is expected—signing a *nikah*, securing religious approval for divorce—by their family and community. None saw this as diminishing or detracting from their personal identification as American or Canadian citizens. This finding attacks the assumption that by using Islamic marriage and divorce processes North American Muslims are being "disloyal" citizens.

Regardless of their attachment to parallel informal processes, and no matter what their obligations under *shari'a*, Muslims are obligated to obey the law of the land.[84] Respondent after respondent made this point. For example, "After my court hearing, I felt truly divorced. For Muslims the law of the land must take precedence over Islamic law so this was what I had to do in order to be 'properly' divorced." However, the two processes are seen and experienced very differently. I discovered very early on in the study that there was no interest among the divorced men and women I interviewed in having the courts review a decision or an agreement made with an imam or other third party according to religious principles. They regard this advice as their religious duty—"this is what Allah expects of us"—and not attributable to the imam—"I'm not following the imam, I'm following what Allah says." When I asked them about whether they might take such advice to the court for review, they uniformly dismissed the question, saying that it was not for the courts to evaluate the word of Allah (as they understood either the advice of the imam or their own reading of their religious obligations). This explains why there were no applications for review from a Muslim "arbitration" (in contrast, for example, to the dozen or so applications over the same period from the Jewish Bet Din) under the Ontario Arbitration Act when it still recognized religious arbitrations.[85]

How American Muslims Use the Courts

In chapter seven I described how those respondents who could not reach agreement about the terms of their divorce typically ask the courts to adjudicate an outcome (just as non-Muslim couples do). For example, some of those ending shorter marriages and seeking a "clean break" appealed to the courts—usually unsuccessfully—when they were unable to obtain their *mahr* and, in the small number of shorter marriages which produced children, applied to the court for child support when it was not paid voluntarily. All but one of those marriages that lasted more than fifteen years was eventually resolved in court. Almost all the applicants were women. They had no compunction about using the courts to obtain a fair outcome when they could not reach agreement with their husband and/or with a supportive imam; they saw it as their right as Americans or Canadians and compatible with the principles of justice espoused by their faith. In a few cases, women recognized that the courts gave them greater protection and security than either their husbands or their imams.

> Hanin asked her imam repeatedly over many years to give her a religious divorce from her alcoholic husband. He told her, "Wait, be patient, he may change." Eventually Hanin went to court and got a divorce. She returned to the imam with her divorce decree. Only now—after asking her one more time, "Are you sure you want a divorce?"—did he give her a religious divorce.
>
> Hanin commented: "He was scared of the court, but not of God." Now she advises other women to go straight to the court."

I could not get help from my religion; I had to go outside my religion to get help."

"The Courts Don't Understand or Respect Muslims"

While Muslims use the courts, they make a number of criticisms of the justice system. Some of the imams and a number of divorced men and women criticized what they saw as the adversarial and unsympathetic nature of court processes, as well as the tendency of the legal system to escalate conflict and make people greedy.

> "Lawyers . . . make their money out of conflict and divorce."
> "When people want more, they go to court."
> "The courts don't want reconciliation. . . . We are just a number in the docket; there is no personal attachment."
> "[The court] is a blunt instrument which suffers from attention-deficit disorder. . . . I feel at the mercy of an arbitrary machine which will punch out a verdict at some point."

Many of these comments and experiences are shared by non-Muslims. Other complaints center on a lack of respect and knowledge regarding Muslims, or sometimes a generalized grievance that the courts are unfriendly and arbitrary places that do not understand Islam.

> "If the lawyer or the judge is not a Muslim, they are not sensitive to Muslim issues."
> "I went to court, but the judge is not a Muslim, and he does not know Allah."

There is a strong sense among some respondents that their choices as Muslims—and the reasons for those choices—are not always taken seriously by the justice system or system officials, or seen as worthy of understanding. There was a feeling among some respondents that legal advisers, courts and other justice officials too often tell Muslims, "We know what is best for you."

When they agreed to divorce, Amjad and his wife Ameera made an agreement covering financial support, payment of the *mahr*, custody and access. Initially the arrangement was that Amjad would have custody of their three children with access by Ameera, and both parents would have an equal say in decision making regarding the children.

This agreement collapsed, and Ameera applied to the court for an order on custody. The children's lawyer in their jurisdiction became involved in carrying out an assessment of the best interests of the children.

Amjad accepted that the court must now make a determination about custody. However, he told me that he felt that the officials from the office of the children's lawyer did not appreciate the religious and cultural issues involved on both sides. He complained that the two social workers who worked on the case regarded him as a "dangerous Muslim man," unsuited to raising his children, especially his two daughters.

Their original agreement had included a dispute resolution clause, and when I asked whether there was any reference to it by the court or the social worker, Amjad laughed. "They were completely dismissive [of it].... They said, "We engage the law." They did this without even a nod to the existing agreement. I felt that they had contempt for us as Muslims."

Court Orders and Islamic Obligations

The great majority of respondents had no qualms about seeking the jurisdiction of the court when they needed an adjudicative solution and accepted that they would comply with any court order. However, two residual questions arise, the most significant of which is whether a civil decree releases Muslim from their *nikah*; in other words, is it a complete substitute for a religious divorce? A relatively small number of respondents were concerned about a second question.

Should a Muslim Comply with a Court Order That Is "Un-Islamic"?

A small number of respondents were conflicted about a court order which appeared to contradict their Islamic obligations. This issue came up in two contexts—receiving and paying benefits—and a number of stories already told illustrate the dilemma. In relation to receiving benefits, a small group of religious women felt strongly that they should not claim anything beyond their Islamic entitlement, preferring to return anything that might appear to be "double-dipping." In relation to paying benefits, two women told me that they were uncomfortable with being ordered by a court to pay spousal support to their husbands. Umbrime—whose story is told in chapter three—worked out a solution with their imam to pay the money owed as *zagat* (a charity contribution) to avoid what they believed would otherwise result in shame and embarrassment. Another female professional ordered to pay support to her husband was furious at the judge for refusing to accept her explanation of spousal support in Islam, and spent a fortune on legal costs, attempting (unsuccessfully) to have the judgment reversed. These stories appear to be the exception. Most imams told me that there was no problem with a woman paying support if that was what was deemed fair. Each emphasized that Muslims have a duty to obey a court order, both as Muslims and as Americans or Canadians.

Does Civil Divorce Release Muslims from their *Nikah*?

If civil divorce were regarded as equivalent to a religious divorce, there would no longer be a need for Muslims in North America to seek out an imam or other third party—or to follow their own procedure—for religious approval. A *fatwa* from the European Council for Fatwa and Research does just this, recognizing an uncontested civil divorce as the equivalent of a religious divorce, with no further steps necessary in order to release an individual from their *nikah* promises (the "equivalency" *fatwa*).[86] The purpose of a *fatwa* is to clarify the appropriate Islamic behavior or response to a new or unfamiliar situation, and the Council is a recognized authority, referring questions to a group of distinguished Islamic scholars and clerics. The rationale behind the equivalency *fatwa* is that "due to the absence of an Islamic judicial system in non-Muslim countries, it is imperative that a Muslim who conducted his marriage by virtue of those countries' respective laws . . . comply with the rulings of a non-Muslim judge in the event of a divorce." A leading American scholar offers the same opinion, and for the same reasons.[87]

> "The dilemma that Muslims in America face is that there are no Muslim courts or Muslim judges in this country, and even if some Muslim scholars or imams of some Islamic centers dissolve a marriage according to Islamic laws, the American courts do not recognize Islamic divorces. Until the American court dissolves the marriage, the parties are considered legally married."

Dr. Siddiqi further advises that if possible the spouses should first agree the terms of their divorce with a Muslim scholar or arbitrator (usually an imam) and file it as a consent order in the family court. If a consent order is not possible, then either the husband or the wife should file for divorce in the family court. They should accept the ruling of a non-Muslim judge, as long as nothing in this order requires the parties to act contrary to Islamic law. When the wife obtains the decree, she should bring it to a mosque or Islamic center. "The Islamic centers should recognize it and should give the woman a letter confirming the American court's decision. They may say that under the present circumstances we have no objection to the court's decision and consider this couple no more husband and wife under the Islamic law as well." This is consistent with the practice of many imams who advise that a civil decree should be obtained first.

I heard frequent references from imams to the substance of this *fatwa*. However, some also noted that the community might be skeptical. "Even if some scholars say so, most of Muslim community does not accept this"; another remarked, "It is not always seen this way by the parties." Imams who are aware of the *fatwa* and similar advice from authoritative sources continue to offer parties an additional religious approval. Many work with couples to meet their particular needs in assuring them that their divorce is valid in Islam. This practice recognizes that for many Muslim men and women it is important for them to have some type of additional ritual or symbolic "release" granted by the imam (and sometimes to provide separate documentation, as Dr. Siddiqi suggests). Just one imam whom I interviewed advised parties that if they obtained a legal divorce, there was nothing further for him to do. The practice of others who recognize the *fatwa* appears to be to still work with the parties either to reach agreement on a consent order, or simply to offer reassurance, guidance and closure. Others will provide written approval for divorce, described as *faskh* or judicial cancellation of the marriage and based on the same reasoning as the *fatwa*, but without reference to the *fatwa* (see the example in appendix C). Further evidence that the *fatwa* has not ended the debate over the need for some form of additional religious approval can be found in the emergence of regional panels of imams in a few jurisdictions that consider paper applications for divorce and issue approvals. Again, this would be unnecessary if the *fatwa* were universally and literally accepted.

Approximately 10 percent of respondents told me that their imam told them about the equivalency *fatwa*. One woman described how she understood the *fatwa* in an e-mail to me:

> "X [an imam] told me that we have to step back and look at what an Islamic divorce really means [the spirit of a divorce]. He said that a divorce is the affirmation of one's intention to dissolve a marriage. So he confirmed that since we both signed our names on a divorce document . . . that this would be just as good as an Islamic divorce . . . since the document clearly stated both of our intentions to jointly end our marriage."

Others received quite different advice. One woman told me that she had been advised by several imams that a civil decree was insufficient to release her Islamically. "Only the liberal imam would say that a civil divorce is equivalent—if you live in a conservative community this [perspective] does not work—the community will still regard you as a married woman."

Most of those who were aware of or were advised about the *fatwa* accepted it with relief. A few told me that although they were aware of the *fatwa*, it did not give them satisfaction or closure. Several others—reflecting the comment above—said that whatever the status of the *fatwa*, they did not think that their family or community would accept a civil decree as equivalent to a religious divorce. In a few cases, the husband was simply unprepared to accept a civil divorce as the end of the Islamic marriage, giving rise to some alarming accounts of continuing harassment. One woman whose husband continued to pursue her for five years after their civil divorce, asserting that she was still his wife, was forced to obtain a series of protection orders. At one hearing he was asked by the judge, "Sir, do you recognize that you are divorced from this woman?" He replied, contemptuously, "Well, yeah, under the laws of [state]." The harassment ended only when she obtained a religious divorce.

Attachment to the need for religious approval in addition to a legal process in order to complete a divorce is reflected in many respondent stories. One man continued to sleep with his wife after their civil divorce because "I felt that she was still my wife Islamically, so it was OK for us to see each other still." One woman—civilly divorced three years earlier—was told by her fiancé's family that he could not marry her until she obtained religious approval for her divorce—something that took months of imam-shopping and some very difficult negotiations with her ex-husband to achieve. Eman's story illustrates the continuing uncertainty and confusion over the adequacy of civil divorce for Muslims.

> Eman was divorced in an American court. She had consulted with an imam before her civil divorce, and he had advised her not to stay with her husband. Her husband was not able to take care of Eman and their two children—one of whom was disabled—either financially or emotionally. The imam did not tell her about *fatwa*, but, empowered by his advice, Eman filed for divorce. When I spoke to her it had been six years since she had received her civil divorce decree.
>
> Her husband continued to assert that they were still religiously married, and some of her friends had also raised this question with her. Eman was worried that she was still tied to her ex-husband in some way and planned to return to the imam to ask for his advice. "It bothers me that there could be still a religious connection with this guy. I don't want to feel like I am doing something wrong if I want to get remarried. . . . I feel I need to ask my imam. But I have been divorced six years—don't tell me I am not divorced! How can I live in America and obey their laws and then be told that is not good enough for Islamic law?"

What's Next For the Courts?

The variable impact of the equivalency fatwa on the actual practice of Islamic divorce illustrates perfectly the nature of a private ordering system. Folk knowledge and inconsistent practice abounds. The psycho-social nature of Islamic marriage and divorce means that their legitimacy and meaning is connected to individual belief rather than any particular aspect of how they are practiced. This only deepens the quandary faced by the courts in North America which are struggling with which, if any, of these processes they should recognize, in order to respect genuine commitments made voluntarily and yet maintain a distance from religious laws and traditions.

How far should the courts go in giving effect to religious and cultural traditions practiced in private ordering? The stories and examples described in this chapter illustrate over and over again the dilemma of balance. As we expand the forms of legally recognized partnership to include common law and same-sex relationships, should the courts also recognize alternative forms of religious marriage? Can this commitment be understood in the same way as a legal commitment in obtaining a marriage license? Is it necessary for the courts to apply the same understandings about the consequences of marriage (for example, the merging of property, shared responsibility for children) to all couples? What evidence of voluntary "contracting out" of legal entitlements—a long established and central feature of the common law system—is necessary? Can we devise sufficient safeguards, including full and informed consent, that would allow a *nikah* ceremony to substitute for a legal marriage? As an immediate practical matter, can jurisprudence develop to allow for the enforcement of a promise to pay the *mahr* when there is a clear meeting of the minds, despite the fact that the promise arises in the context of a "religious" obligation? What would family court judges need to know about Islamic law and culture to enable consistent and fair decision making in relation to the legal status of a *nikah* and the enforcement of the *mahr*?

Recognizing Islamic divorce is even more complex. Since Islamic divorce in North America is a procedure that derives its meaning from the belief of those who participate in it, what would constitute evidence of religious divorce for legal purposes? How far are the intentions of the parties a substitute for formal procedures and documentation? What if those intentions diverge, with one party considering himself/herself formally divorced and the other not?

A further problem arises when a religious or overseas divorce deals in a markedly different way with the financial and legal consequences of divorce. In my study the most common manifestation of this problem was when a claim of an earlier overseas divorce was used to avoid financial obligations due in the United States or Canada. Private agreements made following religious divorce in North

America could, in principle, raise the same question of divergence from legal norms. While it seems just to recognize a genuinely self-determined divorce wherever (in North America or overseas) and however (according to whatever terms) it is conducted, what if the standards set for subsequent responsibilities (for example, support and property division, financial responsibility for children) are widely divergent from public expectations and the standards applied by the courts? This study suggests that domestically, this concern is limited to a very small group of cases. Only a few women were determined to forgo entitlements, with most divorced men and women ending up with outcomes either agreed or imposed which did not depart significantly from the legal norms. Nonetheless, the question of what the court should and can recognize as legally enforceable remains perplexing and contentious. The same cases often raise questions about procedural justice. What elements of "due process" are necessary for it to be a fair process? The use of unilateral *talaq* and a failure of notice raise obvious problems for this standard, already recognized by many of the imams and other leaders in the Muslim community.

The study also found a lacuna of expertise inside the legal profession in dealing with many of the unresolved legal issues described in this chapter, and a clear need for further education for lawyers and judges so that they can be better prepared to give good service to Muslim clients. A case could be made for a legal defense fund to assist indigent clients in their efforts to assert rights—to entitlements as a common law spouse, payment of the *mahr* and protection from claims of comity when they are being used to deprive them of financial support—which are hampered by lack of both expertise and, often, resources.

The final chapter of this book considers alternatives in the development of public policy regarding Islamic marriage and divorce, as well as some of the challenges raised by present practices for the Muslim community. It explores possible models for the interaction between Islamic private ordering processes and the political and legal structure of the secular state. While the development of political solutions does not directly resolve the tensions seen in the case law, it is essential that future policy-making reflect the experiences of Muslim Americans and the reality of their private ordering system, rather than suspicion and speculation. A better informed public discourse and a political debate grounded in facts not fear sets an important tone for a continuing discussion over how the courts can protect basic rights, while maximizing cultural and religious choices.

9 LOOKING FORWARD

"Before members of a liberal democratic polity can truly understand what the values of liberty, equality and multiculturalism can and cannot accommodate . . . , they must also make an effort to understand the Other that seeks accommodation."[1]

Religion and Secularism

At first glance, religion and secularism appear to be opposites, with the former a matter of private practice and the latter a public ideology adopted by the state. When the concept of secularism first emerged in the nineteenth century it was understood as an alternative to religion—the word "secular" in Arabic (*'almaniyya)* means "the worldly"—then the dominant ideology of the nation-state in both the West and parts of the postcolonial world. Secularism offered the possibility of thinking of the nation as a political territory, rather than a religious community. But the commitment of the secular state to protect the space in which religious practice can take place means that the two concepts are inevitably co-dependent.[2] In the United States and Canada constitutional guarantees charge the courts with protecting individual rights to freedoms of speech, conscience and religion, but the state is prohibited from promoting (or "establishing") any particular religion. The result is a public commitment to protecting private religious practices but a parallel commitment (in the name of secularism) to avoid vesting legal authority in religious processes such as Muslim marriage and divorce, or allowing these to give rise to legal rights and obligations. This is a difficult balance to find, as we saw in chapter eight.

Because secularism defines itself as an alternative to religion, it is profoundly affected by the changing nature of "religious" (as opposed to familial, or cultural) practice. Public observance is declining among the general population in North America. That population is also much more diverse in terms of its religious practice than in the nineteenth century. Instead of being understood as a means of holding a (Christian) church at arm's length from the state, secularism in the twenty-first century is increasingly seen in the West as a bulwark against "Other" religions, and particularly Islam since 9/11. Secularism has come to be associated with modernity and Western values, and religion with "traditional" or even "backward" values.[3] Many different approaches to secularism have emerged. For example, an "assertive secularism" prohibits public totems of faith such as the *hijab*; in contrast, the "passive secularism" that prevails in the United States and Canada withholds legal recognition from religious processes but struggles to accommodate the public face of religion and takes a more tolerant approach to visible symbols of religiosity.[4] Because our understanding of "secular" must evolve in relation to our understanding of "religion," both definitions are fluid and dynamic. Far from being oppositional or contradictory, there is a dynamic relationship between them.

As a result, the legal-political status quo in the United States and Canada in relation to Islamic marriage and divorce operates in a constant state of flux and with some underlying unresolved tensions. Historically, American and Canadian jurisprudence has focused on how to protect individual religious beliefs. However, a right to practice one's religion is not the same as a right to have one's religious beliefs recognized as normative or legally enforceable. This is the crux of the struggle to keep religion and the state at arm's length from one another in a secular state. A secular state cannot legislate in a manner that reflects a particular religious doctrine—but at the same time the secular state must protect the right of each citizen to hold and express a religious belief. A further paradox is that the protections of the secular state are essential to enabling discussion and dissension within religious traditions and perhaps to modernizing these traditions.[5] At the heart of this dilemma is what we understand as "having a religion" or "practicing a faith" in twenty-first-century North America.

The Changing Nature of "Religious" Practice

The separation of church and state in Canada and the United States rests on a traditional concept of religion defined by external observance and devotion. One hundred and fifty years ago, as secularism was emerging as an organizing principle for law and governance,[6] most of the colonizer population in North America would have described themselves as having a religion (almost always Protestant Christian), and would have attended church. Religious practice was a central part of individual identity, with religious observance a key aspect of a series of formal obligations and duties—including work for men and housekeeping for women—considered essential to community and family membership. Today, one in seven Americans say that they have "no religion" at all, inconceivable even as recently as fifty years ago. Survey data shows the extent of organized religion—measured by the number of individuals identifying themselves as "having" a religion, attending church or other places of worship, and the number of church congregations—declining significantly.[7]

To those who see themselves as on a religious or spiritual journey, the assumption that religious practice is focused on external observance and sustained by a sense of duty is clearly outdated. So-called New Age religions, adherence to particular physical or nutritional regimes (yoga, reflexology, veganism) and various reform movements (such as Jewish Renewal or Catholic liberation theology) are broadening our understanding of how higher spirituality may be sought. A movement away from traditional religious commitment (characterized by external practices underpinned by a sense of duty and obligation) towards forms of personal spirituality (oriented towards psychological well-being) is a reorientation away from organized religion and towards more private practices, sometimes shared among small communities of like-minded individuals.[8] Sociologists Paul Heelas and Linda Woodhead describe this as religion practiced as "subjective-life," where the focus is on achieving inner peace and knowledge of self—in short, a subjective, private experience. At the same time these forms of religious practice sometimes create and sustain communities—sometimes diverse, sometimes culturally specific—whose membership loosely adopts these practices. Unlike a traditional religious congregation, however, membership is fluid and not dependent upon public signs of piety or observance (religion practiced as "life-as," or obligation towards a higher authority). Identity in this new paradigm is less focused on "sameness" among group members and more on what Talal Asad describes as "the other's recognition of the self," which emphasizes individual characteristics ("old certainties"[9]) which set that person apart rather than join them with others.[10]

The experiences of many of the respondents illustrate the phenomenon of "subjective-life" religious practice. The "religious practice" described by the respondents is more complex and diverse than simple observance. It encompasses spiritual beliefs, cultural traditions and a sense of Islamic identity. It attaches to rituals, beliefs and hopes for the future. It reflects the need to find "the source of significance," as Charles Taylor puts it.[11] Martha Nussbaum describes the search for spirituality as "the faculty with which people search for life's ultimate meaning—frequently called 'conscience'—[this] is a very important part of people, closely related to their dignity."[12] This faculty may be more likely to be exercised when people confront crises; a search for meaning was plain in the stories told by the respondents about how they came to terms with their divorce in light of their faith, however practiced.

Modifying our understanding of the nature of contemporary religious practice as it moves towards private spirituality and away from organized religion affects how we think about the secular state's commitment to remove any consideration of "religion" from lawmaking and judicial decision making. Without a clear definition, or in light of multiple and expanding definitions, the identification of what is a "religious practice" (as opposed to cultural or familial, or a practice that is deeply personal) becomes much more difficult. This lack of clarity exposes the evolving relationship between "culture" and "religion" in a multicultural secular democracy, lacking "a way of distinguishing purely cultural habits from seriously-rooted matters of faith and discipline, and distinguishing uninformed prejudice from religious prescription."[13] Courts and legislators are expected to respect cultural norms and sometimes defer to them, and may draw on their knowledge of cultural differences to fashion legal and political solutions. On the other hand, "purely cultural habits" do not attract the same constitutional protections as "seriously-rooted matters of faith." Culture is understood as a universally shared characteristic, less intrusive to the beliefs of others than a religious creed (which may seek converts, or otherwise threaten the impartiality of the state). Support for multiculturalism—which broadly recognizes and supports cultural identities and practices—is often held up alongside secularism as a political mantra for the modern state. If secularism is pro-culture but anti-religion, how does that translate into terms of judicial or political policy? For example, when religious obligations are owed to a cultural community—when signing a *nikah* or making an agreement to divorce with the assistance of an imam may be an effort to satisfy the expectations of family, community and one's own sense of duty and tradition, regardless of whether an individual will ever again set foot in a mosque - are these still "religious" obligations that the courts must stay away from enforcing? Should informal community fora for resolving disputes—for example, over child support following divorce, or payment of the *mahr*—be recognized by the state, or would such a policy effectively endorse a particular religious faith?

As the nature of religious practice changes, it is increasingly difficult to maintain a clear distinction between religion and culture. A new and nuanced understanding of the relationship between religion and cultural, group and individual norms is needed in order to find the balance between the protection of identity (religious, cultural) rights, and limits on privileging any particular religious practice in a public space, whether by the legislature, the courts, schools or any other public institutions.

Legal-Political Strategies

The changing nature of religious practice and the evolution of state secularism suggest four possible approaches to this dilemma. Each of these is considered below in light of the study data.

Maintaining the Status Quo

At present, neither Islamic marriage nor divorce is recognized as legally effective in either Canada or the United States. The absence of legal recognition reflects the state's commitment to universalism and secularism. The "religion-neutral" approach adopted by the courts prevents legal recognition of any process or contract that has a intention or motivation, removing consideration of any such alternatives from the ambit of the courts. The assumption is that a universal "religion-neutral" standard is critical to ensuring the equal protection of all citizens. Members of minority communities are expected to subjugate their loyalty to different traditions and beliefs about family life to the universal laws of the state in order to avail themselves of state-protected rights and freedoms.[14] Vulnerable members of these communities can use the universal law to assert themselves against discrimination and injustice within their own communities, but they must also embrace how the dominant group understands justice—for example, protection from domestic abuse but also shared matrimonial property and formal gender equality—and the outcomes it advocates.

The effect of state commitment to this understanding of secularism is to force Islamic marriage and divorce processes—along with other informal, customary processes without legal force that represent religious and cultural rites of passage, such as Hmong marriage rituals, the Jewish "get" or divorce, or birth customs such the "bris"—"below the radar" of state oversight (where they continue to flourish as an expression of religious, cultural and community identity.) There is an assumption, reflected in court jurisprudence, that religious belief is the sole explanation for participation in these processes, and so the court must enquire into the sincerity of this belief. As this study shows, this is an incomplete understanding of what motivates individuals to continue to practice these traditions. Choices over actions reflect multiple affiliations of belief, tradition, commitments to family and personal preferences which cannot be collapsed into a single motivation. This reality belies any judicial attempt to define and then discern a "genuine" religious motivation.[15]

By adopting the religion-neutral approach the courts impose "one law for all," a formulation advanced by Premier Dalton McGuinty in Ontario when he announced the "banning" of *shari'a* law in 2005. Ayelat Shachar describes this approach as "secular absolutism."[16] This formula expects Muslims to choose between Islamic values and loyalties and those of the state system. It assumes an inevitable conflict between two systems, and the possibility of just one choice—a "zero-sum" equation or what Shachar describes as an "either/or" dichotomy. Set alongside the results of this study, the stark choice posited by secular absolutism is a simplistic understanding of how citizens actually manage loyalties to different normative systems. The majority of respondents saw no conflict between their Islamic beliefs and values and the civil law system. They used the courts for legitimacy and enforcement and sometimes for adjudication of unresolved issues. When the community cannot provide justice—for example, when a woman repeatedly seeks a religious divorce in the face of intense marital conflict and even abuse but is turned away—its members seek redress in the courts. Tension between the Islamic and the state family law system is experienced for the most part in relation to discrete issues, for example, whether a wife should meet the terms of a court order for paying spousal support (the vast majority believe that she should). Almost none of the respondents advocated the legal recognition of private Islamic processes, accepting that they would operate without the force of law. At the same time, acceptance of and access to a secular legal system does not obviate the desire for informal community processes and traditions. Almost all divorcés and divorcées obtained both a civil and a religious marriage and divorce. A British researcher has observed that "all ethnic minorities in Britain marry twice, divorce twice and do many other things several times in order to satisfy the demands of concurrent legal systems."[17] The same is true for North American Muslims, the vast majority of whom accept the secular absolutist model offered by the legal system and will access this system when the need arises—as long as they can still practice their own traditions.

The real limitations of this model for Muslim communities in North America are less its conceptualization as a part of their civil and political life, and more its limitations in respecting and understanding their traditions and beliefs. Far from mounting a lobby to establish a system of legally recognized "*shari'a* law" in North America, the real source of dissatisfaction among Muslims relates to the way in which the courts understand "Muslim questions" and traditional processes, or credibly assess the sincerity and motivations behind religious belief. While greater knowledge and familiarity with Islamic values and customs would be welcomed by many Muslims who use the courts, and could enable more informed and sensitive decision-making, the problem that remains is the avowed "agnostism" of the court which "will always clash with those who see questions of right religious conduct as necessarily permeating all aspects of human life."[18] Can contemporary secularism accommodate contemporary "religious practice"?

It could be argued that universalism can and should protect access to basic rights for individuals and communities without needing to dissolve or ignore the private spaces within which individuals practice religion, custom and habit.[19] Fear of what happens in those spaces is an obstacle to a more informed debate. The failure of the status quo to recognize attachment to Islamic marriage and divorce as culturally and identity-significant processes must be seen in this light. Muslims are not frustrated because the courts deny these processes legal recognition—which few expect or advocate—but because legal and public discourse excludes any real consideration of the meaning of these rituals to Muslims. This frustration is aggravated by—and sometimes conflated with—anger at growing Islamophobia.

Convergence

Strategies to enhance understanding and cooperation between Islamic and civil law, stopping short of affording legal status to Islamic law, constitute a form of "dialectical interaction between two legal or cultural systems which may result in innovation and change."[20] Sometimes described as a "modified absolutist" or "integration" approach, this means there is mutual influence between the two systems. Shachar describes this as "transformative accommodation." I have described this process elsewhere as "convergence."[21] As a consequence of convergence, each system takes on some of the ideas and values and practices of the other. This process might be compared to a chemical combination, where the essential properties of each process or culture are significantly changed as a result. An example of this phenomenon is the growing use of dispute resolution processes such as mediation in the courts, requiring lawyers to adopt new strategies and approaches to bargaining over the settlement of a lawsuit which fuse some of their traditional skills (legal research and analysis) with some new and less unfamiliar ones (persuasive advocacy, relationship-building, creative problem solving).[22] Another is the evolution of circle-sentencing procedures in some criminal courts sitting in aboriginal and Native American communities, where a judge presides and applies the state law but uses a process model which invites the community to contribute their ideas about an appropriate sentence.[23]

Formally, the courts in the United States and Canada can already consider other legal systems, including Islamic law, when they are relevant to a decision. For example, a transnational contract dispute might prompt the court to review rights and obligations in contract law in the other jurisdiction. This doctrine was subject to sustained criticism in the Oklahoma referendum, although many protagonists did not appear to understand that the doctrine allowed consideration of any other legal system—not just Islamic law—and is essential to the courts being able to determine fair outcomes that reflect the parties' expectations. On the other side of the equation, some imams have incorporated many of the norms and expectations of the civil system into their advice to divorcing couples—for example, deciding custody according to "best interests" and property division so as to recognize joint ownership. In the United Kingdom, Menski[24] suggests that English and Islamic law have combined to form what he calls "Agrezi Sharia." This builds some English legal requirements—for example, the registration of marriage—into customary procedures, creating hybrid laws and processes. As Bano describes it, "Asians learnt to adapt to English law but rather than abandon their customary traditions, they built the requirements of English law into them."[25] While the practice of Islamic divorce has been formalized (although not legalized) in the United Kingdom for more than thirty years via the *Shari'a* Council (a network of regional panels offering a paper-based process for religious divorce), the work of the imams in North America is generally more ad hoc and less centralized, aside from a few urban centers (including Detroit, Toronto and Los Angeles) where panels are emerging. This makes monitoring the emergence of hybrid laws and practices difficult and the phenomenon perhaps less advanced; nonetheless, this study provides several clear examples, including the use of child support guidelines and support for spousal support beyond the period of the *iddat*. The practice of some imams who approve religious divorce but send the parties to lawyers or the courts to resolve other divorce consequences is itself a type of hybrid where each system takes responsibility for a different, but essentially complimentary, aspect of the divorce process.

A sustained process of convergence and cross-fertilization could eventually extend to the limited legal recognition of Islamic marriage and divorce. The courts already occasionally recognize Islamic and other forms of religious marriage (subject to existing laws on the legal age of marriage, and bigamy) when there is evidence of a clear belief in (and reliance upon) a marital commitment.[26] Recognition of Islamic divorce is more problematic, given that there is no established procedure or documentation. If Muslim communities want the courts to recognize such processes as legally dissolving marriage without the need for further recourse to a civil decree, consistent forms, procedures and outcomes will need to be developed.

Practically speaking, conflict is as or more common over the enforcement of agreements made between the couple in the course of Islamic marriage and divorce (for example, a promise to pay a *mahr*, or an agreement to limit spousal support to the *iddat*) than the legal recognition of the act of marriage or divorce itself. If the courts are to consider these agreements in something other than an ad hoc, case-by-case manner (described in chapter eight), the legal basis for an enforceable agreement in such circumstances needs to be clearly established and consistently applied. Many of these principles already exist in contract law. The process of convergence or "dialectical interaction" would reconcile common law standards with Islamic family processes using principles drawn from contract law regarding notice, fair process, coercion, fraud, informed consent (perhaps underpinned by independent advice or a mandatory "cooling-off" period), as well as the possibility of striking down an agreement seen as "oppressive" (denoting cruel and burdensome rather than unbalanced, which is a matter of freedom of contract provided other safeguards are met). If agreements made regarding marriage and divorce passed these tests they could be enforced as legal contracts by the courts.

A new jurisprudence would require both judicial and imam education to ensure shared understanding of the appropriate principles and responsibilities. Some limited legal recognition of Islamic marriage and divorce and subsequent agreements, subject to clear common law safeguards, would generally understand such processes as culturally and personally significant rather than "religious" procedures which are excluded from the consideration of the court. This approach would offer a more nuanced understanding of the significance of Muslim marriage and divorce and reflect the motivations of many of the respondents in this study. It may also encourage some formalizing of both *nikah* and Islamic divorce procedures and the development of "best practices" (for example, explicit negotiation and acceptance of the terms of the *nikah,* notice for *talaq,* fair child and spousal support payments).

Recognized Islamic Tribunals

During the Ontario *shari'a* debate, some legal and Islamic scholars argued that a private system of Muslim family dispute resolution could not be expected to develop consistent, fair processes without an institutional context. "Law without an institutional context is an abstract doctrine," reducing the discussion to "a postcolonial search for identity"[27] in which many competing visions of Islamic law jostle for space, with different approaches privileged by particular cultural perspectives. The development of an institutional framework to enable the emergence of a vibrant and authoritative *shari'a* for North American Muslims requires more than an ad hoc system of individual imams and arbitrators reaching unreported decisions. One option would be to allow independent religious tribunals to determine issues of personal family religious law. The creation of a legally competent Islamic tribunal for family matters would be a significant formalization of the private ordering practices in Muslim communities. The objective would be to preserve the identity of the Muslim community by protecting and legitimating the space in which they conduct marriage and divorce processes.

A parallel legal system is similar to the approach taken by colonial authorities—for example, the British in India and the French in Egypt—when they implemented legal systems based on their own laws, but left a parallel system of alternative courts (usually focused on family disputes) intact. It vests legal authority in religious and cultural communities to make their own determinations regarding family matters by establishing an Islamic tribunal that has legal jurisdiction over marriage and divorce. There are no contemporary examples of this model in the West; the closest is the U.K. Shari'a Council, which is not a formally recognized legal tribunal but a registered charity, although it has many of the characteristics of a tribunal (for example, clear procedural rules, a system of reporting and precedent). Public and political anxiety about the implications of a parallel Islamic legal system has curtailed discussions about the viability of this option in both the United Kingdom and in North America.

There are well-established norms for the structure of a parallel legal forum. The work of such a tribunal would be primarily adjudicative—that is, it would hear disputes and impose decisions—but in common with most contemporary tribunal systems it could also offer mediation or other settlement opportunities. The existence of a separate tribunal would not compel Muslims to use this avenue for their family disputes, but would offer them a choice. Such choices are an established part of citizenship in a society where members hold multiple loyalties and identities. A right of appeal from the tribunal into the formal court system would mean that rulings made by the tribunal would be subject to judicial review by the courts, potentially bringing the two systems into much closer contact. It is questionable how much such an appeal route would be used (in Ontario the now-repealed provisions of the Arbitration Act allowing appeals from any religious arbitrator were never used by the Muslim community).[28] It is possible that with the development of a more formal hearings structure—with reported decisions and the development of precedent—Muslims would become more comfortable over time challenging certain outcomes than they presently are in challenging the advice of the imams. In this way, formally recognizing the role of Islamic tribunals and establishing some oversight may address some of the concerns expressed in Ontario and the United Kingdom about the operation of a private dispute resolution system outside the legal system.

Concerns about a parallel system recognized in law crystallize around two closely related issues—denial of rights promoted by the mainstream system and voluntariness. Differences in the rights and responsibilities framework between the Islamic and civil systems raise questions over whether the state should recognize a parallel jurisdiction that does not offer the same rights offered by the mainstream system, for example, ongoing spousal support and property equalization. An Islamic tribunal may hand control to forces within the community that are oppressive to vulnerable groups; in a highly patriarchal culture, there is a larger risk that women will suffer if their rights are adjudicated according to internal norms. At the same time it is important to recognize that the same choice—between seeking maximal legal entitlements or coming to a private agreement in the "shadow of the law"—is offered to women of other faiths, and none. As Natasha Bakht pointed out in her commentary on the Ontario debate, "It is disingenuous to speak of 'one law for all' when Ontario's family law permits parties to opt out of the default statutory regime such as the equal division of matrimonial property. Parties can, through negotiation, mediation or arbitration, based on the right to contract freely, agree to almost any resolution of their marital affairs. . . . Couples' decisions to settle their family law affairs are generally left un-reviewed by the courts."[29]

In this way concerns over waiving legal entitlements available in the civil courts dovetail with concerns over voluntariness. As Bakht argues, adults can and frequently do consent to waive or reduce legal entitlements in the mainstream system, but a critical question is how much pressure to conform to community norms is inherently oppressive to women, or others with relatively less power. An additional concern is the pressure that may be exerted by religious proscription: "If following the Sharia route is presented as a matter of duty and loyalty to the group, then the argument is essentially that 'to be a good Muslim' one must live under Muslim family law."[30] While this study found no evidence of coercion among any of the respondents who sought religious divorce, many were subject to some family pressure to "do the right thing." A number of women described seeking a religious divorce following a civil divorce to demonstrate to the community—and sometimes to their ex-husbands—that they were "really" divorced. The small group of particularly religious women who refused larger financial settlements due to them in the civil system appeared to be making a free and informed choice, although within a context where their expectations were shaped by their faith and upbringing. Samia Bano's study of experiences in the U.K. Shari'a Council[31] and Ghena Krayem's study of community processes in western Australia[32] have similarly found no evidence of overt compulsion. Voluntariness here is complex and contextual and raises a host of practical questions. Dominant values in family life inevitably color what are seen as expected behaviors for us all. But just how much family (or community) pressure is acceptable, and how much is unacceptably coercive—for example, closing off other viewpoints? At the same time, a legally recognized Islamic tribunal could address some concerns about voluntariness by requiring free and informed participation, overseen and monitored by the state.

Another danger is that the existence of a tribunal may provide a focus for more conservative ideologies promoting the view that only divorces approved by the tribunal are truly "Islamic" and the reassertion of traditional principles regarding property and support. This study suggests that a conservative tribunal would have little appeal to those many respondents whose commitment to Islam is personal and cultural and solidified at a time of crisis or transition, rather than formally religious. On the other hand, a tribunal which debates these and other questions could reach for a more progressive and contemporary approach to gender and other family issues and offer men and women more choices—for example, a progressive Islamic approach—than are presently available between the justice system and the private ordering system. Much would depend on how such a tribunal was constituted and its major players and influences. One obvious question is whether a tribunal would include adjudicators (and mediators) of both genders. In addition to its religious identity, a further challenge for a single tribunal is that it might be seen as representative of some groups—who would prefer it—and not of others—who would reject it.[33] The U.K. Shari'a Council makes an effort to be representative of all Muslims but is widely regarded as most closely connected to the Pakistani community.[34] Establishing regional panels of imams in North America faces the same problem.

The respondents in this study regularly brought issues they considered to be unresolved to a court for adjudication, accepting civil law principles. This finding suggests that even if a parallel system were available to them, men and women will make up their own minds—subject, inevitably, to a degree of family and community influence—over which route best serves their interests and meets their needs.

A Regulated "Marketplace" of Private Ordering

A different approach is to support and encourage the development of a network of competing Muslim family service organizations that together constitute an institutional framework in which Muslims are offered choices of both service providers and processes. Instead of or as well as a single recognized tribunal, a private marketplace model could offer Muslims a range of services in addition to formal adjudication, including counseling, assessment, mediation and arbitration (both binding and non-binding). Services such as premarital and marital counseling would educate Muslims about their Islamic rights and duties in marriage, and crisis intervention would offer families critical practical assistance from Muslim professionals. Some professionals might offer their services as mediators, others as arbitrators. These roles could be expanded beyond the imams to others in the community with appropriate skills and qualifications, including women. Muslim family lawyers, whose work is presently largely disconnected from the private ordering processes within their communities, could choose to offer services and to work in coordination with third-party mediators or arbitrators. Marketing, as well as internal and independent monitoring of such programs, would provide the Muslim community with important information about access to available services that at present is almost entirely lacking. Systematic data collection from service providers could begin to address some of the problems identified by this study—inconsistent access and advice and in particular a lack of proper attention to allegations of domestic abuse and violence. Future researchers would be able to examine established service programs and access data on usage and satisfaction, instead of relying on word of mouth to identify who is offering what type of process. At its best, such a marketplace would enhance services, encourage diversity and enable the development of needs-based Muslim family services.

The development of such a marketplace would be a transformation of the status quo in North America. It has not emerged organically—the few exceptions are a handful of Muslim therapists and counselors, mostly serving non-Muslim clients, online advice on marriage and divorce laws, and agencies offering Muslim "dating." Services for couples in crisis are at present almost exclusively in the hands of a small group composed almost entirely of imams, which exacerbates the problem of access to services; some respondents were unwilling to go to an imam, perceiving him as unsympathetic, lacking in skill or knowledge or just too remote from their everyday life. Some of those respondents who did seek religious divorce from an imam complained that it was an unpleasant and sometimes dehumanizing experience. These individuals would prefer to seek help from other quarters, but presently see no alternative if they want to obtain religious approval for divorce.

In the absence of alternatives, power and credibility within the community remain with traditional authority figures such as the imam or male family members. They are neither expected nor required to carry any further professional qualifications. When the law in Ontario began requiring credentials for family arbitrators there was zero interest within the Muslim community. It is highly unlikely that an imam approached for advice on marital conflict would ever be asked by a Muslim if he is qualified as an arbitrator under the Ontario Arbitration Act—and thus there is no motivation to acquire such a qualification. At the same time, many respondents—and some imams—recognized that intervening in serious family conflicts, especially domestic abuse, requires a high level of skill for which they are largely unprepared and untrained. This suggests a level of recognition from within the leadership that additional and more sophisticated services for Muslim families are necessary.

The critical question is how to develop the necessary momentum within the community to drive the development of appropriate institutions and the professionalization of services. This study has noted a number of environmental factors that constrain the development of services, including taboos on talking openly about divorce and an emphasis on resolving marital conflict within the family system. There is reluctance among many Muslims to seek professional therapy and counseling, and a strong preference for looking for help inside the family. Among other Muslim professionals—including therapists and marriage counselors, social workers, shelter workers and even lawyers—anxiety is frequently expressed about stepping on the toes of the imams, who occupy a position of significant power, especially in newer immigrant communities where they are relied upon for a range of practical and psychological supports. All these factors impede the development of an alternative system of service providers which is more diverse, accessible and accountable and not limited to the mosques, despite the many unmet needs I heard about in interviews. The number of hits on the study website—often asking for relatively simple advice on divorce laws, or seeking a referral to a sympathetic imam—was a constant reminder of the absence of accessible services to meet the community's level of need. To counter these constraining forces, an intentional effort by Muslim leaders is needed to promote the development of service institutions staffed by appropriately credentialed professionals—including but not limited to the imams—and give them a clear role within the community. Before this can happen, however, other challenges must first be confronted.

Challenges for Muslim Communities

In order to protect—and evolve—a distinctive approach that reflects their values, Muslim communities in North America need to begin to talk more openly about marital conflict and divorce. Whether promoted by mosques, community centers or social services organizations, an inclusive debate is a critical first step. I found that some women were afraid to even participate in meetings about marital conflict and divorce that I facilitated for fear of being marked as a divorced woman or a woman considering divorce. Hopefully, as these discussions become more commonplace, and as influential leaders take a role in them, the tendency to stigmatize those who participate will also diminish.

Talking is very important, but it is not all that is needed. This study collected data in four areas of Muslim life that are already in transition, but must continue to adjust to contemporary conditions in order to safeguard the identity, cohesion and stability of North American Muslim communities.

The Role of the Family

As divorce becomes more and more commonplace, intolerance towards divorced women and efforts to exclude them from family and community systems become more noticeable, and less socially acceptable. Most people now know at least one divorced person. Divorced women are drawing strength from one another as they come to realize that they are no longer so exceptional. They are discovering that their worst fears about rejection by their family and future suitors do not (in most cases) materialize. Yet the assumption of rejection persists in many quarters. This is not surprising given wider community attitudes towards divorce and divorced women. A perspective that was frequently articulated in community meetings during the course of this project was that a divorced woman is "to blame" for the break-up of her family. A further judgment heard frequently is that divorced couples (particularly young people) "didn't try hard enough" to make marriage work. Each of these judgments is being increasingly challenged by individuals courageous enough to explain why they felt they needed to end their marriages, and by imams willing to moderate an open discussion about marital conflict and divorce. The data gathered for this study—for example, revealing the reasons for divorce, which for one in three women includes domestic violence, and describing the efforts made by younger people matched to incompatible partners to make their marriages succeed—may also be useful in dispelling some of these tenacious myths about marriage and divorce, which are not limited to the Muslim community.

An important source of more tolerant attitudes towards divorce is the family, which will usually come to the aid of their daughter or son in the event of conflict. A number of respondents expressed surprise and pleasure at the support they received from their parents—perhaps not immediately, but over time—whom they had anticipated would be extremely critical of their decision to divorce. Some were less fortunate—but family ties usually supplant fear and shame. It is also within the family that norms and expectations about marriage are first established and these are often reflected in how the family handles the marriage of their sons and daughters. This study shows that arranged marriages between a spouse born and raised in North America and another born and raised in an overseas country (so-called transnational marriages) frequently face insuperable difficulties. Parents should use caution when arranging these types of marriages and be willing to listen to young women who speak up in an effort to discourage such unions (as some of the respondents poignantly did, but were overruled). While some of the traditions of arranged or semi-arranged marriage are likely to continue in many communities, it is important to recognize that a woman educated in North America and expecting a professional career is unlikely to be able to make a marriage work with a man who has grown up in a Muslim country and is seeking a traditional Muslim wife.

Other marriages foundered on the fact that one of the spouses was the product of a family system that was significantly more traditional—and as a consequence often more interventionist and influential—than the other. In an effort to achieve greater independence from their parents, some young Muslim couples are starting to challenge the expectations of their extended family (for example, over sharing a residence, or seeking their advice) and to focus on establishing norms and values between the two spouses. It is not possible to know whether this change will reduce marital conflict and the rate of divorce—indeed, some may argue that without the guiding hand of their parents, young couples may find themselves more quickly and more frequently in conflict. However, some of the marriages in this study demonstrate that the ability of the spouses to negotiate their own agreed norms for marriage and family life separately from those of their two families is often crucial to their ability to resolve conflict and succeed in their marriage. This suggests that greater independence in both choice of partner and how the couple will live together as a married couple is important for the creation of a contemporary partnership. Younger women respondents—especially those under the age of thirty-five—are leading vastly different lives than their mothers and grandmothers did. They are mostly without family role models for their own access to higher education, professional credentials, work outside the home and sharing housekeeping and child care with a working husband. The inevitable negotiation over roles and responsibilities that occurs throughout a marriage is greatly complicated by societal changes in the role of women inside and outside the home. The reconfiguration of gender roles between husband and wife is challenging even without the overlay of a traditional, rigid or disapproving extended family system. For young men and women whose families wish to dictate the norms of their marital and family life, there are many more conflicts ahead.

Changes are also needed within some family systems regarding attitudes towards domestic abuse and the ill treatment of women. Some women reported telling their family about domestic violence in their marriage but were "returned" to their husband again and again. In some of these cases the family eventually came around and helped the woman leave, but sometimes only after many years of abuse. These families regard divorce as closing off all future social options for a young woman. As one young female respondent, how had been abused by her husband, described it, "I feel like my life is over because I am going to have to get divorced." Muslim families who assume that divorce is unthinkable and will bring social shame on the family create situations of extreme danger for women who are being physically abused by their partners. A greater awareness of the patterns of power that sustain domestic abuse is critical (see the further discussion below).

Some among the older generation recognize the emerging empowerment of women. They are speaking out about their needs in marriage, and welcome changes in gender roles and expectations. Many of the older female respondents spoke about their own passive acceptance of unhappiness and sometimes abuse in their marriages as a symptom of their repression—a condition that they do not wish on their own daughters. These older men and women are open to debate over marriage and divorce and have a great deal to contribute from their own experience.

The Work of the Imams

There is a wide variation in the skill, commitment and attitudes of North American imams. These differences become particularly noticeable when an imam is asked to intervene in a marital conflict or—a crucial litmus test—is approached about a religious divorce. The attitude of imams regarding the place of women in the family system and the community is far more significant than their beliefs about jurisprudence in determining how sympathetic and sensitive they will be in offering marital counseling and divorce services. Sometimes these attitudes derive from norms regarding women's roles in their country of origin, rather than the North American community in which they are now working. A large percentage of imams are raised and educated overseas. The president of a federation of sixty mosques representing 500,000 Muslims told me that 80 percent of the imams in the federation are immigrants, whereas 80 percent of the community members were born in the United States. A recent survey of 300 mosques in the United Kingdom found that 84 percent of the imams were born in South Asia, while only 8 percent were British-born.[35] As the stories in this book show, adjustment to changing gender roles continues to be a challenge for men and women born and raised in North America, but even more traditional assumptions prevail among imams born and trained in (for example) Saudi Arabia or Pakistan, where the social and legal systems remain extremely patriarchal. The resulting culture clashes take place on both a personal level—for example, when women ask for divorce—and an organizational level: "You have men and women actively in the leadership positions of Islamic centers and these imams who came from overseas could not reconcile themselves with the fact that women were running the Islamic centers."[36]

A further debate is developing over the disconnect between some immigrant imams who are unfamiliar with North American culture and Muslim youth who are born and raised in Canada and the United States. It is difficult for these imams to relate to young people and families experiencing crises with, for example, drugs, gang culture, unemployment, or even being drawn towards the jihadist movement. One young Swedish Muslim put the problem this way: "What good is a Saudi Arabian imam to me? I am a Swedish Muslim. The Saudi Arabian imam does not understand my life and who I have become."[37] Two younger imams, born in North America, told me that they saw older community members and immigrant imams coalescing around "baggage from the old country," which they saw as getting in the way of developing solutions in the context of contemporary North America. Efforts are under way to increase the number of "home-grown" imams such as these two young men, but there are further challenges. One is the relative unattractiveness of choosing to become an imam, a position that often lacks job security (most imams are hired and fired on the whim of the trustees of the mosque) and social status. One scholar pointed out that "immigrant parents want their children to become doctors, engineers, computer scientists; if you suggested that they might want their kid to study to become an imam, they would hold a funeral procession."[38] Some caution that if overseas imams are rejected as future community leaders the tradition of deep training in Islamic thought may be lost.

This study, as well as other research,[39] makes it obvious that the workload of the imam in modern North American mosques requires religious training to be supplemented by other practical skills—principally communication and counseling skills to enable them to engage with young people and others in their community. Otherwise, they risk being seen as irrelevant and out of touch: "imams who only knew the Koran, but could not relate themselves to the people."[40] Traditional attitudes surrounding the recruitment, qualifications and employment terms of imams must catch up with the changing needs of this community and recognize the multiple social as well as spiritual roles played by an imam in the West. An immediately achievable objective that would enhance services for Muslim families would be to improve access to training for imams. Traditionally, imams have been educated in Islamic law and theology. Many imams expressed to me a need for more training, and a few had embarked on programs on their own initiative. Respondents in this study, including a number of imams, repeatedly emphasized the need for the development of expertise in conflict resolution and counseling, as well as understanding family systems, the dynamics of domestic violence, youth culture and other aspects of North American culture. This scope of training—and its implications for the re-envisioned role of the imam in their communities—may mean that some imams would benefit from attending local college and university programs directed at a wider spectrum of helping professionals.

As a practical matter, mosque boards can do more to encourage and promote training for imams. Boards have the power to make participation in relevant training a normative expectation for all imams, whatever their background, and should fund participation in the same way as any other employer funds professional development. Programs designed specifically for imams are beginning to emerge, sometimes attached to colleges and sometimes sponsored by imam organizations.[41] Better-trained imams can offer a wider range of services, including premarital counseling and appropriate intervention in family disputes. Better-trained imams are also more likely to be able to realistically appraise gaps in their own expertise and knowledge and identify critical resource support. For example, some mosques use professional counselors and social workers to conduct initial interviews with individuals seeking assistance with a marital conflict, and in a few places experienced domestic violence counselors screen cases. These roles need to be expanded and inclusion broadened to other professionals and referral options such as local family lawyers and shelters.

Important though this is, stepping up the level and range of training for imams is not a complete answer to the provision of more effective and appropriate Muslim family services. Many Muslims would not consider going to an imam for assistance at all, however well trained he might be. For these individuals, whose Muslim identity is still critical to their choice of intervention, access to a diverse marketplace of professionals who operate outside mosques and religious communities is essential.

Tolerance of Domestic Violence

A serious problem that demands the urgent attention of the Muslim community is the persistence of uninformed and often dismissive attitudes towards marital abuse, whether emotional, verbal or physical. Fear and shame about reporting abuse, discouragement from seeking help, limited faith in public agencies and a host of other cultural and environmental barriers add to the dangers of women enduring domestic abuse inside Muslim marriages. Tolerance of domestic violence creates dangers for women and children who may remain in unsafe situations because they have no place to turn for sympathetic support within their community. As some of the stories told here make clear, some women are pressured by their family and their imam to accept ill treatment from their husbands in order to stay married. In some communities there is one imam who is widely known to be sympathetic towards women in such desperate situations, and social networks of women generally identify that individual as the "go-to" person in such situations.[42] I was contacted numerous times by women for a referral to an imam who would take their allegations of domestic violence seriously, and sometimes I was unable to confidently identify any such imam within a fifty- to one-hundred-mile radius. These gaps in service are sometimes filled by Muslim agencies that offer assistance to women reporting domestic violence. Examples include lobbying and educational organizations—for example, the Peaceful Families Initiative and the Healthy Marriage Covenant, an initiative of the Muslim Alliance for North America—generalist social services agencies—for example, the Islamic Social Services Association of Canada—and programs directed specifically at battered women—for example, the Domestic Violence Prevention Program in Dearborn, Michigan, and the London, Ontario–based Muslim Family Safety Project. However, these organizations do not share the same resources and staff numbers as public agencies and are often based locally. Coverage is spotty.

These agencies—as well as non-Muslim public agencies doing parallel work—face the problem of how to encourage women to come forward and report abuse. Family loyalties often constrain disclosure. As two researchers studying domestic violence in the Arab-American community in Dearborn observed, "A woman's failure or success at her marriage is perceived as a reflection on her natal family. . . . Family pressure may reinforce the battered woman's sense of shame. The idea of exposing herself or her family to the gossip of community members and the ensuing sense of shame prevents women from leaving abusive marriages."[43] A decision over leaving an abusive marriage must be weighed against the likelihood of future social isolation with an at-best uncertain prospect of personal safety, in addition to the other (financial, emotional) challenges of leaving a partner. Some imams raise further barriers by discouraging women from contacting outside authorities. When it comes to domestic violence some imams manifest a deep mistrust of both North American legal processes and law enforcement authorities, seeing their intervention as antithetical to Islamic values. (It is notable that there is far less evidence of this attitude among the imams when they advise couples to use the courts to resolve contentious divorce matters.)

Inside non-Muslim agencies, there is often little knowledge of Islam or familiarity with its practices and culture. These service providers may unintentionally raise further barriers by their use of culturally specific policies, procedures, operational practices and interactional styles. Negative public stereotyping of Muslims since 9/11 and evidence of discrimination at the hands of public agencies makes some Muslims even more hesitant about accessing such services.

Conventional education and outreach strategies deployed with some success in non-Muslim communities over the last twenty years to encourage women to seek help when facing domestic violence seem unlikely to eliminate these particular barriers, or to deepen access to services by Muslim women. Because community tolerance is at the heart of this problem, innovative prevention strategies need to engage the entire community—including imams and other leaders—and challenge norms that permit male violence against women by using leadership role models, charters and declarations (for example, asking imams and other leaders to sign a public statement condemning domestic violence),[44] and training programs to raise awareness of the manifestations and dynamics of domestic abuse. The role of leadership in raising awareness of this issue cannot be overstated. The following statement, excerpted from an "Open Letter to the Leaders of American Muslim Communities," written by Imam Magid, a long-time campaigner against domestic violence and the current president of the Islamic Society of North America, shortly after the murder of Aasiya Hassan exemplifies the type of leadership that is needed on this issue.

> "Domestic violence is a behavior that knows no boundaries of religion, race, ethnicity, or social status. . . . We, the Muslim community, need to take a strong stand against domestic violence. . . . I call upon my fellow imams and community leaders to never second-guess a woman who comes to us indicating that she feels her life to be in danger. We should provide support and help to protect the victims of domestic violence by providing

for them a safe place and inform them of their rights as well as refer them to social service providers in our areas. . . . Women who seek divorce from their spouses because of physical abuse should get full support from the community and should not be viewed as someone who has brought shame to herself or her family. The shame is on the person who committed the act of violence or abuse. . . . Our community needs to take a strong stand against abusive spouses and we should not make it easy for them to remarry if they chose a path of abusive behavior."[45]

Institutions and Capacity-Building

One direction for capacity-building is the expansion of professional services available in the mosque, including ensuring that the imams of the future are better trained to deal with the reality of family and marital conflicts in North America. But new institutions—redolent of the private marketplace described above—are also badly needed. Only around one in four North American Muslims attend mosque regularly, and many single and divorced women report feeling unwelcome or uncomfortably scrutinized (regarding their marital status) at the mosque. Others go to the mosque for divorce because they see no alternative if they want religious approval for their decision. "People . . . appear not to be that much attached to Islam but when it comes to divorce, they want that Islamic divorce. They may dress in a western way and eat and drink whatever they want but when it comes to divorce, they want a religious divorce." They may also go to the mosque for help because they have no family to turn to and feel little comfort with non-Muslim agencies. As the stories in this book demonstrate, some of these same men and women are dissatisfied with the advice they have been given and the treatment they have received from the imam. At the same time as strengthening and enlarging the scope and expertise of services based in the mosque, it is critical to develop services outside the mosque that feel welcoming and accessible for a wider cross-section of the community. This study demonstrates a real need for premarital counseling, crisis intervention for families and couples, couples counseling and marriage guidance, post-divorce counseling and conflict resolution, and support for victims of domestic abuse, services that are presently at best patchy and often confined to the mosque.

In developing and supporting a more diverse range of service organizations, it is important for community leaders to avoid characterizing any one approach to resolving family and marital conflict—whether it is related to a particular process, ideology or organization—as "*the* Islamic way." Throughout the public debates in Ontario and the United Kingdom there has been a persistent theme that Muslims who use Islamic divorce are "better" Muslims than those who do not. This rigidity and judgment discourages the open dialogue that is needed about these issues, and about the types of processes and institutions that may offer help to individual spouses and their families. The movement towards private rather than public observance and an emphasis on personal spiritual values rather than the "givens" of traditional religiosity further underscores the importance of maintaining an inclusive and diverse approach to the development of Muslim family services in order to ensure participation by any individual for whom it is important to understand and protect what they identify as "Islamic" values in relation to marriage and divorce.

The uncertain state of legal jurisprudence on issues that affect some Muslim families—the legal status of Islamic marriage and divorce, both domestic and overseas, and the enforcement of promises made in Muslim marriage contracts and divorce agreements—leads to many individual cases of injustice. Many of those affected are those least able to fund legal advice and representation. They often struggle to find a representative who can help them in an area of law unfamiliar to many experienced lawyers. There is no overall strategy within the Muslim community on how to address these issues or, at minimum, how to reduce uncertainty and progress resolution. One area in which capacity needs to be built is legal advice and representation for these cases, possibly in the form of a legal advocacy fund. As well as offering litigants advice and representation, such an organization should also monitor case law and track developments across jurisdictions.

There is a related need for capacity-building outside Muslim communities. Enhanced judicial and legal education would enable judges and lawyers to be better informed about and aware of issues that are important to Muslim families. I found a very low level of general knowledge about Islam among family court judges. Understanding Islamic marriage and divorce as a component of cultural identity that reaches beyond traditional religious expression would enhance the prospects of developing appropriate judicial legal education, and encourage family judges to consider the meaning and values that underlie these practices when they adjudicate disputes involving Muslim couples. A better-informed judiciary would also enable Muslim men and women to feel that their traditions and beliefs were understood and respected in the courts.[46]

A *Shari'a* for North America?

Whichever political and legal model is adopted in the United States and Canada—whether the status quo continues with little change, or an alternate approach evolves—one thing seems certain. Recourse to Islamic marriage and divorce is bound to continue. Individuals for whom it is important to feel that their marriage union is conducted appropriately and with God's blessing will want to use a *nikah*. Those who feel that they need release from these vows when they end their marriage beyond anything that the court can offer them will continue to seek religious permission for divorce. The ways in which religious practice is changing do not appear to diminish this commitment—the fluidity and diversity of Islamic marriage and divorce customs is highly compatible with a more personalized approach to faith and spiritual meaning. At a time when Muslim identity in the West is regarded by many in this community as in need of protection and affirmation, it seems unlikely that these customs will disappear any time soon. The combination of ongoing commitment and increasing diversity suggests a new *shari'a* for North America that reflects contemporary conditions, aspirations and values for men and women alike. As one younger North American–born imam explained to me:

> "We have a hope for the future. We cannot expect divorce law and practice to develop the same way here as it does in Muslim countries, but in a way that fits the context of [North America]. The cultural baggage—for example the belief of some men that they have power and control over their wives—will not disappear overnight. But eventually it will balance out."

A new *shari'a* needs to be supported by modern services for families that reflect the reality of their lives in North America, while respecting and nurturing their Islamic values. Its shape is already emerging in progressive and creative approaches towards restructuring family and spousal relationships, the renegotiation of gender roles within the family and how Muslims manage—using both Islamic and civil law principles—the consequences of marriage breakdown.

Respondents told me over and over during the course of this study that they felt both Muslim and Canadian, or Muslim and American, and that each part of this shared identity was important to their sense of self and their place in wider society. This means that they wish to continue to practice their traditions, but also understand themselves to be participating via citizenship in a Western culture to which—not without pain—they are adapting. To accept this image of how North American Muslims view themselves, their non-Muslims neighbors as well as some members of their own community must move past their stereotypes and fears. If this could happen, the idea of a *shari'a* for North America would not raise "the specter of women being stoned in the streets, and thieves' hands being cut off,"[47] but rather the aspiration of a diverse North American Muslim community to hold onto its core norms and values while adapting to contemporary conditions—a very Islamic aspiration.

MARRIAGE CONTRACTS

All Dulles Area Muslim Society
46903 Sugarland Road, Sterling, Virginia 20164

Pre-Marital Contract

We, the undersigned, _____ (Groom) and

_____(Bride) have agreed on this

_____ day, in the month of _____, in the year _____, to the following terms so

that Almighty Allah (God) may bless our marriage and make it last forever with happiness:

1. *We'll marry in the name of Almighty Allah, the Creator of the Universe.*
2. *We agree that the Groom will give the Bride the following Mahr (marriage gift):*

_____

3. *Our marriage shall be in accordance to Shari'ah (Islamic Law).*
4. *Our children shall be raised as Muslims.*
5. *Our living habits (inside and outside the home) shall be in accordance with Islam.*
6. *All inheritance shall be according to Islamic Jurisprudence.*
7. *Rites of burial shall be according to established Islamic rituals, or in accordance with previously expressed wishes of the deceased spouse, if in an interfaith marriage.*
8. *When confronted with insoluble marital disagreements between ourselves and/or between ourselves and others, we shall go to an Imam, a Muslim celebrant, a Muslim Council of Jurisprudence/Arbitration/Reconciliation, or a Muslim Marriage Counselor.*
9. *In all legal affairs, including but not limited to, divorce, child custody and/or financial settlement, we shall seek the help, advice and opinion of a legitimate Muslim religious leader to execute and enforce the teachings of Islam.*
10. *In case of irreconcilable differences or any type of abuse, the wife has the right to an Islamic divorce with all the guarantees, implicit and explicit, that the Shari'ah (Islamic Law) grants her. This right will not affect the jurisdiction that a Court of Law (Civil Law and/or Criminal Law) may have in this matter.*
11. *We understand marriage is a strong Covenant before Almighty Allah. We shall strive always to maintain this Covenant through constant devotion to Him and dedication to our relationship.*

We the undersigned pray to Almighty Allah to help us honor this contract, and we take Almighty Allah (God), The Creator of the universe, as our Witness. We make this pledge and agreement in front of the following witnesses:

Groom	_____	Signature	_____
Bride	_____	Signature	_____
Witness	_____	Signature	_____
Witness	_____	Signature	_____

_____   _____
Signature of Marriage Celebrant   Date

MARRIAGE CONTRACT

In the name of Allāh, the Beneficent, the Merciful
O Allāh, send His blessings upon Muhammad & his progeny.

"And among His signs is that He created spouses for you from among yourselves
so that you may find tranquility in them;
and He placed between you love & compassion. In these are signs for the people who reflect."
(The Qur'ān 30:21)

This agreement made on the _____ day of _____ in the year _____ CE corresponding to the _____ day

of _____ in the year _____ AH between the "Groom" and "Bride" outlined below.

I. BRIDEGROOM

Full Name: _____

Father's Name: _____

Mother' Name: _____

Date & Place of Birth: _____

Marital Status: *never married / divorcé / widower*

Address : _____

_____

Tel: (___ ___ ___) ___ ___ ___ — ___ ___ ___ ___

Groom's *wakil ('āqid)* whom he hereby
authorizes to perform the *'aqd*:

_____

II. BRIDE

Full Name: _____

Father's Name: _____

Mother's Name: _____

Date & Place of Birth: _____

Marital Status: *never married / divorcee / widow*

Address: _____

_____

Tel: (___ ___ ___) ___ ___ ___ — ___ ___ ___ ___

Bride's *wakil ('āqid)* whom she hereby
authorizes to perform the *'aqd*:

_____

The Groom and the Bride enter into this agreement to provide for circumstances relating to their marriage; and both have read and agreed to the following conditions by way of signing each term or part.

III. *MAHR* / DOWRY

The Groom agrees to give the following marriage consideration (*mahr*/dowry) to the Bride:

_____

_____

_____   _____
Signature of the Groom   Signature of the Bride

IV. OPTIONAL CONDITIONS PERTAINING TO DISSOLUTION OF MARRIAGE

1. If the Husband and Wife divorce without any fault of the latter, then the Husband agrees to give to his Wife half of all the "net family property" (as defined by section 4(1) & (2) of Ontario's *Family Law Act*, R.S.O. 1990, c. F.3) that he acquired during the marriage period, excluding property that the Husband acquired by gift or inheritance from a third person after the date of the marriage.

   In the case of dispute about the cause for divorce, the Shi'a Ithnā-'Ashari religious authority (such as the Resident *'Alim* of the Islamic Shi'a Ithna-Asheri Jamaat of Toronto or the *wakil* of the *marja'* or the *marja'*) will make such a determination. (Note that the religious authority would have to determine whether or not the cause for divorce was the fault of the Wife, and in if that is determined positively, then the Wife will be prevented from receiving the aforementioned property. If the examination as to the cause for divorce is found to be inconclusive, the Wife will have a right to the aforementioned property. Also note that the Wife does not have to give any of her property to the Husband in the event of a divorce.)

ANOTHER VARIATION OF CONDITION # 1

1. If the Husband and the Wife divorce, there will be an equalization of net family properties as described in s. 5(1) of Ontario's *Family Law Act* (R.S.O. 1990, c. F.3) which is reproduced below under "Definitions".

_____   _____
Signature of the Groom   Signature of the Bride

2. The Husband hereby delegates to the Wife an irrevocable authorization to appoint an agent (*wakil*) for divorcing her on behalf of the Husband after giving a Shi'a Ithnā-Ashari religious authority (the Resident *'Ālim* or the *wakil* of the *marja'* or the *marja'*) reason to believe the occurrence of any one of the following:
   (a) if the Husband solemnizes a "religious marriage" with another woman without permission of the Wife named in this contract; ("Religious marriage" a marriage that has been solemnized only basis of Islamic laws which allows polygyny, a practice which is not legal in Canadian family law.)
   (b) if the Husband ill treats or physically abuses the Wife;
   (c) if the Husband abandons the Wife and does not provide for her for more than three months continuously;
   (d) if the Husband divorces the Wife in a secular court, but does not give her the religious divorce; or
   (e) if the Wife obtains a divorce in a secular court, but the Husband does not give the Wife a religious divorce.

_____   _____
Signature of the Groom   Signature of the Bride

3. This Agreement constitutes the entire agreement between the Bride and the Groom, and cancels and supercedes any prior understandings and agreements between them. There are no representations, warranties, terms, conditions, undertakings or collateral agreements, express or implied, between the Bride and the Groom other than expressly set forth in this Agreement.

4. This Agreement shall endure for the duration of the marriage of the Bride and the Groom.

5. If any provision of this Agreement is found to be invalid or unenforceable in whose or in part, such invalidity or unenforceability shall attach only to such provision or part thereof and the remaining part of such provision and all other provisions of the Agreement shall continue in full force and effect.

6. This Agreement shall be governed by and construed in accordance with the laws of the Province of Ontario and the applicable laws of Canada, and in accordance with Ontario's *Family Law Act*.

7. No amendment, supplement, modification or waiver or termination of this Agreement and, unless otherwise specified, no consent or approval by either Husband or Wife, shall be binding unless executed in writing by both Husband and Wife to be bound thereby.

_____   _____
Signature of the Groom for items 3 to 7.   Signature of the Bride for items 3 to 7.

V. CERTIFICATION

This is to certify that the marriage of the bride and the groom named above was solemnized in accordance with the Shi'a Ja'fari laws of Islam on

the _____ day of the month of _____ in the year _____ AH

the _____ day of the month of _____ in the year _____ CE

_____
Wakil ('Āqid) of the Groom   and witnessed by: _____

_____
Wakíl ('Āqid) of the Bride   and witnessed by: _____

Number of the marriage License issued by the city: _____ on: _____

Name & Registration Number of the person solemnizing the marriage: _____

VI. DEFINITIONS

1. "Agreement" means this Marriage Contract.
2. "'Aqd" means the religious marriage vows that are performed in accordance with Shí'a laws of Islam.
3. "Mahr", although also used to denote 'dowry', means the consideration that the Groom must give to the Bride.
4. "Marja" is highest religious authority and jurist of Shí'a laws of Islam.
5. "Husband" is the Groom set out above.
6. "Wife" is the Bride set out above.
7. "Resident 'Alim" is the religious authority of the "Islamic Shí'a Ithna-Asheri Jamaat of Toronto".
8. "Shí'a Ithna-Ashari" is the particular sect of the Islamic religion to which both the Bride and the Groom belong.
9. "Shí'a laws of Islam" or "Shí'a Ja'fari laws" are the set of religious laws that underlie the Shí'a Ithna-Ashari faith.
10. "Islamic Shí'a Ithna-Asheri Jamaat of Toronto" is a well known Shí'a organization of Greater Toronto Area.
11. "Wakíl ('Āqid)" means the representative of the Bride or the Groom for purpose of performing the religious marriage vows ('aqd).
12. Section 5(1) of Ontario's Family Law Act (R.S.O. 1990, c. F.3) is as following:
    When a divorce is granted or a marriage is declared a nullity, or when the spouses are separated and there is no reasonable prospect that they will resume cohabitation, the spouse whose net family property is the lesser of the two net family properties is entitled to one-half the difference between them.
13. "Net Family Property" in Family Law Act is defined as follows:
    4(1) "net family property" means the value of all the property, except property described in subsection (2), that a spouse owns on the valuation date, after deducting,
        (a) the spouse's debts and other liabilities, and
        (b) the value of property, other than a matrimonial home, that the spouse owned on the date of the marriage, after deducting the spouse's debts and other liabilities, calculated as of the date of the marriage;
    4(2) The value of the following property that a spouse owns on the valuation date does not form part of the spouse's net family property:
        1. Property, other than a matrimonial home, that was acquired by gift or inheritance from a third person after the date of the marriage.
        2. Income from property referred to in paragraph 1, if the donor or testator has expressly stated that it is to be excluded from the spouse's net family property.
        3. Damages or a right to damages for personal injuries, nervous shock, mental distress or loss of guidance, care and companionship, or the part of a settlement that represents those damages.
        4. Proceeds or a right to proceeds of a policy of life insurance, as defined in the Insurance Act, that are payable on the death of the life insured.
        5. Property, other than a matrimonial home, into which property referred to in paragraphs 1 to 4 can be traced.
        6. Property that the spouses have agreed by a domestic contract is not to be included in the spouse's net family property.

DIVORCE RULING ON VERBAL DELEGATED *TALAQ*

Al-Falah Islamic Centre

391 Burnhamthorpe Road East, Oakville, ON L6H 7B4
Phone: 905-257-4262, Fax: 905-257-9996, email: admin@alfalah.ca

بسم الله الرحمن الرحيم

ISLAMIC RULING ON AUTHORIZATION OF DIVORCE (KHAYAR)

This is to verify that Ms _____ married to Mr. _____ on August 22, 2006. Islamic and legal marriage was performed by me. At the time of marriage it was a verbal agreement that though Islamically husband has a right to divorce, but he may surrender his authority to his wife, so the wife can use the right to divorce herself if needed.

Mr. _____ agreed to surrender his authority to divorce to his wife Ms _____

Ms _____ has approached me to verify this verbal agreement and she is in the opinion that due to the circumstances, she has no option except to be divorced. Mr. _____ is not willing to divorce her so she has decided to use the authority to divorce herself.

Based on my discussion with Ms _____ I am writing this to confirm that Ms ____ under the authority given to her by Mr. _____ , has divorced herself. A copy of this letter is being sent to Mr. _____ for information.

Dr. Mohammad Iqbal Al-Nadvi
Imam Al-Falah Islamic Centre

February 08, 2007

FASKH RULING

Al-Falah Islamic Centre

391 Burnhamthorpe Road East, Oakville, ON L6H 7B4
Phone: 905-257-2192, Fax: 905-257-9996, email: info@alfalah.ca

بِسْـــمِ اللّٰهِ الرَّحْمٰنِ الرَّحِيْـــمِ

ISLAMIC RULING ABOUT CANCELLATION OF MARRIAGE

It is to confirm that Ms _____ who married to Mr. _____ on September 19, 2001. Due to negligence of Mr. _____ and his refusal to divorce her Islamically, Ms _____ filed a lawsuit in Superior Court of Ontario against her husband to get divorce from her husband. Ontario Superior Court granted divorce to Ms _____ in the absence of her husband Mr. _____.

According to Islamic rules of divorce, husband has the right to divorce or approve it in case wife asks for 'Khula'. In this case husband has refused both the options so wife has the right to go to the court and ask for divorce through judicial system. If the judge is convinced, he can cancel the marriage even husband refuses to divorce. In this case the Judge has granted divorce (superior Court file # FS-05-053258-00 dated July 17, 2005) in the absence of husband.

I was asked to give a ruling on this Islamically.

Looking into the matter thoroughly it is my opinion based on my knowledge of Islam and its family system that Superior Court's ruling will be taken as 'Faskh', especially when husband was aware of the court proceedings and he deliberately avoided to appear in the court to face the charges. His absence from the court indicates his tacit approach to the divorce.

Based on the facts, I declare that the marriage between _____ and _____ has been cancelled from the date of August 18, 2005 and _____ will remain in 'Iddah' for the period of 3 months and she can re-marry to another person after this period.

This is my opinion on the bases of my knowledge of Quran and Sunnah of Prophet Mohammad (PBUH) and Allah (SWT) knows the best.

Dr. Mohammad Iqbal Al-Nadvi
Imam Al-Falah Islamic Centre   August 17, 2005

NOTES

INTRODUCTION

1. According to the 2007 Pew study "Muslim Americans: Middle Class and Mostly Mainstream" (available at http://pewresearch.org/pubs/483/muslim-americans), 23 percent of American Muslims demonstrate a "high commitment" to religious observance, and 26 percent "rarely engage" in formal religious practices. The remainder fall somewhere in between, occasionally attending prayers and participating in formal religious rituals. In Canada, the numbers of Muslims attending mosque are somewhat higher, according to a Canadian Institute of Policy Studies survey conducted in 2009. This survey found that 37 percent attend mosque more than twice a week, 31 percent go once a week, 31 percent attend only for special programs or on special occasions such as Eid. Two percent never attend the mosque. Available at http://www.c-ips.ca/docs/CIPS_Survey_Report.pdf.

2. What one Islamic scholar described as "The Great Theft" (K. A. El Fadl, *The Great Theft: Wrestling Islam from the Extremists* [New York: HarperSanFrancisco, 2005]).

3. Among numerous examples in leading newspapers and reinforced in other media reports, see "Pressing Deeper into Pakistan," *Globe & Mail* (26 October 2007); "In Pakistan, Radio Amplifies Terror of Taliban," *New York Times* (26 October 2009); "Leave Every Stone Unturned," *Globe & Mail* (28 September 2010).

4. Widely used by qualitative researchers for data coding and analysis; see www.qsr.org (accessed 27 August 2011).

5. There are four Sunni schools—Hanifi, Hanbali, Mailki and Shafi—and one Shia school (Jafri), favored in particular regions of the Islamic world.

6. E. Patel, *Being Muslim in America* (U.S. Department of State and Bureau of International Programs, 2009), 49, estimates that 27 percent of Muslim Americans are African Americans.

7. K. Brice, *A Minority within a Minority: A Report on Converts to Islam in the United Kingdom*, a report on behalf of Faith Matters (28 December 2010). Available at http://faith-matters.org/resources/publicationsreports/218-report-on-converts-to-islam-in-the-uk-a-minority-within-a-minority (accessed 27 August 2011).

8. Samia Bano has analysed *Shari'a* Council processes in the United Kingdom, using file analysis, observation and interviews with Council officials and women applicants. See Samia Bano, "Islamic Family Arbitration, Justice and Human Rights in Britain," *Law, Social Justice & Global Development Journal* 1 (2007). See also earlier work on *Shari'a* Council files by S. Shah-Kazemi, *Untying the Knot: Muslim Women Divorce and the Shariah* (London: Nuffield Council, 2001).

9. G. Krayem, "To Recognize or Not to Recognize, That Is NOT the Question: Family Law and the Muslim Community in Australia" (Ph.D. diss., University of Sydney, 2011).

10. Of particular note is the careful advice (rooted in Sunni jurisprudence) provided at www.sunnipath.com (accessed 27 August 2011)

CHAPTER I

1. Statistics from "Questions and Answers: Islam and Europe," *New York Times* (14 July 2005).

2. 2001 Census of Canada, Statistics Canada, Ottawa, available at http://www12.statcan.ca/english/census01/home/index.cfm (accessed 27 August 2011).

3. K. Brice, *A Minority within a Minority: A Report on Converts to Islam in the United Kingdom*, a report on behalf of Faith Matters (28 December 2010). Available at http://faith-matters.org/resources/publicationsreports/218-report-on-converts-to-islam-in-the-uk-a-minority-within-a-minority (accessed 27 August 2011).

4. I. Bagby, *The Mosque in America: A Report from the Mosque Study Project* (Washington, D.C.: Council on American-Islamic Relations, 2001), 20–22.

5. J. Esposito, "Muslims in America or Muslim Americans?," in *Muslims on the Americanization Path?*, ed. Y. Haddad and J. Esposito (New York: Oxford University Press, 2000), 3.

6. M. Akhtar, "Identity Conflict for Muslims in the West," in *Muslim Family in a Dilemma: Quest for a Western Identity*, ed. M. Akhtar (Lanham, Md.: University Press of America, 2007), 77.

7. *Ethnic Diversity Study: Portrait of a Multicultural Society*, Statistics Canada Catalogue No. 89-593-XIE, Minister of Industry, Ottawa (2003), 11–12.

8. M. Gordon, *Assimilation in American Life: The Role of Race, Religion, and National Origins* (New York: Oxford University Press, 1964).

9. See for example Jonathan Okamura's theory of situational ethnicity (J. Okamura, *Filipino Voluntary Associations and the Filipino Community in Hawaii* [Honolulu, 1981]).

10. K. Tran, J. Kaddatz, and P. Allard, "South Asians in Canada: Unity through Diversity," *Canadian Social Trends*, Statistics Canada Catalogue 11-008 20 (Autumn 2005), 22.

11. "Muslim Americans: Middle Class and Mostly Mainstream," Pew Research Center, Washington D.C. (May 2007), 31.

12. Pew Global Attitudes Report 2006, available at http://pewglobal.org/commentary/display.php?AnalysisID=1010 (accessed 27 August 2011).

13. "Muslim Americans: Middle Class and Mostly Mainstream," Pew Research Center, Washington D.C. (May 2007), 3.

14. CNN/Opinion Research Corp (2007), available at http://articles.cnn.com/2007-08-22/us/gw.poll_1_younger-muslims-sampling-error-pew-research-center?_s=PM:US.

15. "Patriotic, Respectful and Homophobic: A Portrait of British Muslims' State of Mind," Gallup and Coexist Foundation, 8 May 2009

16. J. Nagel, "Constructing Ethnicity: Creating and Recreating Ethnic Identity and Culture," *Social Problems* 41(1) (1994): 152–76.

17. Tran, Kaddatz, and Allard, "South Asians in Canada," 22.

18. Akbar Ahmed, quoted in "Questions and Answers," *New York Times*.

19. Y. Haddad, "The Dynamics of Islamic Identity," in Esposito and Haddad, *Muslims on the Americanization Path?*, 23.

20. S. Razack, *Casting Out: The Eviction of Muslims from Western Law and Politics* (Toronto: University of Toronto Press, 2008), 3–11.

21. Ibid., 9–10.

22. A 2011 Pew study found that 55 percent of Muslim Americans say that life as a Muslim in the United States is harder since 9/11. Pew Research Center 2011 Muslim American Survey, available at http://people-press.org/2011/08/30/muslim-americans-no-signs-of-growth-in-alienation-or-support-for-extremism/?src=prc-number.

23. M. Amis, "The Age of Horrorism," *The Observer* (10 September 2006); "Martin Amis Launches Fresh Attack on Muslim Faith Saying Islamic States Are 'Less Evolved,'" *Daily Mail* (18 October 2007).

24. M. Steyn, "The Future Belongs to Islam," *Maclean's Magazine* (20 October 2006).

25. Herman Cain and Newt Gingrich. See John Esposito, "Muslim Bashing by GOP Candidates? Nothing New Here," *Washington Post*, 17 June 2011.

26. "The Rush Limbaugh Show," 17 July 2010.

27. See, for example, "Qur'an Burning: Pastor Jones's Moment in the Spotlight," *The Guardian* (8 September 2010).

28. This is a project of the American Freedom Defense Initiative (http://freedomdefense.typepad.com). See http://news.michiganradio.org/post/leaving-islam-anti-muslim-group-wins-legal-round-against-suburban-detroit-bus-system. The advertisement references a website, LeavingIslam.com.

29. N. Feldman, "Why Shariah?," *New York Times* (16 March 2008).

30. Akhtar, "Identity Conflict for Muslims in the West," 83.

31. A. An-Na'im, *Islam and the Secular State: Negotiating the Future of Shari'a* (Cambridge, Mass.: Harvard University Press, 2008), 2–3, 13–14, 267–74.

32. See, for example, A. An-Na'im, "Reforming Islam," *National Review* 14(2) (Spring 1997); J. Bowen, *Islam, Law and Equality in Indonesia* (Cambridge: Cambridge University Press, 2003); and Jamail A. Kamlian, "Islam, Women and Gender Justice," *Muslim World Journal of Human Rights* 21(1) (2005).

33. For a discussion of the origins and development of *fiqh* see W. Hallaq, *The Origins and Evolution of Islamic Law* (Cambridge: Cambridge University Press, 2006), 29–56.

34. See the discussion in S. H. Nasr, *The Heart of Islam* (San Francisco: Harper Collins, 2002), 114–20.

35. M. Mirza, A. Senthilkumarn and Z. Ja'far Z, *Living Apart Together* (London: Policy Exchange, 2007).

36. "Newsnight Exposes Policy Exchange Anti-Muslim Propaganda," *Newsnight* (BBC2) (12 December 2007).

37. *Shari'a* prohibits the payment or collection of interest, or "riba." See the Holy Qur'an, verses 275, 276, 278, 279.

38. "Legislator's Proposal Would Ban Use of Sharia Law," *Tulsa World* (18 July 2010).

39. Z. Latif, "The Silencing of Women from the Pakistani Muslim Mirupi Community in Violent Relationships," in *Honour, Violence, Women and Islam*, ed. M. Idrriss and T. Abbas (London: Routledge, 2010), 29.

40. See, for example, R. Ayyub, "Domestic Violence in the South Asian Muslim Immigrant Population in the United States," *Journal of Social Distress and the Homeless* 9(3) (2000): 238, and D. Hassouneh-Phillips, "Marriage If Half Faith the Rest Is Fear of God," *Violence against Women* 7(8) (2001): 927.

41. See for example P. Heelas and L. Woodhead, *The Spiritual Revolution: Why Religion Is Giving Way to Spirituality* (Oxford: Blackwells, 2005).

42. P. Heelas and L. Woodhead, *The Spiritual Revolution: Why Religion Is Giving Way to Spirituality* (Oxford: Blackwells, 2005).

43. T. Asad, *Formations of the Secular: Christianity, Islam, Modernity* (Stanford, Calif.: Stanford University Press, 2003), 139–40.

44. Y. Birt, "The Trouble with Shariah," 8 February 2008, available at http://www.yahyabirt.com/?p=139 (accessed on 27 August 2011).

45. A. Emon, "Islamic Law and the Canadian Mosaic: Politics, Jurisprudence, and Multicultural Accommodation," *Canadian Bar Review* 87 (2008): 421.

46. J. Van Rhijn, "First Steps Taken Towards Sharia Law in Canada," *Canadian Law Times* (25 November 2003).

47. C. Morris, "Media's Mediation and Other Matters: Faith-Based Dispute Resolution in Canada," Speaking Notes for a Panel Presentation, ADR Subsection, British Colombia Branch, Canadian Bar Association, Vancouver, Canada.

48. M. McAteer, "Muslims Seek Jurisdiction over Family Law," *Toronto Star* (30 May 1991).

49. M. Jiménez, "Islamic Law in Civil Disputes Raises Questions: Judicial Tribunal Based on Sharia to Decide Disagreements among Ontario Muslims," *Globe and Mail* (11 December 2003); L. Scrivener, "New Islamic Institute Set Up for Civil Cases System Would Reduce Court Time [and] Move Worries," *Toronto Star* (12 December 2003).

50. Ontario Statutes, 1991 c. 17, s. 32 (1), "In deciding a dispute, an arbitral tribunal shall apply the rules of law designated by the parties or, if none are designated, the rules of law it considers appropriate in the circumstances."

51. J. Gaudreault-DesBiens, "The Limits of Private Justice? The Problem of State Recognition of Arbitral Awards in Family and Personal Status Disputes in Ontario," *Perspectives* 16(1) (January 2005): 19.

52. S. Harkipal Singh, "Religious Law Undermines Loyalty to Canada," *Vancouver Sun* (10 December 2003), A23; and G. Harris, "*Shari'a* Is Not a Law by Canadian Standards," *Vancouver Sun* (15 December 2003), A15.

53. The platform of the Canadian Council for Muslim Women is set out at http:// http://www.ccmw.com/activities/act_no_religious_arb.html.

54. H. Mallick, "Boutique Law: It's the Latest Thing," *Globe and Mail* (15 May 2004).

55. *Dispute Resolution in Family Law: Protecting Choice, Promoting Inclusion*, Ontario Ministry of the Attorney-General, Toronto, December 2004, prepared by Marion Boyd, a former attorney-general of Ontario. See http://www.attorneygeneral.jus. gov.on.ca/english/about/pubs/boyd (accessed 27 August 2011).

56. See, for example, S. Chotalia, "Arbitration Using Sharia Law in Canada: A Constitutional and Human Rights Perspective," *Constitutional Forum* 15(6) (2006): 63; M. Jiménez, "A Muslim Woman's *Shari'a* Ordeal," *Globe and Mail* (8 September 2005); M. Jiménez, "Debate Stirs Hatred, *Shari'a* Activists Say: Controversy over Faith-Based Tribunals Feeds Negative Stereotypes, Group Warns," *Globe and Mail* (15 September 2005), A6; K. Howlett and M. Valpy, "Female MPP's Concerns Delay Shar'ia Decision," *Globe and Mail* (8 September 2005). There were a few efforts to balance the debate; see for example S. Khan, "The *Shari'a* Debate Deserves a Proper Hearing," *Globe and Mail* (15 September 2005).

57. See M. Campbell, "McGuinty's Sharia Move Is Bold—But More Must Be Done," *Globe and Mail* (13 September 2005); M. Jiménez, "Decision on *Shari'a* Sparks Jewish Protest," *Globe and Mail* (13 September 2005); K. Howlett and C. Freeze, "McGuinty Government Rules Out Use of *Shari'a* Law," *Globe and Mail* (12 September 2005); Editorial, "Of Common Values and the *Shari'a* Fight," *Globe and Mail* (13 September 2005).

58. N. Greenaway, "63 Per Cent Oppose Faith-Based Arbitration," *Ottawa Citizen* (31 October 2005).

59. Bill 27, Family Statute Law Amendment Act, 2006, amended the 1991 Arbitration Act and the Family Law Act.

60. "New Ontario Bill Partially Strips Bet Din's Powers," *Canadian Jewish News* (18 November 2005).

61. For the speech that precipitated this debate, see Rowan Williams, "Is *Shari'a* Law Unavoidable in England?" (7 February 2008), available at www.archbishopof-canterbury.org/1581/ (accessed 27 August 2011). For selected media coverage, see P. Wintour and R. Butt, "Sharia Law Could Have UK Role Says Lord Chief Justice," *The Guardian* (4 July 2008); E. Sciolino, "Britain Grapples with Role for Islamic Justice," *New York Times* (19 November 2008); and for a comment, see T. Modood, "Within the Law," *The Guardian* (15 February 2008).

62. Editorials in the *Daily Mail* and the *London Standard* (9 February 2008).

63. R. Gledhill and P. Webster, "Archbishop of Canterbury Argues for Islamic Law in Britain," *Times* (London) (8 February 2008).

64. See, for example, "Archbishop Sparks *Shari'a* Law Row," *BBC News* (7 February 2008). The BBC quotes Member of Parliament Mark Pritchard as saying, "The Archbishop should be standing up for our Judeo-Christian principles that under-mine British criminal law that have been hard fought for."

65. BBC interview, Radio 4 World at One, 7 February 2008, conducted by Christo-pher Landau. Available at http://www.archbishopofcanterbury.org/1573 (accessed 27 August 2011).

66. Rowan Williams, quoted in "Profile: Dr Rowan Williams," *BBC News* (8 February 2008).

67. Catherine Heseltine, quoted in "Archbishop Denies Asking for Islamic Law," *New York Times* (8 February 2008).

68. BBC Interview, 7 February 2008, conducted by Christopher Landau.

CHAPTER 2

1. See the discussion in S. H. Nasr, *The Heart of Islam* (San Francisco: Harper Collins, 2002), 114–20. For a discussion of the origins and development of *fiqh* see W. Hal-laq, *The Origins and Evolution of Islamic Law* (Cambridge: Cambridge University Press, 2006), 29–56.

2. Z. Mir-Hosseni, *Marriage on Trial: A Study of Islamic Family Law* (London: I. B. Taurus, 1993), 9.

3. M. Iszzi Dien, *Islamic Law: From Historical Foundations to Contemporary Practice* (South Bend, Ind.: University of Notre Dame Press, 2007), 27.

4. See, for example, A. An-Na'im, *Toward an Islamic Reformation: Civil Liberties, Human Rights and International Law* (Syracuse, N.Y.: Syracuse University Press, 1990), 20 (noting that some scholars consider between 500 and 600 of the verses in the Qur'an to have some legal relevance). However, as Anver Emon points out, most of these deal with worship rituals which would not find their way into a legal system; A. Emon, "Islamic Law and the Canadian Mosaic: Politics, Jurisprudence, and Multicultural Accommo-dation," University of Toronto, Legal Studies Research Paper, No. 947149 (2006).

5. Hallaq, *Origins and Evolution of Islamic Law*, 42.

6. Ibid., 47

7. B. S. Stowasser and Y. Haddad, "Introduction," in *Islamic Law and the Challenges of Modernity*, ed. B. S. Stowasser and Y. Haddad Alta (Walnut Creek, Calif.: Mira Press, 2006), 5.

8. See the account in N. Feldman, *The Fall and Rise of the Islamic State* (Princeton, N.J.: Princeton University Press, 2008), especially 27–40.

9. N. J. Coulson, *Conflicts and Tensions in Islamic Jurisprudence* (Chicago: Center for Middle Eastern Studies, University of Chicago Press, 1969), 80.

10. For a comprehensive review, see Hallaq, *Origins and Evolution of Islamic Law*, and K. A. El Fadl, *Speaking in God's Name: Islamic Law, Authority and Women* (Oxford: One World Publications, 2003).

11. El Fadl, *Speaking in God's Name*, 149–50.

12. M. Iszzi Dien, *Islamic Law: From Historical Foundations to Contemporary Practice* (South Bend, Ind.: University of Notre Dame Press, 2007), 40–48.

13. M. Muslehuddin, *Philosophy of Islamic Law and Orientalists* (Columbia, Mo.: South Asia Books, 1992), 135.

14. Coulson, *Conflicts and Tensions in Islamic Jurisprudence*, 6.

15. A. An-Na'im, ed., *Islamic Family Law in a Changing World: A Global Resource Book* (London and New York: Zed Books, 2002), 6.

16. L. Rosen, *The Anthropology of Justice: Law as Culture in Islamic Society* (Cambridge: Cambridge University Press, 1989).

17. An-Na'im, *Islamic Family Law in a Changing World*, 2.

18. A. Emon, "Natural Law and Natural Rights in Islamic Law," *Journal of Law and Religion* 20 (2004–2005): 352.

19. See, for example, A. I. Rahman, *Shari'ah: The Islamic Law* (London: Taha, 1984).

20. El Fadl, *Speaking in God's Name*, 38.

21. El Fadl, *Speaking in God's Name*; Emon, "Natural Law and Natural Rights in Islamic Law," 351–95.

22. T. Ramadan, *Western Muslims and the Future of Islam* (New York: Oxford University Press, 2004), 34.

23. See, for example, M. Abu-Nimer M., *Nonviolence and Peace Building in Islam: Theory and Practice* (Gainesville: University of Florida Press, 2003), 48–74.

24. Ramadan, *Western Muslims and the Future of Islam*, 35.

25. Z. Mir-Hosseni, *Marriage on Trial: A Study of Islamic Family Law* (London: I. B. Taurus Publishers, 1993), 5.

26. K. A. El Fadl, *The Great Theft* (San Francisco: Harper Collins, 2007), 150.

27. Ramadan, *Western Muslims and the Future of Islam*, 34.

28. El Fadl, *The Great Theft*, 45–48. The most traditional school of law is the Hanbali school. See also M. Izzi Dien, *Islamic Law: From Historical Foundations to Contemporary Practice* (South Bend, Ind.: University of Notre Dame Press, 2004), 147.

29. See, for example, A. El Fadl, *Speaking in God's Name: Islamic Law, Authority and Women* (Oxford: One World Publications, 2003); J. Schacht, "Problems of Modern Islamic Legislation," *Studia Islamica* 12 (1960): 100–101; and W. Hallaq, "Can the Shari'a Be Restored? in *Islamic Law and the Challenges of Modernity*, ed. B. S. Stowasser and Y. Haddad (Walnut Creek, Calif.: Alta, 2004): 21, especially 41–45.

30. Mir-Hosseni, *Marriage on Trial*, 10.

31. J. Esposito with N. DeLong-Bas, *Women in Muslim Family Law* (Syracuse, N.Y., Syracuse University Press, 2001), 47–49, 70–74.

32. For a review, Esposito and DeLong-Bas, *Women in Muslim Family Law*, 47–126.

33. For more information on modern family law in Muslim countries see An-Na'im, *Islamic Family Law in a Changing World*.

34. Rahman, *Shari'ah: The Islamic Law*, 123.

35. M. J. Maghniyyah, *The Five Schools of Islamic Law* (Qum, Iran: Ansariyan Publications, 1995), 266–67.

36. Hanifi jurisprudence allows for an adult woman to dispense with the consent of a guardian.

37. Maghniyyah, *Five Schools of Islamic Law*, 264.

38. See A. Nadir, "I Should Have Read My Islamic Marriage Contract," *Slate*, 25 February 2010. Available at http://www.slate.com/id/2245908/ (accessed 20 September 2011).

39. The U.K. Model Muslim Marriage Contract, Muslim Institute, London, August 2008. A copy of the model *nikah* is embedded in Cassandra Balchin's online article "Negotiating Bliss," available at http://www.muslimparliament.org.uk/articles.htm.

40. Materials provided by the Adams Center, All Dulles Area Muslim Society, Fairfax County, Va., on file with the author.

41. Esposito and DeLong-Bas, *Women in Muslim Family Law*, 23.

42. Canadian Criminal Code, R.S.C. 1985, c. C-46, ss. 290, makes bigamy an indictable offence; the Canadian Civil Marriage Act, S.C. 2005, c. 33, s.2, stipulates that marriage, for civil purposes, is the lawful union of two persons to the exclusion of all others. In the United States laws vary from state to state, but most states base their polygamy laws on the Model Penal Code, section 230.1, which provides for a charge of third-degree felony for polygamy. In 1878 the U.S. Supreme Court ruled that plurality of wives is not defensible as an exercise of religious liberty and is void and grounds for annulment in *Reynolds v. United States*, 98 U.S. 145 (1878).

43. Holy Qur'an, verse 4:34, from M. Pickthall, *The Qur'an Translated* (Washington, D.C.: International Committee for the Support of the Final Prophet, 2005).

44. Holy Qur'an, verse 4:34, from A. Y. Ali, *The Meanings of the Holy Qur'an* (Brentwood, Md.: Amana Corporation, 1992).

45. See B. F. Stowasser, "Women and Citizenship in the Qur'an," in *Women, the Family, and Divorce Laws in Islamic History*, ed. A. E. A. Sonbol (Syracuse, N.Y.: Syracuse University Press, 1996), 32–33.

46. Esposito and DeLong-Bas, *Women in Muslim Family Law*, 22.

47. On Egypt, see ibid., 60–61.

48. The classical law still governs disobedience in Lebanon. See An-Na'im, *Islamic Family Law in a Changing World*, 128.

49. K. Ali, "Marriage in Classical Islamic Jurisprudence," in *The Islamic Marriage Contract: Case Studies in Islamic Family Law*, ed. A. Quraishi and F. Vogel (Cambridge, Mass.: Harvard University Press, 2008).

50. Holy Qur'an, verse 4:19.

51. Esposito and DeLong-Bas, *Women in Muslim Family Law*, 32.

52. See Holy Qur'an, verse 4:3.

53. Hadith of Abu-Daud, verse 13:3.

54. See Holy Qur'an, verses 2:226–32 and 65:1–7.

55. Cited in M. A. Syed, *The Position of Women in Islam: A Progressive View* (Albany: State University of New York Press, 2004), 67, and attributed to Al-Bukhari (the *hadith* author).

56. Shi'ism requires witnesses. See Maghniyyah, *Five Schools of Islamic Law*, 388, citing Quranic verse 65:2–3. This *may* mean that Shia men are more likely to seek the advice of their imam before divorcing their wives (respondent 68).

57. Holy Qur'an, verses 2:228, 65:1.

58. Holy Qur'an, verse 65:1.

59. Holy Qur'an, verse 2:230.

60. For example, in the view of Ibn Hanbal (and therefore the Hanbali school), a triple divorce uttered at the same time is valid. In contrast, Shia (represented by the Jafiri school) is clear that a triple utterance is not valid as a divorce. See Maghniyyah, *Five Schools of Islamic Law*, 381. Mohammed Ali Syed maintains that there is "no mention of triple *talaq* in one sitting in the Quran or the Hadith" (*Position of Women in Islam*, 64), while Safia Iqbal states that "triple talaq (three times uttering talaq in a single utterance) though sinful, remains effective" (*Women and Islamic Law* [New Delhi: Adam Publishers, 2004], 192).

61. S. Spectorsky, trans., *Chapters on Marriage and Divorce: Responses of Ibn Hanbal and Ibn Rahwayh* (Austin: University of Texas Press, 1993), 28–31.

62. Rahman, *Shari'ah: The Islamic Law*, 173–74.

63. Holy Qur'an, verse 2:229.

64. Holy Qur'an, verses 2:230–31.

65. Holy Qur'an, verse 2:228.

66. Spectorsky, *Chapters on Marriage and Divorce*, 51–52; and see Holy Qur'an, verses 2:229, 231; 4:19, 34. Contemporary versions of *shari'a* practiced in some Islamic courts may in fact be harsher in removing the *mahr* than earlier jurisprudence: see the two Egyptian cases contrasted in Sonbol's introduction to *Women, the Family, and Divorce Laws in Islamic History*, 1–2.

67. *Hadith* of Sahih Al-Bukhari, vol. 7, bk. 63, no. 206.

68. In some Islamic courts the expression *khula* is used to refer to any divorce initiated by the wife, with or without her husband's permission, and even where a judge overrides the view of the husband. See for example the discussion of the approach of the Egyptian courts during the Ottoman period. See A. Abdal-Rehim, "The Family and Gender Laws in Egypt during the Ottoman Period," in Sonbol, ed., *Women, the Family, and Divorce Laws in Islamic History*, 105–6 (the same paper also points out that there is no record of a *qadi ever* refusing a wife's request for divorce even when her husband did not agree to it).

69. See Maghniyyah, *The Five Schools of Islamic Law*, 425; L. Bakhtiar, *Encyclopedia of Islamic Law: A Compendium of the Major Schools* (Chicago: ABC International Group, 1996), 539–42; and the many contemporary examples in An-Na'im, *Islamic Family Law in a Changing World*.

70. L. Rosen, *The Anthropology of Justice: Law as Culture in Islamic Society* (Cambridge: Cambridge University Press, 1989), 79.

71. Ramadan, *Western Muslims and the Future of Islam*, 36.

72. Mir-Hosseni, *Marriage on Trial*, 14.

CHAPTER 3

1. Of these two exceptions, one had no "formal *nikah*" (although she did have a *mahr*), and the other was a convert-to-convert marriage in which the parties were still "in transition" towards adopting Islam as their shared faith.

2. See, for example, http://www.world-federation.org/Family+Affairs/Marriage+Contract/Marriage_Contract.htm . . . /, (accessed 20 September 2011); http://www.nikahsearch.com/marriage/contract.htm and http://www.jaffari.org/resources/alim.asp?id=11 and http://www.muslimparliament.org.uk/articles.htm (embedded in article) (accessed 20 September 2011).

3. M. J. Maghniyyah, *The Five Schools of Islamic Law* (Qum, Iran: Ansariyan Publications, 2000), 260.

4. J. Esposito with N. DeLong-Bas, *Women in Muslim Family Law* (Syracuse, N.Y.: Syracuse University Press, 2001), 15.

5. Some jurisdictions allow religious authorities to function simultaneously as the officiators of civil marriages at the same time they sanctify these unions religiously. For example, Ontario, Marriage Act, R.S.O. 1990, c.M.3; Newfoundland and Labrador, Solemnization of Marriage Act, R.S.N.L. 1990, c.S-19; Nova Scotia, Solemnization of Marriage Act, R.S.N.S. 1989, c.436; California Family Code § 400 (1994); Code of Alabama § 30-1-7 (1975).

6. Paternity Act, Act 205 of 1956, Eff. 11 August 1956.

7. All Canadian provinces recognize some form of common law marriage, which gives property division and spousal support rights to these couples in the same way as married couples. See, for example, in Ontario, Family Law Act, R.S.O. 1990, c.F.3, part 3; in Manitoba, support is determined by the Family Maintenance Act,

C.C.S.M., c.F20; in Nova Scotia by Maintenance and Custody Act, R.S.N.S. 1989, c.160, s.4; and in Saskatchewan the division of property, the Family Property Act, S.S. 1997, c.F-63.

8. Currently only nine states (Alabama, Colorado, Iowa, Kansas, Montana, Oklahoma, Rhode Island, South Carolina and Texas) and the District of Columbia recognize common law marriages. Five other states have grandfathered in common law marriage (Georgia, Idaho, Ohio, Oklahoma and Pennsylvania). New Hampshire recognizes common law marriage for purposes of probate, while Utah recognizes it only if validated by a court or administrative order (National Conference on State Legislature, http://www.ncsl.org [accessed 31 August 2011]).

9. Michigan Act 295 of 1982, Support and Parenting Time Enforcement Act.

10. Holy Qur'an, verses 2:220–21.

11. Note that the motivation and practice of "trial marriage" is not the same as a "temporary marriage" (*mut'aa nikah*), a Shia practice which contracts for a sexual relationship for a specified period of time, involves no religious figures and is often associated with the sex trade. See S. M. Al Serat, "Temporary Marriage in Islamic Law," *Journal of Islamic Studies* (available at http://www.al-islam.org/al-serat/muta [accessed 31 August 2011]).

12. Holy Qur'an, verse 4:3, and see Esposito and DeLong-Bas, *Women in Muslim Family Law*, 136.

13. Holy Qur'an, verse 17:34. The "covenant" here is understood by Muslim jurists as the relationship between the citizen and the state.

14. In about half of these cases the wives referred to these women as mistresses; however, the husband may have considered this person to be a second wife. See also the discussion in chapter five.

15. "100 Premarital Questions," prepared by S. Faraz Rabbani. Available at http://qa.sunnipath.com/issue_view.asp?HD=1&ID=588&;CATE=10 (accessed 31 August 2011).

16. For example, Holy Qur'an, verses 7:80–81 and 26:165; *hadith* of Sahih Al-Bukhari, vol. 7, bk. 72, no. 774.

17. Iran is a well-known example. See J. Sofer and A. Schmitt, eds., *Sexuality and Eroticism among Males in Moslem Societies*, vol. 2 (London: Routledge & Kegan Paul, 1992). See also the documentaries *Inside Iran's Secret Gay World* (Canadian Broadcasting Corporation, 2007) and *A Jihad for Love* (Parvez Sharma, 2007).

18. Attributed to Muzzamil Siddiqi, a former two-term president of the Islamic Society of North America and the present chair of the Fikh Council of North America, in A. Akram, "Muslim Gays Seek Lesbians for Wives," *Religion News Service* (24 June 2006); available at http://www.washingtonpost.com/wp-dyn/content/article/2006/06/23/AR2006062301417.html (accessed 31 August 2011).

19. See, for example, K. Bullock, *Rethinking Muslim Women and the Veil* (Herndon, Va.: International Institute of Muslim Thought, 2007), 208–9.

20. A. Bouhdiba, *Sexuality in Islam*, trans. A. Sheridan (London: Routledge & Kegan Paul, 1985), 31.

21. See Sofer and Schmitt, eds., *Sexuality and Eroticism among Males in Moslem Societies*, xiii,

22. See, for example, S. O. Murray, "Some Nineteenth-Century Reports of Islamic Homosexualities," in *Islamic Homosexualities: Culture, History, and Literature*, ed. S. O. Murray and W. Roscoe (New York: New York University Press, 1997); B. Dunne, "Power and Sexuality in the Middle East," *Middle East Report*, no. 206 (Spring 1998).

23. Hadith, attributed to Bayhaqi, Al-Tirmidhi # 3096, narrated by Anas ibn Malik.

24. F. Mernissi, *Beyond the Veil: Male-Female Dynamics in Modern Muslim Society* (Bloomington: Indiana University Press, 1987), 31, 41–42.

25. Esposito and Delong-Bas, *Women in Muslim Family Law*, 15.

26. Holy Qur'an, verse 24:33.

27. H. Hartford, *Initiating and Upholding an Islamic Marriage* (Amman, Jordan: Al-Fath, 2007), 27.

28. Numerous examples of this advice exist on websites for young Muslims seeking marriage partners or advice on marriage. See, for example, www.nikah.com; www.islamonline.net; www.jannah.org/sisters/index.html; www.zawaj.com (all accessed 31 August 2011).

29. R. W. Maqsood, *Muslim Marriage Guide* (Beltsville, Md.: Amana Publications, 2000), 3.

30. Y. K. Greenberg, *Encyclopedia of Love in World Religions*, vol. 1 (Santa Barbara, Calif.: ABC-CLIO, 2008), 7.

31. Z. Shakir, "The Ethics of Chivalry," *Emel Magazine*, no. 67 (April 2010).

32. See, for example, Hartford, *Initiating and Upholding an Islamic Marriage*, 26–27.

33. S. Razack, *Casting Out: The Eviction of Muslims from Western Law and Politics* (Toronto: University of Toronto Press, 2008), 115–16.

34. Attributed to Bukhari and cited in M. Ali Mohammed, *A Manual of Hadith* (Dublin, Ohio: Ahmadiyya Anjuman Ishaat Islam, 1941), 223.

35. A. Bredal, "Arranged Marriages as a Multicultural Battlefield," in *Youth, Otherness, and the Plural City: Modes of Belonging and Social Life*, ed. M. Andersson, Y. Lithman and O. Sernhede (Gothenburg: Daidalos, 2005).

36. Y. Samad and J. Eade, *Community Perceptions of Forced Marriage* (London: Foreign and Commonwealth Office, 2002).

37. T. Modood and R. Berthoud, *Ethnic Minorities in Britain* (London: Fourth National Survey of Ethnic Minorities Policy Studies Institute, 1997), chap. 9.

38. "It's Muslim Boy Meets Girl, but Don't Call It Dating," *New York Times* (19 September 2006).

39. Samad and Eade, *Community Perceptions of Forced Marriage*, 85.

40. Attributed to Abu-Dawad and reported in Ali Mohammed, *A Manual of Hadith*, 233.

41. Holy Bible, Ephesians 5:22.

42. A. Bredal, "Arranged Marriages as a Multicultural Battlefield," paper prepared for the conference Youth in the Plural City: Individualized and Collectivized Identity Projects (Rome, May 1999), cited in Razack, *Casting Out*, 105.

43. M. Minow, "Is Pluralism an Ideal or a Compromise? An Essay for Carol Weisbrod," *Connecticut Law Review* 40 (2007–2008): 1287.

44. See the exposition in J. Bowen, *Why the French Don't Like Headscarves: Islam, the State, and Public Space* (Princeton, N.J.: Princeton University Press; Oxford: Woodstock, 2007).

45. See, for example, the New Marriage Contract of Egypt (first draft) in M. Zulficar, "The Islamic Marriage Contract in Egypt," in *The Islamic Marriage Contract: Case Studies in Islamic Family Law*, ed. A. Quraishi and F. Vogel (Cambridge, Mass.: Harvard University Press, 2008), 256–50.

46. The U.K. Model Muslim Marriage Contract, Muslim Institute, London, August 2008 available at http://www.muslimparliament.org.uk/articles.htm (embedded in article) (accessed 20 September 2011).

47. A. al-Hibri, "Muslim Women's Rights in the Global Village: Challenges and Opportunities," *Journal of Law and Religion* 15 (2000–2001): 52 (citing Abu Hanifah, Malik and al-Shafi'i).

48. For example, the Malaysian Islamic Family Law Act (1984) allows the defence of *nushuz* (disobedience) to be raised against a wife's application for divorce based on breach of the marriage contract: see N. B. Badli Shah, "The Islamic Marriage Contract in Malaysia," in Quraishi and Vogel, *Islamic Marriage Contract*, 185–86.

49. See, for example, M. A. Syed, *The Position of Women in Islam: A Progressive View* (Syracuse: State University of New York Press, 2004), 51–54.

50. T. Ramadan, *Western Muslims and the Future of Islam* (New York: Oxford University Press, 2004), 139.

51. "10 Qualities to Make a Husband Happy," muslimmarriageadvice.com, 29 January 2011, available at www.muslimmarriageadvice.com/2011/01/10-qualities-to-make-a-husband-happy (accessed 31 August 2011).

52. Hartford, *Initiating and Upholding an Islamic Marriage*, 82.

53. S.C.Code Ann. § 16-3-615 (2004).

54. N.C. Gen. Stat. § 14-27.8 (2005).

55. See J. Kelly and M. Johnson, "Differentiation among Types of Intimate Partner Violence," *Family Court Review* 46(3) (2008): 483, describing "Coercive Controlling Violence," which is perpetuated primarily by men and may include sexual violence and/or forced sex.

56. Hartford, *Initiating and Upholding an Islamic Marriage*, 66.

57. *Muslim Americans: A National Portrait* (Washington, D.C.: Muslim West Facts Project, a partnership between Gallup and the Coexist Foundation, 2009), chap. 2, fig. 14.

58. See C. Weisbrod, "Universals and Particulars: A Comment on Women's Human Rights and Religious Marriage Contracts," *Southern California Review of Law and Women's Studies* 9 (1999–2000): 77.

59. On the ability of *shari'a* to evolve and change, see A. Emon, "Natural Law and Natural Rights in Islamic Law," *Journal of Law and Religion* 20 (2004): 351.

60. M. Zulficar, "The Islamic Marriage Contract in Egypt," in Quraishi and Vogel, *Islamic Marriage Contract*, 237.

61. A. Nadir, "I Should Have Read My Islamic Marriage Contract," *Slate*, 25 February 2010, note 181, Available at http://www.slate.com/id/2245908/ (accessed 20 September 2011); quote attributed to Pakistani women's rights activist Rubina Sehagal.

CHAPTER 4

1. Based on the Holy Bible, Romans 7:2 (St. James translation): "For the woman which hath an husband is bound by the law to her husband so long as he liveth; but if the husband be dead, she is loosed from the law of her husband."

2. Vedic marriage (marriage according to the principles of the Vedas, the original scriptures of the Hindu religion) is a lifelong commitment. See P. Lal, *The Vedic Hindu Marriage Ceremony* (Sanskrit text with English trans.) (Calcutta: Writer's Workshop, 1996).

3. A sect of the Mormon church, which otherwise banned polygamy in 1890.

4. Samana Siddiqui reports that conflict with in-laws is the number-one reason for marital strife. See "Divorce among American Muslims: Statistics, Challenges and Solutions," available at www.soundvision.com/info/marriage/conflict/muslimdivorcestats.asp (accessed 2 September 2011).

5. Holy Qur'an, verse 37:105.

6. See J. Macfarlane, *The Emerging Phenomenon of Collaborative Family Law (CFL): A Qualitative Study of CFL Cases* (Department of Justice, Canada, 2005). Available at http://www.justice.gc.ca/eng/pi/fcy-fea/lib-bib/rep-rap/2005/2005_1/index.html#a01 (accessed 21 September 2011).

7. A. Thornton, "Changing Attitudes towards Separation and Divorce: Causes and Consequences," *American Journal of Sociology* 90 (1985): 856.

8. N. Gerstel, "Divorce and Stigma," *Social Problems* 34(2) (1987): 172.

9. C. Moore, *The Mediation Process* (San Francisco: Jossey-Bass, 1996): 104–8.

10. R. Blake, H. A. Shepard and J. Mouton, *Managing Intergroup Conflict in Industry* (Houston, Tex.: Gulf Publishing, 1964).

11. One researcher found that after a divorce, women and children on average experience an approximately 30 percent decline in income, while men experience about a 30 percent increase on average; see A. Crittenden, *The Price of Motherhood: Why the Most Important Job in the World Is Still the Least Valued* (New York: Metropolitan Books, Henry Holt, 2001).

12. M. Abu-Nimer, *Nonviolence and Peace Building in Islam: Theory and Practice* (Gainesville: University of Florida Press, 2003), 60.

13. Holy Qur'an, verse 4:128.

14. See, for example, Holy Qur'an, verse 42:37: "God fills with peace and faith the heart of one who swallows his anger"; Holy Qur'an, verse 2:153: "Allah is with those who patiently persevere." See also Abu-Nimer, *Nonviolence and Peace Building in Islam*, 72–73.

15. Holy Qur'an, verse 4:35.

16. Holy Qur'an, verse 4:128; M. Hathout with U. Jamil, G. Hathout, and N. Ali, *The Pursuit of Justice: The Jurisprudence of Human Rights in Islam* (Los Angeles, Calif.: Muslim Public Affairs Council, 2006), 178.

17. S. H. Nasr, *The Heart of Islam: Enduring Values for Humanity* (London: Harper Collins, 1994), 184.

18. See, for example, J. L. Young, E. E. H. Griffith and D. R. Williams, "The Integral Role of Pastoral Counseling by African-American Clergy in Community Mental Health," *Psychiatric Services* 54 (2003): 688; P. S. Wang, P. A. Berglund, and R. C. Kessler, "Patterns and Correlates of Contacting Clergy for Mental Disorders in the United States," *Health Services Research* 38 (2003): 647.

19. W. Abu-Ras, A. Gheith and F. Cournos, "The Imam's Role in Mental Health Promotion: A Study at Twenty-Two Mosques in New York City's Muslim Community," *Journal of Muslim Mental Health* 3 (2008): 169.

20. S. Bano, "Islamic Family Arbitration Justice and Human Rights in Britain," *Journal of Law, Social Justice and Global Development*, special issue (2007): 20.

21. E. Peters, *Heresy and Authority in Medieval Europe* (Philadelphia: University of Pennsylvania Press, 1980).

22. R. G. Bringle and D. Byers, "Intentions to Seek Marriage Counseling," *Family Relations* 46(3) (July 1997) 299–304.

23. Holy Qur'an, verse 2:177.

24. Abu-Ras, Gheith and Cournos, "Imam's Role in Mental Health Promotion," 161; and see A. Mohit, "Mental Health and Psychiatry in the Middle East: Historical Development," *Eastern Mediterranean Health Journal* 7 (2001): 336.

25. T. Asad, *Formations of the Secular: Christianity, Islam, Modernity* (Stanford, Calif.: Stanford University Press, 2003), 10.

CHAPTER 5

1. Idiom, loosely translated as uptight and "uppity."

2. For a detailed analysis of this relationship and its roots in Islamic tradition, see F. Mernissi, *Beyond the Veil: Male-Female Dynamics in Modern Muslim Society* (South Bend: Indiana University Press, 1987), 121–36, writing about contemporary Moroccan society.

3. A central tenet of feminist writing from the 1970s onwards. See, for example, C. McKninnon, *Feminism Unmodified: Discourses on Life and Law* (Cambridge, Mass.: Harvard University Press, 1987), arguing that gender is a matter of power and dominance, not simply difference, and A. Dworkin, *Intercourse* (New York: Free Press, 1997), arguing that the act of sexual intercourse is an expression of male power and authority over women.

4. For alternative views, see M. Daly, *Beyond God the Father* (Oxford: Blackwell, 1973), and C. Christ, *She Who Changes: Re-imagining the Divine in the World* (London: Palgrave Macmillan, 2004).

5. D. Hassouneh-Phillips, "Marriage If Half Faith the Rest Is Fear of God," *Violence against Women* 7(8) (2001): 939.

6. See, for example, "10 Qualities to Make a Husband Happy," muslimmarriageadvice.com, 29 January 2011, available at www.muslimmarriageadvice.com/2011/01/10-qualities-to-make-a-husband-happy (accessed 31 August 2011).

7. See, for example, A. al-Hibri, "Muslim Women's Rights in the Global Village: Challenges and Opportunities," *Journal of Law and Religion* 15 (2000–2001): 37.

8. See A. al-Hibri, "Quranic Foundations of the Rights of Muslim Women in the Twenty-First Century," in *Women in Indonesian Society: Access, Empowerment, and Opportunity*, ed. M. A. Mudzhar et al. (Yogyakarta: Sunan Kalijaga Press, 2002), 16–19.

9. See M. Badran, *Feminism in Islam: Secular and Religious Convergences* (Oxford: One World Press, 2009), tracing the history and interaction of Islam and feminism.

10. B. Friedan, *The Feminist Mystique* (New York: Dell Publishing, 1964), 54.

11. According to Betty Friedan, the average age at which girls were married in late 1950s America was twenty (*Feminist Mystique*, 12).

12. G. H. Gallup and C. F. Kettering, *Human Needs and Satisfactions—A Global Survey*, research report (C. F. Kettering Foundation and Gallup International Research Institutes, 1976).

13. See also C. De Boer, "The Polls—Women at Work," *Public Opinion Quarterly* 41(2) (1977): 268.

14. G. Guilder, "Women in the Workforce," *Atlantic Monthly*, September 1986.

15. *Muslim Americans: A National Portrait* (Washington, D.C.: Gallup American Muslim Report, 2009), chap. 2, fig. 14.

16. C. B. Mulligan, "A Milestone for Working Women?" *New York Times* (14 July 2009).

17. J. Hagan and F. Kay, "Hierarchy in Practice: The Significance of Gender in Ontario Law Firms," in *Inside the Law: Canadian Law Firms in Historical Perspective*, ed. C. Wilton Osgoode (Toronto: Society for Canadian Legal History and University of Toronto Press, 1996).

18. *Muslim Americans: A National Portrait*, chap. 2, fig. 15.

19. See http://countrystudies.us/egypt/71.htm (accessed 3 September 2011).

20. Mernissi, *Beyond the Veil*, xxvi.
21. G. Esfandiari, "Iran: Number of Female University Students Rising Dramatically," Radio Free Europe (2003), available at http://www.parstimes.com/women/women_universities.html (accessed 3 September 2011).
22. See Farzaneh Roudi-Fahimi and Valentine M. Moghadam, "Empowering Women, Developing Society: Female Education in the Middle East and North Africa," Population Reference Bureau, MENA Policy Brief (2003), 4, 5.
23. *Muslim Americans: A National Portrait*, chap. 1, fig. 3.
24. Ibid., chap. 2, fig. 1.
25. A. L. al-Sayyid Marsot, "Women and Modernisation," in *Women, the Family, and Divorce Laws in Islamic History*, ed. A. E. A. Sonbol (Syracuse, N.Y.: Syracuse University Press, 1996), 50.
26. See, for example, J. H. Greenhaus and N. J. Beutell, "Sources of Conflict between Work and Family Roles," *Academy of Management Review* 10(1) (1985): 76, and L. E. Duxbury and C. A. Higgins, "Gender Differences in Work-Family Conflict" *Journal of Applied Psychology* 76(1) (Feb. 1991): 60.
27. A term used to describe those born between 1961 and the end of the 1970s—after the so-called baby Boomer generation and before Generation Y (those born in the 1980s and 1990s). The novel which first popularized the term was D. Coupland, *Generation X: Tales for an Accelerated Culture* (London: St. Martin's Press, 1991).
28. See, for example, N. J. Beutell and U. Wittig-Berman, "Work-Family Conflict and Work-Family Synergy for Generation X, Baby Boomers, and Matures: Generational Differences, Predictors, and Satisfaction Outcomes," *Journal of Managerial Psychology* 23(5) (2008): 507.
29. See K. Tran, J. Kaddatz and P. Allard, "South Asians in Canada: Unity through Diversity," *Canadian Social Trends* 78 (Autumn 2005). Reporting on the Ethnic Diversity Study, Statistics Canada, 2002, shows that South Asians are the least likely of all visible minority groups to marry someone outside their population group. Of the 232,010 married and common-law couples that included at least one South Asian partner in 2001, only about 13 percent were mixed unions. These figures include common-law partnerships; in the United Kingdom one study found just 1 percent of the Pakistani and Bangladeshi community married outside their ethnic group (T. Modood and R. Berthoud, *Ethnic Minorities in Britain*, Fourth National Survey of Ethnic Minorities [London: Policy Studies Institute, 1997]). Interestingly. African Americans and African Canadians consistently post the highest rates of marriage with members of other minority groups.
30. Y. Samad and J. Eade, *Community Perceptions of Forced Marriage* (London: Foreign and Commonwealth Office, 2002), chap. 5.
31. See A. Bredal, "Arranged Marriages as a Multicultural Battlefield," in *Youth, Otherness, and the Plural City: Modes of Belonging and Social Life*, ed. M. Andersson, Y. Lithman and O. Sernhede (Gothenburg: Daidalos, 2005).

32. See, for example, the many different experiences of arranged marriage for Indian-born women now living in North America described in C. B. Divakaruni, *Arranged Marriage* (New York: Doubleday, 1995).

33. S. Siddiqui, "Divorce among American Muslims: Statistics, Challenges and Solutions," available at http://jannah.org/halfmydeen/index.php?topic=193.0 (accessed 20 September 2011).

34. Mernissi, *Beyond the Veil*, 21.

35. Holy Qur'an, verse 4:3.

36. R. Bachman, *Violence against Women: A National Crime Victimization Survey Report* (Washington, D.C.: U.S. Department of Justice, Bureau of Justice Statistics, 1994), 6.

37. See N. Faizi, "Domestic Violence in the Muslim Community," *Texas Journal of Women and the Law* 10 (2000–2001): 211.

38. Also similar to the findings of Ruksana Ayub. See "Domestic Violence in the South Asian Muslim Population," *Journal of Social Distress and the Homeless* 9(3) (2000): 1.

39. This is an ongoing debate. See, for example, D. Coleman and M. A. Straus, "Alcohol Abuse and Family Violence," in *Alcohol, Drug Abuse and Aggression*, ed. E. Gottheil (Springfield: Charles C. Thomas, 1983); C. B. Cunradi, R. Caetano, C. L. Clark and J. Schafer, "Alcohol-Related Problems and Intimate Partner Violence among White, Black, and Hispanic Couples in the U.S.," *Alcoholism: Clinical and Experimental Research* 23 (1999): 1492.

40. Department of Health and Human Services, *Domestic Violence Fact Sheet* (Washington, D.C.: Department of Health and Human Services, 1994).

41. K. Reihing, "Protecting Victims of Domestic Violence and Their Children after Divorce: The American Law Institute Model," *Family and Conciliation Courts Review* 37 (1999): 393.

42. Federal Bureau of Investigation, *Uniform Crime Reports* (Washington, D.C.: Federal Bureau of Investigation, 1990).

43. A. D. Kulwicki and J. Miller, "Domestic Violence in the Arab American Population: Transforming Environmental Conditions through Community Education," *Issues in Mental Health Nursing* 20(3) (1999): 199.

44. Holy Qur'an, verse 4:34. I have used one version throughout unless otherwise stipulated: *The Qur'an Translated: Message for Humanity*, trans. Marmaduke Pickthall (Washington, D.C.: International Committee for the Support of the Final Prophet, 2005). This particular verse however is from a different translation: Muhammed Asad, *The Message of the Qur'an*, 2nd ed. (Watsonville, Calif.: Book Foundation, 2008).

45. See the examples given by al-Hibri, "Muslim Women's Rights in the Global Village," 64.

46. See N. H. Ammar, "Wife Battery in Islam: A Comprehensive Understanding of Interpretations," *Violence against Women* 13(5) (2007): 519–23.

47. "The Prophet never beat any of his wives or servants" (*hadith* attributed to An-Nasaa'i).

48. According to the Al-Musnadu Al-Sahihu bi Naklil Adli, attributed to Muslim ibn al-Hajjaj, the Prophet advised one woman, whose name was Fatimah bint Qais, not to marry a man named Abul Jahm because he was known for beating women.

49. *Religion and Domestic Violence: Information and Resources: Interpretation of Religious Doctrine* (Harrisburg, Penn.: National Resource Center on Domestic Violence, 2007), 1.

50. See, for example, Hassouneh-Phillips, "Marriage If Half Faith the Rest Is Fear of God," 927; and Ayyub, "Domestic Violence in the South Asian Muslim Immigrant Population in the United States," 237.

51. Z. Latif, "The Silencing of Women from the Pakistani Muslim Mirupi Community in Violent Relationships," in *Honour, Violence, Women and Islam*, ed. M. Idriss and T. Abbas (London: Routledge, 2010), 29.

52. *Religion and Domestic Violence*, 2.

53. See M. K. Barnett, "The Relationship between Violence, Social Support, and Self-Blame in Battered Women," *Journal of Interpersonal Violence* 11(2) (1996): 221.

54. Ayyub, "Domestic Violence in the South Asian Muslim Immigrant Population in the United States," 242.

55. See generally R. Thiara and A. Gill, *Violence against Women in South Asian Communities: Issues for Policy and Practice* (London: Jessica Kingsley, 2001).

56. M. Mamdani, *Good Muslim, Bad Muslim: America, the Cold War, and the Roots of Terror* (New York: Pantheon Press, 2004), 18; and see also M. Mamdani, ed., *Beyond Rights Talk and Culture Talk: Comparative Essays on Rights and Culture* (London: St. Martin's Press, 2000).

57. Z. Grewal, *Death by Culture? How Not to Talk about Islam and Domestic Violence* (Clinton, Mich.: Institute for Social Policy and Understanding, 2009), 5.

58. S. Razack, *Casting Out: The Eviction of Muslims from Western Law and Politics* (Toronto: University of Toronto Press, 2008), 146.

59. Grewal, *Death by Culture?*, 7.

60. See, for example, Idriss and Abbas, *Honour, Violence, Women and Islam*.

61. Latif, "The Silencing of Women from the Pakistani Muslim Mirupi Community in Violent Relationships," 29, 34–37.

62. "Justice Minister: No 'Honour Crime' Criminal Code Change," 8 August 2010, available at http://www.ctv.ca/CTVNews/Canada/20100808/canada-honour-killings-law-100808/ (accessed 3 September 2011).

63. See, for example, leading Muslim scholar Zaid Shakir's call for clarity that Islam does not condone or support "honor killing" and that any such claims simply disguise a criminal act: "Islam and Honor Killing," available at http://ezinearticles.com/?Islam-and-Honor-Killings&;id=758099 (accessed 3 September 2011).

64. Grewal, *Death by Culture?*, 13.

65. Latif, "The Silencing of Women from the Pakistani Muslim Mirupi Community in Violent Relationships," 30.

66. Ayyub, "Domestic Violence in the South Asian Muslim Immigrant Population in the United States," 238.

67. See, for example, W. Abu-Ras and S. Abu-Bader, "The Impact of the September 11, 2001, Attacks on the Well-Being of Arab Americans in New York City," *Journal of Muslim Mental Health* 3 (2008): 217.

68. Ayyub, "Domestic Violence in the South Asian Muslim Immigrant Population in the United States," 242.

69. See http://www.isna.net/Services/pages/Domestic-Violence-Forum.aspx (accessed 20 September 2011).

70. See www.peacefulfamilies.org (accessed 3 September 2011).

CHAPTER 6

1. The divorce rate in India is 15 percent. I. Ba-Yunus, "How Do Muslims in America Divorce?" in *Muslim Family in a Dilemma: Quest for a Western Identity*, ed. M. Akhtar (Lanham, Md.: University Press of America, 2007), 10.

2. See http://www1.albawaba.com/en/news/high-divorce-rates-alarm-gulf-states (accessed 5 September 2011).

3. See, for example, S. Tamale and J. Okumu-Wengi, "The Legal Status of Women in Uganda," in *Women, Laws, Customs and Practices in East Africa: Laying the Foundation*, ed. J. W. Kabeberi-Macharia (Nairobi: Women and Law in East Africa, 1995), 24–45; and A. An-Na'im, ed., *Islamic Family Law in a Changing World: A Global Resource Book* (New York: Zed Books, 2002), 72.

4. *Hadith* attributed to Abu-Dawood.

5. Holy Quran, verse 1:228.

6. Ba-Yunus, "How Do Muslims in America Divorce?," 11. See also I. Ba-Yunus, "Divorce among Muslims," *Islamic Horizons* 29 (Spring 2001): 52–53.

7. Ba-Yunus, "How Do Muslims in America Divorce?," 12.

8. Ibid., 15–17.

9. Conducted by Sound Vision (an Islamic media information foundation). See the results at www.soundvision.com/info/marriage/conflict/muslimdivorcesurvey2010.asp (accessed 5 September 2011).

10. See http://divorcemag.com/statistics/statsUS2002.shtml (accessed 5 September 2011).

11. See M. M. Keshavjee, "Arbitration and Mediation in the Shi'a Imami Ismaili Muslim Community," paper presented at the Fourth International Conference of the World Mediation Forum, 10 May 2003, available at iis.ac.uk/SiteAssets/pdf/mediation.pdf (accessed 5 September 2011).

12. See F. Kniss, *Disquiet in the Land: Cultural Conflict in American Mennonite Communities* (New Brunswick, N.J.: Rutgers University Press, 1997).

13. On the differences between private and formal systems of law, see J. Macfarlane, "Working towards Restorative Justice in Ethiopia: Integrating Traditional Conflict Resolution Systems with the Formal Legal System," *Cardoza Journal of Conflict Resolution* 8(2) (2007): 489–94.

14. S. H. Nasr, *The Heart of Islam: Enduring Values for Humanity* (London: Harper Collins, 1994), 277.

15. See A. Quarashi, "Who Says *Shari'a* Demands the Stoning of Women? A Description of Islamic Law and Constitutionalism," *Berkeley Journal of Middle Eastern and Islamic Law* 1(1) (2008): 63, for an articulation of the relationship between religious law and personal conscience.

16. Nasr, *The Heart of Islam*, 7.

17. See P. Heelas and L. Woodhead, *The Spiritual Revolution: Why Religion Is Giving Way to Spirituality* (Oxford: Blackwells, 2005), and the further discussion in chapter nine.

18. On the use and prevalence of kitchen-table agreements, see S. Gamache, "Collaborative Practice: A New Opportunity to Address Children's Best Interest in Divorce," *Louisiana Law Review* 65 (2004–2005): 1445.

19. Such panels often function according to their own written rules of procedure (see, for example, the Canadian Council of Muslim Theologians at http://ccmt.jucanada.org). I am aware of just three such panels offering divorce processes in North America (in Toronto, Detroit and Southern California), although more are pending. At the time of this writing, none includes an oral hearing or presentation of evidence, simply a written application.

20. See Holy Qur'an, verses 2:226–32 and 65:1–7.

21. M. A. Syed, *The Position of Women in Islam: A Progressive View* (Syracuse: State University of New York Press, 2004), 67–68.

22. For references, see An-Na'im, *Islamic Family Law in a Changing World*, in particular pp. 78, 113, 234 and 271.

23. See M. J. Maghniyyah, *The Five Schools of Islamic Law* (Qum, Iran: Ansariyan Publications, 1995), 388, citing the Holy Qur'an, verse 65:2–3.

24. See the results at http://www.soundvision.com/info/marriage/conflict/muslimdivorcesurvey2010.asp.

25. An-Na'im, *Islamic Family Law in a Changing World*, 255.

26. Ibid., 78

27. Simple incompatibility is a ground for divorce in Pakistan since the enactment of the reformist Muslim Family Laws Ordinance of 1961 and subsequent case law. See ibid., 235.

28. This is this imam's interpretation of the Holy Qur'an, verse 4:34.

29. European Council on Fatwa and Research, Fatwa (17) Resolution 3/5, "Ruling on a Divorce Issued a Non-Muslim Judge," in *Resolutions and Fatwas, Second Collection*, trans. Shakir Nasif Al-Ubaydi and Anas Osama Altikriti, ed. Anas Osama Altikriti and Mohammed Adam Howard (2008). Available at http://www.e-cfr.org/en/index.php?ArticleID=285.

CHAPTER 7

1. B. Mayer, *The Dynamics of Conflict Resolution* (San Francisco: Jossey Bass, 2000), 98–108.
2. K. Pargament and M. Rye, "Forgiveness as a Method of Religious Coping," in *Dimensions of Forgiveness: Psychological Research and Theological Perspectives*, ed. E. Worthington (Philadelphia: Templeton Foundation Press, 1998), 61.
3. See, for example, S. Macintyre, *Single and Pregnant* (London: Redwood Burn Ltd., 1977).
4. Holy Bible, Matthew 5:32.
5. See, for example, K. Pargament, *The Psychology of Religion and Coping: Theory, Research, Practice* (London: Guilford, 1997).
6. R. H. Mnookin and L. Kornhauser, "Bargaining in the *Shadow of the Law*: The Case of Divorce," *Yale Law Journal* 88 (1979): 950.
7. See *Bracklow v. Bracklow* ([1995] 1 S.C.R. 420), where the court discusses the "clean-break" model as recognizing the social reality of shorter marriages and successive relationships. The parties are entitled to what they contracted for and what they have lost as a result of the marriage and its subsequent breakdown.
8. *Moge v. Moge* ([1992] 3 S.C.R. 813).
9. Holy Qur'an, verses 1:228, 65:1, 65:4.
10. S. Iqbal, *Women and Islamic Law* (New Delhi: Adam Publishers, 2004), 212.
11. A. al-Hibri, "Muslim Women's Rights in the Global Village: Challenges and Opportunities," *Journal of Law and Religion* 15 (2000–2001): 48.
12. Holy Qur'an, verses 2:229, 33.
13. Some jurisdictions provide for "children of the family." In Canada, the *Federal Child Support Guidelines*, SOR/97–175, s.5, provides for support obligations of a stepparent, when a spouse "stands in the place of a parent for a child." In the United States, see *Miller v. Miller* (478 A.2d 351 [N.J. 1984]; New Jersey Supreme Court).
14. B. J. Fidler, "Child Custody Disputes: Private and Public Assessments," *Canadian Family Law Quarterly* 25 (2006): 137.
15. In the United States, see A. Schepard, *Children, Custody and Courts: Interdisciplinary Models for Divorcing Families* (Cambridge: Cambridge University Press, 2004), 2; and in Canada see the Divorce Act 1985 (2nd Supp.), c.3 s16(4) and 16(8).
16. M. Gordon, "Infants and Toddlers: An Update of Canadian Law on Post-Separation Parenting Agreements," *Canadian Family Law Quarterly* 29 (2010): 95; M. Brinig, "Penalty Defaults in Family Law: The Case of Child Custody" *Florida State University Law Review* 33 (2006): 779.
17. A. Schepard, "The Evolving Judicial Role in Child Custody Disputes: From Fault Finder to Conflict Manager to Differential Case Management," *University of Arkansas at Little Rock Law Journal* 22(3) (1999–2000): 406–12.

18. There are differing views among the different schools on the period of custody; see L. Bakhtiar (adapted by), *Encyclopedia of Islamic Law: A Compendium of the Major Schools* (Chicago: ABC International Group, 1996), 471–72.

19. A. An-Na'im, ed., *Islamic Family Law in a Changing World: A Global Resource Book* (London and New York: Zed Books, 2002), 235–36

20. In the United States see *re Marriage of Heath*, 18 Cal. Rptr. 3d 760 (Cal. App. 2004); and Principles of the Law of Family Dissolution: Analysis and Recommendations § 2.08(1) (c) (2002). In Canada, the situation is slightly different. See *Re: King and King*, 1979, 2 A.C.W.S., p. 202. The Court held that in parental custody disputes there is only one standard to apply, namely, the best interest principle. Therefore, any forms of presumption, such as "the tender years doctrine, non-separation of siblings, girls to mothers, boys to fathers, etc.," are only significant factors to consider and not operative presumptions to be rebutted.

21. Mnookin and Kornhauser, "Bargaining in the *Shadow of the Law*," 982–83.

22. Some Islamic scholars approve of abortion up to 115 days. See M. Al-Kawthari, *Birth Control and Abortion in Islam* (Santa Barbara, CA: White Thread Press, 2006).

23. *Michelle Marvin v. Lee Marvin* 557 P.2d 106 (Cal 1976). Most states will enforce trusts or agreements between cohabitants.

24. See, for example, in Ontario, *Family Law Act*, S.O. 1990, c. F.3; in Manitoba support is determined by *The Family Maintenance Act*, C.C.S.M., c. F.20; in Nova Scotia by *Maintenance and Custody Act*, R.S.N.S. 1989, c.160, s.4; and in Saskatchewan the division of property, *The Family Property Act*, S.S. 1997, c. F-63.

25. http://divorcemag.com/statistics/statsUS2002.shtm.

26. See the 1970 Uniform Divorce and Marriage Act, 9A Unif L.Ann 161 (1979) and *Marriage of Huntington* (1992) 10 CA4th 1513, 1522.

27. *Pelech v Pelech* (1987) 1SCR 803, and C. Rogerson, "The Canadian Law of Spousal Support," *Family Law Quarterly* 38(1) (2004) (suggesting that enthusiasm for the "clean break" approach in Canada has been modified by concerns over fairness and a movement towards a compensatory principle; see *Moge v. Moge* (1992) 3 SCR 813.

CHAPTER 8

1. A. L. Estin, "Embracing Tradition: Pluralism in American Family Law," *Maryland Law Review* 63 (2004): 556.

2. P. Fournier, "The Erasure of Islamic Difference in Canadian and American Family Law Adjudication," *Journal of Law and Policy* 10 (2001): 94.

3. §§ 1–33, 7 U.L.A. 9–94 (2000).

4. 9 U.S.C. §§ 1–16 (2000).

5. M. Grossman, "Is This Arbitration? Religious Tribunals, Judicial Review and Due Process," *Columbia Law Review* 107 (2007): 169.

6. *New York Civil Practice Law & Rules Law* § 7501 (2010).

7. The 2009 Florida Statutes: *Florida Arbitration Code*, Ch. 682.02.

8. J. F. Gaudreault-DesBiens, "The Limits of Private Justice? The Problems of the State Recognition of Arbitral Awards in Family and Personal Status Disputes in Ontario," *World Arbitration & Mediation Report* 16 (2005): 1.

9. *Family Law Reform Act*, R.S.O. 1980, c.152.

10. *Commercial Arbitration Act*, R.S.B.C. 1996, c. 55.

11. *Commercial Arbitration Act*, S.N.S. 1999, c. 5.

12. Text from the ballot question posed in Oklahoma. Enrolled Joint House Resolution 1056, State Question Number 755, Legislative Referendum Number 355, 25 May 2010.

13. http://xmwcnews.net/focus/analysis/6496-oklahoma-ban-on-shariah-is-unconstitutional.html (accessed 28 September 2011).

14. http://tpmlivewire.talkingpointsmemo.com/2010/06/oklahoma-state-senator-aims-to-stop-liberal-judges-from-imposing-sharia-law.php (accessed 28 September 2011). See also http://www.tulsaworld.com/news/article.aspx?subjectid=14&articleid=20100718_18_A1_Viewsd561266 (accessed 28 September 2011).

15. See http://morallaw.org/news/roy-moore-and-foundation-for-moral-law-file-brief-defending-oklahomas-anti-sharia-save-our-state-amendment (accessed 4 October 2011), case no. CIV-10-1186-M. An amicus curiae brief was filed in support of the amendment by the Foundation for Moral Law on 4 April 2011. Its argument appears to be that had the amendment referred only to international and foreign law it would have been constitutional but that it was necessary to refer to *shari'a* law because of its indeterminate meaning and status as a legal system (p. 4).

16. The Foundation for Moral Law amicus curiae brief filed 4 April 2011 states that there is a "reasonable fear" that "sharia Law could be imposed in Oklahoma." The rationale is that as the Muslim population has grown in the United States, so has "the threat of Sharia Law."

17. A. Wajahat, E. Clifton, M. Duss, L. Fang, S. Keyes and F. Shakir, "Fear, Inc.: The Roots of the Islamophobia Network in America," Centre for American Progress (August 2011).

18. In the United States, see the Restatement (second) of Conflict of Laws § 98. In Canada, see the *Divorce Act*, R.S.C. 1985, c.3 (2nd Suppl.), s. 22.

19. D. F. Forte, "Islamic Law in American Courts," *Suffolk Transnational Law Journal* 7 (1983): 3.

20. For example, in Ontario, *Marriage Act*, R.S.O. 1990, c.M.3, s. 20.

21. Estin, "Embracing Tradition," 560–61.

22. 724 NYS2d (2001) 560.

23. *Ayoub v. Osman* (2006) O.J. No. 1176 (S.C.J.Fam.Ct.). An earlier example of similar reasoning is *Aghili v. Saadatnejadi* (1997) 958 S.W.2d 784; 1997 Tenn. App. LEXIS 415.

24. (2000) T.C.J. No. 371.
25. *Nurmi v. Nurmi* (1988), 16 R.F.L (3d) 201 (Ont. U.F.C.). The agreement must be in writing, signed and witnessed by the parties. There is no need for any special wording or format.
26. *Michelle Marvin v. Lee Marvin* 557 P.2d 106 (Cal 1976).
27. Courts in the United Kingdom have historically been unwilling to enforce prenuptial agreements, but recent case law suggests that this may be changing. See *MacLeod v. MacLeod* (2008) UKPC 64, (2010) 1 AC 298; *Radmacher (formerly Granatino) v. Granatino (Rev 4)* (2010) UKSC 42 (20 October 2010); http://www.guardian.co.uk/money/2010/oct/20/prenuptial-agreement-enforced-uk-law (accessed 28 September 2011).
28. Uniform Pre-Marital Agreement Act (UPAA), National Conference of Commissioners on Uniform State Law, August 1983 State.
29. *Uniform Marriage and Divorce Act*, M.S.A. §§ 518.002 to 518.66.
30. *California Family Law Code*, § 1612 (2009).
31. *Dougherty v. Dougherty* (2008) O.J. No. 1502.
32. In a study of 349 family cases in Dane County, Madison, Wisconsin, only 32 required the adjudication of a judge on one or more issues. See M. Melli, H. Erlanger, and E. Chambliss, "The Process of Negotiation: An Exploratory Investigation in the Context of No-Fault Divorce," *Rutgers Law Review* 40 (1987–1988): 1142–43. See also J. Singer, "The Privatization of Family Law," *Wisconsin Law Review* 5 (1992): 1443.
33. In the Dane County study only 1 of the 349 agreements submitted to the court for approval was turned down. This agreement was found to be insufficient in relation to child support. See Melli, Erlanger, and Chambliss, "The Process of Negotiation," 1145.
34. *Aziz v. Aziz* (1985) 488 N.Y.S.2d 123; 1985 N.Y.
35. (2008) A.J. No. 390, para. 11.
36. *Akileh v. Elchahal* (1996) 666 So. 2d 246, 1996 Fla. App. LEXIS 123, 21 Fla. L. Weekly D 162 (Fla. Dist. Ct. App. 2d Dist. 1996).
37. *In re Marriage of Shaban* (2001) 2001 Cal. App. LEXIS 273.
38. *Obaidi v. Qayoum* 154 Wn. App. 609; 226 P.3d 787; 2010 Wash. App.
39. *Attia v. Amin*, New Jersey Ch. Div., 12 June 2006. Available at http://www.internationalfamilylawfirm.com/2007/10/*mahr*-islamic-marriage-contract-held-to.html (accessed 28 September 2011).
40. *Zawahiri v. Alwattar*, Ohio Ct. App., No. 07AP-925, 7/10/08, available at http://pub.bna.com/fl/07825.pdf (accessed 28 September 2011).
41. (2009) O.J. No. 2245, para. 67.
42. *Cannon v. Cannon* 156 Md. App. 387; 846 A.2d 1127; 2004 Md. App. LEXIS 54 and see also *Zawahiri v. Alwattar* in n. 39. In Canada see *Hartshorne v. Hartshorne* (2004) 1 S.C.R. 550.

43. M.A.K. v. E.I.B (2008) N.B.J. No. 514, para. 58.

44. J. Coles in *Richmond v. Dubuque* 23 Iowa 191 (1861).

45. J. Issacs in *Wilkinson v. Osborne* (1915) 21 CLR 89.

46. *Crowther v. Crowther* 2010 NY Slip Op 50677U; 27 Misc. 3d 1211A; 910 N.Y.S.2d 404; 2010 N.Y. Misc. LEXIS 786; 243 N.Y.L.J. 80.

47. *Skotnicki v. Skotnicki* N.Y.S. 2d 904, at 905 (N.Y. App. Div. 1997).

48. (1995) N.S.J. No. 354; 144 N.S.R. (2d) 223; 57 A.C.W.S. (3d) 974.

49. J. *Experiences of Collaborative Law: Preliminary Results from the Collaborative Lawyering Research Project*, 2004 J. Disp. Resol. 179, 191 (2004); R. E. Emery, *Marriage, Divorce, and Children's Adjustment* (Thousand Oaks, Calif.: SAGE Publications, 1999).

50. U.S. Constitution, Bill of Rights, Amendment I.

51. *Watson v. Jones* 80 US (13 Wall) 679 (1871). See the discussion in Grossman, "Is This Arbitration?" 169, and K. Greenwalt, "'Hands Off' Civil Court Involvement in Conflicts over Religious Property," *Columbia Law Review* 98 (1998): 1843.

52. Estin, "Embracing Tradition," 542.

53. G. Qaisi, "Religious Marriage Contracts: Judicial Enforcement of *Mahr* Agreements in American Courts," *Journal of Law and Religion* 15 (2001–2002): 76.s

54. *Serbian Eastern Orthodox Diocese v. Milivojevich* 426 US 696 (1976); see also Grossman, "Is This Arbitration?" 185.

55. *Aziz v. Aziz* 488 N.Y.S. 2d 123 (NY Sup Ct 1985) at 124.

56. *Kaddoura v. Hammoud* (1998), 168 D.L.R. (4th) 503.

57. http://religionclause.blogspot.com/2007/10/ohio-court-refuses-to-enforce-muslim.html and http://www.internationalfamilylawfirm.com/2007/10/*mahr*-islamic-marriage-contract-held-to.html (both accessed 28 September 2011).

58. *Bruker v. Marcovitz*, 2007 SCC 54.

59. Abella J. at 47. See also R. Moon, "*Bruker v. Marcovitz*: Divorce and the Marriage of Law and Religion," *Supreme Court Law Review* 42 (2008): 38–62.

60. *Lakeside Colony of Hutterian Brethren v. Hofer* (1992) 3 S.C.R. 165 per J. Gonthier at 191.

61. New York Domestic Relations, Article 13, §253.

62. *Nathoo v. Nathoo* (1996) B.C.J. No. 2720 (S.C.), *Amlani v. Hirani* (2000) B.C.J., *N.M.M. v. N.S.M.* (2004) B.C.J. No. 642 (S.C.).

63. *Rashid v. Shaher* (2010) O.J. No. 3490.

64. *Aziz v. Aziz* 488 N.Y.S. 2d 123 (NY Sup Ct 1985) and *Avitur v. Avitur* 58 N.Y. 2d 108 (N.Y. 1983).

65. *Odatalla v. Odatalla* 810 A.2d 93 (N.J. Super.Ch. 2002).

66. J. S. C. Selser in *Odatalla*, at 98.

67. *Rahman v. Obhi Hossain*, 2010 N.J. Super. Unpub. LEXIS 1326.

68. Signed by Portugal, Luxembourg, Egypt, Australia, Finland and the Netherlands on 14 March 1978. Note that other states (including Canada and the United States) have long observed the principle of comity.

69. *Hyde v. Hyde and Woodmansee* 1866 L.R. 1 P.& D. 132.

70. Divorce Act s.22(1). "In my opinion, the arrival of a person in a new locality with the intention of making a home in that locality for an indefinite period makes that person ordinarily resident in that community." J. A. Evans, in *MacPherson v. MacPherson* (1976), 28 R.F.L. 106.

71. *Jahangiri-Mavaneh v. Taheri-Zengekani* (2003) O.J. No. 3018.

72. *Hilton v. Guyot*, 159 U.S. 113, 163–64 (1895), and see more recently *Litvaitis v. Livaitis*, 162 Conn. 540 (1972) and *Winick v. Winick*, 153 Conn. 294 (1965).

73. *Indyka v. Indyka* (1969) 1 AC 33 (decision of the English House of Lords).

74. *Holub v. Holub* (1976) 71 DLR (3d) 698, (1976) 5 WWR 527.

75. *Moustafa v. Moustafa* (2005) 166 Md. App. 391, 888 A.2d 1230, 2005 Md. App.

76. A. An-Na'im, ed., *Islamic Family Law in a Changing World: A Global Resource Book* (New York: Zed Books, 2002), 234.

77. In the United States, see *Bruneau v. Bruneau*, 3 Conn.App. 453, 455, 489 A.2d 1049, and in Canada, the Divorce Act s.22.

78. *Aleem v. Aleem* (2007) 175 Md. App. 663, 931 A.2d 1123, 2007 Md. App.

79. *The Hague Convention of October 25, 1980 on the Civil Aspects of International Child Abduction.*

80. *Navani v. Shahani*, F.3d, 2007 WL 2171355 (C.A. 10, 30 July 2007) (U.S. District Court [New Mexico]).

81. *Hosain v. Malik* (1995) 108 Md. App. 284; 671 A.2d 988 at 535. See also In re Marriage of Donboli, No. 53861-6-I (Wash. Ct. App. 2005) in which the court refused to recognize the custody order of an Iranian court because they did not adequately take account of the best interests of the child.

82. S. A. Warraich and C. Balchin, *Recognizing the Unrecognizable: Inter-Country Cases and Muslim Marriages and Divorces in Britain: Women Living under Muslim Laws* (Nottingham, U.K.: Russell Press, 2006).

83. (2003) O.J. No. 3018, (2005) O.J. No. 2055; (2005) O.J. No. 2055.

84. The Holy Qur'an, verse 17:34.

85. J. Gaudreault-DesBiens, "The Limits of Private Justice? The Problem of State Recognition of Arbitral Awards in Family and Personal Status Disputes in Ontario," *Perspectives* 16(1) (Jan. 2005): 19.

86. European Council on Fatwa and Research, Fatwa (17) Resolution 3/5, "Ruling on a Divorce Issued a Non-Muslim Judge," in *Resolutions and Fatwas*, Second Collection, trans. Shakir Nasif Al-Ubaydi and Anas Osama Altikriti, ed. Anas Osama Altikriti and Mohammed Adam Howard (2008), available at www.e-cfr.org/en/index.php?ArticleID=285.

87. Muzammil H. Siddiqi is a former president of the Islamic Society of North America. See http://www.islamopediaonline.org/fatwa/dr-muzammil-h-siddiqi-former-president-fiqh-council-north-america-rules-validity-american-cour (accessed 4 October 2011).

CHAPTER 9

1. A. Emon, "Islamic Law and the Canadian Mosaic: Politics, Jurisprudence, and Multicultural Accommodation," *Canadian Bar Review* 87 (2008): 421.
2. T. Asad, *Formations of the Secular: Christianity, Islam and Modernity* (Stanford, Calif.: Stanford University Press, 2003), 200–202.
3. A distinction drawn by A. Tkuru, *Secularism and State Policies towards Religion: The United States, Turkey and France* (Cambridge: Cambridge University Press, 2010).
4. M. Badra, *Feminism in Islam: Secular and Religious Convergences* (Oxford: One-World, 2009), 304–5.
5. A. An-Na'im, (2008) *Islam and the Secular State: Negotiating the Future of Shari'a* (Cambridge: Mass.: Harvard University Press, 2008), 36–37.
6. The expression *secularism* was coined by G. J. Holyoake, *Origin and Nature of Secularism* (1896; London: Watts & Co., 1986).
7. B. A. Kosmin and A. Keysar, *American Religious Identification Survey Trinity College* (2008), Hartford, Connecticut, available at http://b27.cc.trincoll.edu/weblogs/AmericanReligionSurvey-ARIS/reports/ARIS_Report_2008.pdf (accessed 28 September 2011).
8. P. Heelas and L. Woodhead, *The Spiritual Revolution: Why Religion Is Giving Way to Spirituality* (Oxford: Blackwells, 2005).
9. Asad, *Formations of the Secular*, 161.
10. Ibid., 139, 160–61.
11. C. Taylor, *Sources of the Self: The Making of Modern Identity* (Cambridge: Cambridge University Press, 1989).
12. M. Nussbaum, "Veiled Threats?" *New York Times*, 11 July 2010, available at http://opinionator.blogs.nytimes.com/2010/07/11/veiled-threats.
13. R. Williams, "Civil and Religious Law in England: A Religious Perspective" (7 February 2008), available at http://www.archbishopofcanterbury.org/articles.php/1137/archbishops-lecture-civil-and-religious-law-in-england-a-religious-perspective#Lecture (accessed 4 October 2011).
14. A. Shachar, *Multicultural Jurisdictions: Cultural Differences and Women's Rights* (Cambridge: Cambridge University Press, 2001), 76–77, and see S. Okin, "Is Multiculturalism Bad for Women?" *Boston Review* 22 (1997): 22, 25–28.
15. A. Bradney, "Faced by Faith," in *Faith in Law: Essays in Legal Theory*, ed. P. Oliver, S. D. Scott, and V. Tadros (Portland, Ore.: Hart Publishing, 2000), 89–105.
16. Shachar, *Multicultural Jurisdictions*, 12–13.
17. D. Pearl and W. Menski, *Muslim Family Law* (London: Sweet & Maxwell, 1998), 75.
18. Bradney, "Faced by Faith," 104.
19. Williams, "Is *Shari'a* Law Unavoidable in England?" p. 6.
20. S. L. Stone, "The Intervention of American Law in Jewish Divorce: A Pluralist Analysis," *Israel Law Review* 34 (2000): 190.

21. J. Macfarlane, "Commentary: When Cultures Collide," in *Intercultural Dispute Resolution in Aboriginal Contexts: Canadian and International Perspectives*, ed. C. Bell and D. Kahane (Vancouver: University of British Columbia Press, 2004), 99–100.

22. J. Macfarlane, *The New Lawyer: How Settlement Is Transforming the Practice of Law* (Vancouver: University of British Colombia Press, 2008).

23. See for example C. LaPrairie, "The 'New' Justice: Some Implications for Aboriginal Communities," *Canadian Journal of Criminology* 40(1) (1998): 61.

24. Pearl and Menski, *Muslim Family Law*.

25. S. Bano, "Muslim Family Justice and Human Rights: The Experience of British Muslim Women," *Journal of Comparative Law* 1(4) (2007): 8.

26. For example, *Persaud v. Balram* 724 NYS2d (2001) 560.

27. Emon, "Islamic Law and the Canadian Mosaic," 423.

28. See J. F. Gaudreault-DesBiens, "The Limits of Private Justice? The Problem of State Recognition of Arbitral Awards in Family and Personal Status Disputes in Ontario," *Perspectives* 16(1) (Jan. 2005): 19.

29. N. Bakht, "Were Muslim Barbarians Really Knocking on the Gates of Ontario? The Religious Arbitration Controversy—Another Perspective," fortieth anniversary edition, *Ottawa Law Review* 67 (2006): 78.

30. A. Shachar, "Religion, State and Problem of Gender: New Modes of Citizenship and Governance in Diverse Societies," *McGill Law Journal* 50 (2005): 74.

31. See S. Bano, "Islamic Family Arbitration Justice and Human Rights in Britain," *Journal of Law, Social Justice and Global Development*, special issue (2007): 1.

32. G. Krayem, "To Recognize or Not to Recognize, That Is NOT the Question: Family Law and the Muslim Community in Australia" (Ph.D. diss., University of Sydney, 2011).

33. S. Poulter, "The Claim to a Separate Islamic System of Personal Law for British Muslims," in *Islamic Family Law*, ed. C. Mallat and J. Connors Graham (London: Trotman, 1990), 147.

34. Bano, "Islamic Family Arbitration Justice and Human Rights in Britain," 12–13.

35. "British Imams Failing Young Muslims," *The Times* (London), 7 January 2008.

36. S. Syeed, quoted in "Young Muslims in US Seek Home Grown Imams," 31 March 2011, news.com, available at http://www.voanews.com/english/news/usa/Young-Muslims-in-US-Seek-Homegrown-Imams-91147399.html (accessed 28 September 2011).

37. J. Klausen, "Is There an Imam Problem?" *Prospect* 98 (20 May 2004), available at http://www.prospectmagazine.co.uk/issue/98/ (accessed 28 September 2011).

38. H. Bazian, quoted in "A Growing Demand for the Rare American Imam," *New York Times*, 1 June 2007.

39. See for example W. Abu-Ras, A. Gheith and F. Cournos, "The Imam's Role in Mental Health Promotion: A Study at Twenty-two Mosques in New York City's Muslim Community," *Journal of Muslim Mental Health* 3 (2008): 155.

40. Syeed, quoted in "Young Muslims in US Seek Home Grown Imams."

41. For example, the Islamic Institute of Toronto (www.islamicinstitute.ca); the Salam Institute for Justice and Peace (www.salaminstitute.org); the ILDC, a branch of the Islamic Society for North America (www.isna.net/Leadership/pages/ILDC.aspx); the North American Imams Federation (NAIF) (www.imansofamerica.org); and a Shia organization, the Imam Mahdi Association of Maryaeya (www.imam-us.org). The largest North American Muslim organization (ISNA) promotes training for imams and Muslim chaplains on its website and throughout its materials.

42. For a progressive perspective, see Imam Mohammed Magid, "Affecting Change as an Imam," in *Change from Within: Diverse Perspectives on Domestic Violence in Muslim Communities*, ed. Salma Elkahdi Abugidieri and Maha Alkhateeb (Great Falls, Va.: Peaceful Families Project, 2007), 187. Note also that three of the four survivor accounts in this book do not mention the support or assistance of an imam.

43. See L. Cainkar and S. Del Toro, "An Investigation into the Social Context of Domestic Violence in the Arab/Muslim-American Community: Identifying Best Practices for Effective Prevention and Intervention," A Study for the Arab-American Action Network (2010), 26, available at http://www.aaan.org/wp-content/uploads/DV-report1.pdf.

44. See for example the Michigan Peaceful Families Proclamation, Arab-American News, 1 December 2007, available at %3Ca href=http://www.arabamericannews.com/news/index.php?mod=article&cat=Community&;article=387 (accessed 30 October 2010).

45. "Responding to the Killing of Aasiya Hassan: An Open Letter to the Leaders of American Muslim Communities," available at http://www.isna.net/articles/News/RESPONDING-TO-THE-KILLING-OF-AASIYA-HASSAN-AN-OPEN-LETTER-TO-THE-LEADERS-OF-AMERICAN-MUSLI.aspx.

46. Bradney, "Faced by Faith," 99–100.

47. F. Kutty, "The Myth and Reality of 'Sharia' Courts in Canada: A Delayed Opportunity for the Indigenization of Islamic Legal Rulings," *University of St. Thomas Law Journal* 7 (2010): 38.

GLOSSARY

Caliph: the ruler or head of state of a Muslim community or *umma* (below). The last formal caliphate was dissolved in 1924, but the authority and influence of the caliphate model was diminished by the end of the 13th century with the emergence of independent rulers in many Muslim countries and regions.

Faskh: judicial annulment of marriage, commonly used where the husband refuses to give consent to *khula* (below)

Fatwa: legal decision or interpretation of Islamic law for guidance, provided by a mufti or another recognized authority

Fiqh: literally "understanding", *fiqh* are laws or the system of Islamic law. *Fiqh* was created by jurists and is derived from the central textual sources of Islam, namely the Qur'an and the Sunna. There are five major schools of Islamic jurisprudence or laws, four of which are Sunni (Maliki, Hanbali, Hanifi and Shafi'i)and one Shia school (Jafri)

Hadith: a report of a saying or action of the Prophet Mohammed or one of his Companions. The complex process of authentication of *hadith* turns on the authority of the author. There are different collections of *hadith* accepted by Sunnis and Shias.

Iddat: the "waiting period" following her husband's death or divorce, during which the wife cannot remarry. Usually lasts for three menstrual cycles or the equivalent to ensure that the wife is not pregnant.

Ijma: principle of Islamic jurisprudence and analysis meaning consensus

Ijtihad: principle of Islamic jurisprudence and analysis meaning independent reasoning

Imam: literally "one who stands in front", a religious leader in Muslim communities. In the West, an imam will lead prayers at the mosque and is usually appointed by the mosque board of trustees

Islam: literally "surrender" or "submission" to the will of God

Khula: divorce initiated by the wife, usually only secured with her husband's permission

Mahr: consideration for the wife's promise to marry, usually monetary but could be anything of value (eg a poem, a promise). *Mahr* may be deferred and payable upon death or divorce, or paid immediately.

Muta: Shia temporary marriage contract, not accepted by Sunnis

Nikah: a Muslim marriage contract, binding the couple together legally and in the eyes of God.

Qadi: a Muslim judge

Qiyas: principle of Islamic jurisprudence and analysis meaning reasoning by analogy

Shari'a: literally "the path", *shari'a* comprises rules of behavior for living as a good Muslim. It includes acts of piety and observance, but also expectations regarding *zagat* (charitable gifts), family affairs (for example marriage and divorce), business affairs (for example borrowing and debt) as well as many other aspects of a Muslim's relationship with God, and with others. Some parts of *shari'a* is formalized as *fiqh* or law

The Qur'an: the central religious text of Islam, regarded by Muslims to be the word of God revealed to the Prophet Mohammed

Shia: Shia Muslims believe that the leadership of the Muslim community rests with the descendants of Ali. They accept many of the same sources of Islam – for example the Qur'an – as Sunni Muslims but adopt some different *hadiths* and some differences in Islamic law (following the Jafri school)

Sunna: reports of the words and actions of the Prophet Mohammed, usually contained in *hadith*

Sunni: the largest branch of Islam

Sura: a chapter of the Quran

Talaq: divorce initiated by the husband, this does not require the wife's consent but usually requires at least formal notice. In practice dialogue is encouraged

Ulama: learned men, scholars, guardians of religious and legal traditions

Umma: a Muslim community that accepts *shari'a*

Zagat: charitable contribution, often a fixed proportion of income

INDEX

Abu-Nimer, Mohammed, 81, 277n23, 285n12, n14
accommodation strategy, 80
adultery, 53, 59, 128, 145, 181, 228
  Islamic law, 14, 168
  marital conflict, 126–29
African Americans/Canadians, 4, 5, 44, 148
African Muslims, 4, 77, 141
Agrezi Sharia, English and Islamic law, 246
Ahmed v. Canada, 219
Al-Falah Islamic Centre, 267, 269
al-Hibri, Azizah, 61
alimony, divorce, 158
All Dulles Area Muslim Society, 51, 263–66
American Freedom Defense Initiative, 273n28
An-Na'im, Abdullahi, 8, 23, 276n4
annulment. *See also faskh*
  faskh, 37–38, 176
  judicial *khula*, 168
anti-*shari'a* movement, 16, 215–17, 294n15
Archbishop of Canterbury, Williams, 16–18, 214, 276n61
arranged marriage, 53–58, 102, 119–22
Asad, Talal, 98, 242
assertive secularism, 241
authority, 59–65, 103–9
Ayoub v. Osman, 218
Ayyub, Ruksana, 138

Baby boomers, 113, 287n37
Bakht, Natasha, 249–50

Bangladesh, 56, 287n29
Bano, Samia, 87, 247, 250, 272n8
Ba-Yunus, Ilyas, 142
Bet Din. *See* Jewish Bet Din
Boyd, Marion, 275n55
Bradney, Anthony, 244
breadwinner, women as, 27, 33, 66–67, 109, 113, 131, 190
Bredal, Anja, 56, 60
British Muslims, 5, 17
burkah, debate over, 60

CAIR (Council on American-Islamic Relations), 9, 214
CAIR-CAN (Canadian Council on American-Islamic Relations), 15
caliphs, 20, 301
Canada
  best interests of siblings, 194
  child support, 192–93
  civil divorce, 144
  comity, principle of, 227, 230
  community property, 191
  courts and *mahr*, 33
  dress legislation, 60
  freedoms of speech, conscience and religion, 240
  Muslim tribunals in Ontario, 216–17
  political and legal model, 261–62
  recognition of marriage, 197–98
  recognizing overseas marriage and divorce, 227–28, 230

Canadian Census- Muslims, 4
Canadian Charter of Rights and Freedoms,
    15, 217
Canadian Civil Marriage Act, 278n42
Canadian Council for Muslim Women,
    275n53
Canadian Council of Muslim Theologians,
    291n19
Canadian Council of Muslim Women
    (CCMW), 15
Canadian Institute of Policy Studies, 271n1
Canadian Islamic Congress, 15
Catholicism, 63, 107
Caucasian converts, Islam, 148
Center for American Progress, 216
children
    where *nikah* marriage only, 44–45
    consequences of divorce, 159
    Islamic vs. civil law, 192–93
    joint custody, 195
    support, care and custody of, 30, 31, 192–97
child support. *See also* children
    guidelines, 292n13
civil divorce. *See also* divorce; Islamic
    divorce; religious divorce
    combining Islamic divorce with, 144–46
    release from *nikah*, 204, 235–37
"clean break" approach
    divorce, 292n7
    religious divorce, 199–02
Coexist/Pew study, 5, 271n1, 273n11,
    273n12, 273n22
comity, principle of
    Canada and United States, 217–18,
    229–30, 297n68
common law partnerships, 45, 197–98,
    287n29
    Canada, 280–81n7
    United States, 281n8
communities
    family and, 78–79, 178
    response to divorce, 78, 179–82
community property. *See* property
Companions of the Prophet, Sunna, 20
conflict. *See also* marital conflict
    family finances, 108–9
    freedoms, 117–19
    gender roles, 102–3
    going to school, 116–17

religious or cultural differences, 124–25
religious practice, 129–30
working wives, 114–16
consent order, 212, 235–36, 173, 186, 220
convert marriages, conflicts, 124–25, 280n1
"co-operative traditional" marriage, 119
counseling. *See also* marital counseling
    imams, 83–84
    marital conflict, 35, 162
    premarital, 49–51
courts. *See also* comity
    American, relative to other legal systems,
        217–18
    civil divorce and *nikah*, 235–37
    claims after divorce, 186–87
    orders and Islamic obligations, 234–37
cross-cultural marriages, 122–25
custody. *See also* children
    children, 30, 31, 192–97
    country differences, 229
    presumption in disputes, 293n20

Darul-Qada, Ontario-based group, 14, 15
dialogue process, religious divorce, 161–63
divorce. *See also* civil divorce; divorce
        consequences; Islamic divorce;
        religious divorce; *talaq*
    annulment of marriage, 37–38
    combining Islamic, and civil, 144–46
    consequences of, 158–60
    cultural and family attitudes, 76–79
    decision to, 73–82, 143–44
    husband requesting, 37–38, 163–67
    Muslim countries, 141
    permission for, 157–58
    religious law regarding, 35–38, 74–76
    ruling on verbal delegated *talaq*, 267
    social stigma against women, 141
    spousal support, 31
    tolerance, 45, 253–55
    wife requesting, 36–37
divorce consequences, 158–60
    accepting reality of, 177–79
    asking for eventual release, 202–5
    goal of pleasing God, 206–8
    legal-financial outcomes, 185–98
    looking for "clean break," 199–202
    outcomes of religious divorce, 198–208
    property division, 191–92

social, 179–82
spiritual, 177, 182–85, 208–9
spousal support, 187–91
support, care and custody of children, 192–97
Domestic Relations Law, 253, 225
domestic violence, 16, 132–34, 136–39, 258–60
    barriers to reporting, 136–39
    changing attitudes, 255
    emotional or verbal abuse, 59, 103, 107, 137
    honor-based violence (HBV), 135–36
    imam granting divorce, 170
    imams offering services for, 137–39, 257–58
    physical abuse, 130–32
    and reconciliation, 86–87
    safety of children, 131
Domestic Violence Forum, 139, 290n69
Domestic Violence Prevention Program, Dearborn, Michigan, 258

Eade, John, 56, 57, 282nn36, 39, 287n30
East Europeans, Muslim communities, 4
education
    conflict over, 116–17
    women, 31, 110–12
    women and domestic violence, 259
Egypt, 28, 31–32, 123, 145, 168
    divorce, 228
    legal system, 248, 280n68
    New Contract Marriage of Egypt, 61
El Fadl, Khalid., The Great Theft, 271n2, 277n28
equivalency fatwa, 235–37, 238
Esposito, John, 273n25
Establishment Clause, 224, 225
Ethiopia, 77, 164, 168, 291n13
Ethnic Diversity Study, Canada, 287n29
European Council for Fatwa and Research, 235

faith, impact of divorce, 177, 182–85, 208–9
family
    arbitrations and Jewish Bet Din, 16
    attitudes to divorce, 76–79, 178
    conflicts, 85, 105–6, 112–14, 125–29
    court and religious divorce agreement, 159–60

extended, and reconciliation, 91–93
service organizations, 251–53
faskh, 37–38, 168–69, 176, 269, 301
fatwa
    definition, 301
    equivalency fatwa, 235–37
    imam's knowledge of, 169–70
    rulings forming law, 20–21
Federal Arbitration Act (FAA), United States, 213
feminist Muslim scholars, 108, 112
fidelity, marital, 30–31
financial responsibilities
    disputes over family finances, 108–9
    in marriage, 65–68
financial settlement
    children after divorce, 36
    common law status, 45
    Islamic divorce, 150–51, 158–59, 185–87
    mahr, 32–34, 158–59, 162, 164, 168, 171–72, 178–79, 185, 187–90, 200–202, 205–7
fiqh, 8, 20–23
    definition, 301
    "God-given," 25
    human intellect and, 26
    Islamic laws
fitna, single women, 52
forced marriage, 29, 119
forced sex, domestic abuse, 130
forum-shopping, religious divorce, 160–61
Fournier, Pascale, 211
France, dress legislation, 60
Friedan, Betty, 110
Fundamentalist Church of Jesus Christ of Latter-Day Saints, marriage, 70

Gallup survey, 110, 112, 273n15, 283n57, 286nn12, 15
gender roles
    breadwinner and homemaker, 109
    challenge of changing, 255–56
    conflict, 102–19
    power and dominance, 286n3
    societal changes in, 109–12
    women as primary breadwinner, 27, 33, 66–67, 109, 113, 131, 190
    working wives, 114–16

generational changes, power and gender roles, 112–14
Generation X, 113
Generation Y, 287n27
Grewal, Zareena, 136

hadith
  authenticity, 20
  criteria of wife for Muslim man, 56
  definition, 301
  divorce, 34, 58, 85, 141
  source of Islamic law, 20
Hague Convention on the Celebration and Recognition of the Validity of Marriages, 227
Hague Convention on the Civil Aspects of International Child Abduction, 229
haj, pilgrimage to Mecca, 41
Hanbali, school of law, 22–23, 271n5, 277n28, 279n60
Hanifi school of law, 22–23, 141, 271n5, 278n36
Hassan, Aasiya, murder, 135, 259
Hassouneh-Phillips, Dena, 107
Healthy Marriage Covenant, 50, 258
Healthy Marriage Initiative, 50
Heelas, Paul, 242
heterosexual relationship, marriage, 51–52
Highland Green, Michigan, 44, 46
Hijab, 4, 6, 13, 133, 185
Hindus, 70, 284n2
Hmong marriage ritual, 244
Holy Bible, 284n1
homosexuality, 51–52
honor-based violence (HBV), 135–36, 289n63
Horn of Africa, 148
houses of obedience, Egypt, Lebanon and Iran, 31
husbands
  authority and wifely obedience, 31, 60–65
  breadwinner role, 109
  control as religious principle, 118
  divorce by, 35–36
  failing to consent to religious divorce, 172–74
  financial responsibility of children, 36
  mismatched expectations, 103–6

Qur'an encouraging kindness, 46–47, 189
religious rights to violence, 133
tolerance of male infidelity, 128–29

iddat, 154, 159, 161, 187
  definition, 301
  separation period, 35, 36, 46
  spousal support beyond, 189, 247
ijma, 21, 30, 301
ijtihad, 21, 27, 301
imams
  approach to marital relations, 24
  barriers to reporting violence, 136–38
  counseling, 84–86
  home grown, 299n36
  imam-shopping, 160–61, 171–72
  intervening in family conflict, 252–53, 257–58
  intervening in marital conflict, 84–86, 90–93, 255–58
  male anger against, 89–90
  obedience, 63
  overseeing religious divorce, 38, 155–60, 162, 168–69, 170, 172–74
  polygamy, 48
  premarital counseling 49, 51, 257, 260, 281n15
  promoting unilateral *talaq*, 165
  social welfare role in North America, 82–84
  standard marriage contracts, 226–27
  working with women, 87–90, 137–38
India, 22, 79, 99, 141, 248, 290n1
individual, marriage as completion of, 52–54
in-laws, relations with, 125–26, 284n4
Interfaith Domestic Violence Coalition, 139
Iran, 28, 31, 111, 164, 230
Islamic divorce. *See also* divorce; religious divorce, *khula, talaq, faskh*
  combining with civil divorce, 144–46
  equivalency *fatwa*, 235–37
  informal private ordering, 146–48
  motivations for seeking, 148–55
  process in North America, 155–60, 161–74
  recognition of overseas, 227–31, 238–39
Islamic dress. *See hijab*
Islamic family law, 29–38, 176, 187–95, 211–12

Islamic identity, religious divorce, 151–53
Islamic Institute of Toronto, 300n41
Islamic law. *See also fiqh*
  ability to change, 26–28
  child custody, 195–96
  child support, 192–93
  development from *shari'a*, 20–21
  family law, 9–10, 28–38, 187–96
  Islamic legal method, 21–22
  jurisprudence and decision making,
    22–24
  khula, 36–37, 167–72, 175
  personal moral code, 19–20
  primary sources, 20–21
Islamic marriage, 29–34
  agreements, 219–27
  arranged marriages, 119–22
  cross-cultural/convert marriages,
    122–25
  lack of legal recognition, 44–47, 197–98,
    247
  public policy considerations, 222–24
  recognizing overseas, 227–31
  as religious contracts, 224–27
  and *shari'a*, 9–10
Islamic Social Services Association of
  Canada, 258
Islamic Society of North America (ISNA),
  139, 259, 300n41

Jafri, school of law, 271n5, 279n60
Jahangir-Mavaneh v. Taheri-Zengekani,
  overseas divorce, 230
Jewish Bet Din, arbitrations, 16, 213, 232
Jewish Women International, 139
Judeo-Christian traditions, legal system,
  210, 211
judges. *See qadis*
judicial *khula*. See *faskh*

Khanis v. Noormohamed, Ontario, 221
khula
  "clean break" approach and, 200–202
  definition, 301
  divorce requested by wife, 36–37,
    167–72, 280n68
  overseas divorce, 228
kitchen-table divorce, 186, 220, 291n18
Krayem, Ghena, 250, 272n9

laissez-faire approach, freedom of contract,
  223
Langille v. Dossa, religious expectation, 223
Last Day, 85
Latif, Zahira, 136
Lebanon, 31, 117, 121, 160, 279n48
legal issues
  American Muslims use of courts, 205–8,
    232–35
  general contractual requirements, 221–22
  Islamic marriage and divorce, procedures,
    218–19,
  Islamic marriage and divorce agreements,
    219–27
  public policy considerations, 222–24
  recognition of overseas Islamic marriage
    and divorce, 227–31
  religious contracts, 224–27
legal method, Islamic, 21–22
legal-political strategies
  cooperation between Islamic and civil law,
    246–48
  Muslim family service organizations,
    251–53
  parallel legal system, 248–51
  religion-neutral approach, 244
  universalism and secularism, 244–46
license, *nikah* and, 42–44

McGuinty, Dalton, 15–16, 244
Maclean's Magazine, Mark Steyn, 6
Magid, Imam, 259
Mahr,
  definition, 302
  divorce without husband's permission,
    171
  element of marriage contract, 32–34, 65,
    66
  financial outcome of divorce, 150–51,
    158–59, 162, 178, 179, 185, 187–91
  imam-shopping for opinions on, 171–72
  relinquishment of deferred, 168, 206
  spousal support as alternative to, 205
  wedding gift from husband to wife, 10
Malaysian Islamic Family Law Act, 283n48
male infidelity, tolerance of, 128–29
Maliki, school of law, 21, 22–23, 271n5
Mamdani, Mahmood, 135
Marcovitz, 225, 226

marital conflict. *See also* conflict
  adultery and second wives, 126–29
  arranged marriages, 119–22
  cross-cultural/convert marriages,
    122–25
  freedoms, 117–19
  generational changes, 112–14
  mismatched expectations of husband and
    wife, 103–19
  personal style, 80–81
  relationship power and authority,
    106–9
  relations with in-laws, 125–26
  societal changes in gender roles, 109–12
  women going to school, 116–17
  working wives, 114–16
marital counseling
  professionals, 97–98
  role of imam in, 84–86
marital fidelity, 30–31, 53, 126–29
marital rape, Muslim legal system, 62–63
marriage. *See also* staying married
  bazaars, 54, 57
  between man and women, 51–52
  between Muslims, 104
  celebrating Muslim, 40–42
  choosing "right" partner, 54–58
  completion of individual, 52–54
  financial responsibilities, 65–68
  legal recognition of, 197–98
  lifelong commitment, 58–59,
    70–205
  nikah and civil license, 231
  obedience and authority, 59–65
  relations with in–laws, 125–26
marriage contract. *See also nikah*
  general requirements, 221–22
  marriage, 264–66
  pre-marital, 263
  religious, 224–27
  recognition of 197–98
matchmaking websites, Muslim, 54, 282n28
Mayer, Bernard, 292n1
Mernissi, Fatima, 111
Michigan Peaceful Families Proclamation,
    300n44
Middle East, 111, 122, 148
Miles-Lagrange, Vicky, 214, 215, 217
Mir-Hosseni, Ziba, 26

mubaraa, mutual aversion, 168
multiple marriages, 47–49
  adultery and second wives, 126–29
  nikah, 47–49
Mumtaz Ali, Syed, *Darul-Qada*, 14
Muslim Alliance for North America, 258
Muslim communities
  celebrating marriage, 40–42
  divorce rate, 142
  establishment in West, 3–5
  expansion of professional services, 260–61
  family service organizations, 251–53
  intolerance toward divorced women,
    253–55
Muslim Family Safety Project, London,
    Ontario, 258
Muslim marriage contract. *See nikah*
Muslim Public Affairs Committee UK, 17
muta, 302
mut'aa nikah, 281n11
mutual consent, *khula*, 37

Nasr, Seyyed, 150
Nassin v. Nassin, 221
National Conciliation and Arbitration
    Boards of the Ismaili Muslim
    Community, 146
natural law, God, 25
negotiations
  Islamic divorce settlement, 27–28
  marital conflict, 80
  premarital counseling, 49–51
neutral principles approach, 224, 226
New Age religions, 242
New Marriage Contract of Egypt, 61
nikah
  acquisition of, 40–42
  All Dulles Area Muslim Society, 263–66,
    278n40
  arranged marriage, 120
  availability of, 40
  civil divorce and, 235–37
  convert-to-convert marriage, 280n1
  future of, 68–69
  gender inequality, 32
  including property agreement, 192
  legal treatment, 219–27
  mahr or wedding gift, 32–34, 200–202,
    205, 206–7

marriage contract, examples, 263–66
multiple marriages, 47–49
premarital counseling, 49–51
procedure, 29
promises, 219
"real" marriage, 42–44
reliance on, alone, 44–47, 153–54
terms, 30–32, 221–22
trial marriage, 47
niqab, debate over veil, 60
North Africa, 45, 111, 122, 141, 148
North America
    divorce rate among Muslims, 142
    feminism emergence, 110
    Muslim population, 5
    new *shari'a* for, 261–62
    shari'a law imposition and
        enforcement, 9
    social welfare role of imam, 82–84
North American Council for Muslim
    Women, 131, 139
North American Imams Federation (NAIF),
    300n41
nushuz, disobedience, 61
Nussbaum, Martha, 242

obedience, wife, 31–32, 102
Oklahoma referendum
    American courts and other legal systems,
        217–18
    public debate, 215–17
    "Save Our State" amendment SQN755,
        214, 294n15
    shari'a law, 9, 246
Old Testament, 75
Ontario
    Al-Falah Islamic Centre, 267, 269
    Marriage Act, 218, 280n5
    media reporting Islamic divorce, 146
    Muslim tribunals in, 216–17,
        275n50
    Ontario Arbitration Act, 14, 16, 213,
        232, 249, 252
    shari'a law debate, 14–16, 244, 248, 260
    Somalian Canadian community, 44
overseas, marriage and divorce, 227–31, 254

Pakistan, 17, 106, 118
    arranged marriage, 121–22

common-law partnerships, 287n29
custody laws, 229
divorce application, 228
divorce rate, 141
education, 116
incompatibility and divorce, 291n27
male control, 118–19
parental consent for marriage, 56
unilateral *talaq*, 166–67
palimony, *Marvin* case, 197
panel of imams, 89, 155–56
parental choices
    arranged marriages, 119–20
    marriage, 56–58
Peaceful Families Initiative, 139, 258
Persaud v. Balram, 218
personal conflict style, marital conflict,
    80–81
personal freedoms, conflict over, 117–19
personal moral code, *shari'a*, 19–20
police, 77, 84, 85
    assistance, 199
    domestic violence, 86–87, 136–37,
        138
    honor code, 135–36
    underreporting, 131
polygamy
    Canada, 278n42
    Fundamentalist Church of Jesus Christ of
        Latter-Day Saints, 70
    Mormon church, 284n3
    nikah, 47–49
    second wives, 126–29
power
    generational changes, 112–14
    relationship, and authority, 106–9
premarital contract, *See nikah*, Islamic
    marriage
premarital counseling, 49–51
prenuptial agreements, 212, 295n27
principle of comity
    Canada and United States, 217–18,
        297n68
    overseas divorces, 229–30
private ordering systems
    Islamic divorce, 146–48
    nikah, 210
property
    after divorce, 158, 175

property (*continued*)
common or shared, 30
community, 30, 178
division after divorce, 191–92
Islamic vs. civil law, 191
Muslim couples and community, 178
Prophet Mohammed
divorce at time of, 142
Kajidha, first wife of, 55
love-based marriages, 55
Sunna, 7
treatment for women, 132
wife Khadija supporting, 67
Protestants, 70, 211

qadis, 20, 302
Qatar, divorce rate, 141
Qiwama, 60, 62, 107–8, 170
qiyas
definition, 302
jurisprudence, 22
standard *nikah*, 30
Qur'an, 302
burning stunts, 7
culture, 125
dialogue and negotiation, 166
divorce, 34, 168
domestic violence, 132
exhortation for ending relationship,
46–47, 189
"man is above woman," 88
marital fidelity, 126–27
polygamy, 48
reconciliation, 81–82
source of Islamic law, 20

Ramadan, Tariq, 25, 38–39, 61
Razack, Sherene, 6, 55
reconciliation, 35
domestic violence and, 86–87
experiences, 94–96
extended family, 91–93
Islamic tradition, 81–82
marriage counseling, 84–86, 97–98
period of counseling, 162
process and practice, 90–93
social welfare role of imam, 82–84
working with women, 87–90
regional panels, *faskh* annulment, 176

religion
Muslims in West, 11–13
and secularism, 240–41
symbolism and good Muslim, 130
religion-neutral approach, courts, 244
religious contracts, marriage and divorce,
224–27
religious divorce. *See also* divorce;
Islamic divorce, *khula, talaq, faskh*
affirmation of having "done the right
thing," 152
asking for eventual release, 202–5
consequences, 158–60
dialogue process, 161–63
failure to obtain, 172–74
finding closure, 153–54
forum-shopping, 160–61
imam-shopping, 160–61
imams overseeing, 155–57
Islamic identity, 151–53
looking for "clean break," 199–202
no interest in, 174–75
outcomes, 198–208
practical considerations, 154–55
process, 155–61
recourse to third party, 155–57
religious obligation, 149–51
seeking "Islamic" outcomes, 205–8
unilateral *talaq*, 163–67
wife-initiated divorce, 167–72
religious freedom, 215–16
religious practice
changing nature of, 241–43
conflicts over, 129–30
Muslims in West, 11–13, 271n1
religious proscriptions, male power and
authority, 132–33
remarriage, 193, 225
romantic love, 54–55
Rosen, Laurence, 23

Samad, Yunus, 56
Saudi Arabia, 3, 27, 31, 123
"Save Our State" amendment, SQN755 in
Oklahoma, 214, 294n15
scholars. *See ulama*
second wives, marital conflict, 126–29
secular absolutism, 244–45
secularism

legal-political system, 244–46
  Muslim marriage or divorce, 226
  religion and, 240–41
sexual abuse. *See* domestic violence
Shachar, Ayelat, 224–45, 246
Shafi'I, school of law, 21, 22–23, 271n5
Shakir, Zaid, 289n63
shared property. *See* property
shari'a
  debate in Ontario, 244, 248
  definition, 302
  lobby for system in North America, 245
  Muslims in West, 7–9
  new, for North America, 261–62
  personal conscience of Muslim, 19–20
  Qur'an and Sunna, 7–8
  seeking "Islamic" outcomes, 205–6
Shari'a Council of the United Kingdom,
    214, 247, 248–49, 250, 251
Sharia Law, 215
Shia, 302
Shia jurisprudence, 165, 279n56
Shi'ism,
Siddiqi, Muzzamil, 281n18, 297n87
Siddiqui, Samana, 125, 235–36, 284n4
Somalian Canadian community, Ontario, 44
Sound Vision, 290n9
South Asia, 4
  arranged marriages, 119
  common-law partnerships, 287n29
  cross-cultural marriage, 122
  divorce, 76, 142
  domestic violence, 136, 138
spirituality
  impact of divorce, 177, 182–85, 208–9
sponsorship, arranged marriage, 121
spousal support
  alternative to *mahr*, 205
  divorce, 31, 187–91
SQN755, Oklahoma's "Save Our State"
    amendment, 214, 294n15
stare decisis, "let the decision stand," 22
Statistics Canada, 4, 5
Statute of Frauds, public policy, 222
staying married. *See also* reconciliation
  case studies, 98–101
  cultural and family attitudes on divorce,
    76–79
  individual decision making, 79–81

individual decisions, 98–101
  influences, 73–81
  religious law and divorce, 74–76
stereotypes
  divorced women, 181–82
  Muslims since 9/11, 241, 259
stigma
  divorced persons, 179–81
  divorced women, 141, 181–82
"subjective-life" model, religious practice, 12,
    242
Sunna, 7, 20, 30, 81–82, 302
Sunni schools of law, jurisprudence and
    decision making, 22–24

talaq
  definition, 302
  divorce by husband, 35–36
  divorce ruling on verbal delegated, 267
  husband pronouncing, 149, 150
  imams and, 24
  Qur'an exhorting kindness, 161
  triple, 279n60
  unilateral, 161–67, 239
Taylor, Charles, 242
transnational marriages, 104, 120, 254
trial marriages, 47, 281n11

U.K. Model Muslim Marriage Contract,
    283n46
U.K. Shari'a Council, 16–17, 87, 89
Ulama
  claim as mouthpiece of God, 25
  definition, 302
  discretionary judgment, 24–25
  Muslim jurists, 20
umma, 301, 302
Uniform Arbitration Act, 213
Uniform Pre-Marital Agreement Act,
    219–20, 222
unilateral *talaq*. *See talaq*
  religious divorce,
United Kingdom. *See also* Shari'a Council of
    the United Kingdom
  debates (2008), 16–18, 260
  domestic violence, 138
  nikah template, 61
  overseas marriage, 227
  prenuptial agreements, 295n27

United States
    child support, 192–93
    community property, 191
    courts and *mahr*, 33, 221–22, 226
    freedoms of speech, conscience and
        religion, 240
    legal-political status quo, 241, 261–62
    overseas marriage and divorce, 227–28
    recognition of marriage, 197–98
    religious arbitrations, 213–14
universalism, legal-political system, 244–46
U.S. Census, religious identification, 4
U.S. Federal Bureau of Investigation,
    domestic violence, 131

Vedic marriage, 284n2
victimization, women, 137

Wahhabist sect, Saudi Arabia, 27
wali, marriage consent, 29, 65
websites
    Muslim marriage advice, 286n6
    Muslim matchmaking, 54, 282n28
wife-initiated divorce. *See also khula*
Williams, Rowan, Archbishop of
    Canterbury, 16–18, 214, 276n61
women
    accusation of being "bad Muslim woman,"
        133–34
    barriers to escape domestic abuse, 139–40
    breadwinner, 27, 33, 66–67, 109, 113,
        131, 190
    domestic violence, 133, 134, 136, 137–38
    economics of older, vs. younger, 204
    education and work, 31, 111
    failing to obtain religious divorce, 172–74
    homemaker role, 109
    imam and marital counseling, 87–90
    intolerance for divorced Muslim, 77,
        253–55
    Islamic entitlement and double-dipping,
        234
    Islamic law and financial independence of,
        191
    lacking Islamic education, 63–64
    reconciliation process, 96
    sexual "property," 53
    social segregation, 115
    social stigma, 141, 179–82
    stereotype of divorced, 181–82
    Western education, 116–17
    working outside home, 31, 66–68,
        114–16
Woodhead, Linda, 242
working wives, conflict, 114–16
World Wide Web, *nikah*, 40

zagat, 41, 190, 234, 302